The purpose of this book is to present, in a unified, completely algorithmic form, a description of fourteen calendars and how they relate to one another: the present civil calendar (Gregorian), the recent ISO commercial calendar, the old civil calendar (Julian), the Coptic and Ethiopic calendars, the Islamic (Moslem) calendar, the modern Persian (solar) calendar, the Bahá'í calendar, the Hebrew (Jewish) calendar, the Mayan calendars, the French Revolutionary calendar, the Chinese calendar, and both the old (mean) and new (true) Hindu (Indian) calendars. Easy conversion among these calendars is a by-product of the approach, as is the determination of secular and religious holidays. *Calendrical Calculations* makes accurate calendrical algorithms readily available for computer use.

This volume will be a valuable resource for working programmers, as well as a source of useful algorithmic tools for computer scientists. It also includes a wealth of historical material of value to anyone interested in chronology.

CALENDRICAL CALCULATIONS

CALENDRICAL CALCULATIONS

NACHUM DERSHOWITZ
EDWARD M. REINGOLD

Department of Computer Science
University of Illinois at Urbana-Champaign
1304 West Springfield Avenue
Urbana, Illinois 61801-2987, USA

PUBLISHED BY THE PRESS SYNDICATE OF THE UNIVERSITY OF CAMBRIDGE
The Pitt Building, Trumpington Street, Cambridge CB2 1RP, United Kingdom

CAMBRIDGE UNIVERSITY PRESS
The Edinburgh Building, Cambridge CB2 2RU, United Kingdom
40 West 20th Street, New York, NY 10011-4211, USA
10 Stamford Road, Oakleigh, Melbourne 3166, Australia

See page xxi for licensing and other legal information
regarding the code and calculations presented in this book.

First published 1997

Printed in the United States of America

Library of Congress Cataloging-in-Publication Data

Dershowitz, Nachum.
Calendrical calculations / Nachum Dershowitz, Edward M. Reingold.
p. cm.
Includes bibliographical references and index.
ISBN 0-521-56413-1 (hc). — ISBN 0-521-56474-3 (pbk.)
1. Calendar—Mathematics. I. Reingold, Edward M., 1945– .
II. Title.
CE12.D47 1997
529′.3—dc20 96-45964
CIP

A catalog record for this book is available from the British Library

ISBN 0-521-56413-1 hardback
ISBN 0-521-56474-3 paperback

לקהלות הקדש
שמסרו נפשם על קדשת השם
יהי זכרם ברוך

Contents

List of Illustrations

Figures

Frontspieces

List of Tables

Abbreviations

Abbreviation	Meaning	Explanation
A.D.	Anno Domini (= C.E.)	In the year of the Lord
A.H.	Anno hegiræ	In the year of Mohammed's emigration to Medina
A.M.	Anno mundi	In the traditional year of the world since creation
a.m.	Ante meridiem	Before noon
A.P.	Anno persico	Persian year
A.U.C.	Ab urbe condita	From the traditional founding of the city of Rome
B.C.	Before Christ (= B.C.E.)	
B.C.E.	Before the common era (= B.C.)	
B.E.	Bahá'í era	
C.E.	Common era (= A.D.)	
J.D.	Julian day number	Elapsed days since noon on Monday, January 1, 4713 B.C.E. (Julian); sometimes J.A.D., Julian Astronomical Day
K.Y.	Kali Yuga	"Iron Age" epoch of the traditional Hindu calendar
S.E.	Śaka era	Epoch of the modern Hindu calendar
p.m.	Post meridiem	After noon
R.D.	Rata die	Fixed date—elapsed days since the onset of Monday, January 1, 1 (Gregorian)
U.T.	Universal Time	Mean solar time at Greenwich, England (0° meridian), reckoned from midnight; sometimes G.M.T., Greenwich Mean Time
V.E.	Vikrama era	Alternative epoch of the modern Hindu calendar

Notation	Name	Meaning
$\lfloor x \rfloor$	Floor	Largest integer not larger than x
$\lceil x \rceil$	Ceiling	Smallest integer not smaller than x
$\text{round}(x)$	Round	Nearest integer to x, that is, $\lfloor x + 0.5 \rfloor$
$x \bmod y$	Remainder	$x - y\lfloor x/y \rfloor$
$x \text{ amod } y$	Adjusted mod	y if $x \bmod y = 0$, $x \bmod y$ otherwise
$\text{signum}(x)$	Sign	-1 when x is negative, $+1$ when x is positive, 0 when x is 0
$\sin x$	Sine	Sine of x, given in degrees
$\cos x$	Cosine	Cosine of x, given in degrees
$\tan x$	Tangent	Tangent of x, given in degrees
$\arcsin x$	Arc sine	Inverse sine of x, in degrees
$\arccos x$	Arc cosine	Inverse cosine of x, in degrees
$\arctan x$	Arc tangent	Inverse tangent of x, in degrees
$\sum_{i \geq k}^{p(i)} f(i)$	Summation	The sum of $f(i)$ for all $i = k, k+1, \ldots$, continuing only as long as the condition $p(i)$ holds
$\underset{\xi \in [\mu : \nu]}{\textbf{MIN}} \{\psi(\xi)\}$	Minimum value	The value x such that ψ is false in $[\mu : x)$ and is true in $[x : \nu]$; see equation (12.21) on page 148 for details
$\langle x_0, x_1, x_2, \ldots \rangle$	List formation	The list containing $x_0, x_1, x_2, \ldots$
$\langle\, \rangle$	Empty list	A list with no elements
$L_{[i]}$	List element	The ith element of list L; 0-based
$A \Vert B$	Concatenation	The concatenation of lists A and B
bogus	Error	Invalid calendar date

Preface

> You ought to know that no one has the right to speak in public before he has rehearsed what he wants to say two, three, and four times, and learned it; then he may speak. . . . But if a man . . . puts it down in writing, he should revise it a thousand times, if possible.
>
> —Moses Maimonides: *The Epistle on Martyrdom* (circa 1165)

This book has developed over a ten-year period during which the calendrical algorithms and our presentation of them have continually evolved. Our initial motivation was to create Emacs-Lisp code that would provide calendar and diary features for GNU Emacs [12]; this version of the code included the Gregorian, Islamic, and Hebrew calendars. A deluge of inquiries from around the globe soon made it clear to us that there was keen interest in an explanation that would go beyond the code itself, leading to our paper [1] and encouraging us to rewrite the code completely, this time in Common Lisp [1]. The subsequent addition—by popular demand—of the Mayan and French Revolutionary calendars to GNU Emacs prompted a second paper [5]. We received many hundreds of reprint requests for these papers. The response engendered far exceeded our expectations and provided the impetus to write a book in which we could more fully address the multifaceted subject of calendars and their implementation.

The subject of calendars has always fascinated us with its cultural, historical, and mathematical wealth, and we have occasionally employed calendars as accessible examples in introductory programming courses. Once the book's plan took shape, our curiosity turned into obsession. We began by extending our programs to include other calendars, such as the Chinese, Coptic, modern Hindu, and modern Persian. Then, of course, the code for these newly added calendars needed to be rewritten, in some cases several times, to bring it up to the standards of the earlier material. We have long lost track of the number of revisions, and, needless to say, we could undoubtedly devote another decade to polishing what we have, tracking down minutæ, and implementing and refining additional interesting calendars. As much as we might be tempted to, circumstances do not allow us to follow Maimonides' dictum quoted above.

We give a unified, algorithmic presentation for fourteen calendars of current and historical interest: the Gregorian (current civil), ISO (International Organization for Standardization), Julian (old civil), Coptic, Ethiopic, Islamic (Moslem), modern Persian, Bahá'í, Hebrew (Jewish), Mayan, French Revolutionary, Chinese, old Hindu, and modern Hindu. Easy conversion among these calendars is a natural outcome of the approach, as is the determination of secular and religious holidays.

Our goal in this book is twofold: to give precise descriptions of each calendar and to make accurate calendrical algorithms readily available for computer use. The complete workings of each calendar are described both in prose and in mathematical/algorithmic form. Working computer programs are included in an appendix.

Calendrical problems are notorious for plaguing software, as shown by the following examples:

1. The COBOL programming language usually allocates only two decimal digits for internal storage of years, so untold numbers of programs are expected to go awry on New Year's Eve of the coming millennium [3].
2. Many programs err in, or simply ignore, the century rule for leap years on the Gregorian calendar (every 4th year is a leap year, except every 100th year, which is not, except every 400th year, which is). For example, early releases of the popular spreadsheet program Lotus® 1-2-3® treated 2000 as a nonleap year—a problem eventually fixed. However, all releases of Lotus® 1-2-3® take 1900 as a leap year; by the time this error was recognized, the company deemed it too late to correct: "The decision was made at some point that a change now would disrupt formulas which were written to accomodate [*sic*] this anomaly" [9]. Excel®, part of Microsoft Office®, has the same flaw.
3. Various programs calculate the Hebrew calendar by first determining the date of Passover using Gauss's method [7] (see [6]); this method is correct only when sufficient precision is used, so such an approach often leads to errors.
4. At least one modern, standard source for calendrical matters, Parise [4], has many errors, some of which are presumably due to the algorithms used to produce the tables. For example the Mayan date 8.1.19.0.0 is given incorrectly as February 14, 80 (Gregorian) on page 290; the dates given

on pages 325–327 for Easter for the years 1116, 1152, and 1582 are not Sundays; the epact for 1986 on page 354 is wrongly given as 20; Chinese New Year is wrong for many years.

5. Printed and computerized dates for religious holidays are often erroneous. Delrina Technology's 1994 Daily Planner, for example, has three days for Rosh HaShanah.

Though some of the calendars described in this book are mainly of historical interest, all but the Bahá'í and Hindu calendars are incorporated in version 19 of GNU Emacs [12]. The algorithms presented also serve to illustrate all the basic features of nonstandard calendars: The Mayan calendar requires dealing with multiple, independent cycles and exemplifies the kind of reasoning often needed for calendrical-historical research. The French and Chinese calendars are examples in which accurate astronomical calculations are paramount. The Hindu calendar is an example of one in which the cycles (days of the month, months of the year) are irregular.

We hope that in the process of reworking classical calendrical calculations and rephrasing them in the algorithmic language of the computer age, we have also succeeded in affording the reader a glimpse of the beauty and individuality of diverse cultures, past and present.

The Web Page

To facilitate electronic communication with our readers, we have established a home page for this book on the World Wide Web:

`http://emr.cs.uiuc.edu/home/reingold/calendar-book/index.html`

This home page gives easy access to the Lisp functions from the book.

An errata document for the book is available via that home page. Try as we have, at least one error remains in the book.

Acknowledgments

We thank Reza Abdollahy, Liu Baolin, Ahmad Birashk, the late LeRoy E. Doggett, Jacques Dutka, Denis A. Elliott, John S. Justeson, Tzvi Langermann, Denis B. Roegel, Robert H. Stockman, and Robert H. van Gent for their comments on various parts of the book, and Srinathan Kadambi and Lynne Yancy for their help. Stewart M. Clamen wrote an early version of the Mayan calendar code.

Shigang Chen, Howard Jacobson, Claude Kirchner, the late Gerhard Nothmann, and Roman Waupotitsch helped us with various translations. Charles

Hoot labored hard on the program for automatically transforming Lisp code into arithmetic expressions and provided general expertise in Lisp. Mitchell Harris helped with fonts, star names, and the automatic translation; Marla Brownfield helped with various tables. Erga Dershowitz, Idan Dershowitz, Schulamith Halevy, Christine Mumm, Deborah Reingold, Eve Reingold, Rachel Reingold, Ruth Reingold, and Joyce Woodworth were invaluable in proofreading tens of thousands of dates, comparing our results with published tables. We are grateful to all of them.

Portions of this book appeared, in a considerably less polished state, in our papers [1] and [5]. We thank John Wiley & Sons for allowing us to use that material here.

R.D. 728841 N.D.
Urbana, Illinois E.M.R.

References

[1] N. Dershowitz and E. M. Reingold, "Calendrical Calculations," *Software—Practice and Experience*, volume 20, no. 9, pp. 899–928, September, 1990.

[2] C. F. Gauss, "Berechnung des jüdischen Osterfestes," *Monatliche Correspondenz zur Beförderung der Erd- und Himmels-Kunde*, Herausgegeben vom Freiherrn von Zach (May, 1802). Reprinted in Gauss's *Werke*, Herausgegeben von der Königlichen Gesellschaft der Wissenschaften, Göttingen, volume 6, pp. 80–81, 1874.

[3] P. G. Neumann, "Inside Risks: The Clock Grows at Midnight," *Communications of the ACM*, volume 34, no. 1, p. 170, January, 1991.

[4] F. Parise, ed., *The Book of Calendars*, Facts on File, New York, 1982.

[5] E. M. Reingold, N. Dershowitz, and S. M. Clamen, "Calendrical Calculations, Part II: Three Historical Calendars," *Software—Practice and Experience*, volume 23, no. 4, pp. 383–404, April, 1993.

[6] I. Rhodes, "Computation of the Dates of the Hebrew New Year and Passover," *Computers & Mathematics with Applications*, volume 3, pp. 183–190, 1977.

[7] R. M. Stallman, *GNU Emacs Manual*, 6th ed., Free Software Foundation, Cambridge, MA, 1986.

[8] G. L. Steele, Jr., *Common Lisp: The Language*, 2nd ed., Digital Press, Bedford, MA, 1990.

[9] Letter to Nachum Dershowitz from Kay Wilkins, Customer Relations Representative, Lotus Development Corporation, Cambridge, MA, April 21, 1992.

Credits

Quote on p. xvii from *Epistles of Maimonides: Crisis and Leadership*, A. Halkin, trans., Jewish Publication Society, 1993. Used with permission. Letter on p. 84 reprinted with permission.

License and Limited Warranty and Remedy

The Functions (code, formulas, and calendar data) contained in this book were written by Nachum Dershowitz and Edward M. Reingold (the "Authors"), who retain all rights to them except as granted in the License and subject to the warranty and liability limitations below. These Functions are subject to this book's copyright and a Patent Pending on certain of them.

The Authors' public service intent is more liberal than suggested by the License below, as are their licensing policies for otherwise nonallowed uses such as—without limitation—those in commercial, web-site, and large-scale academic contexts. Please see the above mentioned web site for all uses not authorized below; in case there is cause for doubt about whether a use you contemplate is authorized, please contact the Authors.

1. LICENSE. The Authors grant you a license for personal use only. This means that for strictly personal use you may copy and use the code, and keep a backup or archival copy also. Any other uses, including without limitation, allowing the code or its output to be accessed, used, or available to others, is not permitted.
2. WARRANTY.
   (a) *The Authors and Publisher provide no warranties of any kind, either express or implied, including without limiting the generality of the foregoing, any implied warranty of merchantability or fitness for a particular purpose.*
   (b) *Neither the Authors nor Publisher shall be liable to you or any third parties for damages of any kind, including without limitation, any lost profits, lost savings, or other incidental or consequential damages arising out of or related to the use, inability to use, or accuracy of calculations of the code and functions contained herein, or the breach of any express or implied warranty, even if the Authors or Publisher have been advised of the possibility of those damages.*
   (c) *The foregoing warranty may give you specific legal rights which may vary from state to state in the U.S.A.*
3. LIMITATION OF LICENSEE REMEDIES. You acknowledge and agree that your exclusive remedy (in law or in equity), and Authors' and Publisher's entire liability with respect to the material herein, for any breach of representation or for any inaccuracy shall be to petition for a refund of the price of this book. *Some States in the U.S.A. do not allow the exclusion or limitation of liability for incidental or consequential damages, so the above exclusions or limitation may not apply to you.*
4. DISCLAIMER. Except as expressly set forth above, Authors and Publisher:
   (a) make no other warranties with respect to the material and expressly disclaim any others;
   (b) do not warrant that the functions contained in the code will meet your requirements or that their operation shall be uninterrupted or error-free;
   (c) license this material on an "as is" basis, and the entire risk as to the quality, accuracy, and performance herein is yours, should the code or functions prove defective (except as expressly warranted herein). You alone assume the entire cost of all necessary corrections.

CALENDRICAL CALCULATIONS

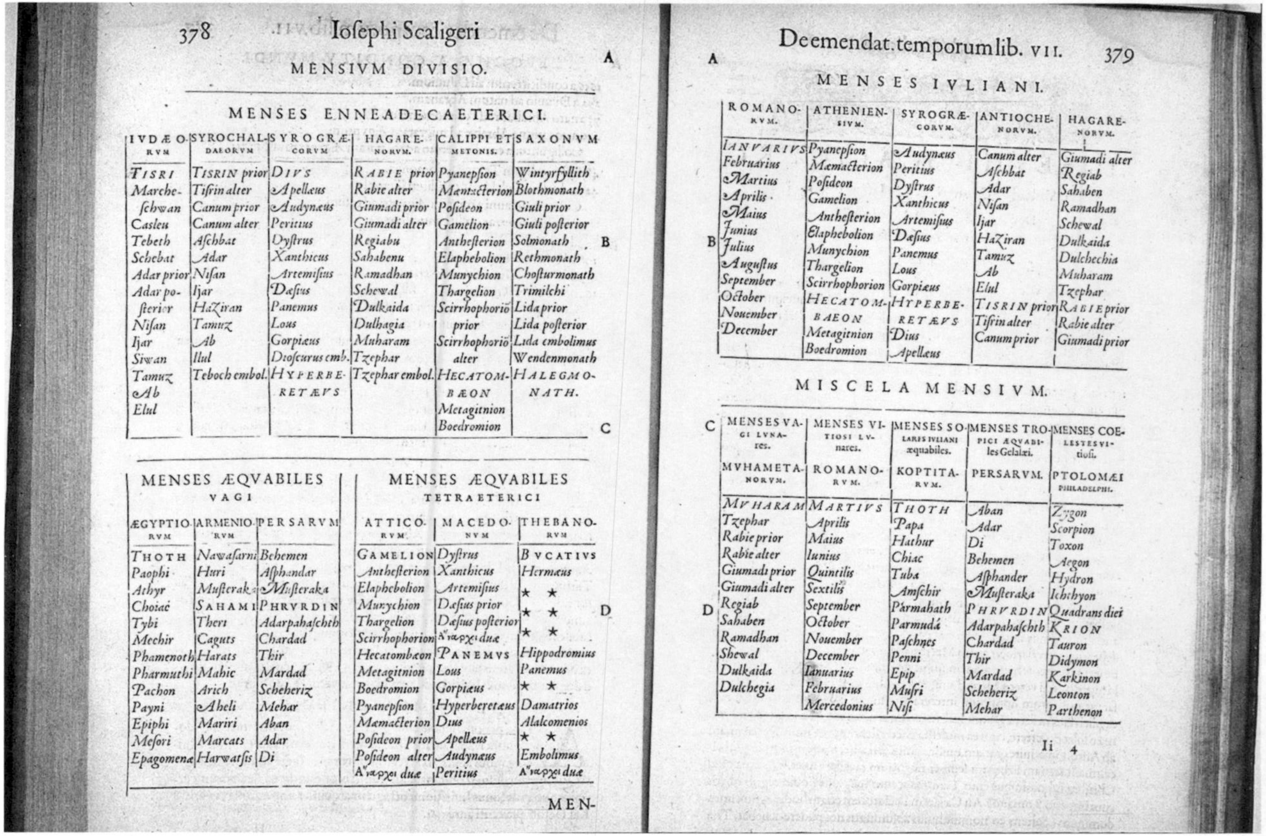

MENSIVM DIVISIO.

MENSES ENNEADECAETERICI.

IVDÆORVM	SYROCHALDÆORVM	SYROGRÆCORVM	HAGARENORVM	CALIPPI ET METONIS	SAXONVM
Tisri	Tisrin prior	Dius	Rabie prior	Pyanepsion	Wintyrfyllith
Marche-	Tisrin alter	Apellæus	Rabie alter	Mæmacterion	Blothmonath
schwan	Canum prior	Audynæus	Giumadi prior	Posideon	Giuli prior
Casleu	Canum alter	Peritius	Giumadi alter	Gamelion	Giuli posterior
Tebeth	Aschbat	Dystrus	Regiabu	Anthesterion	Solmonath
Schebat	Adar	Xanthicus	Sahabenu	Elaphebolion	Rethmonath
Adar prior	Nisan	Artemisius	Ramadhan	Munychion	Chosturmonath
Adar po-	Ijar	Dæsius	Schewal	Thargelion	Trimilchi
sterior	HaZiran	Panemus	Dulkaida	Scirrhophoriō	Lida prior
Nisan	Tamuz	Lous	Dulhagia	prior	Lida posterior
Ijar	Ab	Gorpiæus	Muharam	Scirrhophoriō	Lida embolimus
Siwan	Ilul	Dioscurus emb.	Tzephar	alter	Wendenmonath
Tamuz	Teboch embol.	Hyperbe-	Tzephar embol.	Hecatom-	Halegmo-
Ab		retæus		bæon	nath.
Elul				Metagitnion	
				Boedromion	

MENSES ÆQVABILES VAGI			MENSES ÆQVABILES TETRAETERICI		
ÆGYPTIORVM	ARMENIORVM	PERSARVM	ATTICORVM	MACEDONVM	THEBANORVM
Thoth	Nawasarni	Behemen	Gamelion	Dystrus	Bucatius
Paophi	Huri	Asphandar	Anthesterion	Xanthicus	Hermæus
Athyr	Musterak	Musteraka	Elaphebolion	Artemisius	* *
Choiac	Sahami	Phrurdin	Munychion	Dæsius prior	* *
Tybi	Thert	Adarpahaschth	Thargelion	Dæsius posterior	* *
Mechir	Caguts	Chardad	Scirrhophorion	Ἄναρχοι duæ	
Phamenoth	Harats	Thir	Hecatombæon	Panemus	Hippodromius
Pharmuthi	Mahic	Mardad	Metagitnion	Lous	Panemus
Pachon	Arich	Scheheriz	Boedromion	Gorpiæus	* *
Payni	Aheli	Mehar	Pyanepsion	Hyperberetæus	Damatrios
Epiphi	Mariri	Aban	Mæmacterion	Dius	Alalcomenios
Mesori	Marcats	Adar	Posideon prior	Apellæus	* *
Epagomenæ	Harwatsis	Di	Posideon alter	Audynæus	Embolimus
			Ἄναρχοι duæ	Peritius	Ἄναρχοι duæ

MEN-

MENSES IVLIANI.

ROMANORVM	ATHENIENSIVM	SYROGRÆCORVM	ANTIOCHENORVM	HAGARENORVM
Ianuarius	Pyanepsion	Audynæus	Canum alter	Giumadi alter
Februarius	Mæmacterion	Peritius	Aschbat	Regiab
Martius	Posideon	Dystrus	Adar	Sahaben
Aprilis	Gamelion	Xanthicus	Nisan	Ramadhan
Maius	Anthesterion	Artemisius	Ijar	Schewal
Iunius	Elaphebolion	Dæsius	HaZiran	Dulkaida
Iulius	Munychion	Panemus	Tamuz	Dulchechia
Augustus	Thargelion	Lous	Ab	Muharam
September	Scirrhophorion	Gorpiæus	Elul	Tzephar
October	Hecatom-	Hyperbe-	Tisrin prior	Rabie prior
Nouember	bæon	retæus	Tisrin alter	Rabie alter
December	Metagitnion	Dius	Canum prior	Giumadi prior
	Boedromion	Apellæus		

MISCELA MENSIVM.

MENSES VAGI LVNARES.	MENSES VITIOSI LVNARES.	MENSES SOLARES IVLIANI æquabiles.	MENSES TROPICI ÆQVABILES Gelalæi.	MENSES COELESTES VITIOSI.
MVHAMETANORVM.	ROMANORVM.	KOPTITARVM.	PERSARVM.	PTOLOMÆI PHILADELPHI.
Muharam	Martius	Thoth	Aban	Zygon
Tzephar	Aprilis	Papa	Adar	Scorpion
Rabie prior	Maius	Hathur	Di	Toxon
Rabie alter	Iunius	Chiac	Behemen	Aegon
Giumadi prior	Quintilis	Tuba	Asphander	Hydron
Giumadi alter	Sextilis	Amschir	Musteraka	Ichthyon
Regiab	September	Parmahath	Phrurdin	Quadrans diei
Sahaben	October	Parmudá	Adarpahaschth	Krion
Ramadhan	Nouember	Paschnes	Chardad	Tauron
Shewal	December	Penni	Thir	Didymon
Dulkaida	Ianuarius	Epip	Mardad	Karkinon
Dulchegia	Februarius	Musri	Scheheriz	Leonton
	Mercedonius	Nisi	Mehar	Parthenon

Ii 4

Two pages of Joseph Scaliger's great work, *De Emendatione Temporum* (1593), giving month names on many calendars. (Courtesy of the University of Illinois, Urbana, IL.)

1

Introduction

> A learned man once asked me regarding the eras used by different nations, and regarding the difference of their roots, that is, the epochs where they begin, and of their branches, that is, the months and years, on which they are based; further regarding the causes which led to such difference, and the famous festivals and commemoration-days for certain times and events, and regarding whatever else one nation practices differently from another. He urged me to give an explanation, the clearest possible, of all this, so as to be easily intelligible to the mind of the reader, and to free him from the necessity of wading through widely scattered books, and of consulting their authors. Now I was quite aware that this was a task difficult to handle, an object not easily to be attained or managed by anyone, who wants to treat it as a matter of logical sequence, regarding which the mind of the student is not agitated by doubt.
>
> —Abū-Raiḥān Muḥammad ibn 'Aḥmad al-Bīrūnī:
> *Al-Āthār al-Bāqiyah 'an al-Qurūn al-Khāliyah*, p. 2 (1000)

Calendrical calculations are ubiquitous. Banks need to calculate interest on a daily basis. Computer operating systems need to switch to and from daylight saving time. Dates of secular and religious holidays must be computed for consideration in planning events. Corporations issue paychecks on weekly, biweekly, or monthly schedules. Bills and statements must be generated periodically. Most of these calculations are not difficult, because the rules of our civil calendar (the Gregorian calendar) are straightforward.

Complications begin when we need to know the day of the week on which a given date falls or when various religious holidays based on other calendars occur. These complications lead to difficult programming tasks—not often difficult in an algorithmic sense, but difficult because it can be extremely tedious to delve, for example, into the complexities of the Hebrew calendar and its relation to the civil calendar.

The purpose of this book is to present, in a unified, completely algorithmic form, a description of fourteen calendars and how they relate to one another: the present civil calendar (Gregorian); the recent ISO commercial calendar; the old civil calendar (Julian); the Coptic and (virtually identical) Ethiopic calendars; the Islamic (Moslem) calendar; the (modern) Persian calendar; the Bahá'í calendar; the Hebrew (Jewish) calendar; the Mayan calendars; the French Revolutionary calendar; the Chinese calendar; and both the old (mean) and new (true) Hindu (Indian) calendars. Information that is sufficiently detailed to allow computer implementation is difficult to find for most of these calendars, because the published material is often inaccessible, ecclesiastically oriented, incomplete, inaccurate, based on extensive tables, overburdened with extraneous material, focused on shortcuts for hand calculation to avoid complicated arithmetic or to check results, or difficult to find in English. Most existing computer programs are proprietary, incomplete, or inaccurate.

The need for such a secular presentation in the public domain was made clear to us when the second author, in implementing a calendar/diary feature for GNU Emacs [12], found difficulty in gathering and interpreting appropriate source materials that describe the interrelationships among the various calendars and the determination of the dates of holidays.

The calendar algorithms in this book are presented as function definitions in standard mathematical format; Appendix A gives the types (ranges and domains) of all functions and constants we use. To ensure correctness, all calendar functions were automatically typeset[1] directly from the working Common Lisp [13] functions listed in Appendix B.[2]

We have chosen mathematical notation as the vehicle for presentation because of its universality and easy convertibility to any programming language. We have endeavored to simplify the calculations as much as possible. Many of the algorithms we provide are considerably more concise than previously published ones. This is particularly true of the Persian, Hebrew, and old Hindu calendars.

We chose Lisp as the vehicle for implementation because it encourages functional programming and has a trivial syntax, nearly self-evident semantics, historical durability, and wide distribution. Except for a few short macros, the code uses only a very simple, side-effect-free subset of Lisp. (Were it not for

[1] This has meant some sacrifice in the typography of the book; we hope the reader sympathizes with our decision.

[2] We will gladly provide these Lisp functions in electronic form to those who agree to the terms of the License Agreements and Limited Warranty on page xxi. Send an empty electronic mail message to `reingold@cs.uiuc.edu` with the subject line containing precisely the phrase "`send-cal`"; your message will be answered automatically. The code (and errata for this book) are also available over the World Wide Web at `http://emr.cs.uiuc.edu/home/reingold/calendar-book/index.html`.

the matter of availability and durability, a modern functional language might have been preferable.)

It is not the intention of this book to give a detailed historical treatment of the material, nor, for that matter, a mathematical one; our goal is to give a logical, thorough *computational* treatment. Thus, although we give much historical, religious, mathematical, and astronomical data in the text, the focus of the presentation is algorithmic. Full historical/religious details and mathematical/astronomical underpinnings of the calendars can be pursued in the references.

In the remainder of this chapter, we describe the underlying unifying theme of all the calculations, along with some useful mathematical facts. The details of specific calendars are presented in subsequent chapters. Historically, the oldest of the calendars that we consider are the Chinese and the Mayan (about three thousand years old). Next are the Julian (the roots of which date back to the ancient Roman empire), the Coptic and Ethiopic (third century), the Hebrew (fourth century) and the old Hindu (fifth century), followed by the fixed Islamic calendar (seventh century), the newer Hindu calendars (tenth century), the Gregorian modification to the Julian calendar (sixteenth century), the French Revolutionary calendar (eighteenth century), and the Bahá'í calendar (nineteenth century). Finally, the International Organization for Standardization's ISO calendar and the modern Persian calendar are of twentieth century origin.

For expository purposes, however, we present the Gregorian calendar first, in Part I, because it is the most popular calendar currently in use; then we give the ISO calendar, which is trivial to implement and depends wholly on the Gregorian. Since the Julian calendar is so close in substance to the Gregorian, we present it next, followed by the very similar Coptic and Ethiopic calendars. Then we give the fixed Islamic calendar, which because of its simplicity is easy to implement, followed by the modern Persian calendar, which has some interesting related computational aspects, and the Bahá'í calendar, which depends wholly on the Gregorian calendar. Next, we present the Hebrew calendar, one of the more complicated and difficult calendars to implement. Next, the Mayan calendar (actually three calendars), of historical interest, has several unique computational aspects. To conclude Part I, we describe the ancient Hindu solar and lunisolar calendars; these are simple versions of the modern Hindu solar and lunisolar calendars. All of the calendars described in Part I are "arithmetical," in that they operate by straightforward numerical rules.

In Part II we present calendars that are controlled by astronomical events (or extremely close approximations to them), although these calendars may have an arithmetical component as well. The French Revolutionary calendar, in both its original and modified forms, is first in Part II; then we give the Chinese calendar. Both of these calendars are computationally simple, provided certain astronomical values are available. Finally, we describe the modern Hindu calendars, which are by far the most complicated of the calendars in this book. The French Revolutionary, Chinese, and modern Hindu calendars require some understanding of astronomical events such as solstices and new moons. Where needed in the calendar algorithms, we employ "black-box" astronomical functions, the details of which are included in Chapter 12, which introduces Part II.

As each calendar is discussed, we also provide algorithms for computing holidays based on it. In this regard we take the ethnocentric view that our task is to compute the dates of holidays in reference to a given *Gregorian year*; there is clearly little difficulty in finding the dates of, say, Islamic New Year in a given Islamic year!

The selection of calendars we present was chosen with two purposes: to include all common modern calendars and to cover all calendrical techniques. We do not give all variants of the calendars we discuss, but we have given enough details to make almost any calendar easy to implement.

1.1 Calendar Units and Taxonomy

The sun moves from east to west and night follows day with predictable regularity. This apparent motion of the sun as viewed by an Earthbound observer provided the earliest timekeeping standard for humankind. The day is, accordingly, the basic unit of time underlying all calendars, but various calendars use different conventions to structure days into larger units: weeks, months, years, and cycles of years. Different calendars also begin their day at different times: the French Revolutionary day, for example, begins at midnight; the Islamic, Bahá'í, and Hebrew days begin at sunset; the Hindu day begins at sunrise. The various definitions of "day" are surveyed in Section 12.2.

The purpose of a calendar is to give a name to each day. The mathematically simplest naming convention would be to assign an integer to each day; fixing day 1 would determine the whole calendar. The Babylonians had such a day count (in base 60). Such *diurnal* calendars are used by astronomers (see Section 12.2) and by calendarists (see, for example, Section 11.1); we use a day numbering in this book as an intermediate device for converting from one calendar to another (see the following section). Day-numbering schemes can be complicated by using a mixed-radix system in which the day number is given as a sequence of numbers or names. The Maya, for example, utilized such a method (Section 10.1).

Calendar day names are generally distinct, but this is not always the case. For example, the day of the week is a calendar, in a trivial sense, with infinitely many days having the same day name (see Section 1.8). A seven-day week is almost universal today. In many cultures, the days of the week were named after the seven "wandering stars" (or after the gods associated with those heavenly bodies), namely, the sun, the moon, and the five planets visible to the naked eye—Mercury, Venus, Mars, Jupiter, and Saturn. In some languages—Arabic, Portuguese, and Hebrew are examples—days of the week are just numbered. Other cycles of days have also been used, including four-day weeks (in the Congo), five-day weeks (in Africa and in Russia in 1929), eight-day weeks (in Africa and in the Roman Republic), and ten-day weeks (in ancient Egypt and in France at the end of the eighteenth century; see page 162). The mathematics of cycles of days are described in Section 1.8. Many calendars repeat after one or more years. In one of the Mayan calendars (see Section 10.2), and in many preliterate societies, day names are recycled every year. The Chinese calendar used a repeating 60-name scheme for days and months, and uses it still for years.

An interesting variation in some calendars is the use of two or more cycles running simultaneously. For example, the Mayan tzolkin calendar (Section 10.2) combines a cycle of 13 names with a cycle of 20 numbers. The Chinese cycle of 60 names for years is actually composed of cycles of length 10 and 12 (see Section 14.4). The mathematics of simultaneous cycles are described in Section 1.9.

The notions of "month" and "year," like the day, were originally based on observations of heavenly phenomena, namely the waxing and waning of the moon, and the cycle of seasons, respectively. Some calendars begin each month with the "apparent" new moon, when the crescent moon first becomes visible (as in the Hebrew calendar of classical times and in the religious calendar of the Moslems until today); others begin the month at full moon (in northern India, for example).

Over the course of history, many different schemes have been devised for determining the start of the year. Some are astronomical, beginning at the autumnal or spring equinox, or at the winter or summer solstice. Solstices are more readily observable, either by observing when the shadow of a gnomon is longest (summer solstice in the northern hemisphere) or shortest (winter), or by noting the point in time when the sun rises or sets as far south at it does during the course of the year (which is summer in the northern hemisphere) or maximally north (winter). The ancient Egyptians began their year with the *heliacal rising* of Sirius—that is, on the day that the Dog Star Sirius (the brightest fixed star in the sky), can first be seen in the morning, after a period during which the sun's proximity to Sirius makes the latter invisible to the naked eye. The Pleiades were used by some peoples for the same purpose. Various other natural phenomena have been used to establish the onset of a new year, such as harvests or the rutting seasons of certain animals among North American tribes [2].

The calendars that we consider have an integral number of days in a month and an integral number of months in a year. However, these astronomical periods—day, month, and year—are incommensurate: their periods do not form integral multiples of one another. The lunar month is about $29\frac{1}{2}$ days long, and the solar year is about $365\frac{1}{4}$ days long. (See Chapter 12 for precise definitions and values.) How exactly one coordinates these time periods and the accuracy with which they approximate their astronomical values are what differentiate one calendar from another.

Broadly speaking, solar calendars—including the Gregorian, Julian, Coptic/Ethiopic, ISO, French Revolutionary, and Bahá'í—are based on the yearly solar cycle, whereas lunar and lunisolar calendars—such as the Islamic, Hebrew, Hindu, and Chinese—take the monthly lunar cycle as their basic building block. Most solar calendars are divided into months, but these months are divorced from the lunar events; they are sometimes related to the movement of the sun through the twelve signs of the zodiac.

Because observational methods suffer from the vagaries of weather and chance, they have for the most part been supplanted by calculations. The simplest option is to approximate the length of the year, of the month, or of both. Originally, the Babylonian calendar was based on twelve months of 30 days each, overestimating the length of the month and underestimating the year. Such a calendar is easy to calculate, but each month begins at a slightly later lunar phase than the previous, and the seasons move forward slowly through the year. The ancient Egyptian calendar achieved greater accuracy by having twelve months of 30 days plus five extra days. To achieve better correlation with the motion of the moon, one can alternate months of 29 and 30 days. Twelve such months, however, amount to 354 days—more than eleven days short of the solar year.

Almost every calendar in this book, and virtually all other calendars, incorporate a notion of "leap" year to deal with the cumulative error caused by approximating a year by an integral number of days and months. Solar calendars add a day every few years to keep up with the astronomical year. Calculations are simplest when the leap years are evenly distributed; the Julian, Coptic, and Ethiopic calendars add one day every four years. To get a more precise mean year, one needs somewhat fewer leap years. Formulas for the evenly distributed case, such as when one has a leap year every fourth or fifth year, are derived in Section 1.8. The old Hindu solar calendar (see Chapter 11) follows such a pattern; the Persian calendar almost does (see Chapter 7). The Gregorian calendar, however, uses an uneven distribution of leap years but a relatively easy-to-remember rule (see the next chapter). The modified French Revolutionary calendar (Chapter 13) included an even more accurate rule.

Most lunar calendars incorporate the notion of a year. Purely lunar calendars may approximate the solar year with twelve lunar months (as does the Islamic), though this is about 11 days short of the astronomical year. Lunisolar calendars invariably alternate twelve- and thirteen-month years, either according to some fixed rule (as in the Hebrew calendar) or astronomically determined pattern (Chinese and modern Hindu). The so-called *Metonic cycle* is based on the observation that 19 solar years contain almost exactly 235 lunar months. This correspondence, named after the Athenian astronomer Meton (who published it in 432 B.C.E.) and known much earlier to ancient Babylonian astronomers, makes a relatively simple and accurate fixed solar/lunar calendar feasible. The $235 = 12 \times 12 + 7 \times 13$ months in the cycle are divided into twelve years of twelve months and seven leap years of thirteen months. The Metonic cycle is used in the Hebrew calendar (see Chapter 9) and for the ecclesiastical calculation of Easter (see Section 4.3). The old Hindu calendar is even more accurate, comprising 66,389 leap years in a cycle of 180,000 years (see Chapter 11) to which the leap year formulas of Section 1.10 apply.

1.2 Fixed Day Numbers

Teach us to number our days, that we may attain a wise heart.
—Psalms 90:12

Over the centuries, human beings have devised an enormous variety of methods for specifying dates.[3] None are ideal computationally, however, because all have idiosyncrasies resulting from attempts to coordinate a convenient human labeling with lunar and solar phenomena.

For a computer implementation, the easiest way to reckon time is simply to count days: Fix an arbitrary starting point as day 1 and specify a date by giving a day number relative to that starting point; a single 32-bit integer allows the representation of more than 11.7 million years. Such a reckoning of time is, evidently, extremely awkward for human beings and is not in common use, except among astronomers who use *julian day numbers* to specify dates (see Section 1.4).

We have chosen midnight at the onset of Monday, January 1, 1 (Gregorian) as our fixed date 1, which we abbreviate as R.D.[4] 1, and count forward day-by-day from there. Of course, this is anachronistic because there was no year 1 on the Gregorian calendar—the Gregorian calendar was devised only in the

[3] The best reference is still Ginzel's monumental three-volume work [2]. An exceptional survey can be found in the *Encyclopædia of Religion and Ethics* [8, vol. III, pp. 61–141 and vol. V, pp. 835–894]. A useful, modern summary is [3].

[4] *Rata die*, or fixed date. We are indebted to Howard Jacobson for this coinage.

sixteenth century—so by January 1, 1 (Gregorian) we mean the day we get if we extrapolate backwards from the present; this day turns out to be Monday, January 3, 1 C.E.[5] (Julian).

We should thus think of the passage of time as a sequence of days numbered $\ldots, -2, -1, 0, 1, 2, 3, \ldots$, which the various human-oriented calendars label differently. For example, R.D. 710,347 is called

- Monday, November 12, 1945 on the Gregorian calendar.
- Day 1 of week 46 of 1945 on the ISO calendar.
- October 30, 1945 C.E. on the Julian calendar.
- Hatur 3, 1662 on the Coptic calendar (until sunset).
- Khedār 4, 1939 on the Ethiopic calendar (until sunset).
- Dhu al-Ḥijja 6, 1364 on the Islamic calendar (until sunset).
- Abān 21, 1324 on the modern Persian calendar.
- The day of Asmá', of the month of Qudrat, of the year Abad, of the sixth Vahid, of the first Kull-i-Shay on the Bahá'í calendar (until sunset).
- Kislev 7, 5706 on the Hebrew calendar (until sunset).
- 12.16.11.16.9 on the Mayan long count.
- 7 Zac on the Mayan haab calendar.
- 11 Muluc on the Mayan tzolkin calendar.
- Tulā 29, 5046 Kali Yuga era (elapsed) on the old Hindu solar calendar (after sunrise).
- Day 8 in the bright half of Kārttika, 5046 Kali Yuga era (elapsed) on the old Hindu lunisolar calendar (after sunrise).
- Décade III, Primidi de Brumaire de l'Année 154 de la Révolution on the French Revolutionary calendar.
- Day 8 of the 10th month in the 22nd year (Yi-you) of the 77th sexagesimal cycle on the Chinese calendar.
- Tulā 26, 1866 Śaka era (elapsed) on the modern Hindu solar calendar (after sunrise).
- Day 7 in the bright half of Kārttika, 2002 Vikrama era (elapsed) on the modern Hindu lunisolar calendar (after sunrise).

All that is required for calendrical conversion is to be able to convert each calendar to and from this fixed calendar. Since some calendars begin their day at midnight and others at sunrise or sunset, *we fix the time of day at which conversions are performed to be noon.*

We give, in subsequent chapters, functions to do the conversions for the Gregorian, ISO, Julian, Coptic, Ethiopic, Islamic, Bahá'í, Hebrew, Mayan, French

[5] Common era; or, A.D.

Revolutionary, Chinese, and Hindu calendars. For each calendar x, we write a function **fixed-from-*x***(x-*date*) to convert a given date x-*date* on that calendar to the corresponding R.D. date, and a function ***x*-from-fixed**(*date*) to do the inverse operation, taking R.D. *date* and computing its representation in calendar x. One direction is often much simpler to calculate than the other, and occasionally we resort to considering a range of possible dates on calendar x, searching for the one that converts to the given R.D. date. To convert from calendar x to calendar y, one need only compose the two functions:

$$y\text{-}date = \mathbf{y\text{-}from\text{-}fixed}(\mathbf{fixed\text{-}from\text{-}}\boldsymbol{x}(x\text{-}date)).$$

Each calendar has an *epoch*, the first day of the first year of that calendar (see Section 1.5). To avoid confusion, we generally assign an integer R.D. date to an epoch, even if the calendar in question begins its days at a time other than midnight. All of the algorithms given in this book give mathematically sensible results for dates prior to the calendar's epoch.

1.3 Negative Years

The date Monday, January 1, 1 (Gregorian), though arbitrarily chosen as our starting point, has a desirable characteristic: It is early enough that almost all dates of interest are represented by positive integers of moderate size. However, we cannot avoid dealing with dates before the common era. For example, the Hebrew calendar begins at sunset on Sunday, September 6, -3760 (Gregorian); scholarly literature is replete with such statements. Thus, to aid the reader, we now explain how years before the common era are conventionally handled. This convention is often a source of confusion, even among professional historians.

It is computationally convenient, and mathematically sensible, to label years with the sequence of integers $\ldots, -3, -2, -1, 0, 1, 2, 3, \ldots$ so that year 0 precedes year 1; we do this when extrapolating backward on the Gregorian calendar so that the same leap year rule will apply based on divisibility by 4, 100, and 400 (see Chapter 2). However, on the Julian calendar it is customary to refer to the year preceding 1 C.E. as 1 B.C.E.,[6] counting it as a leap year in accordance with the every-fourth-year leap year rule of the Julian calendar. Thus, the beginning of the Hebrew calendar can alternatively be referred to as sunset October 6, 3761 B.C.E. (Julian). To highlight this asymmetry, in the *prose* of this book we append "B.C.E." *only* to Julian calendar years, reserving the minus sign for Gregorian calendar years. Thus for year $n \geq 0$, the rough

[6] Before the common era; or, B.C.

present-day alignment of the Julian and Gregorian calendars gives

$$-n \text{ (Gregorian)} \approx (n+1) \text{ B.C.E. (Julian)},$$

and, for year $n \geq 1$,

$$n \text{ (Gregorian)} \approx n \text{ C.E. (Julian)}.$$

However, in the few instances that we need a B.C.E. Julian year in the Lisp functions in the appendix, we use negative numbers, with the convention that year n B.C.E. (Julian) is represented as $-n$.

1.4 Julian Day Numbers

Astronomers avoid the confusing situation of specifying moments in time by giving them in "julian days" or J.D. (sometimes "julian astronomical days" or J.A.D.). The "Julian period," introduced in 1583 by Joseph Justus Scaliger,[7] was originally a counting of *years* in a cycle of 7980 years, starting from 4713 B.C.E. (Julian). Neugebauer [9, Appendix A, section 1] explains Scaliger's choice of starting date in detail (see also Asimov's essay [1]). In the nineteenth century, Herschel [8] adapted the system into a strict counting of *days* backward and forward from

$$\begin{aligned}\text{J.D. } 0 &= \text{Noon on Monday, January 1, 4713 B.C.E. (Julian)}\\ &= \text{Noon on Monday, November 24, } -4713 \text{ (Gregorian).}\end{aligned}$$

A fractional part of a julian[8] date gives the fraction of a day beyond noon; switching dates at noon makes sense for astronomers who work through the night. Using this system, for example, the Hebrew calendar begins at J.D. 347,997.25. The literature on the Mayan calendar commonly specifies the beginning of the calendar in julian days. Since noon of R.D. 0 is J.D. 1,721,425, it follows that

$$\text{J.D. } n = \text{Noon on R.D. } (n - 1{,}721{,}425).$$

In other words,

$$\text{Midnight at the onset of R.D. } d = \text{J.D. } (d + 1{,}721{,}424.5). \tag{1.1}$$

We do not use julian days directly, as suggested in [6], because we want our days to begin at civil midnight. *We also use fractional days when we need to calculate with time, but begin each day at midnight.*

[7] It is often claimed that Scaliger named the period after his father, the Renaissance physician Julius Cæsar Scaliger, but this claim is not borne out by examination of Scaliger's great work, *De Emendatione Temporum*, in which he states, at the end of the introductory section to Book V, "Iulianam vocauimus: quia ad annum Iulianum dumtaxat accommodata est." [I have called this the Julian period because it is fitted to the Julian year.]

[8] We use lower case here to avoid any confusion between a julian day number and a date on the Julian calendar.

To distinguish clearly between the Julian calendar and julian days in our functions, we use the abbreviation "jd" instead of "julian." We have

$$\textbf{jd-start} \stackrel{\text{def}}{=} -1721424.5 \tag{1.2}$$

$$\textbf{moment-from-jd}\ (jd) \stackrel{\text{def}}{=} jd + \textbf{jd-start} \tag{1.3}$$

$$\textbf{jd-from-moment}\ (moment) \stackrel{\text{def}}{=} moment - \textbf{jd-start} \tag{1.4}$$

where *jd* can be a fraction, representing time as well as date. We use the term "moment" to mean an R.D. date with a fractional part giving, as a decimal fraction, thc time of day.

1.5 Epochs

Every calendar has an *epoch* or starting date. This date is usually not the date the calendar was adopted, but rather a hypothetical starting point for the first day. For example, the Gregorian calendar was devised and adopted in the sixteenth century, but its epoch is January 1, 1. Since days begin at different hours on different calendars, we adopt the convention that a calendar's epoch is the onset of the (civil) day containing the first noon. Thus, we take September 7, −3760 (Gregorian) as the epoch of the Hebrew calendar, which was codified in the fourth century, though the first Hebrew day began at sunset the preceding evening.

Table 1.1 gives the epochs of the calendars discussed in this book. We express the epochs of all the calendars as integer R.D. dates, that is, the integer R.D. day number at *noon* of the first day of the calendar. Thus, the epoch for the Gregorian calendar is R.D. 1, and that for the Hebrew calendar is R.D. −1,373,427. Using this form of calendar epochs is convenient because

R.D. d is (d − calendar epoch) days since the start of that calendar.

For example,

$$\begin{aligned} 710{,}347 - (\text{Hebrew calendar epoch}) &= 710{,}347 - (-1{,}373{,}427) \\ &= 2{,}083{,}774, \end{aligned}$$

and hence

R.D. 710,347 = 2,083,774 days since the start of the Hebrew calendar.

Because, for the most part, our formulas depend on the number of days elapsed on some calendar, we often use the expression (d − epoch) in our calendar formulas.

Table 1.1 *Epochs for the calendars*

Calendar	Epoch (R.D.)	Equivalents
Julian day number	−1,721,424.5	Noon, November 24, −4713 (Gregorian) Noon, January 1, 4713 B.C.E. (Julian)
Hebrew	−1,373,427	September 7, −3760 (Gregorian) October 7, 3761 B.C.E. (Julian)
Mayan	−1,137,142	August 11, −3113 (Gregorian) September 6, 3114 B.C.E. (Julian)
Hindu (Kali Yuga)	−1,132,959	January 23, −3101 (Gregorian) February 18, 3102 B.C.E. (Julian)
Chinese	−963,099	February 15, −2636 (Gregorian) March 8, 2637 B.C.E. (Julian)
Julian	−1	December 30, 0 (Gregorian) January 1, 1 C.E. (Julian)
Gregorian	1	January 1, 1 (Gregorian) January 3, 1 C.E. (Julian)
ISO	1	January 1, 1 (Gregorian) January 3, 1 C.E. (Julian)
Ethiopic	2,430	August 27, 7 (Gregorian) August 29, 7 C.E. (Julian)
Coptic	103,605	August 29, 284 (Gregorian) August 29, 284 C.E. (Julian)
Persian	226,896	March 22, 622 (Gregorian) March 19, 622 C.E. (Julian)
Islamic	227,015	July 19, 622 (Gregorian) July 16, 622 C.E. (Julian)
French Revolutionary	654,415	September 22, 1792 (Gregorian) September 11, 1792 C.E. (Julian)
Bahá'í	673,222	March 21, 1844 (Gregorian) March 9, 1844 C.E. (Julian)

1.6 Mathematical Notation

The best notation is no notation.
—Paul Halmos: *How to Write Mathematics*, Section 15 (1970)

We use the following mathematical notation (see [5]) when describing the calendar calculations: The *floor function*, $\lfloor x \rfloor$, gives the largest integer less than or equal to x. For example, $\lfloor \pi \rfloor = 3$ and $\lfloor -\pi \rfloor = -4$. The similar *ceiling function*, $\lceil x \rceil$, gives the smallest integer greater than or equal to x. For example, $\lceil \pi \rceil = 4$ and $\lceil -\pi \rceil = -3$. For integers n, $\lfloor n \rfloor = \lceil n \rceil = n$. Using the floor function, we can convert a moment given in julian days to an R.D. date, with no fractional part, with

$$\textbf{fixed-from-jd}\,(jd) \stackrel{\text{def}}{=} \lfloor \textbf{moment-from-jd}\,(jd) \rfloor \tag{1.5}$$

Occasionally we need to *round* values to the nearest integer. We can express this using the floor function as

$$\text{round}(x) \stackrel{\text{def}}{=} \lfloor x + 0.5 \rfloor. \tag{1.6}$$

The *remainder*, or *modulus, function*, $x \bmod y$, is defined for $y \neq 0$ as

$$x \bmod y \stackrel{\text{def}}{=} x - y\lfloor x/y \rfloor, \tag{1.7}$$

which is the remainder when x is divided by y (x and y need not be integers). For example, $9 \bmod 5 = 4$, $-9 \bmod 5 = 1$, $9 \bmod -5 = -1$, and $-9 \bmod -5 = -4$. Definition (1.7) makes sense for any nonzero value of y; for example, $5/3 \bmod 3/4 = 1/6$. When $y = 1$, $x \bmod 1$ is the *fractional part* of x. Thus, in programming languages (including C, C++, and Pascal) without a built-in remainder function that works for nonintegers, the above definition must be used instead.

There are four important consequences of definition (1.7). First, if $y > 0$, then $(x \bmod y) \geq 0$ for all x, even for negative values of x; we use this property throughout our calculations. Care must thus be exercised in implementing our algorithms in computer languages like C and C++ in which the mod operator % has $(x \,\%\, y) < 0$ for $x < 0$, $y > 0$. The second consequence is that the definition of the mod function implies that for $y, z \neq 0$,

$$a = (x \bmod y) \quad \text{if and only if} \quad (az = xz \bmod yz). \tag{1.8}$$

Third,

$$x - (x \bmod y) \text{ is always a multiple of } y. \tag{1.9}$$

Finally, for $y \neq 0$,

$$0 \leq \text{signum}(y) \cdot (x \bmod y) < |y|, \tag{1.10}$$

where

$$\text{signum}(y) \stackrel{\text{def}}{=} \begin{cases} -1 & \text{if } y < 0, \\ 0 & \text{if } y = 0, \\ 1 & \text{if } y > 0. \end{cases} \tag{1.11}$$

We also find it convenient to use an *adjusted remainder function*, x amod y, defined for $y \neq 0$ as

$$x \text{ amod } y \stackrel{\text{def}}{=} \begin{cases} y & \text{if } x \bmod y = 0, \\ x \bmod y & \text{otherwise.} \end{cases} \tag{1.12}$$

The amod function can also be described as

$$x \text{ amod } y = 1 + [(x - 1) \bmod y].$$

Lastly, we use a special summation operator,

$$\sum_{i \geq k}^{p(i)} f(i)$$

whose value is that obtained when $f(i)$ is summed for all $i = k, k+1, \ldots,$ continuing only as long as the condition $p(i)$ holds. The sum is 0 if $p(k)$ is false.

1.7 Lists

> The list could surely go on, and there is nothing more wonderful than a list, instrument of wondrous hypotyposis.
>
> —Umberto Eco: *The Name of the Rose* (1983)

We represent calendar dates by lists of components, usually having the form

month	*day*	*year*

in which *month*, *day*, and *year* are all integers. We use subscripts to select components; for example, if $d =$ | 11 | 12 | 1945 |, then $d_{\mathbf{day}} = 12$. The components of dates differ for some calendars; we explain those particular forms in the individual discussions and use analogously named extraction functions.

We also have occasion to use lists of dates or of other items. Our use of lists requires manipulations such as forming lists, selecting elements from a list, or concatenating lists. We use the following notation in our calendar functions:

- Angle brackets indicate list construction, that is, the formation of a list from individual components. For example, $\langle 11, 12, 1945 \rangle$ is a list of the three components 11, 12, 1945, respectively.
- Subscripts in square brackets indicate list element selection, with the indices of the elements being zero-based. Thus if $b = \langle 11, 12, 1945 \rangle$, then $b_{[0]}$ is 11, $b_{[1]}$ is 12, and $b_{[2]}$ is 1945.
- Empty angle brackets, $\langle\ \rangle$, indicate the list with no elements.
- Double bars indicate concatenation of lists, so that $\langle 11, 12 \rangle || \langle 1945 \rangle = \langle 11, 12, 1945 \rangle$. The identity under concatenation is $\langle\ \rangle$; that is, the concatenation of $\langle\ \rangle$ with any list leaves the list unchanged.

1.8 Cycles of Days

And day by day I'll do this heavy task.
—Shakespeare: *Titus Andronicus* (V, ii)

Since R.D. 1 is a Monday, determining the day of the week amounts to taking the R.D. date modulo seven—zero is Sunday, one is Monday, and so forth. However, to keep all of our discussions independent of the arbitrary starting date, we define the seven constants

$$\textbf{sunday} \stackrel{\text{def}}{=} 0 \tag{1.13}$$

$$\textbf{monday} \stackrel{\text{def}}{=} \textbf{sunday} + 1 \tag{1.14}$$

$$\textbf{tuesday} \stackrel{\text{def}}{=} \textbf{sunday} + 2 \tag{1.15}$$

$$\textbf{wednesday} \stackrel{\text{def}}{=} \textbf{sunday} + 3 \tag{1.16}$$

$$\textbf{thursday} \stackrel{\text{def}}{=} \textbf{sunday} + 4 \tag{1.17}$$

$$\textbf{friday} \stackrel{\text{def}}{=} \textbf{sunday} + 5 \tag{1.18}$$

$$\textbf{saturday} \stackrel{\text{def}}{=} \textbf{sunday} + 6 \tag{1.19}$$

and determine the day of the week with

$$\textbf{day-of-week-from-fixed}\,(date) \stackrel{\text{def}}{=} date \mod 7 \tag{1.20}$$

Many holidays are on the nth occurrence of a given day of the week, counting forward or backward from some date. For example, American Thanksgiving is the fourth Thursday in November, that is, the fourth Thursday on or after November 1st. We handle such specifications by writing a function that encapsulates the formula, derived below,

$$d - [(d - k) \bmod 7] \tag{1.21}$$

to find the kth day of the week ($k = 0$ for Sunday, and so on) that falls in the seven-day period ending on R.D. d:

$$\textbf{kday-on-or-before}\,(date, k) \stackrel{\text{def}}{=} \tag{1.22}$$

$$date - \textbf{day-of-week-from-fixed}\,(date - k)$$

In our functions (and programs) we will generally use the parameter *date* for R.D. dates.

Formula (1.21) is an instance of a more general principle for finding the occurrence of the kth day of a repeating m-day cycle that is closest to but not past day number d, where the enumeration of days begins at day Δ of a cycle:

$$\boxed{d - [(d + \Delta - k) \bmod m]} \tag{1.23}$$

Before proving formula (1.23), let us note that it works equally well for negative and nonintegral dates d (that is, for a time of day) and for nonintegral positions k, shifts Δ, and periods m. We use such computations extensively for the Mayan calendars (Chapter 10) and the Hindu calendars (Chapter 11).

The derivation for formula (1.23) is as follows: We have days numbered $\ldots, -2, -1, 0, 1, 2, \ldots$. Suppose we also have a cycle of labels $0, 1, 2, \ldots, m-1$ for the days, in which day 0 has label Δ. We must determine the last k-label day on or before the start of day number d. (In spite of appearances, there is no assumption that m or k are integers. The labels can be continuous over the range 0 up to, but not including, m.)

Since day number 0 is a Δ-label day, day $-\Delta$ is a 0-label day. Thus the k-label days are the days numbered $k - \Delta + xm$ for any integer x. We want the day number D such that

$$D = k - \Delta + xm \le d \tag{1.24}$$

(because D is to be a k-label day on or before day d) and

$$d < D + m = k - \Delta + (x + 1)m \tag{1.25}$$

(because D is to be the last such k-label day). Inequality (1.24) tells us that

$$x \le (d - k + \Delta)/m,$$

and inequality (1.25) tells us that

$$x + 1 > (d - k + \Delta)/m.$$

That is,

$$x \le (d - k + \Delta)/m < x + 1,$$

so that

$$x = \lfloor (d - k + \Delta)/m \rfloor.$$

But, since $D = k - \Delta + xm$ by (1.24),

$$D = k - \Delta + \lfloor (d - k + \Delta)/m \rfloor \times m,$$

which we can rewrite as

$$\begin{aligned} D &= d - (d - k + \Delta - \lfloor (d - k + \Delta)/m \rfloor \times m) \\ &= d - ((d - k + \Delta) \bmod m), \end{aligned}$$

by definition (1.7). Thus formula (1.23) is verified.

Note that if the cycle of labels is $1, 2, \ldots, m$ (that is, based at one instead of zero), the corresponding formula for the last k-label day on or before day number d is found by simply shifting the label sought by -1:

$$d - ((d + \Delta - 1 - k) \bmod m). \tag{1.26}$$

We never need this, however.

Applying our function **kday-on-or-before** above to $d + 6$ gives us the **kday-on-or-after** R.D. d. Similarly, applying it to $d + 3$ gives the **kday-nearest** to R.D. d, applying it to $d - 1$ gives the **kday-before** R.D. d, and applying it to $d + 7$ gives the **kday-after** R.D. d:

$$\textbf{kday-on-or-after}\,(date, k) \stackrel{\text{def}}{=} \tag{1.27}$$
$$\textbf{kday-on-or-before}\,(date + 6, k)$$

$$\textbf{kday-nearest}\,(date, k) \stackrel{\text{def}}{=} \tag{1.28}$$
$$\textbf{kday-on-or-before}\,(date + 3, k)$$

$$\textbf{kday-after}\,(date, k) \stackrel{\text{def}}{=} \tag{1.29}$$
$$\textbf{kday-on-or-before}\,(date + 7, k)$$

$$\textbf{kday-before}\,(date, k) \stackrel{\text{def}}{=} \tag{1.30}$$
$$\textbf{kday-on-or-before}\,(date - 1, k)$$

1.9 Simultaneous Cycles

Some calendars employ two cycles running simultaneously. Each day is labeled by a pair of numbers $\langle a, b\rangle$, beginning with $\langle 0, 0\rangle$, followed by $\langle 1, 1\rangle$, $\langle 2, 2\rangle$, and so on. Suppose the first component repeats after c days and the second after d days, with $c < d < 2c$, then after day $\langle c - 1, c - 1\rangle$ come days $\langle 0, c\rangle$, $\langle 1, c + 1\rangle$, and so on, until $\langle d - c - 1, d - 1\rangle$, which is followed by $\langle d - c, 0\rangle$. If day 0 of the calendar is labeled $\langle 0, 0\rangle$, then day n is $\langle n \bmod c, n \bmod d\rangle$. The Chinese use such pairs to identify years (see Section 14.4), with cycles of length $c = 10$ and $d = 12$, but since the first component ranges from 1 to 10, inclusive, and the second from 1 to 12, we would use the adjusted mod function: $\langle n \text{ amod } 10, n \text{ amod } 12\rangle$.

More generally, if the label of day 0 is $\langle \Gamma, \Delta\rangle$, then day n is labeled

$$\boxed{\langle (n + \Gamma) \bmod c, (n + \Delta) \bmod d\rangle} \tag{1.31}$$

For the Mayan tzolkin calendar, with $c = 13$, $d = 20$, $\Gamma = 3$, $\Delta = 19$, and beginning the cycles with 1 instead of 0, this is $\langle (n+3) \text{ amod } 13, (n+19) \text{ amod } 20\rangle$. It follows that day 1 of the Mayan calendar is labeled $\langle 4, 20\rangle$ (see Section 10.2).

How many distinct day names does such a scheme provide? If m is the least common multiple (lcm) of c and d, then such a calendar repeats after m days. If the cycle lengths c and d are relatively prime (that is, no integer greater than 1 divides both c and d without remainder), then $m = c \times d$ days. Thus for the Mayan tzolkin calendar, with $c = 13$ and $d = 20$, m is 260. For the Chinese year names $\text{lcm}(10, 12) = 60$, yielding a sexagesimal cycle.

Inverting this representation is much harder. Suppose first that $\Gamma = \Delta = 0$. Given a pair $\langle a, b\rangle$, where a is an integer in the range $0 \ldots c-1$ and b is an integer in the range $0 \ldots d-1$, we are looking for an n, $0 \le n < m$, such that $a = n \bmod c$ and $b = n \bmod d$. This requires the solution to a pair of simultaneous linear congruences:

$$\begin{aligned} n &\equiv a \pmod{c} \\ n &\equiv b \pmod{d}. \end{aligned}$$

The first congruence means that

$$n = a + ic \tag{1.32}$$

for some integer i. Substituting this for n in the second congruence and transposing, we get

$$ic \equiv b - a \pmod{d}.$$

Let g be the greatest common divisor (gcd) of c and d, and let k be the multiplicative inverse of c/g modulo d/g, which is obtained using the Euclidean algorithm (see [6] for details). Then,

$$i \equiv ik\frac{c}{g} \equiv k\frac{b-a}{g} \left(\text{mod } \frac{d}{g}\right).$$

Using this value of i in equation (1.32), we get day number

$$a + c\left[k\frac{b-a}{g} \text{ mod } \frac{d}{g}\right].$$

When day 0 is labeled $\langle \Gamma, \Delta\rangle$, we must subtract Γ from a and Δ from b. To make sure that n is in the range $0 \ldots m-1$, we use

$$\boxed{n = \left(a - \Gamma + \frac{c\,[k(b - a + \Gamma - \Delta) \bmod d]}{\gcd(c, d)}\right) \bmod \text{lcm}(c, d)} \tag{1.33}$$

where k is the multiplicative inverse of $c/\gcd(c, d)$ modulo $d/\gcd(c, d)$. For example, if $c = 10$ and $d = 12$, as in the Chinese calendar, then $\gcd(10, 12) = 2$, lcm(10, 12) = 60, and $k = 1$, since $12/2 \equiv 1 \pmod{10/2}$. Using $\Gamma = \Delta = 0$, but counting from 1 instead of 0, we find that Chinese year name $\langle a, b\rangle$, $1 \le a \le 10$, $b \le b \le 12$, corresponds to year number

$$[a - 1 + 5(b - a) \bmod 12] \bmod 60 + 1$$

of the sexagesimal cycle. Detailed derivations of this sort are given for the Mayan calendars in Section 10.2.

Note that some combinations $\langle a, b\rangle$ are impossible. For example, with the Chinese scheme, the parity of the two components must be the same, since c and d are both even, and only 60 of the 120 conceivable pairs are possible.

1.10 Cycles of Years

At the expiration of the years, come challenge me.
—Shakespeare: *Love's Labour's Lost* (V, ii)

We now derive some general formulas that are useful in calendar conversions for the Julian, Islamic, Coptic, Hebrew, modern Persian, and old Hindu lunisolar calendars (although not in the same way to the Gregorian calendar, unfortunately). These calendars have in common that they follow a simple type of leap year rule in which leap years are spread as evenly as possible over a cycle of years; the particular constants that define these leap year rules are given in Table 1.2.

Suppose we have a sequence of years $\ldots, -2, -1, 0, 1, 2, \ldots$, and we want to place l leap years in a cycle of c years, with year 0 as the first year of the cycle. How can we spread the leap years evenly over the cycle? If l is a divisor of c, our problem is easy: Have year numbers that are multiples of c/l be leap years. If l is not a divisor of c, however, the best we can do is have year numbers that are *roughly* multiples of c/l be leap years—specifically, we have a leap year whenever the year number has reached or just passed a multiple of c/l. Let y be a year number; then it is a leap year if

$$y - 1 < k\frac{c}{l} \le y,$$

for some integer k. Rearranging this inequality we get

$$k\frac{c}{l} \le y < k\frac{c}{l} + 1, \tag{1.34}$$

which is the same as saying that

$$0 \le \left(y \bmod \frac{c}{l}\right) < 1.$$

Multiplying through by l using equation (1.8),

$$0 \le (yl \bmod c) < l.$$

Table 1.2 *Constants describing the simple leap year structure of various calendars*

c is the length of the leap year cycle, l is the number of leap years in that cycle of c years, Δ is the position in the cycle of year 0, L is the length of an ordinary year (hence $L + 1$ is the length of a leap year), $\bar{L} = (cL + l)/c$ is the average length of a year, and $\delta = (\Delta l)/c \bmod 1$ is the time of day (as a fraction of a day) when mean year 0 begins. This cyclic year structure also applies, approximately, to the Gregorian/Julian *months*; see Section 2.2.

Calendar	c	l	Δ	L	$\bar{L} = \frac{cL+l}{c}$	δ
Julian years C.E.	4	1	0	365 days	$\frac{1{,}461}{4}$ days	0 days
Julian years B.C.E.	4	1	1	365 days	$\frac{1{,}461}{4}$ days	$\frac{1}{4}$ day
Coptic/Ethiopic years	4	1	1	365 days	$\frac{1{,}461}{4}$ days	$\frac{1}{4}$ day
Islamic years	30	11	4	354 days	$\frac{10{,}631}{30}$ days	$\frac{7}{15}$ day
Islamic years (variant)	30	11	15	354 days	$\frac{10{,}631}{30}$ days	$\frac{1}{2}$ day
Hebrew years	19	7	11	12 months	$\frac{235}{19}$ months	$\frac{1}{19}$ month
Persian years (partial)	2816	682	38	365 days		
Old Hindu lunisolar years				12 months	$\frac{2{,}226{,}389}{180{,}000}$ months	$\frac{2{,}093{,}611}{2{,}160{,}000}$ month
Gregorian/Julian months (approximate)	12	7	11	30 days	$\frac{367}{12}$ days	$\frac{5}{12}$ day

Because our cycles always have length $c > 0$, the definition of the mod function guarantees that $(yl \bmod c) \geq 0$, so we can drop that part of the inequality to get

$$(yl \bmod c) < l. \tag{1.35}$$

For example, on the Julian calendar for years C.E. (Chapter 4) we want $l = 1$ leap year in the cycle of $c = 4$ years; then year $y > 0$ is a leap year if

$$(y \bmod 4) < 1,$$

or, in other words, if

$$(y \bmod 4) = 0.$$

We can complicate the leap year situation by insisting year 0 be in position Δ in the cycle of c years. In this case, we have the same analysis, but pretend that the cycle begins at year 0 and ask about year $y + \Delta$. Inequality (1.35) becomes,

$$\boxed{[(y + \Delta)l \bmod c] < l} \tag{1.36}$$

For example, the Julian calendar for years B.C.E. (Chapter 4) and the Coptic calendar (Chapter 5) have a cycle of $c = 4$ years containing $l = 1$ leap years with $\Delta = 1$. Inequality (1.36) becomes

$$[(y + 1) \bmod 4] < 1;$$

this is equivalent to

$$(y \bmod 4) = 3.$$

The Islamic calendar (Chapter 6) has a cycle of $c = 30$ years containing $l = 11$ leap years with $\Delta = 4$ (some Moslems have a different leap year structure that corresponds to $\Delta = 15$; see page 64), so the test for an Islamic leap year is

$$[(11y + 14) \bmod 30] < 11.$$

Spreading 11 leap years evenly over 30 years implies gaps of 2 or 3 years between leap years. Since $\frac{30}{11} = 2\frac{8}{11}$, three of the eleven leap years occur after only two years. These three short gaps are also placed at regular intervals within the 30-year cycle, to which formula (1.36) could also be applied (with $c = 11$, $l = 8$, and $\Delta = 8$).

If $\Delta = 0$, inequality (1.34) implies that

$$k = \left\lfloor \frac{y}{c/l} \right\rfloor \tag{1.37}$$

is the number of leap years in the range of years $1 \ldots y$. When $\Delta \neq 0$, we again pretend that the cycle begins at year 0 and ask about year $y + \Delta$ instead of year

y. Thus the number of leap years in the range $1 \ldots y-1$ for $\Delta \neq 0$ is the same as the number of leap years in the unshifted range of years $\Delta+1 \ldots y+\Delta-1$, namely,

$$\boxed{\left\lfloor \frac{y+\Delta-1}{c/l} \right\rfloor - \left\lfloor \frac{\Delta}{c/l} \right\rfloor = \left\lfloor \frac{ly - l + (\Delta l \bmod c)}{c} \right\rfloor} \tag{1.38}$$

the number of years in the unshifted range $1 \ldots y+\Delta-1$ minus the number in the unshifted range $1 \ldots \Delta$. For example, $\lfloor (y-1)/4 \rfloor$ is the number of leap years prior to year y on the Julian calendar, $\lfloor (11y+3)/30 \rfloor$ is the number of leap years prior to year y on the Islamic calendar, and $\lfloor y/4 \rfloor$ is the number of leap years prior to year y on the Coptic calendar.

Using formula (1.38) we immediately get the following formula for the number of days in the years prior to year y—that is, the number of days in the years $1, 2, 3, \ldots, y-1$, assuming there are L days in an ordinary year and $L+1$ days in a leap year:

$$\boxed{n = \left\lfloor \frac{ly - l + (\Delta l \bmod c)}{c} \right\rfloor + L(y-1)} \tag{1.39}$$

For example, for the Julian calendar this yields $\lfloor (y-1)/4 \rfloor + 365(y-1)$, for the Coptic calendar this yields $\lfloor y/4 \rfloor + 365(y-1)$, and for the Islamic calendar it yields $\lfloor (11y+3)/30 \rfloor + 354(y-1)$. Because the Hebrew calendar (and lunisolar calendars in general) adds leap months, formula (1.39) does not apply to days, but it does apply to *months*: The number of months prior to year y on the Hebrew calendar is $\lfloor (7y-6)/19 \rfloor + 12(y-1)$.

Formula (1.39) works for $y \leq 0$. In this case it computes the number of days in years $y \ldots 0$ as a negative number.

Finally, we can derive an inverse to (1.39) to find the year at day n, counting day $n=0$ as the first day of year 1 (the epoch). Because there are L days in an ordinary year and $L+1$ days in a leap year, the average year length is

$$\bar{L} = \frac{cL+l}{c}.$$

In the simple case that $\Delta = 0$, year y begins on day

$$\begin{aligned} n &= (y-1)L + (\text{number of leap years in } 1 \ldots y-1) \\ &= (y-1)L + \left\lfloor \frac{y-1}{c/l} \right\rfloor \\ &= \lfloor (y-1)\bar{L} \rfloor, \end{aligned} \tag{1.40}$$

using (1.38) and simplifying. Day n is in year y provided that it is on or after the first day of year y and before the first day of year $y+1$; that is,

$$\lfloor (y-1)\bar{L} \rfloor \leq n < \lfloor y\bar{L} \rfloor. \tag{1.41}$$

The sequence $\{\lfloor \bar{L} \rfloor, \lfloor 2\bar{L} \rfloor, \lfloor 3\bar{L} \rfloor, \ldots\}$ is called the *spectrum* of $\bar{L}$ (see [5, section 3.2]); in our case, they are the initial day numbers of successive years. Inequality (1.41) is equivalent to

$$(y-1)\bar{L} - 1 < n \leq y\bar{L} - 1,$$

from which it follows that

$$y = \left\lceil \frac{n+1}{\bar{L}} \right\rceil. \tag{1.42}$$

In general, when $\Delta \neq 0$, we must then shift Δ years backward; that is, shift the first day of year 1 to the first day of year $-\Delta + 1$. The number of days in the shifted years $-\Delta + 1, \ldots, 0$ is the same as the number of days in the unshifted years $1, \ldots, \Delta$, which is computed by adding the L ordinary days in each of those Δ years, plus the $\lfloor \Delta/(c/l) \rfloor$ leap days in those years as given by (1.37). The shift of Δ years thus corresponds to a shift of $\Delta L + \lfloor \Delta/(c/l) \rfloor$ days. So the shifted form of (1.42) is

$$y + \Delta = \left\lceil \frac{n + 1 + \Delta L + \left\lfloor \frac{\Delta}{c/l} \right\rfloor}{\bar{L}} \right\rceil,$$

which is the same as

$$\boxed{\begin{aligned} y &= \left\lceil \frac{cn + c - (l\Delta \bmod c)}{cL + l} \right\rceil \\ &= \left\lfloor \frac{cn + cL + l - 1 + c - (l\Delta \bmod c)}{cL + l} \right\rfloor \end{aligned}} \tag{1.43}$$

We usually prefer the latter form because the floor function is more readily available than the ceiling function in computer languages.

For the Julian calendar, formula (1.43) gives day n occurring in year

$$\left\lceil \frac{4n+4}{1461} \right\rceil = \left\lfloor \frac{4n+1464}{1461} \right\rfloor,$$

for the Coptic calendar it gives year

$$\left\lceil \frac{4n+3}{1461} \right\rceil = \left\lfloor \frac{4n+1463}{1461} \right\rfloor,$$

and for the Islamic calendar it gives year

$$\left\lceil \frac{30n+16}{10631} \right\rceil = \left\lfloor \frac{30n+10646}{10631} \right\rfloor.$$

Formula (1.43) does not apply to days on the Hebrew calendar but rather to months, giving the formula

$$\left\lceil \frac{19n+18}{235} \right\rceil = \left\lfloor \frac{19n+252}{235} \right\rfloor$$

for the year in which month n occurs; we have no use for this formula, however.

Formula (1.43) makes sense when $n < 0$, too. In this case it gives the correct year as a negative number (but, as discussed earlier, this is off by one for Julian B.C.E. years).

A more general approach to leap year distribution is to imagine a sequence of *mean years* of (noninteger) length $\bar{L}$, with year 1 starting on day 0 at time δ, $0 \leq \delta < 1$, where δ expresses time as a fraction of a day. We define a *calendar year* y to begin at the start of the day on which mean year y begins; that is, mean year y begins at moment $\delta + (y-1)\bar{L}$, so calendar year y begins on day

$$\boxed{n = \lfloor (y-1)\bar{L} + \delta \rfloor} \tag{1.44}$$

Calendar year y is an ordinary year if

$$\lfloor y\bar{L} + \delta \rfloor - \lfloor (y-1)\bar{L} + \delta \rfloor = \lfloor \bar{L} \rfloor,$$

and a leap year if

$$\lfloor y\bar{L} + \delta \rfloor - \lfloor (y-1)\bar{L} + \delta \rfloor = \lfloor \bar{L} \rfloor + 1.$$

By definition (1.7), this latter equation tells us that calendar year y is a leap year if

$$\left(\delta + (y-1)(\bar{L} \bmod 1)\right) \bmod 1 \geq 1 - \left(\bar{L} \bmod 1\right),$$

or, equivalently, if

$$\boxed{\left(\delta + (y-1)\bar{L}\right) \bmod 1 \geq 1 - \left(\bar{L} \bmod 1\right)} \tag{1.45}$$

For the old Hindu lunisolar calendar, with the year count beginning at 0 (not 1), average year length of

$$\bar{L} = \frac{2{,}226{,}389}{180{,}000} \approx 12.368828$$

months, and

$$\delta = \frac{2{,}093{,}611}{2{,}160{,}000},$$

inequality (1.45) means that y is a leap year if

$$\left(\frac{2{,}093{,}611}{2{,}160{,}000} + y\frac{2{,}226{,}389}{180{,}000}\right) \bmod 1 \geq 1 - \frac{66{,}389}{180{,}000} = \frac{113{,}611}{180{,}000},$$

or, equivalently,

$$(2{,}093{,}611 + 796{,}668y) \bmod 2{,}160{,}000 \geq 1{,}363{,}332.$$

(See page 127.) This test is not, however, needed for other old-Hindu-calendar calculations.

When $\delta = 0$, mean year 1 and calendar year 1 both begin at the same moment, and equation (1.44) tells us that leap years follow the same pattern as for $\Delta = 0$ in our earlier discussion. More generally, given any Δ, choosing

$$\delta = \frac{\Delta l}{c} \bmod 1, \tag{1.46}$$

the leap year test (1.45) simplifies to (1.36), so we have the same leap year structure. For example, the Coptic calendar has $\delta = [(1 \times 1)/4] \bmod 1 = \frac{1}{4}$.

Our δ formulas generalize our Δ formulas, because formula (1.46) gives a corresponding value of δ for each Δ. However, there need not be a value of Δ for arbitrary $\bar{L}$ and δ; indeed, there is no such Δ for calendars in which the mean and calendar years never begin at exactly the same moment. Given $\bar{L}$ and δ, we have $l/c = \bar{L} \bmod 1$, and (1.46) means that Δ exists only if δ is an integer multiple, modulo 1, of $\bar{L}$. In the old Hindu lunisolar calendar, for example, formula (1.36) cannot be used: $\bar{L} \bmod 1 = 66{,}389/180{,}000$, and we must have an integer Δ such that

$$\frac{2{,}093{,}611}{2{,}160{,}000} = \left(\Delta \frac{66{,}389}{180{,}000}\right) \bmod 1,$$

or

$$2{,}093{,}611 = (796{,}668\Delta) \bmod 2{,}160{,}000.$$

No such Δ exists because 796,668 and 2,160,000 are both even, but 2,093,611 is odd.

The generalization of formula (1.43) in terms of δ follows by solving equation (1.44) for y, to yield

$$\boxed{y = \left\lceil \frac{n + 1 - \delta}{\bar{L}} \right\rceil} \tag{1.47}$$

For the Coptic calendar this becomes

$$y = \left\lceil \frac{n + 1 - 1/4}{1461/4} \right\rceil = \left\lceil \frac{4n + 3}{1461} \right\rceil,$$

as we knew before.

For the old Hindu lunisolar calendar, in every 180,000 year cycle there are 66,389 evenly distributed leap years of 13 months. Remembering that it began with year 0, month m falls in year

$$y = \left\lceil \frac{m + 1 - \frac{2{,}093{,}611}{2{,}160{,}000}}{\frac{2{,}226{,}389}{180{,}000}} \right\rceil .$$

The application of these formulas to the old Hindu lunisolar calendar is discussed in Chapter 11.

In the foregoing discussion we have counted days beginning with the epoch of the calendars, so that when formulas (1.39) and (1.43) are used in our calendrical functions, the epoch must be added or subtracted to refer to R.D. dates. For example, to compute the Islamic year of R.D. d, we must write

$$\left\lfloor \frac{30(d - \text{Islamic epoch}) + 10646}{10631} \right\rfloor,$$

since R.D. d is (d − Islamic epoch) elapsed days on the Islamic calendar.

1.11 Warnings about the Calculations

Caveat emptor.
[Let the buyer beware.]
—Latin motto

Our code will not work forever (though it will work for many thousands of years). Specifically, some parts of the code assume that the Gregorian year and the solar year maintain the same alignment, which will not be the case in, say, 200,000 years.

We have chosen not to optimize the algorithms at the expense of clarity; consequently, considerable improvements in economy are possible, some of which are pointed out. In particular, our algorithms are designed to convert individual dates from one calendar to another, so preparation of a monthly or yearly calendar would benefit enormously from the storing of intermediate results and using them for subsequent days. This standard algorithmic technique (called "caching" or "memoization") is ignored in this book.

The functions given in the text are mechanically derived from the working Lisp code in Appendix B. In case of any ambiguity in the functions or discrepancy between the functions and the code, the code should be considered authoritative.

The astronomical code we use is not the best available, but it works quite well in practice, especially for dates near the present time, around which its approximations are centered. More precise code would be more time-consuming and complex and would not necessarily result in more accurate calendars for those calendars that depended on observations, tables, or less accurate calculations.

We do not do any error checking in the code. If one asks for the R.D. date corresponding to a date in Julian year 0, or to February 29, 1990, an answer will be generated despite the nonexistence of such dates. Similarly, the code will not object to the absurdity of asking for the R.D. date corresponding to December 39th, or even the thirty-ninth day of the thirteenth month.

All of our functions give "correct" (mathematically sensible) results for negative years and for dates prior to the epoch of a calendar. However, these results may be *culturally* wrong in the sense that, say, the Copts may not refer to a year 0 or -1. It may be heretical on some calendars to refer to years before the creation of the world.

Except for our summation operator (page 16) and search function (page 148), we avoid iteration and instead use recursion, which is natural, since we use functional notation. The use of recursion, however, is nonessential: it is "tail" recursion and can easily be replaced by iteration.

Our algorithms assume that if $y > 0$, then $(x \bmod y) \geq 0$ for all x, even for negative values of x. Care must thus be exercised in implementing our algorithms in computer languages like C or C++, in which the built-in mod function (often the % operator) gives $(x \bmod y) < 0$ for $x < 0$, $y > 0$. We also assume, in some of the functions, that $x \bmod y$ works for real numbers x and y, as well as for integers.

Checking the results of conversions against the historical record is sometimes misleading because the different calendars begin their days at different times. For example, a person who died in the evening will have a different Hebrew date of death than if he or she had died in the morning of the same Gregorian calendar date; gravestone inscriptions often err in this. All of our conversions are as of noon.

Some of our calculations require extremely large numbers; other calculations depend on numerically accurate approximations to lunar or solar events. All of the calendars in Part I, except the old Hindu, work properly (for dates within thousands of years from the present) in 32-bit integer arithmetic; the Hebrew and Persian calendars approach this limit, so we have indicated how to rephrase the calculations to use only small numbers. On the other hand, double-precision (64-bit arithmetic) is needed to reproduce accurately the results of the astronomical calculations done in Part II. We use exact rational arithmetic, with very large numbers, for the Hindu calendars; double precision can be used to approximate their calculation.

References

[1] I. Asimov, "Let Me Count the Days," *Fantasy and Science Fiction*, October 1981, pp.129–139. Reprinted in Asimov's *Counting the Eons*, Doubleday & Co. Inc., Garden City, New York, 1983, pp. 50–60.

[2] L. Cope, "Calendars of the Indians North of Mexico," *American Archaeology and Ethnology*, volume 16, pp. 119–176, 1919.

[3] 3 L. E. Doggett, "Calendars," *Explanatory Supplement to the Astronomical Almanac*, P. K. Seidelmann, ed., University Science Books, Mill Valley, CA, pp. 575–608, 1992.

[4] F. K. Ginzel, *Handbuch der mathematischen und technischen Chronologie*, J. C. Hinrichs'sche Buchhandlung, Leipzig, 1906 (volume 1), 1911 (volume 2), and 1914 (volume 3).

[5] R. L. Graham, D. E. Knuth, and O. Patashnik, *Concrete Mathematics*, 2nd ed., Addison-Wesley Publishing Company, Reading, MA, 1994.

[6] O. L. Harvey, *Calendar Conversions by Way of the Julian Day Number*, American Philosophical Society, Philadelphia, 1983.

[7] J. Hastings, ed., *Encyclopædia of Religion and Ethics*, Charles Scribner's Sons, New York, 1908–1922.

[8] J. F. W. Herschel, *Outlines of Astronomy*, 5th ed., Longman, Brown, Green, Longmans, and Roberts, London, 1858.

[9] O. Neugebauer, *A History of Ancient Mathematical Astronomy*, Springer-Verlag, Berlin, 1975 (volume 1, pp. 1–555, volume 2, pp. 556–1058, volume 3, pp. 1059–1457).

[10] O. Ore, *Number Theory and Its History*, McGraw-Hill Book Co., Inc., New York, 1948. Reprinted by Dover Publications, Inc., Mineola, NY, 1987.

[11] E. M. Reingold, J. Nievergelt, and N. Deo, *Combinatorial Algorithms: Theory and Practice*, Prentice-Hall, Englewood Cliffs, NJ, 1977.

[12] R. M. Stallman, *GNU Emacs Manual*, 6th ed., Free Software Foundation, Cambridge, MA, 1986.

[13] G. L. Steele, Jr., COMMON LISP: *The Language*, 2nd ed., Digital Press, Bedford, MA, 1990.

[14] W. S. B. Woolhouse, "Calendar," *The Encyclopædia Britannica*, 11th ed., volume 4, The Encyclopædia Britannica Co., New York, 1910, pp. 987–1004. The same article also appears in the eighth through tenth editions.

Part I

Arithmetical Calendars

Lithograph of Pope Gregory from *Biography of Gregory* (1596). (Courtesy of the University of Illinois, Urbana, IL.)

2

The Gregorian Calendar

> Ma prima che gennaio tutto si sverni,
> per la centesma ch'è laggiù negletta.
> [But, ere that January be all unwintered by
> that hundredth part neglected upon earth.]
> —Dante: *Paradiso* (XXVII, 142–143)

2.1 Structure

The calendar in use today in most countries is the *new-style* or Gregorian calendar designed by a commission assembled by Pope Gregory XIII in the sixteenth century. The main author of the new system was the Naples astronomer Aloysius Lilius; see [3], [4], [7], and [11] for mathematical and historical details. This strictly solar calendar is based on a 365-day common year divided into twelve months of lengths 31, 28, 31, 30, 31, 30, 31, 31, 30, 31, 30, and 31 days, and on 366 days in leap years, the extra day being added to make the second month 29 days long:

(1) January	31 days	(7) July	31 days
(2) February	28 {29} days	(8) August	31 days
(3) March	31 days	(9) September	30 days
(4) April	30 days	(10) October	31 days
(5) May	31 days	(11) November	30 days
(6) June	30 days	(12) December	31 days

The leap year structure is given in curly brackets. A year is a leap year if it is divisible by 4 and is not a century year (multiple of 100) or if it is divisible by 400. For example, 1900 is not a leap year; 2000 is. The Gregorian calendar differs from its predecessor, the old-style or Julian calendar, only in that the Julian calendar did not include the century rule for leap years—all century years were leap years. It is the century rule that causes the leap year structure to fall outside the cycle-of-years paradigm of Section 1.10. Days on both calendars begin at midnight.

Although the month lengths seem arbitrarily arranged, they would precisely satisfy the cycle-of-years formulas of Section 1.10 with $c = 12$, $l = 7$, $\Delta = 11$, and $L = 30$, if February always had 30 days. In other words, assuming February has 30 days, formula (1.39) tells us that there are

$$\left\lfloor \frac{7m - 2}{12} \right\rfloor + 30(m - 1) = \left\lfloor \frac{367m - 362}{12} \right\rfloor \tag{2.1}$$

days in the months $1, \ldots, m - 1$, and formula (1.43) tells us that day n of the year falls in month number

$$\left\lfloor \frac{12n + 373}{367} \right\rfloor . \tag{2.2}$$

It is a simple matter to use these formulas and correct for the mistaken assumption that February has 30 days (see the next section).

The Julian calendar was instituted on January 1, 709 A.U.C.[1] (45 B.C.E.) by Julius Cæsar, with the help of Alexandrian astronomer Sosigenes; it was a modification of the Roman Republican and ancient Egyptian calendars. Since every fourth year was a leap or *bissextile* year[2] (see Chapter 4), a cycle of 4 years contained $4 \times 365 + 1 = 1461$ days, giving an average length of year of 365.25 days. This is somewhat more than the mean length of the tropical year, and over the centuries the calendar slipped with respect to the seasons. By the sixteenth century, the date of the vernal (spring) equinox had shifted from around March 21 to around March 11. If this error were not corrected, eventually Easter, whose date depends on the vernal equinox, would migrate through the whole calendar year.

Pope Gregory XIII instituted only a minor change in the calendar—century years not divisible by 400 would no longer be leap years. (He also improved the rules for Easter; see Section 4.2.) Thus, three out of four century years are common years, giving a cycle of 400 years containing $400 \times 365 + 97 = 146{,}097$ days and an average year length of $146097/400 = 365.2425$ days. He also corrected the accumulated 10-day error in the calendar by proclaiming that Thursday, October 4, 1582 C.E., the last date in the old style (Julian) calendar, would be followed by Friday, October 15, 1582, the first day of the new-style (Gregorian) calendar. Catholic countries followed his rule; Spain, Portugal, and Italy adopted it immediately, as did the Catholic states in Germany. However,

[1] *Ab urbe condita*; from the (traditional) founding of the city (of Rome). The counting of years according to the Christian era was instituted by the Roman monk and scholar Dionysius Exiguus in the sixth century, but only became commonplace a few centuries later.

[2] The leap day, originally six days before the start of March, was called *ante diem bis sextum Kalendas Martias*, or *bissextum* [1, page 795].

Protestant countries resisted. The Protestant parts of Germany waited until 1700 to adopt it. Switzerland changed over gradually, by omitting leap years during 1583–1812. Sweden began a gradual changeover in 1699, omitting February 29 in 1700. At that point the plan was abandoned, leaving the Swedish calendar one day off from the Julian. This was only rectified in 1712 by adding a February 30th to that year! The Swedish calendar stayed in tune with the Julian until 1753, when the Gregorian was adopted.[3] Great Britain and her colonies (including the United States) waited until 1752; Russia held out until after the revolution in 1918, and Turkey until 1927. An extensive list of dates of adoption of the Gregorian calendar can be found in [2].

Although the Gregorian calendar did not exist prior to the sixteenth century, we can extrapolate backwards using its rules to obtain what is sometimes called the "proleptic Gregorian calendar,"[4] which we implement in the next section. By our choice of the starting point of our fixed counting of days, we define

$$\textbf{gregorian-epoch} \stackrel{\text{def}}{=} 1 \tag{2.3}$$

2.2 Implementation

We define twelve numerical constants by which we will refer to the twelve months of the Gregorian and Julian calendars:

$$\textbf{january} \stackrel{\text{def}}{=} 1 \tag{2.4}$$

$$\textbf{february} \stackrel{\text{def}}{=} \textbf{january} + 1 \tag{2.5}$$

$$\textbf{march} \stackrel{\text{def}}{=} \textbf{january} + 2 \tag{2.6}$$

$$\textbf{april} \stackrel{\text{def}}{=} \textbf{january} + 3 \tag{2.7}$$

$$\textbf{may} \stackrel{\text{def}}{=} \textbf{january} + 4 \tag{2.8}$$

$$\textbf{june} \stackrel{\text{def}}{=} \textbf{january} + 5 \tag{2.9}$$

$$\textbf{july} \stackrel{\text{def}}{=} \textbf{january} + 6 \tag{2.10}$$

$$\textbf{august} \stackrel{\text{def}}{=} \textbf{january} + 7 \tag{2.11}$$

$$\textbf{september} \stackrel{\text{def}}{=} \textbf{january} + 8 \tag{2.12}$$

$$\textbf{october} \stackrel{\text{def}}{=} \textbf{january} + 9 \tag{2.13}$$

[3] See *Den Svenska Historien*, volume 6, Frihetstiden, 1719–1772. We are indebted to Tapani Tarvainen and Donald Knuth for pointing out this anomaly.

[4] This appellation is really a misnomer, because "proleptic" refers to the future, not the past.

$$\textbf{november} \stackrel{\text{def}}{=} \textbf{january} + 10 \tag{2.14}$$

$$\textbf{december} \stackrel{\text{def}}{=} \textbf{january} + 11 \tag{2.15}$$

To convert from a Gregorian date to an R.D. date, we first need a function that tells us when a year is a leap year. We write

$$\textbf{gregorian-leap-year?}\,(g\text{-}year) \stackrel{\text{def}}{=} \tag{2.16}$$

$$(g\text{-}year \mod 4) = 0$$
$$\text{and } (g\text{-}year \mod 400) \notin \{100, 200, 300\}$$

The calculation of the R.D. date from the Gregorian date (which has been described [7] as "impractical") can now be done by counting the number of days in prior years (both common and leap years), the number of days in prior months of the current year, and the number of days in the current month.

$$\textbf{fixed-from-gregorian}\left(\boxed{month \mid day \mid year}\right) \stackrel{\text{def}}{=} \tag{2.17}$$

$$\textbf{gregorian-epoch} - 1 + 365 \cdot (year - 1) + \left\lfloor \frac{year - 1}{4} \right\rfloor$$
$$- \left\lfloor \frac{year - 1}{100} \right\rfloor + \left\lfloor \frac{year - 1}{400} \right\rfloor + \left\lfloor \frac{367 \cdot month - 362}{12} \right\rfloor +$$
$$\left\{ \begin{array}{ll} 0 & \textbf{if } month \le 2 \\ -1 & \textbf{if } month > 2 \\ & \quad \text{and } \textbf{gregorian-leap-year?}\,(year) \\ -2 & \textbf{otherwise} \end{array} \right\}$$
$$+ \, day$$

The explanation of this function is as follows. We add together the number of days *before* the epoch of the calendar (zero, but we do it explicitly so that the dependence on our arbitrary starting date is clear), the number of nonleap days since the epoch, the number of leap days since the epoch, the number of days in prior months of the given date, and the number of days in the given month up to and including the given date. The number of leap days since the epoch is determined by the mathematical principle of "inclusion and exclusion" [7, chapter 4]: add all Julian-leap-year-rule leap days (multiples of 4), subtract all the century years (multiples of 100), and then add back all multiples of 400. The number of days in prior months of the given year is determined by formula (2.1), corrected by 0, −1, or −2 for the assumption that February always has 30 days.

For example, to compute the R.D. date of November 12, 1945 (Gregorian) we compute $365 \times (1945-1) = 709{,}560$ prior nonleap days, $\lfloor (1945-1)/4 \rfloor = 486$ prior Julian-rule leap days (multiples of 4), $-\lfloor (1945-1)/100 \rfloor = -19$ prior century years, $\lfloor (1945-1)/400 \rfloor = 4$ prior 400-multiple years, $\lfloor (367 \times 11 - 362)/12 \rfloor = 306$ prior days, corrected by -2 because November is beyond February and 1945 is not a Gregorian leap year. Adding these values and the day 12 together gives $709{,}560 + 486 - 19 + 4 + 306 - 2 + 12 = 710{,}347$.

Calculating the Gregorian date from the R.D. *date* involves sequentially determining the year, month, and day of the month. Because of the century rule for Gregorian leap years, allowing an occasional seven-year gap between leap years, we cannot use the methods of Section 1.10—in particular, formula (1.43)—to determine the Gregorian year. Rather, the exact determination of the Gregorian year from the R.D. *date* is an example of base conversion in a mixed-radix system [10]:

$$\textbf{gregorian-year-from-fixed}\ (\mathit{date}) \stackrel{\text{def}}{=} \tag{2.18}$$

$$\begin{cases} \mathit{year} & \textbf{if } n_{100} = 4 \text{ or } n_1 = 4 \\ \mathit{year} + 1 & \textbf{otherwise} \end{cases}$$

where

$$\begin{aligned}
d_0 &= \mathit{date} - \textbf{gregorian-epoch} \\
n_{400} &= \left\lfloor \frac{d_0}{146097} \right\rfloor \\
d_1 &= d_0 \bmod 146097 \\
n_{100} &= \left\lfloor \frac{d_1}{36524} \right\rfloor \\
d_2 &= d_1 \bmod 36524 \\
n_4 &= \left\lfloor \frac{d_2}{1461} \right\rfloor \\
d_3 &= d_2 \bmod 1461 \\
n_1 &= \left\lfloor \frac{d_3}{365} \right\rfloor \\
d_4 &= (d_3 \bmod 365) + 1 \\
\mathit{year} &= 400 \cdot n_{400} + 100 \cdot n_{100} + 4 \cdot n_4 + n_1
\end{aligned}$$

The significance of d_4, which is not needed for the determination of the year, is that if $n_{100} \neq 4$ and $n_1 \neq 4$, then *date* is ordinal day $d_4 + 1$ in *year* + 1; otherwise, it is the last day of a leap year (the 146,097th day of the 400-year cycle or the 1461st day of a 4-year cycle); that is, *date* is December 31 of *year*.

This calculation of the Gregorian year of R.D. *date* is also correct for nonpositive years. In that case, n_{400} gives the number of 400-year cycles from *date* until the start of the Gregorian calendar—*including* the current cycle—as a *negative* number, since the floor function always gives the largest integer smaller than its argument. Then the rest of the calculation yields the number of years from the *beginning* of that cycle, as a *positive* integer, since the modulus is always nonnegative for positive divisor—see equations (1.9) and (1.10).

Now that we can determine the year of an R.D. date, we can find the month by formula (2.2), corrected by 0, 1, or 2 for the assumption that February always has 30 days. Knowing the year and month, we determine the day of the month by subtraction. Putting these pieces together, we have

$$\textbf{gregorian-from-fixed}\,(\textit{date}) \stackrel{\text{def}}{=} \boxed{\textit{month} \mid \textit{day} \mid \textit{year}} \tag{2.19}$$

where

$$\textit{year} = \textbf{gregorian-year-from-fixed}\,(\textit{date})$$

$$\textit{prior-days} = \textit{date} - \textbf{fixed-from-gregorian}\left(\boxed{\textbf{january} \mid 1 \mid \textit{year}}\right)$$

$$\textit{correction} = \begin{cases} 0 & \textbf{if } \textit{date} < \textbf{fixed-from-gregorian}\left(\boxed{\textbf{march} \mid 1 \mid \textit{year}}\right) \\ 1 & \textbf{if } \textit{date} \geq \textbf{fixed-from-gregorian}\left(\boxed{\textbf{march} \mid 1 \mid \textit{year}}\right) \text{ and } \textbf{gregorian-leap-year?}\,(\textit{year}) \\ 2 & \textbf{otherwise} \end{cases}$$

$$\textit{month} = \left\lfloor \frac{12 \cdot (\textit{prior-days} + \textit{correction}) + 373}{367} \right\rfloor$$

$$\textit{day} = \textit{date} - \textbf{fixed-from-gregorian}\left(\boxed{\textit{month} \mid 1 \mid \textit{year}}\right) + 1$$

We can use our fixed numbering of days to facilitate the calculation of the number of days difference between two Gregorian dates:

$$\textbf{gregorian-date-difference}\,(\textit{g-date}_1, \textit{g-date}_2) \stackrel{\text{def}}{=} \tag{2.20}$$
$$\textbf{fixed-from-gregorian}\,(\textit{g-date}_2) - \textbf{fixed-from-gregorian}\,(\textit{g-date}_1)$$

which can then be used to compute the ordinal day number of a date on the Gregorian calendar within its year:

$$\textbf{day-number}\,(g\text{-}date) \stackrel{\text{def}}{=} \tag{2.21}$$

$$\textbf{gregorian-date-difference}\left(\boxed{\textbf{december} \mid 31 \mid g\text{-}date_{\textbf{year}}-1}\,,\, g\text{-}date\right)$$

It is also easy to determine the number of days remaining after a given date in the Gregorian year:

$$\textbf{days-remaining}\,(g\text{-}date) \stackrel{\text{def}}{=} \tag{2.22}$$

$$\textbf{gregorian-date-difference}\left(g\text{-}date,\ \boxed{\textbf{december} \mid 31 \mid g\text{-}date_{\textbf{year}}}\right)$$

2.3 Holidays

> The information in this book has been gathered from many sources. Every effort has been made to insure its accuracy. Holidays sometimes are subject to change, however, and Morgan Guaranty cannot accept responsibility should any date or statement included prove to be incorrect.
>
> —Morgan Guaranty: *World Calendar* (1978)

Secular holidays on the Gregorian calendar are either on fixed days or on a particular day of the week relative to the beginning or end of a month. (An extensive list of secular holidays can be found in [5].) Fixed holidays are trivial to deal with; for example, to determine the R.D. date of American Independence Day in a given Gregorian year we would use

$$\textbf{independence-day}\,(year) \stackrel{\text{def}}{=} \tag{2.23}$$

$$\textbf{fixed-from-gregorian}\left(\boxed{\textbf{july} \mid 4 \mid year}\right)$$

Other holidays are on the nth occurrence of a given day of the week, counting from either the beginning or the end of the month. American Labor Day, for example, is the first Monday in September, and American Memorial Day is the last Monday in May. To find the R.D. date of the nth k-day after/before a given

Gregorian date (counting backward when $n < 0$), we write

$$\textbf{nth-kday}\,(n, k, date) \stackrel{\text{def}}{=} \tag{2.24}$$
$$\begin{cases} 7 \cdot n + \textbf{kday-before}\,(\textbf{fixed-from-gregorian}\,(date)\,,k) & \textbf{if } n > 0 \\ 7 \cdot n + \textbf{kday-after}\,(\textbf{fixed-from-gregorian}\,(date)\,,k) & \\ & \textbf{otherwise} \end{cases}$$

using the functions of Section 1.8 (page 19). It is also convenient to define two constants,

$$\textbf{first} \stackrel{\text{def}}{=} 1 \tag{2.25}$$

$$\textbf{last} \stackrel{\text{def}}{=} -1 \tag{2.26}$$

for use with this function. Now we can define holiday dates, such as American Labor Day,

$$\textbf{labor-day}\,(g\text{-}year) \stackrel{\text{def}}{=} \tag{2.27}$$
$$\textbf{nth-kday}\left(\textbf{first}, \textbf{monday}, \boxed{\textbf{september} \mid 1 \mid g\text{-}year}\right)$$

American Memorial Day,

$$\textbf{memorial-day}\,(g\text{-}year) \stackrel{\text{def}}{=} \tag{2.28}$$
$$\textbf{nth-kday}\left(\textbf{last}, \textbf{monday}, \boxed{\textbf{may} \mid 31 \mid g\text{-}year}\right)$$

American Election Day (the Tuesday after the first Monday in November, which is the first Tuesday on or after November 2),

$$\textbf{election-day}\,(g\text{-}year) \stackrel{\text{def}}{=} \tag{2.29}$$
$$\textbf{nth-kday}\left(\textbf{first}, \textbf{tuesday}, \boxed{\textbf{november} \mid 2 \mid g\text{-}year}\right)$$

or determine the starting and ending dates of American daylight savings time (the first Sunday in April and the last Sunday in October, respectively):

$$\textbf{daylight-savings-start}\,(g\text{-}year) \stackrel{\text{def}}{=} \tag{2.30}$$
$$\textbf{nth-kday}\left(\textbf{first}, \textbf{sunday}, \boxed{\textbf{april} \mid 1 \mid g\text{-}year}\right)$$

$$\textbf{daylight-savings-end}\,(g\text{-}year) \stackrel{\text{def}}{=} \tag{2.31}$$
$$\textbf{nth-kday}\left(\textbf{last}, \textbf{sunday}, \boxed{\textbf{october} \mid 31 \mid g\text{-}year}\right)$$

The main Christian holidays are Christmas, Easter, and various days connected with them (Advent, Ash Wednesday, Good Friday, and others; see the *Encyclopædia of Religion and Ethics* [6, vol. V, pp. 844–853]). The date of

Christmas on the Gregorian calendar is fixed and hence easily computed:

$$\textbf{christmas}\,(g\text{-}year) \stackrel{\text{def}}{=} \tag{2.32}$$
$$\textbf{fixed-from-gregorian}\left(\boxed{\textbf{december} \mid 25 \mid g\text{-}year}\right)$$

The related dates of Advent (Sunday closest to November 30) and Epiphany (twelve days after Christmas)[5] are computed by

$$\textbf{advent}\,(g\text{-}year) \stackrel{\text{def}}{=} \tag{2.33}$$
$$\textbf{kday-nearest}\left(\textbf{fixed-from-gregorian}\left(\boxed{\textbf{november} \mid 30 \mid g\text{-}year}\right), \textbf{sunday}\right)$$

$$\textbf{epiphany}\,(g\text{-}year) \stackrel{\text{def}}{=} 12 + \textbf{christmas}\,(g\text{-}year - 1) \tag{2.34}$$

The date of Assumption (August 15), celebrated in Catholic countries, is fixed and presents no problem.

We defer the calculation of Easter and related "movable" Christian holidays, which depend on lunar events, until Section 4.3.

References

[1] *The Nautical Almanac and Astronomical Ephemeris for the Year 1938*, His Majesty's Stationery Office, London, 1937.

[2] *Explanatory Supplement to the Astronomical Ephemeris and the American Ephemeris and Nautical Almanac*, Her Majesty's Stationery Office, London, 1961.

[3] G. V. Coyne, M. A. Hoskin, and O. Pedersen, *Gregorian Reform of the Calendar: Proceedings of the Vatican Conference to Commemorate Its 400th Anniversary, 1582–1982*, Pontifica Academica Scientiarum, Specola Vaticana, Vatican, 1983.

[4] J. Dutka, "On the Gregorian Revision of the Julian Calendar," *Mathematical Intelligencer*, volume 10, pp. 56–64, 1988.

[5] R. W. Gregory, *Special Days*, Citadel, Secaucus, NJ, 1975. Previous editions appeared under the title *Anniversaries and Holidays*.

[6] J. Hastings, ed., *Encyclopædia of Religion and Ethics*, Charles Scribner's Sons, New York, 1911.

[7] L. Lamport, "On the Proof of Correctness of a Calendar Program," *Communications of the ACM*, volume 22, pp. 554–556, 1979.

[8] C. L. Liu, *Introduction to Combinatorial Mathematics*, McGraw-Hill Book Co., New York, 1968.

[9] G. Moyer, "The Gregorian Calendar," *Scientific American*, volume 246, no. 5, pp. 144–152, May, 1982.

[10] E. M. Reingold, J. Nievergelt, and N. Deo, *Combinatorial Algorithms: Theory and Practice*, Prentice-Hall, Englewood Cliffs, NJ, 1977.

[11] V. F. Rickey, "Mathematics of the Gregorian Calendar," *Mathematical Intelligencer*, volume 7, pp. 53–56, 1985.

[5] Except in the United States, where Epiphany is celebrated on the first Sunday after January 1.

BANKER'S 1881 CALENDAR

And TIMING TABLE

For ascertaining the maturity of bills and notes, and the number of days from one date to another within the year.

Please report PROMPTLY to THE BANKER'S ALMANAC AND REGISTER, *New York*, any changes that may occur in your bank or in others of your vicinity; also the names of new banks or bankers.

	S	M	T	W	T	F	S		S	M	T	W	T	F	S
	....	....	....	....	....	....	1 +		....	....	....	....	....	182 1	183 2
	2 2	3 3	4 4	5 5	6 6	7 7	8 8		184 3	185 +	186 5	187 6	188 7	189 8	190 9
January.	9 9	10 10	11 11	12 12	13 13	14 14	15 15	July.	191 10	192 11	193 12	194 13	195 14	196 15	197 16
	16 16	17 17	18 18	19 19	20 20	21 21	22 22		198 17	199 18	200 19	201 20	202 21	203 22	204 23
	23 23	24 24	25 25	26 26	27 27	28 28	29 29		205 24	206 25	207 26	208 27	209 28	210 29	211 30
	30 30	31 31	32 1	33 2	34 3	35 4	36 5		212 31	213 1	214 2	215 3	216 4	217 5	218 6
	37 6	38 7	39 8	40 9	41 10	42 11	43 12		219 7	220 8	221 9	222 10	223 11	224 12	225 13
February.	44 13	45 14	46 15	47 16	48 17	49 18	50 19	August.	226 14	227 15	228 16	229 17	230 18	231 19	232 20
	51 20	52 21	53 +	54 23	55 24	56 25	57 26		233 21	234 22	235 23	236 24	237 25	238 26	239 27
	58 27	59 28	60 1	61 2	62 3	63 4	64 5		240 28	241 29	242 30	243 31	244 1	245 2	246 3
	65 6	66 7	67 8	68 9	69 10	70 11	71 12		247 4	248 5	249 6	250 7	251 8	252 9	253 10
March.	72 13	73 14	74 15	75 16	76 17	77 18	78 19	September.	254 11	255 12	256 13	257 14	258 15	259 16	260 17
	79 20	80 21	81 22	82 23	83 24	84 25	85 26		261 18	262 19	263 20	264 21	265 22	266 23	267 24
	86 27	87 28	88 29	89 30	90 31	91 1	92 2		268 25	269 26	270 27	271 28	272 29	273 30	274 1
	93 3	94 4	95 5	96 6	97 7	98 8	99 9		275 2	276 3	277 4	278 5	279 6	280 7	281 8
April.	100 10	101 11	102 12	103 13	104 14	105 15	106 16	October.	282 9	283 10	284 11	285 12	286 13	287 14	288 15
	107 17	108 18	109 19	110 20	111 21	112 22	113 23		289 16	290 17	291 18	292 19	293 20	294 21	295 22
	114 24	115 25	116 26	117 27	118 28	119 29	120 30		296 23	297 24	298 25	299 26	300 27	301 28	302 29
	121 1	122 2	123 3	124 4	125 5	126 6	127 7		303 30	304 31	305 1	306 2	307 3	308 4	309 5
	128 8	129 9	130 10	131 11	132 12	133 13	134 14		310 6	311 7	312 +	313 9	314 10	315 11	316 12
May.	135 15	136 16	137 17	138 18	139 19	140 20	141 21	November.	317 13	318 14	319 15	320 16	321 17	322 18	323 19
	142 22	143 23	144 24	145 25	146 26	147 27	148 28		324 20	325 21	326 22	327 23	328 +	329 25	330 26
	149 29	150 +	151 31	152 1	153 2	154 3	155 4		331 27	332 28	333 29	334 30	335 1	336 2	337 3
	156 5	157 6	158 7	159 8	160 9	161 10	162 11		338 4	339 5	340 6	341 7	342 8	343 9	344 10
June.	163 12	164 13	165 14	166 15	167 16	168 17	169 18	December.	345 11	346 12	347 13	348 14	349 15	350 16	351 17
	170 19	171 20	172 21	173 22	174 23	175 24	176 25		352 18	353 19	354 20	355 21	356 22	357 23	358 24
	177 26	178 27	179 28	180 29	181 30	....	....		359 25	360 +	361 27	362 28	363 29	364 30	365 31

+ LEGAL HOLIDAYS in the State of New York.

Banker's calendar, arranged by weeks and including day numbers. From *The Banker's Almanac and Register* (1881). (Courtesy of the publisher.)

3

The ISO Calendar

> O tempora! O mores! [Oh what times! Oh what standards!]
>
> —Cicero: *In Catilinam* (I,1)

The International Organization for Standardization (ISO) calendar, popular in Sweden and other European countries, specifies a date by giving the ordinal day in the week and the "calendar week" in a Gregorian year. The ISO standard [1, section 3.17] defines a *calendar week* as

> A seven day period within a calendar year, starting on a Monday and identified by its ordinal number within the year; the first calendar week of the year is the one that includes the first Thursday of that year. In the Gregorian calendar, this is equivalent to the week which includes 4 January.

It follows that an ISO year begins with the Monday between December 29th and January 4th and ends with a Sunday between December 28th and January 3rd. Accordingly, a year on the ISO calendar consists of 52 or 53 whole weeks, making the year either 364 or 371 days long. The epoch is the same as the Gregorian calendar, namely R.D. 1, because January 1, 1 (Gregorian) was a Monday. Days begin at midnight, as on the Gregorian and Julian calendars.

The week number of a given ISO date gives the number of weeks after the first Sunday on or after December 28th of the preceding year. Hence the determination of the R.D. date corresponding to an ISO date is easy, using **nth-kday** (page 40). The ISO calendar counts Sunday as the seventh day of the week, so we implement this calendar as follows:

$$\textbf{fixed-from-iso}\left(\begin{array}{|c|c|c|}\hline \textit{week} & \textit{day} & \textit{year} \\ \hline\end{array}\right) \stackrel{\text{def}}{=} \tag{3.1}$$

$$\textbf{nth-kday}\left(\textit{week}, \textbf{sunday}, \begin{array}{|c|c|c|}\hline \textbf{december} & 28 & \textit{year}-1 \\ \hline\end{array}\right)$$

$$+\ \textit{day}$$

$$\textbf{iso-from-fixed}\ (\textit{date}) \stackrel{\text{def}}{=} \begin{array}{|c|c|c|}\hline \textit{week} & \textit{day} & \textit{year} \\ \hline\end{array} \tag{3.2}$$

where

$$
\begin{aligned}
\textit{approx} &= \textbf{gregorian-year-from-fixed}\\
&\quad (\textit{date} - 3)\\
\textit{year} &= \begin{cases} \textit{approx} + 1 & \textbf{if } \textit{date} \geq \textbf{fixed-from-iso}\left(\boxed{1 \mid 1 \mid \textit{approx}{+}1}\right) \\ \textit{approx} & \textbf{otherwise} \end{cases}\\
\textit{week} &= \left\lfloor \frac{\textit{date} - \textbf{fixed-from-iso}\left(\boxed{1 \mid 1 \mid \textit{year}}\right)}{7} \right\rfloor\\
&\quad + 1\\
\textit{day} &= \textit{date} \text{ amod } 7
\end{aligned}
$$

The calculation of the ISO day and week numbers from the fixed date are clear, once the ISO year has been found. Because the ISO year can extend as much as three days into the following Gregorian year, we find the Gregorian year for *date* − 3; this approximation is guaranteed to be either the desired ISO year or the prior ISO year. We determine which is the case by comparing the *date* to the R.D. date of the start of the approximate ISO year.

Reference

[1] *Data Elements and Interchange Formats—Information Interchange—Representation of Dates*, ISO 8601, International Organization for Standardization, 1988. This standard replaced ISO 2015, the original document describing the ISO calendar.

CERTISSIMA VERÆ VIRTVTIS

EFFIGIES,

D. JULIUS CÆSAR

DICTATOR.

Imperium, *binis fuerat ſolenne quod olim*
Conſulibus, Cæſar Iulius obtinuit.
Sed breve jus regni, ſola trieteride geſtum,
Perculit armatæ factio ſæva togæ.

CHRI-

Profile of Julius Cæser from *C. Ivlii Cæsaris Quæ Extant*, with emendations of Joseph Scaliger (1635). (Courtesy of the University of Chicago, Chicago, IL.)

4

The Julian Calendar

Thirty days hath September,
April, June and November;
All the rest have thirty-one,
Excepting February alone,
And that has twenty-eight days clear
And twenty-nine in each leap year.
—*Traditional children's rhyme*

4.1 Structure and Implementation

The calculations for the Julian calendar, which we described in introducing the Gregorian calendar in Chapter 2, are nearly identical to those for the Gregorian calendar, but we must change the leap year rule to

$$\textbf{julian-leap-year?}\ (\textit{j-year}) \stackrel{\text{def}}{=} \tag{4.1}$$

$$(\textit{j-year} \mod 4) = \left\{ \begin{array}{ll} 0 & \textbf{if } \textit{j-year} > 0 \\ 3 & \textbf{otherwise} \end{array} \right\}$$

The upper part is formula (1.35), and the lower part is formula (1.36) with $\Delta = 1$. Note that the Julian leap year rule was applied inconsistently for some years prior to 8 C.E.

The months of the Julian calendar are the same as on the Gregorian calendar (see page 33).

Converting from a Julian date to an R.D. date requires a calculation similar to that in the Gregorian case, but with two minor adjustments: We no longer need consider century-year leap days, and we must define the epoch of the Julian calendar in terms of our fixed dating. For the epoch, we know that R.D. 1 is January 3, 1 C.E. (Julian), so the first day of the Julian calendar, January 1,

1 C.E. (Julian) must be December 30, 0 (Gregorian), that is, R.D. −1:

$$\textbf{julian-epoch} \stackrel{\text{def}}{=} \textbf{fixed-from-gregorian}\left(\boxed{\textbf{december} \mid 30 \mid 0}\right) \tag{4.2}$$

Now we can write

$$\textbf{fixed-from-julian}\left(\boxed{\mathit{month} \mid \mathit{day} \mid \mathit{year}}\right) \stackrel{\text{def}}{=} \tag{4.3}$$

$$\textbf{julian-epoch} - 1 + 365 \cdot (y - 1) + \left\lfloor \frac{y-1}{4} \right\rfloor + \left\lfloor \frac{367 \cdot \mathit{month} - 362}{12} \right\rfloor + \begin{cases} 0 & \textbf{if } \mathit{month} \le 2 \\ -1 & \textbf{if } \mathit{month} > 2 \text{ and } \textbf{julian-leap-year?}(\mathit{year}) \\ -2 & \textbf{otherwise} \end{cases} + \mathit{day}$$

where

$$y = \begin{cases} \mathit{year} + 1 & \textbf{if } \mathit{year} < 0 \\ \mathit{year} & \textbf{otherwise} \end{cases}$$

This function is similar in structure to **fixed-from-gregorian**. We add together the number of days before the epoch of the calendar, the number of nonleap days since the epoch, the number of leap days since the epoch, the number of days in prior months of the given date, and the number of days in the given month up to and including the given date. For nonpositive years, we adjust the year to accommodate the lack of year zero.

For the inverse function, we handle the missing year zero by subtracting one from the year as determined by formula (1.43) for dates before the epoch:

$$\textbf{julian-from-fixed}\,(\mathit{date}) \stackrel{\text{def}}{=} \boxed{\mathit{month} \mid \mathit{day} \mid \mathit{year}} \tag{4.4}$$

where

$$\mathit{approx} = \left\lfloor \frac{4 \cdot (\mathit{date} - \textbf{julian-epoch}) + 1464}{1461} \right\rfloor$$

$$year = \begin{cases} approx - 1 \ \textbf{if} \ approx \le 0 \\ approx \qquad\qquad \textbf{otherwise} \end{cases}$$

$$prior\text{-}days = date - \textbf{fixed-from-julian}\left(\boxed{\textbf{january} \mid 1 \mid year}\right)$$

$$correction = \begin{cases} 0 \ \textbf{if} \ date < \textbf{fixed-from-julian}\left(\boxed{\textbf{march} \mid 1 \mid year}\right) \\ 1 \qquad \textbf{if} \ date \ge \textbf{fixed-from-julian}\left(\boxed{\textbf{march} \mid 1 \mid year}\right) \\ \qquad \text{and } \textbf{julian-leap-year?}\,(year) \\ 2 \qquad \textbf{otherwise} \end{cases}$$

$$month = \left\lfloor \frac{12 \cdot (prior\text{-}days + correction) + 373}{367} \right\rfloor$$

$$day = date - \textbf{fixed-from-julian}\left(\boxed{month \mid 1 \mid year}\right) + 1$$

4.2 Holidays

Until 1923 Eastern Orthodox Christmas depended on the Julian calendar. At that time, the Ecumenical Patriarch, Meletios IV, convened a congress at which it was decided to use the Gregorian date instead. By 1968 all but the churches of Jerusalem, Russia, and Serbia adopted the new date, December 25th on the Gregorian calendar. There remain, however, *Palaioemerologitai* groups, especially in Greece, who continue to use the old calendar. Virtually all Orthodox churches continue to celebrate Easter according to the Julian calendar. (See the next section.)

The occurrence of the old Eastern Orthodox Christmas in a given Gregorian year is somewhat involved. Since the Julian year is always at least as long as the corresponding Gregorian year, Eastern Orthodox Christmas can occur at most once in a given Gregorian year, but it can occur either at the beginning or the end; in some years (for example, 1100 C.E.) it does not occur at all. We write a general function that gives a list of the corresponding R.D. dates of occurrence of a given month, day on the Julian calendar (within a given Gregorian year):

$$\textbf{julian-in-gregorian}\,(\textit{j-month}, \textit{j-day}, \textit{g-year}) \stackrel{\text{def}}{=} \tag{4.5}$$

$$\left\{\begin{array}{ll} \langle \textit{date}_1 \rangle & \textbf{if } \textit{jan}_1 \le \textit{date}_1 \le \textit{dec}_{31} \\ \langle\,\rangle & \textbf{otherwise} \end{array}\right\} \;\|\; \left\{\begin{array}{ll} \langle \textit{date}_2 \rangle & \textbf{if } \textit{jan}_1 \le \textit{date}_2 \le \textit{dec}_{31} \\ \langle\,\rangle & \textbf{otherwise} \end{array}\right\}$$

where

$$\begin{array}{lcl} \textit{jan}_1 & = & \textbf{fixed-from-gregorian}\left(\boxed{\textbf{january} \mid 1 \mid \textit{g-year}}\right) \\ \textit{dec}_{31} & = & \textbf{fixed-from-gregorian}\left(\boxed{\textbf{december} \mid 31 \mid \textit{g-year}}\right) \\ y & = & \textbf{julian-from-fixed}\,(\textit{jan}_1)_{\textbf{year}} \\ \textit{date}_1 & = & \textbf{fixed-from-julian}\left(\boxed{\textit{j-month} \mid \textit{j-day} \mid y}\right) \\ \textit{date}_2 & = & \textbf{fixed-from-julian}\left(\boxed{\textit{j-month} \mid \textit{j-day} \mid y+1}\right) \end{array}$$

Recall that || is our notation for list concatenation (see Section 1.7).

For example, we use this function to determine a list of zero or one R.D. dates of December 25 (Julian) for a given year of the Gregorian calendar:

$$\textbf{eastern-orthodox-christmas}\,(\textit{g-year}) \stackrel{\text{def}}{=} \tag{4.6}$$

$$\textbf{julian-in-gregorian}\,(\textbf{december}, 25, \textit{g-year})$$

Other fixed Orthodox holidays are the Nativity of the Virgin Mary (September 8), the Elevation of the Life-Giving Cross (September 14), the Presentation of the Virgin Mary in the Temple (November 21), Epiphany (January 6), the Presentation of Christ in the Temple (February 2), the Annunciation (March 25), the Transfiguration (August 6), and the Repose of the Virgin Mary (August 15). Orthodox periods of fasting include the Fast of the Repose of the Virgin Mary (August 1–14) and the forty-day Christmas Fast (November 15–December 24).

4.3 Easter

The calculation of the date of Easter has a fascinating history, and algorithms and computer programs abound (for example, [1], [6], and [9]; the discussion in

O'Beirne's *Puzzles and Paradoxes* [8] is especially nice); these computations rely on the formulas of Gauss [3], [4] (see also [5]).[1] We include functions here for Easter because its computation was originally tied to the Julian calendar. Our fixed-date approach allows considerable simplification of "classical" algorithms.

The date of Easter was fixed in 325 C.E. by the Council of Nicæa, convened by Constantine the Great, to be

The first Sunday after the first full moon occurring on or after the vernal equinox.

Easter is thus delayed one week if the full moon is on Sunday to lessen the likelihood of its being on the same day as the Jewish Passover. This ruling was contrary to the practice of the Quartodecinians, who celebrated Easter on the day of the full moon, fourteen days into the month, regardless of the day of the week. As the Council wrote to the Church of Alexandria [1, p. 799]:

> We send you the good news concerning the unanimous consent of all in reference to the celebration of the most solemn feast of Easter, for this difference also has been made up by the assistance of your prayers, so that all the brethren in the East, who formerly celebrated this festival at the same time as the Jews, will in future conform to the Romans and to us and to all who have from of old kept Easter with us.

The above definition seems precise, but accurate determination of the full moon and the vernal equinox is quite complex in reality, and simpler approximations are used in practice; as Kepler declared [7], "Easter is a feast, not a planet." As implemented by Dionysius Exiguus in 525 C.E., the date of Easter is based on the presumption that the vernal equinox is always March 21 and on ecclesiastical approximations to the lunar phases, called *epacts*. Epacts are computed based on the fact that new moons occur on about the same day of the solar year (adjusted for leap years) in a cycle of 19 years, called the *Metonic cycle*, comprising 235 lunations (see page 9). Curiously, Kepler's Rudolphine astronomical tables were used to fix the date of Easter by Protestants in Germany between 1700 and 1776 and Sweden used astronomical rules from 1740 to 1844.

Before the Gregorian reform of the Julian calendar, the approximations were fairly crude. If the Metonic cycle were perfectly accurate, the phase of the moon on January 1 would be the same every 19 years. Hence, the epact can be approximated by multiplying the number of years since the start of the current Metonic cycle (the so-called "golden number") by the 11-day difference between a common year of 365 days and 12 lunar months of 29.5 days and adjusting by the epact

[1] Gauss's original paper contained an error that affects the date of Easter first in 4200 C.E.; see [8].

of January 1, 1 C.E. (Julian)—all this done modulo 30. To find the last full moon (that is, day 14 of the monthly cycle) prior to April 19, we subtract the phase of the moon on April 5 (14 days earlier) from the fixed date of April 19. (The number of days between full moon and April 19 is equal to the days between new moon and April 5.) The moon's phase (in days) on April 5, called the *shifted-epact* in the function below, increases by 11 days each year, modulo 30, taking on the values 14, 25, 6, 17, 28, 9, 20, 1, 12, 23, 4, 15, 26, 7, 18, 29, 10, 21, 2, in sequence. Going back that number of days from April 19 gives a date between March 21 and April 18, inclusive, for the (ecclesiastical) "Paschal full moon." Thus the equivalent of the following calculation was used to determine Easter from the end of the eighth century until the adoption of the Gregorian calendar, and it is still used by all Orthodox churches, except those in Finland:

$$\textbf{nicaean-rule-easter}\ (\textit{j-year}) \stackrel{\text{def}}{=} \qquad (4.7)$$

$$\textbf{kday-after}\ (\textit{paschal-moon}, \textbf{sunday})$$

where

$$\begin{aligned} \textit{shifted-epact} &= (14 + 11 \cdot (\textit{j-year} \bmod 19)) \bmod 30 \\ \textit{paschal-moon} &= \textbf{fixed-from-julian}\left(\boxed{\textbf{april} \mid 19 \mid \textit{j-year}}\right) \\ &\quad - \textit{shifted-epact} \end{aligned}$$

Since the shifted epact is never 0, the calculated full moon is never on April 19. The earliest date for Easter Sunday is therefore March 22 and the latest is April 25.

The Julian leap-year cycle of four years contains 208 weeks and 4 days. Only after 28 years do all dates on the Julian calender return to the same day of the week. The combination of this "solar" cycle and the 19-year lunar cycle gives rise to the 532-year "Victorian" or "Dionysian" cycle for the date of Orthodox Easter. The average length of a lunar month according to this method is

$$\frac{19 \cdot 365\frac{1}{4}}{235} \approx 29.530851 \text{ days.}$$

The number of full moons between April 19 of two successive years can be either 12 or 13. The distribution of "leap" years of 13 lunar cycles and ordinary years of 12 follows a regular pattern describable by formula (1.38), namely

$$\left\lfloor \frac{7y - 11}{19} \right\rfloor.$$

This observation leads to an alternative formula for the fixed date of the paschal moon:

$$354y + 30\left\lfloor \frac{7y - 11}{19} \right\rfloor + \left\lfloor \frac{y}{4} \right\rfloor - \left\lfloor \frac{y}{19} \right\rfloor - 243.$$

The minimum twelve lunar months per year contribute 354 days; seven out of nineteen years include a thirteenth lunar month of 30 days; each leap year contributes an extra day to the total number of elapsed days; but every 19 years the lunar cycle is reset to begin one day earlier.

The Gregorian reform of 1582 C.E. included a far more accurate approximation to the lunar phases for the calculation of Easter, developed by German Jesuit astronomer Christoph Clavius, based on the suggestions of Lilius. Two corrections and two adjustments are employed in the Gregorian rule for Easter:

- In three out of four century years, the Gregorian leap-year rule causes a shift of one day forward in the date of the full moon. This is taken into account in the calculation of epacts by subtracting 1 for each non-leap century year.
- The first correction keeps the lunar cycle synchronized with the Julian calendar. But nineteen Julian years of 365.25 days are a fraction longer than 235 mean lunations. So a corrective factor of one day in 8 out of 25 century years is added to the epact. The epacts of the 3rd, 6th, 9th, 12th, 15th, 19th, 22nd, and 25th centuries are affected by this correction. A one-day bias was deliberately introduced in its initial sixteenth-century value of 5 to minimize coincidences of Easter and Passover (also based on the 19-year Metonic cycle; see Section 9.3) as often as possible [8].
- The old limits on the dates of the ecclesiastical full moon were preserved in the reformed calendar. Unfortunately, with the new century-year rule a shifted epact of 0 becomes possible, which, if used, would place the full moon on April 19. Whenever that occurs, the epact is, therefore, adjusted to 1, which pushes the full moon date back to April 18.
- Clavius also strived to retain the property that the date of the Easter moon never repeats within a single 19-year cycle. The problem is that when the previous adjustment is made and the shifted epact is set to 1 instead of 0, the same shifted epact may also occur 11 years later. The solution is to also increase any shifted epact of 1 occurring in the second half of a cycle.

This is the method now used by Catholic and Protestant churches:

$$\mathbf{easter}\,(\textit{g-year}) \stackrel{\text{def}}{=} \tag{4.8}$$

$$\mathbf{kday\text{-}after}\,(\textit{paschal-moon},\ \mathbf{sunday})$$

where

$$\textit{century} \quad = \quad \left\lfloor \frac{\textit{g-year}}{100} \right\rfloor + 1$$

$$
\textit{shifted-epact} = \left(14 + 11 \cdot (\textit{g-year} \bmod 19) - \left\lfloor \frac{3 \cdot \textit{century}}{4} \right\rfloor + \left\lfloor \frac{5 + 8 \cdot \textit{century}}{25} \right\rfloor \right) \bmod 30
$$

$$
\textit{adjusted-epact} = \begin{cases} \textit{shifted-epact} + 1 & \textbf{if } \textit{shifted-epact} = 0 \text{ or } \{ \textit{shifted-epact} = 1 \text{ and } 10 < (\textit{g-year} \bmod 19) \} \\ \textit{shifted-epact} & \textbf{otherwise} \end{cases}
$$

$$
\textit{paschal-moon} = \textbf{fixed-from-gregorian}\left(\boxed{\textbf{april} \mid 19 \mid \textit{g-year}} \right) - \textit{adjusted-epact}
$$

With the new method, the most likely date of Easter is April 19 (almost 4% of the years); the least likely is March 22 (less than 0.5%). The dates of Easter repeat only after 5,700,000 years, the least common multiple of the 19-year Metonic cycle, the 400 years it takes for the Gregorian calendar to return to the same pattern of days of the week, the 4000 years it takes for the Gregorian leap-year corrections to add up to 30 days, and the 9375 years it takes for the correction to the Metonic cycle to amount to 30 days. This cycle comprises 2,081,882,250 days and 70,499,183 months for an average lunar month of approximately 29.530587 days.

Many Christian holidays depend on the date of Easter: Septuagesima Sunday (63 days before), Sexagesima Sunday (56 days before), Shrove Sunday (49 days before), Shrove Monday (48 days before), Shrove Tuesday (47 days before), Ash Wednesday (46 days before), Passion Sunday (14 days before), Palm Sunday (seven days before), Holy or Maundy Thursday (three days before), Good Friday (two days before), Rogation Sunday (35 days after), Ascension Day (39 days after), Pentecost (also called Whitsunday—49 days after), Whitmundy (50 days after), Trinity Sunday (56 days after), and Corpus Christi (60 days[2] after). All

[2] Or 63 days, in the Catholic Church in the United States. Because of the extensive liturgical changes after the Second Vatican Council, the Catholic Church no longer observes Septuagesima, Sexagesima, and Shrove Sunday through Tuesday.

these are easily computed; for example

$$\textbf{pentecost}\,(g\text{-}year) \stackrel{\text{def}}{=} \textbf{easter}\,(g\text{-}year) + 49 \tag{4.9}$$

The forty days of Lent begin on Ash Wednesday. Orthodox Christians begin Lent seven weeks (48 days) before Eastern Orthodox Easter, on Monday. The Eastern Orthodox Church celebrates the Feast of Orthodoxy on the following Sunday (42 days before Eastern Orthodox Easter). The Orthodox Fast of the Apostles begins eight days after Orthodox Pentecost and ends on June 28.

References

[1] *The Nautical Almanac and Astronomical Ephemeris for the Year 1938*, His Majesty's Stationery Office, London, 1937.

[2] E. R. Berlekamp, J. H. Conway, and R. K. Guy, *Winning Ways: Volume 2, Games in Particular*, Academic Press, New York, 1982.

[3] C. F. Gauss, "Berechnung des Osterfestes," *Monatliche Correspondenz zur Beförderung der Erd- und Himmels-Kunde*, Herausgegeben vom Freiherrn von Zach (August, 1800). Reprinted in Gauss's *Werke*, Herausgegeben von der Königlichen Gesellschaft der Wissenschaften, Göttingen, volume 6, pp. 71–79, 1874.

[4] C. F. Gauss, "Noch etwas über die Bestimmung des Osterfestes," *Braunschweigisches Magazin* (September 12, 1807). Reprinted in Gauss's *Werke*, Herausgegeben von der Königlichen Gesellschaft der Wissenschaften, Göttingen, volume 6, pp. 82–86, 1874.

[5] H. Kinkelin, "Die Berechnung des christlichen Osterfestes," *Zeitschrift für mathematik und Physik,* volume 15, pp. 217–238, 1870.

[6] D. E. Knuth, "The Calculation of Easter," *Communications of the ACM*, volume 5, pp. 209–210, 1962.

[7] G. Moyer, "The Gregorian Calendar," *Scientific American*, volume 246, no. 5, pp. 144–152, May, 1982.

[8] T. H. O'Beirne, *Puzzles and Paradoxes*, Oxford University Press, London, 1965. Reprinted by Dover Publications, New York, 1984.

[9] J. V. Uspensky and M. A. Heaslet, *Elementary Number Theory*, McGraw-Hill, New York, 1939.

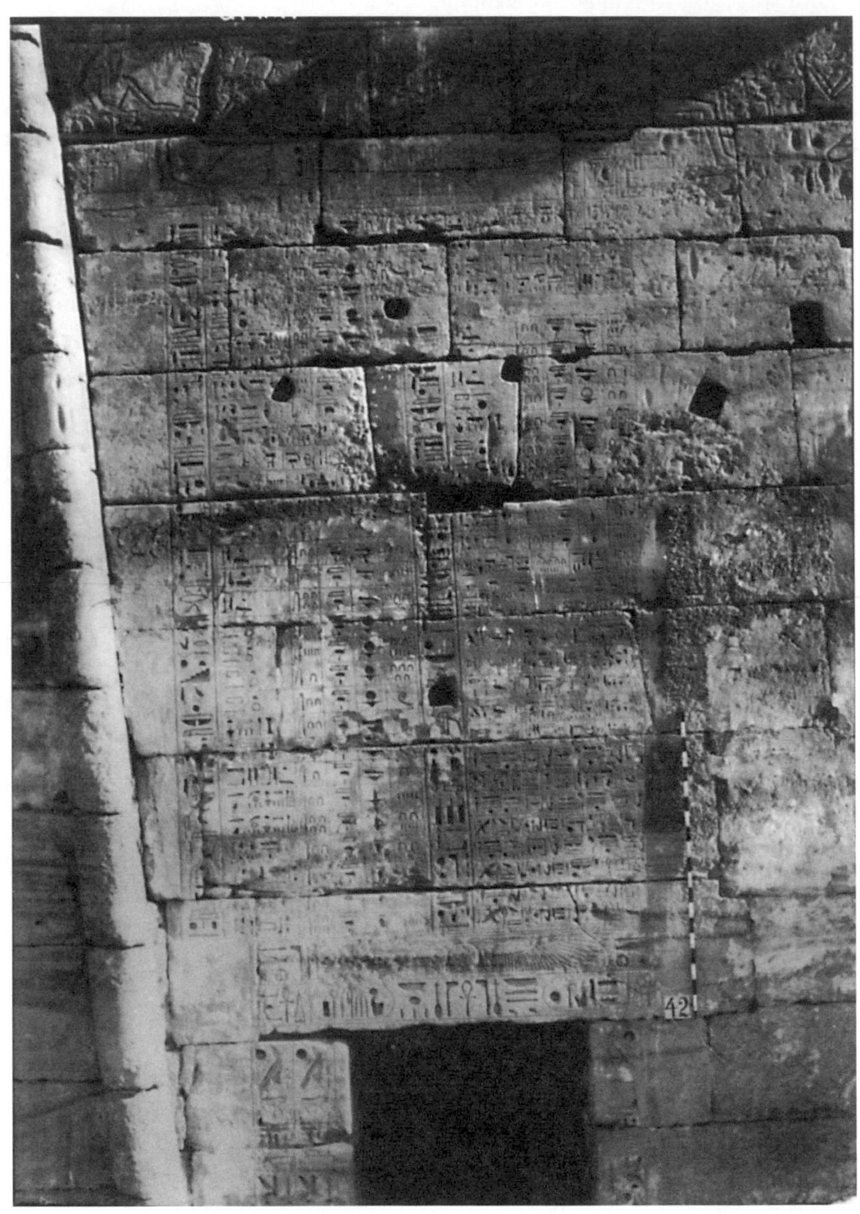

The calendar monument at Medinet Habu, Thebes, including dates of celebrations and sacrifices. From the reign of Ramses III (twelfth century B.C.E.). (Courtesy of the Oriental Institute, University of Chicago, Chicago, IL.)

5

The Coptic and Ethiopic Calendars

Kiyahk: ṣabāḥak misāk
[In Kiyahk, your morning is your evening.]
—*Coptic rhyme about the short days of winter*

5.1 The Coptic Calendar

The Christian Copts, modern descendants of the Pharaonic Egyptians, use a calendar based on the ancient Egyptian solar calendar. Days begin at sunset, and the calendar consists of twelve 30-day months followed by an extra five-day period. Once every fourth year a leap day is added to this extra period to make it six days, making the average year $365\frac{1}{4}$ days long, like the Julian calendar of Chapter 4. The months are called by Arabic names:

(1) Tūt	30 days	(7) Baramhāt	30 days
(2) Bābah	30 days	(8) Baramūndah	30 days
(3) Hātūr	30 days	(9) Bashans	30 days
(4) Kiyahk	30 days	(10) Ba'ūnah	30 days
(5) Ṭūbah	30 days	(11) Abīb	30 days
(6) Amshīr	30 days	(12) Misrā	30 days
		(13) al-Nasī	5 {6} days

(The leap year structure is given in curly brackets.) We treat al-Nasī, the extra five or six days, called *epagomenæ*, as a short thirteenth month. Indeed, they are called "the small month" (*p abot n kouji*) in Coptic.

The Copts count their years from August 29, 284 C.E. (Julian), R.D. 103,605, the beginning of their year 1.[1] Thus we define

[1] This is the year Diocletian ascended the emperorship of Rome. A year on the Coptic calendar is usually indicated by the abbreviation A.M., standing for *anno martyrum* or "Era of the Martyrs." We avoid this usage because it conflicts with the common method of referring to a year on the Hebrew calendar.

$$\textbf{coptic-epoch} \stackrel{\text{def}}{=} \tag{5.1}$$

$$\textbf{fixed-from-julian}\left(\boxed{\textbf{august} \mid 29 \mid 284 \text{ C.E.}}\right)$$

Leap years occur when the Coptic year number leaves a remainder of 3 when divided by 4; this is $c = 4$, $l = 1$, $\Delta = 1$ in formula (1.36). We express this rule by

$$\textbf{coptic-leap-year?}\ (c\text{-}year) \stackrel{\text{def}}{=} (c\text{-}year \bmod 4) = 3 \tag{5.2}$$

but we do not ever need this function.

Considering al-Nasī as a month, to convert a Coptic date

$$\boxed{month \mid day \mid year}$$

to an R.D. date, we do as with the corresponding Gregorian and Julian functions: Add together the days before the start of the Coptic calendar, the number of days since the epoch aside from leap days, the number of leap days, the number of days in prior months in *year*, and the number of prior days in *month*:

$$\textbf{fixed-from-coptic}\left(\boxed{month \mid day \mid year}\right) \stackrel{\text{def}}{=} \tag{5.3}$$

$$\textbf{coptic-epoch} - 1 + 365 \cdot (year - 1) + \left\lfloor \frac{year}{4} \right\rfloor + 30 \cdot (month - 1) + day$$

To convert an R.D. date to a Coptic date, we use formula (1.43) to determine the year. Then, unlike the Gregorian or Julian calendars, the simple month-length structure of the Coptic calendar allows us to determine the month by dividing by 30. As in the other calendars, we determine the day by subtraction:

$$\textbf{coptic-from-fixed}\ (date) \stackrel{\text{def}}{=} \boxed{month \mid day \mid year} \tag{5.4}$$

where

$$year = \left\lfloor \frac{4 \cdot (date - \textbf{coptic-epoch}) + 1463}{1461} \right\rfloor$$

$$month = \left\lfloor \frac{date - \textbf{fixed-from-coptic}\left(\boxed{1 \mid 1 \mid year}\right)}{30} \right\rfloor + 1$$

$$day = date + 1 - \textbf{fixed-from-coptic}\left(\boxed{month \mid 1 \mid year}\right)$$

5.2 The Ethiopic Calendar

The Ethiopic calendar is identical to the Coptic calendar except for the epoch and the month names. The Ethiopic months are

(1) Maskaram	30 days	(7) Magābit	30 days
(2) Teqemt	30 days	(8) Miyāzyā	30 days
(3) Khedār	30 days	(9) Genbot	30 days
(4) Tākhśāś	30 days	(10) Sanē	30 days
(5) Ṭer	30 days	(11) Ḥamlē	30 days
(6) Yakātit	30 days	(12) Naḥasē	30 days
		(13) Pāguemēn	5 {6} days

The Ethiopic calendar starts on August 29, 7 C.E. (Julian), our R.D. 2430:

$$\textbf{ethiopic-epoch} \stackrel{\text{def}}{=} \tag{5.5}$$

$$\textbf{fixed-from-julian}\left(\boxed{\textbf{august}}\boxed{29}\boxed{7\text{ C.E.}}\right)$$

To convert Ethiopic dates to and from R.D. dates, we just use our Coptic functions above, but adjust for the different epoch:

$$\textbf{fixed-from-ethiopic}\left(\boxed{\mathit{month}}\boxed{\mathit{day}}\boxed{\mathit{year}}\right) \stackrel{\text{def}}{=} \tag{5.6}$$

$$\textbf{ethiopic-epoch} +$$
$$\textbf{fixed-from-coptic}\left(\boxed{\mathit{month}}\boxed{\mathit{day}}\boxed{\mathit{year}}\right) - \textbf{coptic-epoch}$$

$$\textbf{ethiopic-from-fixed}\,(\mathit{date}) \stackrel{\text{def}}{=} \tag{5.7}$$

$$\textbf{coptic-from-fixed}$$
$$(\mathit{date} + \textbf{coptic-epoch} - \textbf{ethiopic-epoch})$$

5.3 Holidays

Determining the corresponding Gregorian date of a fixed date on the Coptic or Ethiopic calendars is similar to the corresponding determination for the Julian calendar. Indeed, the Coptic and Julian are consistently aligned, except for a fluctuation of one day caused by the difference in leap year rule. For the Coptic calendar, to determine the R.D. dates of a given Coptic month/day during a

Gregorian year, we use

$$\textbf{coptic-in-gregorian}\,(c\text{-}month,\ c\text{-}day,\ g\text{-}year) \stackrel{\text{def}}{=} \tag{5.8}$$

$$\begin{Bmatrix} \langle date_1 \rangle \ \textbf{if}\ jan_1 \le date_1 \le dec_{31} \\ \langle\,\rangle \qquad\qquad\qquad \textbf{otherwise} \end{Bmatrix} \ \| \ \begin{Bmatrix} \langle date_2 \rangle \ \textbf{if}\ jan_1 \le date_2 \le dec_{31} \\ \langle\,\rangle \qquad\qquad\qquad \textbf{otherwise} \end{Bmatrix}$$

where

$$jan_1 = \textbf{fixed-from-gregorian}\left(\boxed{\textbf{january}}\boxed{1}\boxed{g\text{-}year}\right)$$

$$dec_{31} = \textbf{fixed-from-gregorian}\left(\boxed{\textbf{december}}\boxed{31}\boxed{g\text{-}year}\right)$$

$$y = \textbf{coptic-from-fixed}\,(jan_1)_{\textbf{year}}$$

$$date_1 = \textbf{fixed-from-coptic}\left(\boxed{c\text{-}month}\boxed{c\text{-}day}\boxed{y}\right)$$

$$date_2 = \textbf{fixed-from-coptic}\left(\boxed{c\text{-}month}\boxed{c\text{-}day}\boxed{y+1}\right)$$

For example, the Copts celebrate Christmas on Kiyahk 29 (which is always either December 25th or 26th on the Julian calendar) so we can write

$$\textbf{coptic-christmas}\,(g\text{-}year) \stackrel{\text{def}}{=} \tag{5.9}$$

$$\textbf{coptic-in-gregorian}\,(4,\ 29,\ g\text{-}year)$$

to give us a list of R.D. dates of Coptic Christmas during a given Gregorian year.

Other Coptic holidays include Epiphany (Ṭūbah 11), Mary's Announcement (Baramūndah 29), Jesus's Circumcision (Ṭūbah 6), Jesus's Transfiguration (Mishrā 13), and the Building of the Cross (Tūt 17). The date of Easter is determined by the Nicæan rule (page 52) and converted to the Coptic calendar.

The corresponding determinations for the Ethiopic calendar require only a straightforward modification of **coptic-in-gregorian**, changing all references from the Coptic calendar to the Ethiopic calendar.

References

[1] A. Cody, "Coptic Calendar," *The Coptic Encyclopedia*, volume 2, pp. 433–436, Macmillan, New York, 1991.

[2] F. K. Ginzel, *Handbuch der mathematischen und technischen Chronologie*, volume 3, J. C. Hinrichs'sche Buchhandlung, Leipzig, section 262, 1914.
[3] C. W. Wassef, *Practiques Rituelles et Alimentaires des Coptes*, Publications de L'Institut Français d'Archéologie Orientale du Caire, Bibliothèque d'Études Coptes, Cairo, 1971.

Page containing a discussion of months in the pre-Islamic Arab, Hebrew, Islamic, and Hindu calendars, along with a multicolored illustration of Mohammed instituting the purely lunar calendar. From a seventeenth-century copy of an illuminated fourteenth-century manuscript of the eleventh-century work *Al-Āthār al-Bāqiyah ʻan al-Qurūn al-Khāliyah* by the great Persian scholar and scientist Abū-Raiḥān Muḥammad ibn ʼAḥmad al-Bīrūnī. (Courtesy of Bibliothèque Nationale de France, Paris.)

6

The Islamic Calendar

> The number of months with God is twelve in accordance with God's law since the day he created the heavens and the earth. . . . Intercalating a month is adding to unbelief.
>
> —*Koran* (IX, 36–37)

6.1 Structure and Implementation

The Islamic calendar is a straightforward, strictly lunar calendar, with no intercalation of months (unlike lunisolar calendars). Its independence of the solar cycle means that its months do not occur in fixed seasons, but migrate through the solar year. Days begin at sunset. In this book, we describe only the fixed, civil Islamic calendar, in which months follow a set pattern; for religious purposes, virtually all Moslems follow an observation-based calendar.

The week begins on Sunday; the days of the week are numbered, not named:

Sunday	yawm al-'aḥad	(The first day)
Monday	yawm al-'ithnayn	(The second day)
Tuesday	yawm ath-thalāthā'	(The third day)
Wednesday	yawm al-'arba'ā'	(The fourth day)
Thursday	yawm al-khamīs	(The fifth day)
Friday	yawm al-jum'a	(The sixth day)
Saturday	yawm as-sabt	(The sabbath day)

The calendar is computed, by the majority of the Moslem world, starting at sunset of Thursday, July 15, 622 C.E. (Julian), the year of Mohammed's emigration[1] to Medina. The introduction of the calendar is often attributed to the Caliph 'Umar, in 639 C.E., but there is evidence that it was in use before his succession. In essence, Moslems count R.D. 227,015 = Friday, July 16, 622 C.E.

[1] The term "flight," while commonly used in English to describe the beginning of the Islamic epoch, does not accurately reflect the meaning of the Arabic term *hijra*, which has more a connotation of "breaking of ties" than of "running away."

(Julian) as the beginning of the Islamic year 1, that is, as Muḥarram 1, 1 A.H.,[2] so we define

$$\textbf{islamic-epoch} \stackrel{\text{def}}{=} \qquad (6.1)$$

$$\textbf{fixed-from-julian}\left(\boxed{\textbf{july} \mid 16 \mid 622 \text{ C.E.}}\right)$$

There are twelve Islamic months, which contain, alternately, 29 or 30 days:

(1) Muḥarram	30 days	(7) Rajab	30 days
(2) Ṣafar	29 days	(8) Sha'bān	29 days
(3) Rabī' I	30 days	(9) Ramaḍān	30 days
(4) Rabī' II	29 days	(10) Shawwāl	29 days
(5) Jumādā I	30 days	(11) Dhu al-Qa'da	30 days
(6) Jumādā II	29 days	(12) Dhu al-Ḥijja	29 {30} days

The leap year structure is given in curly brackets—the last month, Dhu al-Ḥijja, contains 30 days in the 2nd, 5th, 7th, 10th, 13th, 16th, 18th, 21st, 24th, 26th, and 29th years of a 30-year cycle. This gives an average month of $29.5305555\cdots$ days and an average year of $354.3666\cdots = 354\frac{11}{30}$ days. The cycle of common and leap years can be expressed concisely by observing that an Islamic year y is a leap year if and only if $(11y + 14) \bmod 30$ is less than 11; this is an instance of formula (1.36) with $c = 30$, $l = 11$, and $\Delta = 4$:

$$\textbf{islamic-leap-year?}\ (\textit{i-year}) \stackrel{\text{def}}{=} \qquad (6.2)$$

$$((14 + 11 \cdot \textit{i-year}) \bmod 30) < 11$$

We never need this function, however. Some Moslems take the 15th year as a leap year instead of the 16th. This variant structure, which is used by Birashk [1], corresponds to $c = 30$, $l = 11$, and $\Delta = 15$ in the cycle formulas from Section 1.10; our functions thus require only minor modification for this variant leap year rule (replacing 14 by $11 \times 15 \bmod 30 = 15$ in **islamic-leap-year?**, for example).

Converting from an Islamic date to an R.D. date is done by summing the days so far in the current month, the days so far in prior months of the current Islamic year [$29.5 \times (\textit{month} - 1)$, rounded up], the days in prior Islamic years

[2] *Anno hegiræ*; in the year of the Hegira (Mohammed's emigration to Medina)—see the previous footnote.

[by formula (1.39)], and the days prior to the Islamic calendar:

$$\textbf{fixed-from-islamic}\left(\boxed{\,\textit{month}\mid\textit{day}\mid\textit{year}\,}\right) \stackrel{\text{def}}{=} \tag{6.3}$$

$$\textit{day} + \lceil 29.5 \cdot (\textit{month} - 1)\rceil + (\textit{year} - 1) \cdot 354 + \left\lfloor \frac{3 + 11 \cdot \textit{year}}{30} \right\rfloor + \textbf{islamic-epoch} - 1$$

Computing the Islamic date equivalent to a given R.D. date is more straightforward than the computations for the Gregorian calendar or the Julian: We calculate the exact value of the year using formula (1.43). Then, since months alternate in length between 30 and 29, they too are easy to calculate directly, except that we must allow for an irregular 30-day twelfth month in leap years:

$$\textbf{islamic-from-fixed}\,(\textit{date}) \stackrel{\text{def}}{=} \boxed{\,\textit{month}\mid\textit{day}\mid\textit{year}\,} \tag{6.4}$$

where

$$\textit{year} = \left\lfloor \frac{30 \cdot (\textit{date} - \textbf{islamic-epoch}) + 10646}{10631} \right\rfloor$$

$$\textit{month} = \min\{12, m\}$$

$$\textit{day} = \textit{date} - \textbf{fixed-from-islamic}\left(\boxed{\,\textit{month}\mid 1\mid\textit{year}\,}\right) + 1$$

$$m = \left\lceil \frac{\textit{date} - 29 - \textbf{fixed-from-islamic}\left(\boxed{\,1\mid 1\mid\textit{year}\,}\right)}{29.5} \right\rceil + 1$$

It is important to realize that to a great extent the foregoing calculations are merely hypothetical because there are many disparate forms of the Islamic calendar [5]. Furthermore, much of the Islamic world relies not on the calculations of this *civil* calendar at all but on proclamation of the new moon by religious authorities based on visibility of lunar crescent. Consequently, the dates given by the functions here can be in error by a day or two from what will actually be observed in various parts of the Islamic world; this is unavoidable. Though one could use astronomical functions (see Chapter 12) to determine the actual date of visibility of a new moon, the calculation of the astronomical Islamic calendar is quite intricate—see [4]—and not universally accepted.

6.2 Holidays

Only approximate positions have been used for predicting the commencement of a Hijri month, as accurate places cannot be computed without a great amount of labour. . . . Users of this Diglott Calendar must, therefore, at the commencement of each year correct the dates with those in the official Block Calendar issued by the Nizamiah Observatory.

—Director of Nizamiah Observatory, quoted by Mazhar Husain: *Diglott Calendar*, volume II, p. iii (1961)

Determining the R.D. dates of holidays occurring in a given Gregorian year is complicated, because an Islamic year is always shorter than the Gregorian year, so each Gregorian year contains parts of at least two and sometimes three successive Islamic years. Hence any given Islamic date occurs at least once and possibly twice in any given Gregorian year. For example, Islamic New Year (Muḥarram 1) occurred twice in 1943: on January 8 and again on December 28. Accordingly, we approach the problem of the Islamic holidays by writing a general function to return a list of the R.D. dates of a given Islamic date occurring in a given Gregorian year:

$$\textbf{islamic-in-gregorian}\ (\textit{i-month}, \textit{i-day}, \textit{g-year}) \stackrel{\text{def}}{=} \tag{6.5}$$

$$\begin{Bmatrix} \langle date_1 \rangle \ \textbf{if}\ jan_1 \le date_1 \le dec_{31} \\ \langle\,\rangle \qquad\qquad \textbf{otherwise} \end{Bmatrix} \parallel \begin{Bmatrix} \langle date_2 \rangle \ \textbf{if}\ jan_1 \le date_2 \le dec_{31} \\ \langle\,\rangle \qquad\qquad \textbf{otherwise} \end{Bmatrix} \parallel \begin{Bmatrix} \langle date_3 \rangle \ \textbf{if}\ jan_1 \le date_3 \le dec_{31} \\ \langle\,\rangle \qquad\qquad \textbf{otherwise} \end{Bmatrix}$$

where

$$jan_1 = \textbf{fixed-from-gregorian}\left(\boxed{\textbf{january} \mid 1 \mid \textit{g-year}}\right)$$

$$dec_{31} = \textbf{fixed-from-gregorian}\left(\boxed{\textbf{december} \mid 31 \mid \textit{g-year}}\right)$$

$$y = \textbf{islamic-from-fixed}\left(jan_1\right)_{\textbf{year}}$$

$$date_1 = \textbf{fixed-from-islamic}\left(\boxed{\textit{i-month} \mid \textit{i-day} \mid y}\right)$$

$$date_2 = \textbf{fixed-from-islamic}\left(\begin{array}{|c|c|c|}\hline \textit{i-month} & \textit{i-day} & y{+}1 \\ \hline\end{array}\right)$$

$$date_3 = \textbf{fixed-from-islamic}\left(\begin{array}{|c|c|c|}\hline \textit{i-month} & \textit{i-day} & 2{+}y \\ \hline\end{array}\right)$$

There is little uniformity among the Islamic sects and countries as to holidays. In general, the principal holidays of the Islamic year are Islamic New Year (Muḥarram 1), 'Ashūrā' (Muḥarram 10), Mawlid an-Nabī (Rabī' I 12), Lailat-al-Mi'rāj (Ascent of the Prophet, Rajab 27), Lailat-al-Barā'a (Sha'bān 15), Ramaḍān (Ramaḍān 1), Lailat-al-Kadr (Ramaḍān 27), 'Īd-al-Fiṭr (Shawwāl 1), and 'Īd-al'-Aḍḥā (Dhu al-Ḥijja 10). Other days, too, have religious significance—for example, the entire month of Ramaḍān. Like all Islamic days, an Islamic holiday begins at sunset the prior evening. We can determine a list of the corresponding R.D. dates of occurrence in a given Gregorian year by using **islamic-in-gregorian** above, as in

$$\textbf{mawlid-an-nabi}\,(\textit{g-year}) \stackrel{\text{def}}{=} \qquad (6.6)$$

$$\textbf{islamic-in-gregorian}\,(3, 12, \textit{g-year})$$

It bears reiterating that the determination of the Islamic holidays cannot be fully accurate, because the precise day of their occurrence depends on proclamation by religious authorities.

References

[1] A. Birashk, *A Comparative Calendar of the Iranian, Muslim Lunar, and Christian Eras for Three Thousand Years*, Mazda Publishers (in association with Bibliotheca Persica), Costa Mesa, CA, 1993.

[2] S. B. Burnaby, *Elements of the Jewish and Muhammadan Calendars, With Rules and Tables and Explanatory Notes on the Julian and Gregorian Calendars*, George Bell and Sons, London, 1901.

[3] G. S. P. Freeman-Grenville, *The Muslim and Christian Calendars*, 2nd ed., Rex Collings, London, 1977. A new addition has been published as *The Islamic and Christian Calendars* A.D. 622–2222 (A.H. 1–1650): *A Complete Guide for Converting Christian and Islamic Dates and Dates of Festivals*, Garnet Publications, Reading, MA, 1995.

[4] M. Ilyas, *A Modern Guide to Astronomical Calculations of Islamic Calendar, Times & Qibla*, Berita Publishing, Kuala Lumpur, 1984.

[5] V. V. Tsybulsky, *Calendars of Middle East Countries*, Institute of Oriental Studies, USSR Academy of Sciences, Moscow, 1979.

[6] W. S. B. Woolhouse, *Measures, Weights, & Moneys of All Nations: And an Analysis of the Christian, Hebrew, and Mahometan Calendars*, 6th ed., Crosby Lockwood, London, 1881.

First fourteen of twenty-eight Arabian lunar mansions from a late fourteenth-century manuscript of *Kitāb al-Bulhān* by the celebrated ninth-century Muslim astrologer Abu-Ma'shar (Albumazar) al-Falaki of Balkh, Khurasan, Persia. (Courtesy of the Bodleian Library, University of Oxford, Oxford.)

7

The Persian Calendar

> It was the custom of the Persians not to begin a march before sunrise. When the day was already bright, the signal was given from the king's tent with the horn; above the tent, from which it might be seen by all, there gleamed an image of the sun enclosed in crystal. Now the order of march was as follows. In front on silver altars was carried the fire which they called sacred and eternal. Next came the Magi, chanting their traditional hymn. These were followed by three hundred and sixty five young men clad in purple robes, equal in number to the days of the whole year; for the Persians also divided the year into that number of days.
>
> —Quintus Curtius Rufus:
> *History of Alexander* (III, iii, pp. 8–10)

The modern Persian calendar, adopted in 1925, is an extremely accurate solar calendar based on the Jalālī calendar designed in the eleventh century by a committee of astronomers including a young Omar Khayyām, the noted Persian mathematician, astronomer, and poet. The Jalālī calendar had twelve months of thirty days each, followed by a five-day period (six in leap years; the leap year structure is simpler than that described below for the modern Persian calendar), just like the Coptic/Ethiopic calendar described in Chapter 5. The lengthy history of Persian calendars is discussed in [3]; [1] gives a briefer history, together with tables and complex computational rules.[1] A calendar identical to the modern Persian calendar, but with different month names, was adopted in Afghanistan in 1957.

[1] Birashk [1] contains some significant numerical errors in the treatment of negative Persian years. For example, his leap year test in Section 2.5.2 works only for positive years. His Table 2.2 shows the subcycle −41 . . . 86, which contains only 127 years, since there is no year zero; this leads to errors in his examples in his Section 2.6.2. His Table I shows −1260 as a leap year, which it is not. There are various other minor errors in his Table I as well.

7.1 Structure

The epoch of the modern Persian calendar is the date of the vernal equinox prior to the epoch of the Islamic calendar; that is,

$$\textbf{persian-epoch} \stackrel{\text{def}}{=} \tag{7.1}$$
$$\textbf{fixed-from-julian}\left(\boxed{\textbf{march} \mid 19 \mid 622\ \text{C.E.}}\right)$$

In theory, the year begins on the day when the vernal equinox (approximately March 21) occurs before noon (the middle point of the day) and is postponed to the next day if the equinox is after noon. However, the time of day of the equinox is location-dependent, so such a rule would lead to location-dependent leap-year determination; Birashk [1, page 38], [2], the premier expert on modern Persian calendars, explicitly rejects such determination in favor of the fixed intercalation scheme described below. To implement the theoretical form of the calendar, we would imitate the method used for the French Revolutionary calendar described in Chapter 13.

There are twelve Persian months, containing 29, 30, or 31 days, as follows:

(1) Farvardīn	31 days	(7) Mehr	30 days
(2) Ordībehesht	31 days	(8) Abān	30 days
(3) Khordād	31 days	(9) Āzar	30 days
(4) Tīr	31 days	(10) Dey	30 days
(5) Mordād	31 days	(11) Bahman	30 days
(6) Shahrīvar	31 days	(12) Esfand	29 {30} days

The leap year structure is given in curly brackets—the last month, Esfand, contains 30 days in leap years. Thus, an ordinary year has 365 days and a leap year has 366 days. Days begin at local zone midnight, just like the Gregorian day.

The intricate leap year pattern of the modern Persian calendar follows a cycle of 2820 years, containing a total of 683 leap years, with the following structure. The 2820-year cycle consists of twenty-one 128-year subcycles, followed by a 132-year subcycle:

$$2820 = 21 \times 128 + 132.$$

Each 128-year subcycle is divided into one 29-year sub-subcycle, followed by three 33-year sub-subcycles:

$$128 = 29 + 3 \times 33.$$

Similarly, the 132-year subcycle is divided into one 29-year sub-subcycle, followed by two 33-year sub-subcycles, followed by one 37-year sub-subcycle:

$$132 = 29 + 2 \times 33 + 37.$$

Finally, a year y in a sub-subcycle is a leap year if $y > 1$ and $y \bmod 4 = 1$. That is, years 5, 9, 13, ... of a sub-subcycle are leap years. Thus, a 29-year sub-subcycle has seven leap years, a 33-year sub-subcycle has eight leap years, and a 37-year sub-subcycle has nine leap years for a total of

$$21 \times (7 + 3 \times 8) + (7 + 2 \times 8 + 9) = 683$$

leap years and a total of

$$2820 \times 365 + 683 = 1{,}029{,}983$$

days in the 2820-year cycle. The true number of days in 2820 solar years is

$$2820 \times 365.242199 = 1{,}029{,}983.00118,$$

so the Persian calendar is in error by only 1.7 *minutes* in 2820 years, or one day in 2.39 *million years*—amazing accuracy!

Years 475 A.P.,[2] 3295 A.P., ... are the first years of the cycle, and there is no Persian year 0 (as on the Julian calendar). To facilitate the use of modular arithmetic, however, it is more convenient for us to view the cycles as beginning in the years 474 A.P., 3294 A.P., ... which we consider the zeroth years of the cycle, rather than the 2820th years.

7.2 Implementation

Unfortunately, the distribution of the 683 leap years in the cycle of 2820 years does not obey the cycle-of-years formulas from Section 1.10, so our implementation must be more complex than in, say, the Islamic calendar described in Chapter 6. Fortunately, the distribution of the leap years in the range of 443–3293 A.P. *does* satisfy the cycle of years formulas with $c = 2816$, $l = 682$, and $\Delta = 38$. This range of years contains a full cycle of 2820 Persian years, 474–3293 A.P., so by shifting into that range we *can* use the cycle-of-years formulas from Section 1.10. First we find the number of years since the zeroth year of Persian cycle that started in 474 A.P.; then we find the equivalent position to that year in the range 474–3293 A.P.; and then we apply formula (1.36). Our test for a Persian leap year is thus

$$\textbf{persian-leap-year?}\ (p\text{-}year) \stackrel{\text{def}}{=} \tag{7.2}$$

$$((year + 38) \cdot 682 \mod 2816) < 682$$

[2] *Anno persico*; Persian year.

where

$$y = \begin{cases} p\text{-}year - 474 & \textbf{if } 0 < p\text{-}year \\ p\text{-}year - 473 & \textbf{otherwise} \end{cases}$$

$$year = (y \bmod 2820) + 474$$

However, we do not need this function to convert Persian dates to and from R.D. dates. We include it because it is much simpler than the rule given in [1]; the simple rule in [3] is wrong.

To convert a Persian date to an R.D. date we first find the equivalent year in the 2820-year cycle 474–3293 A.P.; then we use *that* year and imitate our function for converting from an Islamic date to an R.D. date (page 65): We add together the number of days before the epoch of the calendar, the number of days in 2820-year cycles before 474 A.P., the number of nonleap days in prior years, the number of leap days in prior years—computed using formula (1.38) with $\Delta = 474 + 38 = 512$, the number of days in prior months of the given date, and the number of days in the given month up to and including the given date:

$$\textbf{fixed-from-persian}\left(\boxed{month \mid day \mid p\text{-}year}\right) \stackrel{\text{def}}{=} \tag{7.3}$$

$$\textbf{persian-epoch} - 1 + 1029983 \cdot \left\lfloor \frac{y}{2820} \right\rfloor + 365 \cdot (year - 1) +$$

$$\left\lfloor \frac{682 \cdot year - 110}{2816} \right\rfloor + \begin{cases} 31 \cdot (month - 1) & \textbf{if } month \leq 7 \\ 30 \cdot (month - 1) + 6 & \textbf{otherwise} \end{cases} + day$$

where

$$y = \begin{cases} p\text{-}year - 474 & \textbf{if } 0 < p\text{-}year \\ p\text{-}year - 473 & \textbf{otherwise} \end{cases}$$

$$year = (y \bmod 2820) + 474$$

The inverse problem, determining the Persian date corresponding to a given R.D. date, must be handled as on the Gregorian calendar (page 38). First we must determine the Persian year in which a given R.D. date occurs. This calculation is done as in the Gregorian calendar (page 38), but taking the number of days elapsed since Farvardīn 1, 475 A.P., dividing by 1,029,983 to get the number of completed 2820-year cycles, and using the remainder of that division to get the number of prior days since the start of the last 2820-year cycle. Then we add together 474 (the number of years before the 2820-year cycles), $2820 \times n_{2820}$ (the number of years in prior 2820-year cycles), and the number of years since the start of the last 2820-year cycle. The last of these is computed from formula (1.43). However, that formula is based on a cycle of years numbered 1, 2, ..., $c = 2820$, while the range of applicability of our approximate cycle structure is 474–3293 A.P. which corresponds to years in the cycle numbered 0, 1, ..., 2819; hence formula (1.43) does not apply to the last year. The last year differs from the cycle-of-years formula only because it is a leap year and hence it is only to the last day of that year that the formula does not apply—that is, day 1,029,982, the last day of a 2820-year cycle—and we must handle that as an exception. Thus:

$$\textbf{persian-year-from-fixed}\ (date) \stackrel{\text{def}}{=} \tag{7.4}$$

$$\begin{cases} year & \textbf{if } 0 < year \\ year - 1 & \textbf{otherwise} \end{cases}$$

where

$$d_0 = date - \textbf{fixed-from-persian}\left(\boxed{1 \mid 1 \mid 475}\right)$$

$$n_{2820} = \left\lfloor \frac{d_0}{1029983} \right\rfloor$$

$$d_1 = d_0 \bmod 1029983$$

$$y_{2820} = \begin{cases} 2820 & \textbf{if } d_1 = 1029982 \\ \left\lfloor \dfrac{2816 \cdot d_1 + 1031337}{1028522} \right\rfloor & \textbf{otherwise} \end{cases}$$

$$year = 474 + 2820 \cdot n_{2820} + y_{2820}$$

The computation of y_{2820} in **persian-year-from-fixed** requires a numerator as large as $2816 \times 1{,}029{,}981 = 2{,}900{,}426{,}496$, which approaches our limit of 32-bit arithmetic. We can avoid such large numbers by expressing $d_1 = 366a + b$, $0 \le b < 366$, and rewriting that computation as

$$a = \left\lfloor \frac{d_1}{366} \right\rfloor,$$

$$b = d_1 \bmod 366,$$

$$y_{2820} = 1 + a + \left\lfloor \frac{2134a + 2816b + 2815}{1028522} \right\rfloor.$$

We chose 366 as the divisor because $(2816 \times 366) \bmod 1028522 = 2134$ is small.

Now that we can determine the Persian year of an R.D. date, we can easily find the day number in the Persian year of an R.D. date; from that we can compute the

Persian month number by division. Knowing the year and month, we determine the day of the month by subtraction. Putting these pieces together, we have

$$\textbf{persian-from-fixed}\,(date) \stackrel{\text{def}}{=} \boxed{month \mid day \mid year} \tag{7.5}$$

where

$$\begin{aligned}
year &= \textbf{persian-year-from-fixed}\,(date)\\
day\text{-}of\text{-}year &= date - \textbf{fixed-from-persian}\left(\boxed{1 \mid 1 \mid year}\right)\\
&\quad +1\\
month &= \begin{cases} \left\lceil \dfrac{day\text{-}of\text{-}year}{31} \right\rceil & \textbf{if } day\text{-}of\text{-}year \le 186\\[2ex] \left\lceil \dfrac{day\text{-}of\text{-}year - 6}{30} \right\rceil & \textbf{otherwise} \end{cases}\\
day &= date - \textbf{fixed-from-persian}\\
&\quad \left(\boxed{month \mid 1 \mid year}\right)\\
&\quad +1
\end{aligned}$$

7.3 Holidays

> A philosopher of the Ḥashwiyya-school relates that when Solomon the son of David had lost his seal and his empire, but was reinstated after forty days, he at once regained his former majesty, the princes came before him, and the birds were busy in his service. Then the Persians said, "*Naurôz âmadh*," *i.e.* the new day has come. Therefore that day was called Naurôz.
>
> —Abū-Raiḥān Muḥammad ibn 'Aḥmad al-Bīrūnī: *Al-Āthār al-Bāqiyah 'an al-Qurūn al-Khāliyah*, p. 199 (1000)

As throughout this book, we consider our problem to be the determination of holidays that occur in a specified Gregorian year. Since the Persian year is almost consistently aligned with the Gregorian year, each Persian holiday (as long as it is not near January 1) occurs just once in a given Gregorian year. Holidays that occur on fixed days on the Persian calendar are almost fixed on the Gregorian calendar. They are easy to determine on the Gregorian calendar by observing that the Persian year beginning in the Gregorian year y is given by

$$\text{Persian new year occurring in March of Gregorian year } y$$
$$= y + 1 - \textbf{gregorian-year-from-fixed}(\textbf{persian-epoch}),$$

but we must compensate for the lack of year zero by subtracting one if the above value is not positive. Thus, to find the R.D. date of *Naw Ruz* (Persian New Year, Farvardīn 1), which falls in a Gregorian year, we would use

$$\textbf{naw-ruz}\,(g\text{-}year) \stackrel{\text{def}}{=} \tag{7.6}$$

$$\textbf{fixed-from-persian}\left(\boxed{1 \mid 1 \mid \begin{Bmatrix} persian\text{-}year - 1 & \textbf{if } persian\text{-}year \le 0 \\ persian\text{-}year & \textbf{otherwise} \end{Bmatrix}}\right)$$

where

$$persian\text{-}year = g\text{-}year - \textbf{gregorian-year-from-fixed}(\textbf{persian-epoch}) + 1$$

References

[1] A. Birashk, *A Comparative Calendar of the Iranian, Muslim Lunar, and Christian Eras for Three Thousand Years*, Mazda Publishers (in association with Bibliotheca Persica), Costa Mesa, California, 1993.

[2] Letter to Edward Reingold from A. Birashk, editor of *Dānešnāme-ye Bozorg-e Farsi* (*The Larger Persian Encyclopædia*), Tehran, June 21, 1996.

[3] E. Yarshater, ed., *Encyclopædia Iranica*, Routledge & Kegan Paul, Ltd., London, 1990.

Shrine of the Báb, located on Mt. Carmel, Israel and built in stages from 1899 to 1953. The Báb (d. 1850) was the originator of the nineteen-year cycle of the Bahá'í calendar. (Courtesy of the Bahá'í National Center, Wilmette, IL.)

8

The Bahá'í Calendar

> In the not far distant future it will be necessary that all peoples in the world agree on a common calendar. It seems, therefore, fitting that the new age of unity should have a new calendar free from the objections and associations which make each of the older calendars unacceptable to large sections of the world's population, and it is difficult to see how any other arrangement could exceed in simplicity and convenience that proposed by the Báb.
> —John Ebenezer Esslemont: *Bahá'u'lláh and the New Era: An Introduction to the Bahá'í Faith*, p. 179 (1923)

8.1 Structure and Implementation

The Bahá'í (or Badí') calendar begins its years at sunset on March 20 (the vernal equinox) of the Gregorian calendar, so we consider March 21 to be the first day of the Bahá'í year. Theoretically, if the actual time of the equinox occurs after sunset, then the year should begin a day later [2]; current practice, however, is to begin on March 21 regardless. The calendar is based on the nineteen-year cycle 1844–1863 of the Báb, the martyred forerunner of Bahá'u'lláh and co-founder of the Bahá'í faith.

As in the Islamic calendar, days are from sunset to sunset. Unlike those of the Islamic calendar, years are solar; they are composed of 19 months of 19 days each, with an additional month of four or five days after the eighteenth month. We treat these intercalary days as the nineteenth month of a twenty-month year. Leap years follow the same pattern as in the Gregorian calendar.

The week begins on Saturday; weekdays have the names

Saturday	Jalál	(Glory)
Sunday	Jamál	(Beauty)
Monday	Kamál	(Perfection)

Tuesday	Fiḍál	(Grace)
Wednesday	'Idál	(Justice)
Thursday	Istijlál	(Majesty)
Friday	Istiqlál	(Independence)

The months are called

(1) Bahá	(Splendor)	19 days
(2) Jalál	(Glory)	19 days
(3) Jamál	(Beauty)	19 days
(4) 'Aẓamat	(Grandeur)	19 days
(5) Núr	(Light)	19 days
(6) Raḥmat	(Mercy)	19 days
(7) Kalimát	(Words)	19 days
(8) Kamál	(Perfection)	19 days
(9) Asmá'	(Names)	19 days
(10) 'Izzat	(Might)	19 days
(11) Mashíyyat	(Will)	19 days
(12) 'Ilm	(Knowledge)	19 days
(13) Qudrat	(Power)	19 days
(14) Qawl	(Speech)	19 days
(15) Masáil	(Questions)	19 days
(16) Sharaf	(Honor)	19 days
(17) Sulṭán	(Sovereignty)	19 days
(18) Mulk	(Dominion)	19 days
(19) Ayyám-i-Há	(intercalary days)	4 {5} days
(20) 'Alá'	(Loftiness)	19 days

The leap year structure is given in curly brackets. The days of the month have the same names as the months, except that the 19th day is 'Alá', which is usually considered the 19th month, ignoring the intercalary days.

Years are also named in a 19-year cycle, called *Váḥid*, meaning "unity" and having a numerological value of 19 in Arabic:

(1) Alif (letter A)	(11) Bahháj (Delightful)
(2) Bá' (letter B)	(12) Javáb (Answer)
(3) Ab (Father)	(13) Aḥad (Single)
(4) Dál (letter D)	(14) Vahháb (Bountiful)
(5) Báb (Gate)	(15) Vidád (Affection)
(6) Váv (letter V)	(16) Badí' (Beginning)
(7) Abad (Eternity)	(17) Bahí (Luminous)
(8) Jád (Generosity)	(18) Abhá (Most Luminous)
(9) Bahá (Splendor)	(19) Váḥid (Unity)
(10) Ḥubb (Love)	

There is also a 361-year major cycle, called *Kull-i-Shay* (the name has numerological value $361 = 19^2$ in Arabic). Thus, for example, Monday, April 21, 1930 would be called "Kamál (Monday), the day of Qudrat, of the month of Jalál, of the year Bahháj, of the fifth Váḥid, of the first Kull-i-Shay, of the Bahá'í era."

Accordingly, we represent a Bahá'í date by a list

major	*cycle*	*month*	*day*	*year*

The first component, *major*, is an integer (positive for real Bahá'í dates); the components, *cycle*, *year*, and *day*, take on integer values in the range 1...19; because of our convention of considering the intercalary days to be a defective month and assigning a number to it, *month* is an integer between 1 and 20.

The epoch of the calendar, day 1 of year 1 B.E.,[1] is March 21, 1844 (Gregorian):

$$\textbf{bahai-epoch} \stackrel{\text{def}}{=} \textbf{fixed-from-gregorian}\left(\boxed{\textbf{march} \mid 21 \mid 1844}\right) \tag{8.1}$$

which is R.D. 673,222.

Our functions make use of the Gregorian calendar and are relatively straightforward:

$$\textbf{fixed-from-bahai}\left(\boxed{\mathit{major} \mid \mathit{cycle} \mid \mathit{year} \mid \mathit{month} \mid \mathit{day}}\right) \stackrel{\text{def}}{=} \tag{8.2}$$

$$\textbf{fixed-from-gregorian}\left(\boxed{\textbf{march} \mid 20 \mid \textit{g-year}}\right) + 19 \cdot (\mathit{month} - 1) + \begin{cases} 0 & \textbf{if } \mathit{month} \neq 20 \\ -14 & \textbf{if } \mathit{month} = 20 \\ & \quad \text{and } \textbf{gregorian-leap-year?}\,(\textit{g-year} + 1) \\ -15 & \textbf{otherwise} \end{cases} + \mathit{day}$$

where

$$\textit{g-year} = 361 \cdot (\mathit{major} - 1) + 19 \cdot (\mathit{cycle} - 1) + \mathit{year} - 1 + \textbf{gregorian-year-from-fixed}\,(\textbf{bahai-epoch})$$

We first find the corresponding Gregorian year by counting how many years (361 for each major cycle and nineteen for each minor cycle) have elapsed since

[1] Bahá'í era.

the epoch in 1844. Starting with the R.D. date of the last day of the prior Bahá'í year we add 19 days for each month, plus the number of days in the given month, except that, since the nineteenth month has only four or five days, for dates in 'Alá' we need to subtract 14 or 15, depending on whether February of the Gregorian calendar had a leap day or not.

The inverse function is

$$\textbf{bahai-from-fixed}\ (\mathit{date}) \stackrel{\text{def}}{=} \qquad (8.3)$$

$$\boxed{\mathit{major} \mid \mathit{cycle} \mid \mathit{year} \mid \mathit{month} \mid \mathit{day}}$$

where

$$\mathit{g\text{-}year} = \textbf{gregorian-year-from-fixed}\ (\mathit{date})$$

$$\mathit{start} = \textbf{gregorian-year-from-fixed}\ (\textbf{bahai-epoch})$$

$$\mathit{years} = \mathit{g\text{-}year} - \mathit{start} - \begin{cases} 1 & \textbf{if } \textbf{fixed-from-gregorian}\left(\boxed{\textbf{january} \mid 1 \mid \mathit{g\text{-}year}}\right) \le \mathit{date} \le \textbf{fixed-from-gregorian}\left(\boxed{\textbf{march} \mid 20 \mid \mathit{g\text{-}year}}\right) \\ 0 & \textbf{otherwise} \end{cases}$$

$$\mathit{major} = \left\lfloor \frac{\mathit{years}}{361} \right\rfloor + 1$$

$$\mathit{cycle} = \left\lfloor \frac{\mathit{years} \bmod 361}{19} \right\rfloor + 1$$

$$\mathit{year} = (\mathit{years} \bmod 19) + 1$$

$$\mathit{days} = \mathit{date} - \textbf{fixed-from-bahai}\left(\boxed{\mathit{major} \mid \mathit{cycle} \mid \mathit{year} \mid 1 \mid 1}\right)$$

$$\mathit{month} = \begin{cases} 20 & \textbf{if } \mathit{date} \ge \mathit{last} \\ \left\lfloor \frac{\mathit{days}}{19} \right\rfloor + 1 & \textbf{otherwise} \end{cases}$$

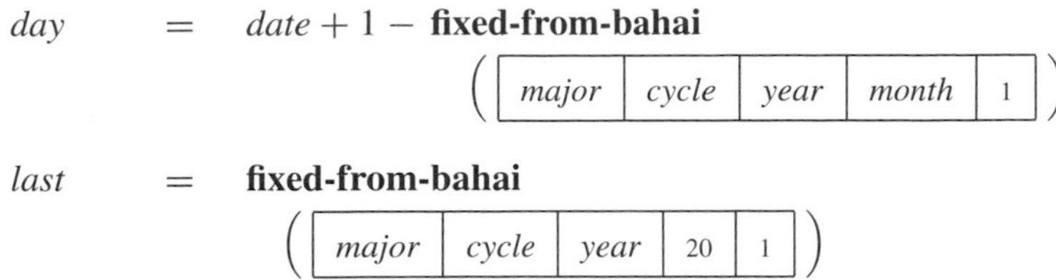

Here we compute the number of years that have elapsed since the start of the Bahá'í calendar, by looking at the Gregorian year number and considering whether the date is before or after Gregorian New Year, and then use the result to get the number of elapsed major and minor cycles and years within the cycle. The remaining days divided by 19 (the length of a month) gives the month number, but again, special consideration must be given for the last month of the Bahá'í year.

8.2 Holidays

Since the Bahá'í calendar is synchronized with the Gregorian (except that Ayyám-i-Há 4 is March 1 in ordinary years, but February 29 in leap years), holidays are a trivial matter. The nine major holidays on which work is proscribed are Bahá'í New Year (Feast of Naw-Rúz) on March 21, Feast of Riḍván (April 21), Riḍván 9 (April 29), Riḍván 12 (May 2), Declaration of the Báb (May 23), Ascension of Bahá'u'lláh (May 29), Martyrdom of the Báb (July 9), Birth of the Báb (October 20), and the Birth of Bahá'u'lláh (November 12). Two other obligatory celebrations are the Birth of 'Abdu'l-Bahá (May 23) and the Ascension of 'Abdu'l-Bahá (November 28). There are additional days of significance, including the first day of each month (a feast day) and the whole last month (fast days).

For example,

$$\textbf{bahai-new-year}\ (g\text{-}year) \stackrel{\text{def}}{=} \textbf{fixed-from-gregorian}\left(\boxed{\textbf{march} \mid 21 \mid g\text{-}year}\right) \tag{8.4}$$

The Bahá'í New Year is always on March 21, the assumed date of the spring equinox. It is called the Feast of Naw-Rúz, as is the Persian New Year, which also celebrates the vernal equinox (see Chapter 7).

8.3 Future Calendar

The Bahá'í year was intended by the official rules [2] to begin at sunset following the vernal equinox. The equinox (in Haifa) is frequently a day before or after

March 21. The calculations for this intended version of the calendar would then involve similar astronomical computations to that of the original French Revolutionary calendar, described in Chapter 13, with the added complication of the need of calculating the time of sunset (which is only approximately 6 p.m., even on the day of the equinox). The functions **bahai-from-fixed** and **fixed-from-bahai** would then be more involved, since they could not depend on the Gregorian. Moreover, to determine the holidays we would then need, for example,

$$\textbf{feast-of-ridvan}\,(g\text{-}year) \stackrel{\text{def}}{=} \textbf{fixed-from-bahai}\left(\begin{array}{|c|c|c|c|c|}\hline major & cycle & year & 2 & 13 \\ \hline\end{array}\right) \tag{8.5}$$

where

$$\begin{aligned}
years &= g\text{-}year - \textbf{gregorian-year-from-fixed}\,(\textbf{bahai-epoch}) \\
major &= \left\lfloor \frac{years}{361} \right\rfloor + 1 \\
cycle &= \left\lfloor \frac{years \bmod 361}{19} \right\rfloor + 1 \\
year &= (years \bmod 19) + 1
\end{aligned}$$

This astronomical version of the calendar is not currently in use, as explained in the following letter [1]:

> Until the Universal House of Justice decides upon the spot on which the calculations for establishing the date of Naw-Rúz each year are to be based it is not possible to state exactly the correspondence between Bahá'í dates and Gregorian dates for any year. Therefore for the present the believers in the West commemorate Bahá'í events on their traditional Gregorian anniversaries. Once the necessary legislation to determine Naw-Rúz has been made, the correspondence between Bahá'í and Gregorian dates will vary from year to year depending upon whether the Spring Equinox falls on the 20th, 21st or 22nd March. In fact in Persia the friends have been, over the years, following the Spring Equinox as observed in Tehran, to determine Naw-Rúz, and the National Spiritual Assembly has to issue every year a Bahá'í calendar for the guidance of the friends. The Universal House of Justice feels that this is not a matter of urgency and, in the meantime, is having research conducted into such questions.

References

[1] Letter written on behalf of the Universal House of Justice to the National Spiritual Assembly of the Bahá'í of the United States, October 30, 1974.

[2] Universal House of Justice, *The Bahá'í World: An International Record*, volume xviii, Bahá'í World Center, Haifa, pp. 598–601, 1986.

Sixteenth-century astrolabe, with zodiac and star names inscribed in Hebrew. (Courtesy of Adler Planetarium & Astronomy Museum, Chicago, IL.)

9

The Hebrew Calendar

Do not take these [astronomical] calculations lightly. . .for they are deep and difficult and constitute the "secret of the calendar" that was [only] known to the great sages. . . . On the other hand, this calendar that is calculated nowadays . . . even school children can master in three or four days.
—Moses Maimonides: *Mishneh Torah, Book of Seasons* (1178)

The Hebrew calendar, promulgated by the Patriarch, Hillel II, in the mid-fourth century[1] and attributed by Maimonides to Mosaic revelation, is more complicated than the other calendars we have considered so far. Its complexity is inherent in the requirement that calendar months must be strictly lunar, whereas Passover must always occur in the spring. Since the seasons depend on the solar year, the Hebrew calendar must harmonize simultaneously with both lunar and solar events, as do all lunisolar calendars, including the Hindu and Chinese calendars described in Chapters 11, 14, and 15. As in the Islamic and Bahá'í calendars, days begin at sunset.

9.1 Structure and History

Of all [methods of intercalation] which exist today the Jewish calculation is the oldest, the most skillful, and the most elegant.
—Joseph Justus Scaliger: *De Emendatione Temporum* Book 7, p. 294 (1593)

[1] Poznański [8, pp. 118–119] disputes the assertion of the tenth-century Hai Gaon that the calendar was formulated in 359 C.E. (year 670 of the Seleucid Era).

The Hebrew year consists of twelve months in a common year and thirteen in a leap ("gravid" or "embolismic") year:

(1) Nisan	30 days	ניסן
(2) Iyyar	29 days	אייר
(3) Sivan	30 days	סיון
(4) Tammuz	29 days	תמוז
(5) Av	30 days	אב
(6) Elul	29 days	אלול
(7) Tishri	30 days	תשרי
(8) Ḥeshvan	29 or 30 days	חשון or מרחשון
(9) Kislev	29 or 30 days	כסלו
(10) Teveth	29 days	טבת
(11) Shevat	30 days	שבט
{(12) Adar I	30 days	{אדר ראשון
(12) {(13)} Adar {II}	29 days	{ואדר or} אדר {שני}

The leap year structure is given in curly brackets—in a leap year there is an interpolated twelfth month of 30 days called "Adar I" to distinguish it from the final month, "Adar II." The length of the eighth and ninth months vary from year to year according to criteria that will be explained below. Our ordering of the Hebrew months follows biblical convention (Leviticus 23:5), in which (what is now called) Nisan is the first month. This numbering causes the Hebrew new year (Rosh HaShanah) to begin on the first of Tishri, which by our ordering is the seventh month—but this too agrees with biblical usage (Leviticus 23:24). Adding up the lengths of the months, we see that a normal year has 353–355 days, whereas a leap year has 383–385 days.

In the Hebrew calendar, leap years occur in the 3rd, 6th, 8th, 11th, 14th, 17th, and 19th years of the 19-year Metonic cycle. This sequence can be computed concisely by noting that Hebrew year y is a leap year if and only if $(7y+1)$ mod 19 is less than 7—another instance of formula (1.36). Thus we determine whether a year is a Hebrew leap year by

$$\textbf{hebrew-leap-year?}\ (\textit{h-year}) \stackrel{\text{def}}{=} \qquad (9.1)$$

$$((7 \cdot \textit{h-year} + 1) \bmod 19) < 7$$

and the number of months in a Hebrew year by

$$\textbf{last-month-of-hebrew-year}\ (\textit{h-year}) \stackrel{\text{def}}{=} \qquad (9.2)$$

$$\begin{cases} 13 & \textbf{if hebrew-leap-year?}\ (\textit{h-year}) \\ 12 & \textbf{otherwise} \end{cases}$$

The number of days in a Hebrew month is a more complex issue. The twelfth month, Adar or Adar I, has 29 days in a common year and 30 days in a leap year, but the numbers of days in the eighth month (Ḥeshvan) and ninth month (Kislev) depend on the overall length of the year, which in turn depends on factors discussed below.

The beginning of the Hebrew new year is determined by the occurrence of the new moon (mean conjunction) of the seventh month (Tishri), subject to possible postponements of a day or two. The new moon of Tishri, 1 A.M.,[2] the first day of the first year for the Hebrew calendar, is fixed at Sunday night at 11:11:20 p.m. Since days begin at sunset, we thus define the epoch of the Hebrew calendar (that is, Tishri 1, 1 A.M.) to be Monday, September 7, −3760 (Gregorian) or October 7, 3761 B.C.E. (Julian).

The Hebrew day is traditionally divided into 24 hours, and the hour is divided into 1080 *parts* (*ḥalaqim*), so a day has 25920 parts of $3\frac{1}{3}$ seconds duration each. These divisions are of Babylonian origin. The new moon of Tishri, 1 A.M., which occurred on Sunday night at 5 hours, 204 parts, is called *molad* ***beharad***, since the numerical value of the letter ***beth*** is 2, signifying, Monday, or Sunday night; ***heh*** is 5 (hours); ***resh*** = 200 parts; ***daleth*** = 4 parts. Other epochs appear in classical and medieval literature. In particular, the initial conjunction of the epoch starting one year later, called ***wayad*** (signifying 6 days, 14 hours), occurred on Friday at exactly 8 a.m. the morning Adam and Eve were created according to the traditional chronology.[3]

The length of a mean lunar period in this representation is 29 days, 12 hours, and 793 parts, or $29\frac{13753}{25920} \approx 29.530594$ days. This is a classical value for the lunar (synodic) month, attributed to Cidenas in about 383 B.C.E. and used by Ptolemy in his *Almagest*.[4] With 354 days, 8 hours, 48 minutes, and 40 seconds for an ordinary year and 383 days, 21 hours, 32 minutes, and $43\frac{1}{3}$ seconds for a leap year, this value gives an average Hebrew year length of 365.2468 days. The start of each new year, Rosh HaShanah (Tishri 1), coincides with the calculated day of the mean conjunction of Tishri—twelve months after the previous new year conjunction in ordinary years, and thirteen in leap years—unless one of four delays is mandated:

[2] *Anno mundi*; in the (traditional) year of the world (since creation).

[3] This ambiguity in the Hebrew epoch has led to some confusion. For example, on account of this, *The Jewish Time Line Encyclopedia*, by M. Kantor, Jason Aronson, Inc., Northvale, NJ (1989), and A. Spier [14] erroneously give 69 C.E., rather than 70 C.E., as the date Titus captured Jerusalem.

[4] The astronomer/mathematician Abraham bar Ḥiyya Savasorda (11th century) suggested that the reason for the choice of 1080 parts per hour is that it is the smallest number that allows this particular value of the length of a month to be expressed with an integral number of parts (in other words, 793/1080 is irreducible).

1. If the mean conjunction is at midday or after, then the new year is delayed. The moment of sunset is *deemed* 6 p.m. and sunrise is *deemed* 6 a.m., so that the "daylight hours" and "nighttime hours" have different lengths that vary according to the seasons (see Section 12.3). Postponement occurs if the conjunction is 18 (variable-length) hours or more after sunset.[5]
2. In no event must the new year be on Sunday, Wednesday, or Friday. Excluding Wednesday and Friday prevents Yom Kippur (Tishri 10) from falling on Friday or Sunday; excluding Sunday prevents Hoshana Rabba (Tishri 21) from falling on Saturday. Maimonides [11, 7:8] ascribes the delay to the need to introduce a correction in the calculated time of appearance of the new moon of the month of Tishri. The real purpose of the delay is moot. If the conjunction is on Saturday, Tuesday, or Thursday afternoon, then this rule combines with the previous rule and results in a two-day delay.
3. In rare cases an additional delaying factor may need to be employed to keep the length of a year within the allowable ranges. (It is the irregular effect of the second delay that makes this necessary.) Were Rosh HaShanah before noon on Tuesday of a common year and the conjunction of the following year at midday or later, then applying the previous two rules would result in delaying the *following* Rosh HaShanah from Saturday or Sunday—the day of the next conjunction for a common year—until Monday. This would require an unacceptable year length of 356 days, so instead the *current* Rosh HaShanah is delayed until Thursday, giving a 354-day year. For the following year's conjunction to fall on Saturday afternoon, the current year's must have occurred after 3:11:20 a.m. The prior year cannot become too long because of this delay, since its new-year conjunction must have been on Friday (in a common year) or Wednesday (in a leap year) and would have been delayed a day by the second rule.
4. Rosh HaShanah on Monday after a leap year can pose a similar problem by causing the year just ending to be too short—when the *prior* new-year conjunction was after midday on Tuesday, and was, therefore, delayed until Thursday. If the conjunction was after midday Tuesday the previous year, then in the current year it would be after 9:32:43$\frac{1}{3}$ a.m. on Monday. In this case, Rosh HaShanah is postponed from Monday to Tuesday, extending the leap year just ending from 382 days to 383.

The precise rules for delays were the subject of a short-lived dispute (921–923 C.E.) between Palestinian and Babylonian Jewish authorities. In 923 C.E.

[5] This is the correct interpretation of Maimonides' code [11, 6:2], but the computation is unaffected, since noon is 18 seasonal hours after true sunset as well as 18 civil hours after mean local sunset.

the calculated conjunction fell just after midday, but the Jerusalem authorities insisted that the first delaying rule applied only when the conjunction was at 12:35:40 p.m. or later. Because of the retroactive effect of the third delay, this already affected dates in 921 (see the sample calculation beginning on page 96). In the end, the Babylonian gaon Saadia ben Joseph al-Fayyūmi prevailed, and the rules have since been fixed as given above. (Some scant details can be found in [8, vol. III, p. 119] and the *Encyclopædia Judaica* [13, vol. 4, col. 539–540]; a full discussion of the controversy appears in [9].) Interestingly, according to Maimonides [11, 5:13], the final authority in calendrical matters is vested in the residents of the Holy Land, and their decision—even if erroneous—should be followed worldwide:

> Our own calculations are solely for the purpose of making the matter available to public knowledge. Since we know that the Palestinians use the same method of calculation, we perform the same operations in order to find out and ascertain what day it is that has been determined by the people of Palestine.

One fairly common misconception regarding the Hebrew calendar is that the correspondence with the Gregorian calendar repeats every nineteen years. This is, however, not the case, on account of the irregular Gregorian leap year rule and the irregular applicability of the above delays. In the seventeenth century, Hezekiah di Silo of Jerusalem, in his book *Peri Ḥadash*, complained about published tables for the Hebrew calendar:

> I have seen disaster and scandal [on the part] of some intercalators who are of the [erroneous] opinion that the character [of years] repeats every thirteen cycles [247 years]. For the sake of God, do not rely and do not lean on them. "Far be it from thou to do after this manner," which will—perish the thought—cause the holy and awesome fast to be nullified, leaven to be eaten on Passover, and the holidays to be desecrated. Therefore, you the reader, "Hearken now unto my voice, I will give thee counsel, and God be with thee." Be cautious and careful lest you forget . . . what I am writing regarding this matter, since it is done according to exact arithmetic, "divided well," and is precise on all counts . . . from the 278th cycle [1521 C.E.] until the end of time. "Anyone who separates from it, it is as if he separates [himself] from life [itself]."

By the "character" of a year he means the day of the week of New Year and the length of the year. In fact, the Hebrew calendar repeats only after 689,472 years, since each 19-year cycle comprises 991 weeks, 2 days, and 17875 parts, which add up to a multiple of a 7-day week (containing 181,440 parts) in 36,288 cycles, as pointed out by the celebrated Persian Moslem writer, al-Bīrūnī [2, p. 154] in 1000 C.E.

9.2 Implementation

> Perhaps a scholar from amongst the Gentile scholars or Jewish scholars who have studied Greek science will examine the methods by which I calculate visibility of the [new] moon and notice an approximation in some of the methods, and then imagine that it eluded me and that I was unaware of the approximation involved. Such should not cross his mind. Rather, anything regarding which we have been inexact is because we knew by clear geometric proofs that it does not invalidate the determination of visibility and is negligible; therefore were we inexact. Similarly, when it appears that there is a small shortfall in a figure from what is appropriate, it is intentional—there being a corresponding excess in another figure, whereby the value comes out correctly via simple methods, without protracted calculations. Thus, someone unversed in these matters will not be daunted by voluminous calculations that do not contribute to [calculations of] visibility of the moon.
>
> —Moses Maimonides: *Mishneh Torah*, *Book of Seasons* 11:5–6 (1178)

The epoch of the Hebrew calendar is R.D. $-1{,}373{,}427$:

$$\textbf{hebrew-epoch} \stackrel{\text{def}}{=} \tag{9.3}$$

$$\textbf{fixed-from-julian}\left(\boxed{\textbf{october} \mid 7 \mid 3761\ \text{B.C.E.}}\right)$$

We can calculate the time elapsed on the Hebrew calendar from the start of this Hebrew day until the new moon of Tishri for Hebrew year y by computing

$$\frac{5604}{25920} + (\text{number of months before year } y) \times 29\frac{13753}{25920}; \tag{9.4}$$

the fraction $\frac{5604}{25920}$ represents the 5 hours, 11 minutes, and 20 seconds from 6 p.m. Sunday evening until the first conjunction. To compute the total number of months, leap and regular, we just apply formula (1.39): $\lfloor(7y-6)/19\rfloor + 12(y-1) = \lfloor(235y-234)/19\rfloor$. Interestingly, Burnaby [3, pp. 237–238] derives a similar formula by ad hoc means.

To implement the first of the four delays (putting off the new year if the calculated conjunction is in the afternoon), all we need to do is add six hours (6480 parts) to the time of conjunction and let the day be the integer part (the floor) of the value obtained. This is analogous to equation (1.44), except that we are counting days in months of average length $29\frac{13753}{25920}$ rather than in years. The initial conjunction is 11 hours, 11 minutes, and 20 seconds—that is, 12084 parts—into the determining period, which began at noon on the day before the epoch.

To test for Sunday, Wednesday, and Friday as required by the second delay, we can use $(3d \bmod 7) < 3$, as in equation (1.35), to determine whether d is one of the three evenly spaced excluded days. These two delays are incorporated in the following function:

$$\textbf{hebrew-calendar-elapsed-days}\ (\textit{h-year}) \stackrel{\text{def}}{=} \tag{9.5}$$

$$\begin{cases} \textit{day} + 1 \textbf{ if } (3 \cdot (\textit{day} + 1) \bmod 7) < 3 \\ \textit{day} & \textbf{otherwise} \end{cases}$$

where

$$\begin{aligned} \textit{months-elapsed} &= \left\lfloor \frac{235 \cdot \textit{h-year} - 234}{19} \right\rfloor \\ \textit{parts-elapsed} &= 12084 + 13753 \cdot \textit{months-elapsed} \\ \textit{day} &= 29 \cdot \textit{months-elapsed} + \left\lfloor \frac{\textit{parts-elapsed}}{25920} \right\rfloor \end{aligned}$$

So that 32 bits suffice for dates in the foreseeable future, whole days and fractional days (parts) are computed separately. The foregoing calculation comes close to the 32-bit limit; if that is a problem, one can compute days, hours, and parts separately:

$$\begin{aligned} \textit{parts-elapsed} &= 204 + 793 \cdot (\textit{months-elapsed} \bmod 1080) \\ \textit{hours-elapsed} &= 11 + 12 \cdot \textit{months-elapsed} \\ &\quad + 793 \cdot \left\lfloor \frac{\textit{months-elapsed}}{1080} \right\rfloor + \left\lfloor \frac{\textit{parts-elapsed}}{1080} \right\rfloor \\ \textit{day} &= 29 \cdot \textit{months-elapsed} + \left\lfloor \frac{\textit{hours-elapsed}}{24} \right\rfloor \end{aligned}$$

The two remaining delays depend on the length of the prior and current years that would result from the putative new year dates suggested by the previous function. If the current year would have 356 days, it is too long, and we delay its start two days. If the prior year is 382 days long, then we delay its end by one day. Rather than check the day of the week, the time of conjunction, and the leap year status of the prior and current year as in the traditional formulation of these delays, we just check for the unacceptable year lengths:

$$\textbf{hebrew-new-year-delay}\ (\textit{h-year}) \stackrel{\text{def}}{=} \tag{9.6}$$

$$\begin{cases} 2 \textbf{ if } ny_2 - ny_1 = 356 \\ 1 \textbf{ if } ny_1 - ny_0 = 382 \\ 0 \qquad\qquad \textbf{otherwise} \end{cases}$$

where

$$\begin{aligned} ny_0 &= \textbf{hebrew-calendar-elapsed-days}\ (\textit{h-year} - 1) \\ ny_1 &= \textbf{hebrew-calendar-elapsed-days}\ (\textit{h-year}) \\ ny_2 &= \textbf{hebrew-calendar-elapsed-days}\ (\textit{h-year} + 1) \end{aligned}$$

Adding the value of this function to the number of elapsed days determines the day the year begins. To get the R.D. date of the new year, we will have to add the (negative) epoch.

As already mentioned, the length of the year determines the length of the two varying months: Ḥeshvan and Kislev. Ḥeshvan is long (30 days) if the year has 355 or 385 days; Kislev is short (29 days) if the year has 353 or 383 days. The length of the year, in turn, is determined by the dates of the Hebrew new years (Tishri 1) preceding and following the year in question:

$$\textbf{last-day-of-hebrew-month}\ (\textit{h-month}, \textit{h-year}) \stackrel{\text{def}}{=} \tag{9.7}$$

$$\begin{cases} 29 \textbf{ if } \textit{h-month} \in \{2, 4, 6, 10, 13\} \\ \qquad \text{or } \{ \textit{h-month} = 12 \\ \qquad\qquad \text{and not } \textbf{hebrew-leap-year?} \\ \qquad\qquad\qquad (\textit{h-year}) \} \\ \qquad \text{or } \{ \textit{h-month} = 8 \\ \qquad\qquad \text{and not } \textbf{long-heshvan?}\ (\textit{h-year}) \} \\ \qquad \text{or } \{ \textit{h-month} = 9 \\ \qquad\qquad \text{and } \textbf{short-kislev?}\ (\textit{h-year}) \} \\ 30 \qquad\qquad\qquad\qquad \textbf{otherwise} \end{cases}$$

$$\textbf{long-heshvan?}\ (\textit{h-year}) \stackrel{\text{def}}{=} \tag{9.8}$$

$$\left(\textbf{days-in-hebrew-year}\ (\textit{h-year}) \bmod 10 \right) = 5$$

$$\textbf{short-kislev?}\ (\textit{h-year}) \stackrel{\text{def}}{=} \quad (9.9)$$

$$\left(\textbf{days-in-hebrew-year}\ (\textit{h-year}) \bmod 10\right) = 3$$

$$\textbf{days-in-hebrew-year}\ (\textit{h-year}) \stackrel{\text{def}}{=} \quad (9.10)$$

$$\textbf{fixed-from-hebrew}\left(\boxed{7 \mid 1 \mid \textit{h-year}{+}1}\right) -$$
$$\textbf{fixed-from-hebrew}\left(\boxed{7 \mid 1 \mid \textit{h-year}}\right)$$

With all the foregoing machinery, we are now ready to convert from any Hebrew date to an R.D. date:

$$\textbf{fixed-from-hebrew}\left(\boxed{\textit{month} \mid \textit{day} \mid \textit{year}}\right) \stackrel{\text{def}}{=} \quad (9.11)$$

$$\begin{aligned}
&\textbf{hebrew-epoch} + \\
&\textbf{hebrew-calendar-elapsed-days}\ (\textit{year}) + \\
&\textbf{hebrew-new-year-delay}\ (\textit{year}) + \textit{day} - 1 + \\
&\begin{cases}
\left(\sum_{m \geq 7}^{p(m)} \textbf{last-day-of-hebrew-month}\ (m, \textit{year})\right) + \left(\sum_{m \geq 1}^{m < \textit{month}} \textbf{last-day-of-hebrew-month}\ (m, \textit{year})\right) & \textbf{if } \textit{month} < 7 \\
\sum_{m \geq 7}^{m < \textit{month}} \textbf{last-day-of-hebrew-month}\ (m, \textit{year}) & \textbf{otherwise}
\end{cases}
\end{aligned}$$

where

$$p(m) \quad = \quad m \leq \textbf{last-month-of-hebrew-year}\ (\textit{year})$$

To the fixed date of the start of the given year we add the number of elapsed days in the given month and the length of each elapsed month. We distinguish between months before and after Tishri, which is the seventh month, though the new year begins with its new moon. For dates in the second half of the year (months 1 . . . 6) we need to include the lengths of all months from Tishri (month 7) until **last-month-of-hebrew-year** (month 12 or 13).

Conversion to Hebrew dates is done as follows:

$$\textbf{hebrew-from-fixed}\,(date) \stackrel{\text{def}}{=} \boxed{month \mid day \mid year} \tag{9.12}$$

where

$$approx = \left\lfloor \frac{date - \textbf{hebrew-epoch}}{\frac{35975351}{98496}} \right\rfloor$$

$$year = approx - 1 + \left(\sum_{y \geq approx}^{p(y)} 1 \right)$$

$$start = \begin{cases} 7 \textbf{ if } date < \textbf{fixed-from-hebrew}\left(\boxed{1 \mid 1 \mid year}\right) \\ 1 \qquad \textbf{otherwise} \end{cases}$$

$$month = start + \left(\sum_{m \geq start}^{q(m)} 1 \right)$$

$$day = date - \textbf{fixed-from-hebrew}\left(\boxed{month \mid 1 \mid year}\right) + 1$$

$$p(y) = date \geq \textbf{fixed-from-hebrew}\left(\boxed{7 \mid 1 \mid y}\right)$$

$$q(m) = date > \textbf{fixed-from-hebrew}\left(\boxed{m \mid \textbf{last-day-of-hebrew-month}\,(m, year) \mid year}\right)$$

We first approximate the Hebrew year by dividing the number of elapsed days by the average year length, $\frac{35,975,351}{98,496}$. (A simpler value—even 365.25—can be used instead.) The irregularity of year lengths means that this estimate *approx* can be off by one in either direction. So we search for the right year, adding 1 to *approx* −1 for each year *y* whose new year (the first day of the seventh month) is not after fixed date *date*. To determine the Hebrew month, we search forward from the new year until the first month that begins after *date*.

9.3 Holidays and Fast Days

As throughout this book, we consider our problem to be the determination of holidays that occur in a specified Gregorian year. Since the Hebrew year is, on the average, consistently aligned with the Gregorian year, each Jewish holiday occurs just once in a given Gregorian year (with a minor exception noted below). The major holidays of the Hebrew year occur on fixed days on the Hebrew calendar but only in fixed seasons on the Gregorian calendar. They are easy to determine on the Gregorian calendar with the machinery developed above, provided we observe that the Hebrew year beginning in the Gregorian year y is given by

$$\begin{aligned}&\text{Hebrew new year occurring in the fall of Gregorian year } y\\ &\quad = y + 1 - \textbf{gregorian-year-from-fixed}(\textbf{hebrew-epoch}).\end{aligned}$$

For example, the Hebrew year that began in the fall of 1 (Gregorian) was 3762 A.M. This means that holidays occurring in the fall and early winter of the Gregorian year y occur in the Hebrew year $y + 1 + 3760$, while holidays in the late winter, spring, and summer occur in Hebrew year $y + 3760$. For example, to find the R.D. date of Yom Kippur (Tishri 10) in a Gregorian year, we would use

$$\textbf{yom-kippur}\,(\textit{g-year}) \stackrel{\text{def}}{=} \tag{9.13}$$
$$\textbf{fixed-from-hebrew}\left(\boxed{7 \mid 10 \mid \textit{hebrew-year}}\right)$$

where

$$\begin{aligned}\textit{hebrew-year} \;=\;& \textit{g-year} - \textbf{gregorian-year-from-fixed}\\ &\qquad\qquad(\textbf{hebrew-epoch})\\ &+ 1\end{aligned}$$

The R.D. dates of Rosh HaShanah (Tishri 1), Sukkot (Tishri 15), Hoshana Rabba (Tishri 21), Shemini Aẓereth (Tishri 22), and Simḥat Torah (Tishri 23, outside Israel) are identically determined.[6] As on the Islamic calendar, all Hebrew holidays begin at sunset the prior evening.

The dates of the other major holidays—Passover (Nisan 15), ending of Passover (Nisan 21), and Shavuot (Sivan 6)—are determined similarly, but because these holidays occur in the spring, the year corresponding to Gregorian year y is $y + 3760$. Conservative and Orthodox Jews observe two days Rosh HaShanah—Tishri 1 and 2. Outside Israel, they also observe Tishri 16, Nisan 16, Nisan 22, and Sivan 7 as holidays.

Thus, for example, we determine the R.D. date of Passover by

$$\textbf{passover}\,(\textit{g-year}) \stackrel{\text{def}}{=} \tag{9.14}$$
$$\textbf{fixed-from-hebrew}\left(\boxed{1 \mid 15 \mid \textit{hebrew-year}}\right)$$

6 See *Winning Ways, Volume 2: Games in Particular* [1, p. 800] for another way to determine the date of Rosh HaShanah.

where

$$\textit{hebrew-year} = \textit{g-year} - \textbf{gregorian-year-from-fixed}\ (\textbf{hebrew-epoch})$$

Gauss [7] developed an interesting formula to determine the Gregorian date of Passover in a given year.

Consider, as an example, the calculation of the date of Passover in 922 C.E.—that is, Nisan 15, 4682 A.M. (See page 88 for the historical significance of this year.) The mean conjunction of the preceding Tishri fell on Thursday, September 6, 921 C.E. (Julian), R.D. 336, 277, at 5:51:46$\frac{2}{3}$ a.m. The mean conjunction of the following Tishri fell on Tuesday, September 24, 922 C.E. (Julian) at 3:24:30 a.m. At the latter time, $57{,}909 = (235 \times 4683 - 234)/19$ months of mean length $29\frac{13753}{25920}$ had elapsed since the primeval conjunction, to which we add $12084/25920$ to count from noon on the Sunday before the epoch. By the traditional reckoning, that is Tuesday, 9 hours and 441 parts since sunset the preceding evening. Hebrew year 4683 was year 9 of the 247th 19-year cycle, which is not a leap year, making 4683 an instance of the third delay. Since this conjunction was later than 9 hours and 204 parts, the conjunction of the following year, 4684, fell on Saturday afternoon, just 237 parts (13.167 minutes) after midday, for which time the first two delays apply. Specifically, equation (9.5) yields

$$\begin{aligned}\textbf{hebrew-calendar-elapsed-days}(4682) &= 1{,}709{,}704,\\ \textbf{hebrew-calendar-elapsed-days}(4683) &= 1{,}710{,}087,\\ \textbf{hebrew-calendar-elapsed-days}(4684) &= 1{,}710{,}443.\end{aligned}$$

With the first two delays, but without the third delay, year 4683 would be $1{,}710{,}443 - 1{,}710{,}087 = 356$ days long, which is unacceptably long. Thus, the first of Tishri 4683 is put off two days to Thursday, September 26, R.D. 336,662. The start of year 4682 is not delayed, making 4682 a "long" leap year with a total of 385 days. Tishri (month 7) and Shevat (month 11) are always 30 days long, Tevet (month 10) is 29 days, Ḥeshvan (month 8) and Kislev (month 9) both have 30 days in a long year, and in a leap year Adar I (month 12) has 30 days and Adar II (month 13) has 29. Adding these ($5 \times 30 + 2 \times 29 = 208$), plus 14 days of Nisan (month 1), to the R.D. date of Rosh HaShanah of 4682, we arrive at R.D. $336{,}277 + 208 + 14 = 336{,}499$ as the starting date of Passover.[7] That date is Tuesday, April 16, 922 C.E. (Julian) and April 21, 922 (Gregorian). Were the first delay not applied in 4684, there would have been no

[7] Dates during the second half of the Hebrew year (from Nisan through Elul) depend *only* on the date of the following Rosh HaShanah, since the intervening months are all of fixed length, so in hand calculations it is easier to count backwards from the following Rosh HaShanah, subtracting 30 days for Sivan and Av, 29 days for Iyyar, Tammuz, and Elul, and 16 for the remainder of Nisan, rather than always starting with the preceding Rosh HaShanah, as in our algorithm.

need for the third delay in 4683. Were it not for the third delay, Hebrew year 4682 would have been "short," and Passover in 922—as well as all other dates between Tevet 1 in late 921 and Elul 30 in the summer of 922—would have occurred two days earlier. Dates in Kislev would have been one day earlier. 45 The seven-week period following the first day of Passover is a period called the *omer* (heave offering); the days of the omer are counted from 1 to 49, with the count expressed in completed weeks and excess days. The following function tells the omer count for an R.D. date, returning a list of weeks (an integer 0–7) and days (an integer 0–6) if the date is within the omer period, and returning **bogus** if not:

$$\textbf{omer}\,(\mathit{date}) \stackrel{\text{def}}{=} \begin{cases} \left\langle \left\lfloor \frac{c}{7} \right\rfloor, c \bmod 7 \right\rangle & \textbf{if } 1 \le c \le 49 \\ \textbf{bogus} & \textbf{otherwise} \end{cases} \tag{9.15}$$

where

$$c = \mathit{date} - \textbf{fixed-from-hebrew}\left(\boxed{1 \mid 15 \mid \textbf{hebrew-from-fixed}(\mathit{date})_{\textbf{year}}}\right)$$

The minor holidays of the Hebrew year are the "intermediate" days of Sukkot (Tishri 16–21) and of Passover (Nisan 16–20); Ḥanukkah (eight days, beginning on Kislev 25); Tu-B'Shevat (Shevat 15); and Purim (Adar 14 in normal years, Adar II 14 in leap years). Ḥanukkah occurs in late fall or early winter, so Ḥanukkah of Gregorian year y occurs in the Hebrew year $y + 3761$, while Tu-B'Shevat occurs in late winter/early spring and hence Tu-B'Shevat of Gregorian year y occurs in Hebrew year $y + 3760$; thus these two holidays are handled as were Yom Kippur and Passover, respectively. Purim also always occurs in late winter or early spring, in the last month of the Hebrew year (Adar or Adar II), so its R.D. date is computed by

$$\textbf{purim}\,(\mathit{g\text{-}year}) \stackrel{\text{def}}{=} \tag{9.16}$$

$$\textbf{fixed-from-hebrew}\left(\boxed{\mathit{last\text{-}month} \mid 14 \mid \mathit{hebrew\text{-}year}}\right)$$

where

$$\mathit{hebrew\text{-}year} = \mathit{g\text{-}year} - \textbf{gregorian-year-from-fixed}(\textbf{hebrew-epoch})$$

$$\mathit{last\text{-}month} = \textbf{last-month-of-hebrew-year}(\mathit{hebrew\text{-}year})$$

The Hebrew year contains several fast days that, though specified by particular Hebrew calendar dates, are shifted when those days occur on Saturday. The fast days are Tzom Gedaliah (Tishri 3), Tzom Teveth (Teveth 10), Ta'anith Esther (the day before Purim), Tzom Tammuz (Tammuz 17), and Tisha B'Av (Av 9). When Purim is on Sunday, Ta'anith Esther occurs on the preceding Thursday, so we can write

$$\textbf{ta-anith-esther}\,(\textit{g-year}) \stackrel{\text{def}}{=} \begin{cases} \textit{purim-date} - 3 & \textbf{if day-of-week-from-fixed}\,(\textit{purim-date}) = \textbf{sunday} \\ \textit{purim-date} - 1 & \textbf{otherwise} \end{cases} \tag{9.17}$$

where

$$\textit{purim-date} = \textbf{purim}\,(\textit{g-year})$$

Each of the other fast days, as well as Shushan Purim (the day after Purim, celebrated in Jerusalem), is postponed to the following day (Sunday) when it occurs on Saturday. Since Tzom Gedaliah is always in the fall and Tzom Tammuz and Tisha B'Av are always in the summer, their determination is easy. For example,

$$\textbf{tisha-b-av}\,(\textit{g-year}) \stackrel{\text{def}}{=} \begin{cases} \textit{ninth-of-av} + 1 & \textbf{if day-of-week-from-fixed}\,(\textit{ninth-of-av}) = \textbf{saturday} \\ \textit{ninth-of-av} & \textbf{otherwise} \end{cases} \tag{9.18}$$

where

$$\textit{hebrew-year} = \textit{g-year} - \textbf{gregorian-year-from-fixed}\,(\textbf{hebrew-epoch})$$

$$\textit{ninth-of-av} = \textbf{fixed-from-hebrew}\left(\boxed{5 \mid 9 \mid \textit{hebrew-year}}\right)$$

Tzom Teveth, which can never occur on Saturday, should be handled like Islamic holidays (Section 6.2), because Teveth 10 can fall on either side of January 1, so a single Gregorian calendar year can have zero, one, or two occurrences of Tzom Teveth. For example, Tzom Teveth occurred twice in 1982, but not at all in 1984. We leave it to the reader to work out the details. For the foreseeable future, other Jewish holidays and fasts occur exactly once in each Gregorian year, since the Hebrew leap months and Gregorian leap days keep the two calendars closely aligned.

Yom HaShoah (Holocaust Memorial Day) is Nisan 27 (which cannot fall on Saturday). Yom HaZikaron, normally on Iyar 4, is advanced to Wednesday if it falls on Thursday or Friday. The first delay precludes that date being a Saturday (or Monday or Wednesday). Thus we can write

$$\textbf{yom-ha-zikaron}\ (\textit{g-year}) \stackrel{\text{def}}{=} \tag{9.19}$$

$$\begin{cases} \textbf{kday-before}\ (h, \textbf{wednesday}) & \\ \quad \textbf{if wednesday} & \\ \quad\quad < \textbf{day-of-week-from-fixed}\ (h) & \\ h & \textbf{otherwise} \end{cases}$$

where

$$\textit{hebrew-year} = \textit{g-year} - \textbf{gregorian-year-from-fixed}\ (\textbf{hebrew-epoch})$$

$$h = \textbf{fixed-from-hebrew}\left(\boxed{2 \mid 4 \mid \textit{hebrew-year}}\right)$$

On the Hebrew calendar, the first day of each month is called Rosh Ḥodesh and has minor ritual significance. When the preceding month has 30 days, Rosh Ḥodesh includes also the last day of the preceding month. The determination of these days is elementary.

Some other dates of significance depend on the Julian approximation of the tropical year (equinox to equinox), in which each of the four seasons is taken to be $91\frac{5}{16}$ days long: By one traditional Hebrew reckoning, the vernal equinox of year 5685 A.M. was at 6 p.m. Wednesday evening, March 26, 1925 C.E. (Julian). It recurs on that day of the Julian calendar and at that hour of the week every 28 years, in what is called the *solar cycle*, and is celebrated as *birkath haḥama*.

Since 1925 mod 28 = 21, we can write

$$\textbf{birkath-ha-hama}\ (g\text{-}year) \stackrel{\text{def}}{=} \begin{cases} mar_{26} & \textbf{if } mar_{26} \neq \langle\,\rangle \\ & \quad\text{and } \left(\textbf{julian-from-fixed}\left(mar_{26[0]}\right)_{\textbf{year}} \bmod 28\right) = 21 \\ \langle\,\rangle & \textbf{otherwise} \end{cases} \tag{9.20}$$

where

$$mar_{26} = \textbf{julian-in-gregorian}\ (\textbf{march}, 26, g\text{-}year)$$

(The bracketed subscript 0 extracts the first element of a list.) This function returns an empty list for the 27 out of 28 years in which this event does not occur.

The beginning of *sh'ela* (request for rain) outside Israel, meant to correspond to the start of the 60th Hebrew day since the autumnal equinox, is November 22 (Julian), except in the year prior to a Julian leap year, when it is a day later. That date is always the 124th day before March 26 of the following Julian year. This circumlocution aligns the rule for sh'ela with the Julian leap year structure. Hence we write

$$\textbf{sh-ela}\ (g\text{-}year) \stackrel{\text{def}}{=} \textbf{julian-in-gregorian}\ (\textbf{march}, 26, g\text{-}year + 1)_{[0]} - 124 \tag{9.21}$$

which is either December 5th or 6th (Gregorian) during the twentieth and twenty-first centuries (see [14]). As with most other Jewish holidays and events, sh'ela actually begins the prior evening.

9.4 Days of Personal Interest

Finally, the Hebrew calendar contains what we might term "personal" days: One's birthday according to the Hebrew calendar determines the day of one's *Bat* (for girls) or *Bar* (for boys) *Mitzvah* (the twelfth or thirteenth birthday). Dates of death determine when *Kaddish* is recited (*yahrzeit*, *naḥala*) for parents (and sometimes for other relatives). These are ordinarily just anniversary dates, but the leap year structure and the varying number of days in some months require that alternative days be used in certain years, just as someone born

February 29 on the Gregorian calendar has to substitute an alternative day in common years.

The birthday of someone born in Adar of an ordinary year or Adar II of a leap year is also always in the last month of the year, be that Adar or Adar II. Someone born on the thirtieth day of Ḥeshvan, Kislev, or Adar I has his/her birthday postponed until the first of the following month in years when that day does not occur. Since the problem here is the determination of an anniversary date in a given Hebrew year, we write the function in that way:

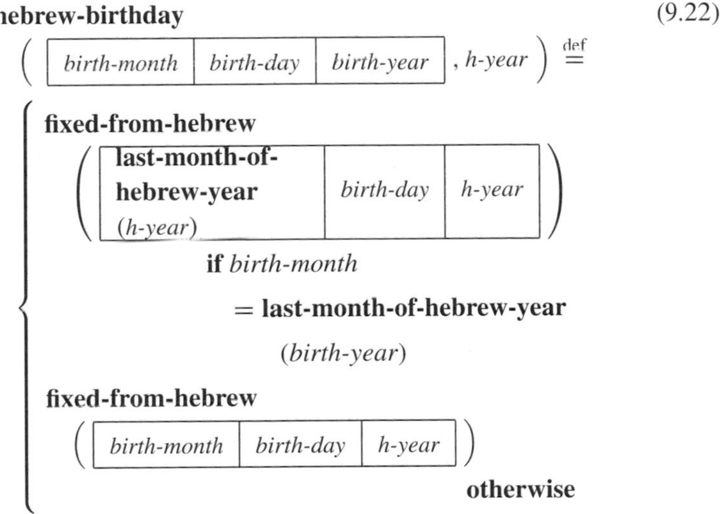

Note this function and the following take advantage of the fact that **fixed-from-hebrew** works for dates *month*, *i* of *year* and always gives the R.D. date of the $(i-1)$st day after *month*, 1, even if the month has fewer than *i* days.

The customary anniversary date of a death is more complicated and depends also on the character of the year in which the first anniversary occurs. There are several cases:

- If the date of death is Ḥeshvan 30, the anniversary in general depends on the *first* anniversary; if that first anniversary was not Ḥeshvan 30, use the day before Kislev 1.
- If the date of death is Kislev 30, the anniversary in general again depends on the first anniversary—if that was not Kislev 30, use the day before Teveth 1.
- If the date of death is Adar II, the anniversary is the same day in the last month of the Hebrew year (Adar or Adar II).
- If the date of death is the 30th in Adar I, the anniversary in a Hebrew year that is not a leap year (in which Adar has only 29 days) is the last day in Shevat.
- In all other cases, use the normal anniversary of the date of death.

Perhaps these rules are best expressed algorithmically:

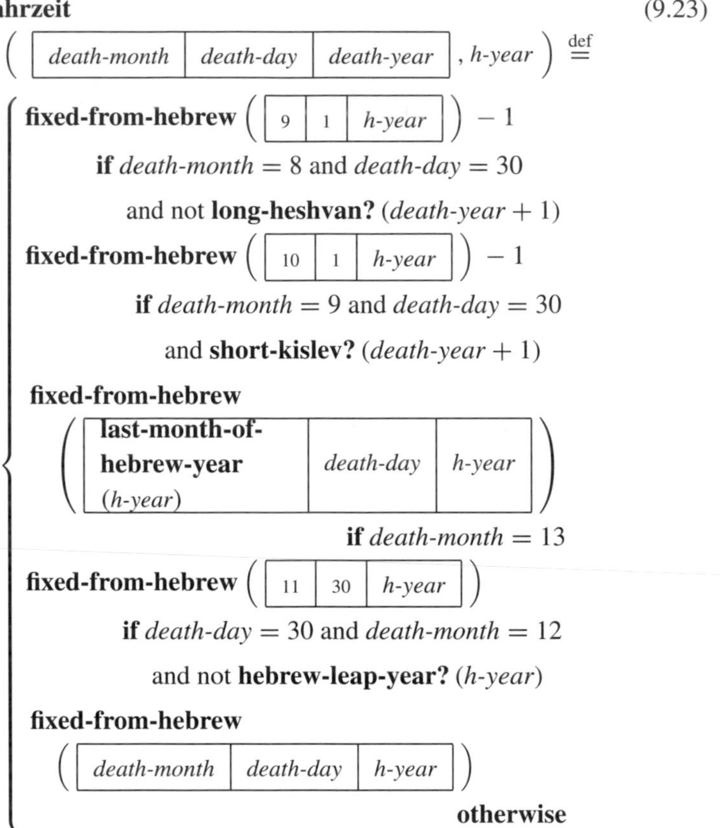

$$\textbf{yahrzeit}\left(\boxed{\textit{death-month} \mid \textit{death-day} \mid \textit{death-year}}, \textit{h-year}\right) \stackrel{\text{def}}{=} \tag{9.23}$$

$$\begin{cases}
\textbf{fixed-from-hebrew}\left(\boxed{9 \mid 1 \mid \textit{h-year}}\right) - 1 & \textbf{if } \textit{death-month} = 8 \text{ and } \textit{death-day} = 30 \text{ and not } \textbf{long-heshvan?}\,(\textit{death-year} + 1) \\
\textbf{fixed-from-hebrew}\left(\boxed{10 \mid 1 \mid \textit{h-year}}\right) - 1 & \textbf{if } \textit{death-month} = 9 \text{ and } \textit{death-day} = 30 \text{ and } \textbf{short-kislev?}\,(\textit{death-year} + 1) \\
\textbf{fixed-from-hebrew}\left(\boxed{\textbf{last-month-of-hebrew-year}\,(\textit{h-year}) \mid \textit{death-day} \mid \textit{h-year}}\right) & \textbf{if } \textit{death-month} = 13 \\
\textbf{fixed-from-hebrew}\left(\boxed{11 \mid 30 \mid \textit{h-year}}\right) & \textbf{if } \textit{death-day} = 30 \text{ and } \textit{death-month} = 12 \text{ and not } \textbf{hebrew-leap-year?}\,(\textit{h-year}) \\
\textbf{fixed-from-hebrew}\left(\boxed{\textit{death-month} \mid \textit{death-day} \mid \textit{h-year}}\right) & \textbf{otherwise}
\end{cases}$$

There are minor variations in custom regarding the anniversary date in some of these cases. For example, Spanish and Portuguese Jews never observe the anniversary in Adar I. The specifics need not concern us here.

References

[1] E. R. Berlekamp, J. H. Conway, and R. K. Guy, *Winning Ways: Volume 2, Games in Particular*, Academic Press, New York, 1982.

[2] al-Bīrūnī (= Abū-Raiḥān Muḥammad ibn 'Aḥmad al-Bīrūnī), *Al-Āthār al-Bāqiyah 'an al-Qurūn al-Khāliyah*, 1000. Translated and annotated by C. E. Sachau as *The Chronology of Ancient Nations*, William H. Allen and Co., London, 1879; reprinted by Hijra International Publishers, Lahore, Pakistan, 1983.

[3] S. B. Burnaby, *Elements of the Jewish and Muhammadan Calendars, With Rules and Tables and Explanatory Notes on the Julian and Gregorian Calendars*, George Bell and Sons, London, 1901.

[4] N. Bushwick, *Understanding the Jewish Calendar*, Moznaim Publishing Corp., New York, 1989.

[5] W. M. Feldman, *Rabbinical Mathematics and Astronomy*, M. L. Cailingold, London, 1931; 3rd corrected ed., Sepher-Hermon Press, New York, 1978.

[6] M. Friedländer, "Calendar," *The Jewish Encyclopedia*, Funk and Wagnalls, New York, pp. 501–508, 1906.

[7] C. F. Gauss, "Berechnung des jüdischen Osterfestes," *Monatliche Correspondenz zur Beförderung der Erd- und Himmels-Kunde*, Herausgegeben vom Freiherrn von Zach (May 1802). Reprinted in Gauss's *Werke*, Herausgegeben von der Königlichen Gesellschaft der Wissenschaften, Göttingen, volume 6, pp. 80–81, 1874.

[8] J. Hastings, ed., *Encyclopædia of Religion and Ethics*, Charles Scribner's Sons, New York, 1911.

[9] M. M. Kasher, Appendix to "Exodus," *Torah Shelemah (Complete Torah): Talmudic-Midrashic Encyclopedia of the Pentateuch*, volume 13, American Biblical Encyclopedia Society, Inc., New York, 1949.

[10] L. Levi, *Jewish Chrononomy: The Calendar and Times of Day in Jewish Law*, Gur Aryeh Institute for Advanced Jewish Scholarship, Brooklyn, NY, 1967. A revised edition has been published under the title *Halachic Times for Home and Travel*, Rubin Mass, Ltd., Jerusalem, 1992.

[11] Maimonides (= Moshe ben Maimon), *Mishneh Torah: Sefer Zemanim—Hilḥot Kiddush HaḤodesh*, 1178. Translated by S. Gandz (with commentary by J. Obermann and O. Neugebauer), as *Code of Maimonides, Book Three, Treatise Eight, Sanctification of the New Moon*, Yale Judaica Series, volume XI, Yale University Press, New Haven, CT, 1956. Addenda and corrigenda by E. J. Wiesenberg appear at the end of *Code of Maimonides, Book Three, The Book of Seasons*, translated by S. Gandz and H. Klein, Yale Judaica Series, volume XIV, Yale University Press, New Haven, CT, 1961.

[12] L. A. Resnikoff, "Jewish Calendar Calculations," *Scripta Mathematica*, volume 9, pp. 191–195, 274–277, 1943.

[13] C. Roth, ed., *Encyclopædia Judaica*, Macmillan, New York, 1971.

[14] A. Spier, *The Comprehensive Hebrew Calendar*, 3rd ed., Feldheim Publishers, New York, 1986.

[15] E. J. Wiesenberg, "Calendar," *Encyclopædia Judaica*, volume 5, col. 43–50, Macmillan, New York, 1971.

Sketch of the Mayan Tablet of the Sun, at Palenque, with symbols of the Mundane Era, Historical Era, and Era of the Chronicles. (Courtesy of the Peabody Museum of American Archeology and Ethnology, Cambridge, MA.)

10

The Mayan Calendars

> The invention of the Central American calendar in the Seventh century before Christ may be described with all propriety as one of the outstanding intellectual achievements in the history of man. This calendar solved with conspicuous success the great problem of measuring and defining time which confronts all civilized nations. Moreover it required the elaboration of one of the four or five original systems of writing the parts of speech in graphic symbols, and it conjoined with this supplementary invention of hieroglyphs the earliest discovery of the device of figures with place values in the notation of numbers. This time machine of ancient America was distinctly a scientific construction, the product of critical scrutiny of various natural phenomena by a master mind among the Mayas. It permitted a school of astronomer-priests to keep accurate records of celestial occurrences over a range of many centuries, with the ultimate reduction of the accumulated data through logical inferences to patterns of truth.
>
> —Herbert J. Spinden: "The Reduction of Mayan Dates," p. v (1924)

The Mayans, developers of an ancient Amerindian civilization in Central America, employed three separate, overlapping calendrical systems, called by scholars the *long count*, the *haab*, and the *tzolkin*. Their civilization reached its zenith during the period 250–900 C.E., and the Mayans survive to this day in Guatemala and in the Yucatan peninsula of Mexico and Belize; some groups have preserved parts of the calendar systems. What is known today has been recovered through astro-archeological and epigraphic research. There is general agreement on the Mayan calendrical rules and the correspondence between the three Mayan calendars; however, the exact correspondence between the Mayan calendars and

Western calendars is still a matter of some slight dispute. Correspondences are proposed by date equivalences in Spanish sources and by interpreting Mayan recordings of astronomical phenomena, such as new moons. In this book, we give the details for the most popular (and nearly universally accepted) of the correspondences, the *Goodman-Martinez-Thompson correlation* [11]. Another correlation is due to Spinden [8], [9], [10].[1] A superb discussion of Mayan mathematics, astronomy, and calendrical matters is given by Lounsbury [4] (see also [3]).

10.1 The Long Count

The long count is a strict counting of days from the beginning of the current cycle, each cycle containing 2,880,000 days (about 7885 solar years); the Mayans believed that the universe is destroyed and recreated at the start of every cycle. The units of the long count are

1 kin	=	1 day	
1 uinal	=	20 kin	(20 days)
1 tun	=	18 uinal	(360 days)
1 katun	=	20 tun	(7200 days)
1 baktun	=	20 katun	(144,000 days)

Thus, the long count date 12.16.11.16.6 means 12 baktun, 16 katun, 11 tun, 16 uinal, and 6 kin, for a total of 1,847,486 days from the start of the Mayan calendar epoch. (It is uncertain when the Mayan day began; there is evidence that the tzolkin day began at sunset and the haab day at sunrise, or in any case that they began at different times of day.)

Although not relevant here, the Mayans used the following larger units for longer time periods:

1 pictun	=	20 baktun	(2,880,000 days)
1 calabtun	=	20 pictun	(57,600,000 days)
1 kinchiltun	=	20 calabtun	(1,152,000,000 days)
1 alautun	=	20 kinchiltun	(23,040,000,000 days)

An alautun is about 63,081,377 solar years!

The starting epoch of the long count, according to the Goodman-Martinez-Thompson correlation, is taken as Wednesday, August 11, −3113 (Gregorian).

[1] Some of Spinden's date calculations are wrong. Here are three examples: on page 46 of "Maya Dates and What They Reveal" [10], he gives the equivalence J.D. 1,785,384 = February 10, 176 (Gregorian), but it should be February 11, 176 (Gregorian); on top of page 55 several Gregorian dates are off by one day; on page 57 he gives the equivalence J.D. 2,104,772 = August 30, 1050 (Gregorian), but it should be July 27, 1050 (Gregorian).

This date equals September 6, 3114 B.C.E. (Julian),[2] which equals J.D. 584,282.5; that is, R.D. −1,137,142:[3]

$$\textbf{mayan-epoch} \stackrel{\text{def}}{=} \textbf{fixed-from-jd}\,(584282.5) \tag{10.1}$$

In other words, our R.D. 0 is long count 7.17.18.13.2.

Thus, to convert from a Mayan long count date to an R.D. date we need only compute the total number of days given by the long count and subtract the number of days before R.D. 0 by adding the epoch:

$$\textbf{fixed-from-mayan-long-count}\left(\boxed{\mathit{baktun}\mid\mathit{katun}\mid\mathit{tun}\mid\mathit{uinal}\mid\mathit{kin}}\right) \stackrel{\text{def}}{=} \tag{10.2}$$

$$\textbf{mayan-epoch} + \mathit{baktun}\cdot 144000 + \mathit{katun}\cdot 7200 + \mathit{tun}\cdot 360 + \mathit{uinal}\cdot 20 + \mathit{kin}$$

In the opposite direction, converting an R.D. date to a Mayan long count date, we need to add the number of days in the long count before R.D. 0 and then divide the result into baktun, katun, tun, uinal, and kin:

$$\textbf{mayan-long-count-from-fixed}\,(\mathit{date}) \stackrel{\text{def}}{=} \tag{10.3}$$

$$\boxed{\mathit{baktun}\mid\mathit{katun}\mid\mathit{tun}\mid\mathit{uinal}\mid\mathit{kin}}$$

where

$$\begin{aligned}
\mathit{long\text{-}count} &= \mathit{date} - \textbf{mayan-epoch}\\
\mathit{baktun} &= \left\lfloor \frac{\mathit{long\text{-}count}}{144000} \right\rfloor\\
\mathit{day\text{-}of\text{-}baktun} &= \mathit{long\text{-}count} \bmod 144000\\
\mathit{katun} &= \left\lfloor \frac{\mathit{day\text{-}of\text{-}baktun}}{7200} \right\rfloor\\
\mathit{day\text{-}of\text{-}katun} &= \mathit{day\text{-}of\text{-}baktun} \bmod 7200\\
\mathit{tun} &= \left\lfloor \frac{\mathit{day\text{-}of\text{-}katun}}{360} \right\rfloor
\end{aligned}$$

[2] Thompson [11] errs in referring to this date as "3113 B.C.," confusing the two systems of dealing with years before the common era. His error has been reproduced by many scholars.

[3] Almost all experts believe this correlation, or possibly J.D. 584,284.5 is correct. Spinden's value, now no longer used, is J.D. 489,383.5.

$$day\text{-}of\text{-}tun = day\text{-}of\text{-}katun \bmod 360$$

$$uinal = \left\lfloor \frac{day\text{-}of\text{-}tun}{20} \right\rfloor$$

$$kin = day\text{-}of\text{-}tun \bmod 20$$

10.2 The Haab and Tzolkin Calendars

The Mayans used a civil calendar, the haab, based approximately on the solar year, consisting of 18 "months" of 20 days each, together with 5 additional days at the end. Because the haab calendar accounts for only 365 days (as compared to the mean length of the solar tropical year, 365.2422 days), the civil calendar slowly drifted with respect to the seasons. The months were called[4]

(1) Pop	(7) Yaxkin	(13) Mac
(2) Uo	(8) Mol	(14) Kankin
(3) Zip	(9) Chen	(15) Muan
(4) Zotz	(10) Yax	(16) Pax
(5) Tzec	(11) Zac	(17) Kayab
(6) Xul	(12) Ceh	(18) Cumku

The five additional days were an unlucky period called Uayeb. The pictographs for the haab names are shown in Figure 10.1. Unlike Gregorian months, the days of the haab months begin at 0 and indicate the number of *elapsed days* in the current month. Thus, 0 Uo follows 19 Pop, and the fifth monthless day is followed by 0 Pop. This method of counting is also used for years in the Hindu calendar discussed later in this book (Chapters 11 and 15).

The long count date 0.0.0.0.0 is considered to be haab date 8 Cumku (there is no disagreement here between the various correlations), which we specify by

$$\textbf{mayan-haab-at-epoch} \stackrel{\text{def}}{=} \boxed{8 \mid 18} \tag{10.4}$$

representing haab dates as pairs

$$\boxed{day \mid month},$$

where *day* and *month* are integers in the ranges 0 to 19 and 1 to 19, respectively. Thus we treat Uayeb as a defective nineteenth month and can convert an R.D. date to a haab date by

$$\textbf{mayan-haab-from-fixed}\ (date) \stackrel{\text{def}}{=} \boxed{day \mid month} \tag{10.5}$$

[4] The haab month names and tzolkin day names are transliterated from the Yucatan (Yucatec) Mayan language. The Guatemalan (Quiché) Mayans used slightly different names.

	Carving	Codex		Carving	Codex
Pop			Yax		
Uo			Zac		
Zip			Ceh		
Zotz			Mac		
Tzec			Kankin		
Xul			Muan		
Yaxkin			Pax		
Mol			Kayab		
Chen			Cumku		
			Uayeb		

Figure 10.1 The haab month signs. Adapted from Spinden [9, Fig. 3].

where

$$\begin{aligned} \textit{long-count} &= \textit{date} - \textbf{mayan-epoch} \\ \textit{day-of-haab} &= \Big(\textit{long-count} + \textbf{mayan-haab-at-epoch}_{\textbf{day}} + 20 \cdot \big(\textbf{mayan-haab-at-epoch}_{\textbf{month}} - 1 \big) \Big) \bmod 365 \\ \textit{day} &= \textit{day-of-haab} \bmod 20 \\ \textit{month} &= \left\lfloor \frac{\textit{day-of-haab}}{20} \right\rfloor + 1 \end{aligned}$$

It is not possible to convert a haab date to an R.D. date, because without a "year" there is no unique corresponding R.D. date. We can ask, though, for the number of days between two dates on the haab calendar—the calculation is elementary:

$$\textbf{mayan-haab-difference}\left(\boxed{\textit{day}_1 \mid \textit{month}_1}, \boxed{\textit{day}_2 \mid \textit{month}_2} \right) \stackrel{\text{def}}{=} \big(20 \cdot (\textit{month}_2 - \textit{month}_1) + \textit{day}_2 - \textit{day}_1\big) \bmod 365 \qquad (10.6)$$

The function **mayan-haab-difference** can be used as follows to compute the R.D. date of the Mayan haab date on or before a given R.D. date:

$$\textbf{mayan-haab-on-or-before}\,(\textit{haab}, \textit{date}) \stackrel{\text{def}}{=} \textit{date} - \Big(\big(\textit{date} - \textbf{mayan-haab-difference}\big(\textbf{mayan-haab-from-fixed}(0), \textit{haab} \big) \big) \bmod 365 \Big) \qquad (10.7)$$

This is an instance of formula (1.23).

The third Mayan calendar, the tzolkin (or sacred) calendar, was a religious calendar consisting of two cycles: a thirteen-day count and a cycle of twenty names:

(1) Imix	(5) Chicchan	(9) Muluc	(13) Ben	(17) Caban
(2) Ik	(6) Cimi	(10) Oc	(14) Ix	(18) Etznab
(3) Akbal	(7) Manik	(11) Chuen	(15) Men	(19) Cauac
(4) Kan	(8) Lamat	(12) Eb	(16) Cib	(20) Ahau

The pictographs for the tzolkin names are shown in Figure 10.2.

	Carving	Codex		Carving	Codex
Imix			Chuen		
Ik			Eb		
Akbal			Ben		
Kan			Ix		
Chicchan			Men		
Cimi			Cib		
Manik			Caban		
Lamat			Eznab		
Muluc			Cauac		
Oc			Ahau		

Figure 10.2 The tzolkin name signs. Adapted from Spinden [9, Fig. 1].

Unlike the haab months and days, the counts and names cycle *simultaneously*, so, for example, 13 Etznab precedes 1 Cauac, which precedes 2 Ahau, which precedes 3 Imix, and so on. Since 20 and 13 are relatively prime, this progression results in 260 unique dates, forming the divine year.

The long count date 0.0.0.0.0 is taken to be tzolkin date 4 Ahau. (The different correlations agree on this, too.) Representing tzolkin dates as pairs of positive integers

$$\boxed{\textit{number} \mid \textit{name}},$$

where *number* and *name* are integers in the ranges 1 to 13 and 1 to 20, respectively, we specify

$$\textbf{mayan-tzolkin-at-epoch} \stackrel{\text{def}}{=} \boxed{4 \mid 20} \tag{10.8}$$

As with the haab, we can convert from an R.D. date to a tzolkin date with

$$\textbf{mayan-tzolkin-from-fixed}\ (\textit{date}) \stackrel{\text{def}}{=} \tag{10.9}$$

$$\boxed{\textit{number} \mid \textit{name}}$$

where

$$\begin{aligned}
\textit{long-count} &= \textit{date} - \textbf{mayan-epoch} \\
\textit{number} &= \big(\textit{long-count} + \\
&\qquad \textbf{mayan-tzolkin-at-epoch}_{\textbf{number}}\big) \text{ amod } 13 \\
\textit{name} &= \big(\textit{long-count} + \\
&\qquad \textbf{mayan-tzolkin-at-epoch}_{\textbf{name}}\big) \text{ amod } 20
\end{aligned}$$

Just as with the haab calendar, it is impossible to convert a tzolkin date to an R.D. date. Unlike the haab calendar, however, because day numbers and day names cycle simultaneously, to calculate the number of days between two given tzolkin dates requires the solution to a pair of simultaneous linear congruences, as we did in Section 1.9. (See [6] for a general discussion of this topic and [4] for a specific discussion relating to the Mayan calendars.) Suppose we want to know the number of days x from tzolkin date $\boxed{d_1 \mid n_1}$ until the next occurrence of tzolkin date $\boxed{d_2 \mid n_2}$. We must have

$$d_1 + x \equiv d_2 \pmod{13},$$

or, equivalently, $x = d_2 - d_1 + 13i$, for some integer i. Similarly, we must have

$$x \equiv n_2 - n_1 \pmod{20},$$

which becomes

$$d_2 - d_1 + 13i \equiv n_2 - n_1 \pmod{20}.$$

Hence we need to know the values of i satisfying

$$13i \equiv n_2 - n_1 - d_2 + d_1 \pmod{20}.$$

Multiplying each side by -3, the multiplicative inverse of 13 modulo 20, gives

$$i \equiv 3(d_2 - d_1 - n_2 + n_1) \pmod{20},$$

from which we conclude that

$$x = d_2 - d_1 + 13\,[3(d_2 - d_1 - n_2 + n_1) \bmod 20]\,.$$

However, because we want the *next* occurrence of $\boxed{d_2 \mid n_2}$, we must guarantee that x is nonnegative. Thus, we write

$$\textbf{mayan-tzolkin-difference} \tag{10.10}$$
$$\left(\boxed{\textit{number}_1 \mid \textit{name}_1}, \boxed{\textit{number}_2 \mid \textit{name}_2} \right) \stackrel{\text{def}}{=}$$
$$\Big(\textit{number-difference} + 13 \cdot \big(3 \cdot (\textit{number-difference} - \textit{name-difference}) \bmod 20 \big) \Big) \bmod 260$$

where

$$\textit{number-difference} = \textit{number}_2 - \textit{number}_1$$
$$\textit{name-difference} = \textit{name}_2 - \textit{name}_1$$

As with the haab calendar, this function can be used to compute the R.D. date of the Mayan tzolkin date on or before a given R.D. date:

$$\textbf{mayan-tzolkin-on-or-before}\,(\textit{tzolkin}, \textit{date}) \stackrel{\text{def}}{=} \tag{10.11}$$
$$\textit{date} - \Big(\big(\textit{date} - \textbf{mayan-tzolkin-difference} \big(\textbf{mayan-tzolkin-from-fixed}\,(0), \textit{tzolkin} \big) \big) \bmod 260 \Big)$$

This is another instance of formula (1.23).

A popular way for the Mayans to specify a date was to use the haab and tzolkin dates together, forming a cycle of the least common multiple of 365 and 260 days: 18,980 days; or approximately 52 solar years. This cycle is called a *calendar round*, and we can ask for the most recent R.D. date, on or before a given R.D. date, that falls on a specified date of the calendar round.

Suppose the haab date of interest is $\boxed{D \mid M}$ and the tzolkin date of interest is $\boxed{d \mid n}$; we seek the latest R.D. x, on or before the given R.D. date, that satisfies

$$x + D_0 \equiv D \pmod{20},$$
$$x + M_0 \equiv M \pmod{18},$$
$$x + d_0 \equiv d \pmod{13},$$
$$x + n_0 \equiv n \pmod{20},$$

where $\boxed{D_0 \mid M_0}$ is the haab date of R.D. 0, and $\boxed{d_0 \mid n_0}$ is the tzolkin date of R.D. 0. The first two of these congruences combine to become

$$x \equiv \Delta_H \pmod{365}, \tag{10.12}$$

where

$$\Delta_H = \textbf{mayan-haab-difference} \text{ applied to } \boxed{D \mid M} \text{ and } \boxed{D_0 \mid M_0}.$$

The last two of these congruences combine to become

$$x \equiv \Delta_T \pmod{260}, \tag{10.13}$$

where

$$\Delta_T = \textbf{mayan-tzolkin-difference} \text{ applied to } \boxed{d \mid n} \text{ and } \boxed{d_0 \mid n_0}.$$

Congruence (10.12) means that

$$x = \Delta_H + 365i, \tag{10.14}$$

and combining this with congruence (10.13) we get

$$365i \equiv \Delta_T - \Delta_H \pmod{260}.$$

This has a solution *only* if $\Delta_T - \Delta_H$ is divisible by 5; otherwise the haab–tzolkin combination cannot occur. So, dividing by 5, we get

$$73i \equiv \frac{\Delta_T - \Delta_H}{5} \pmod{52},$$

and multiplying this by the multiplicative inverse of 73 modulo 52 (which, by coincidence, is 5), we find

$$i \equiv \Delta_T - \Delta_H \pmod{52},$$

so that $i = \Delta_T - \Delta_H + 52u$, for some u. Plugging this into equation (10.14) yields

$$x = \Delta_H + 365(\Delta_T - \Delta_H) + 18980u.$$

Thus we want the last date on or before the given R.D. date that is congruent to $\Delta_H + 365(\Delta_T - \Delta_H)$ modulo 18,980. This is computed using formula (1.23):

mayan-haab-tzolkin-on-or-before (10.15)

$$(\mathit{haab}, \mathit{tzolkin}, \mathit{date}) \stackrel{\text{def}}{=}$$

$$\begin{cases} \mathit{date} - ((\mathit{date} - \mathit{haab\text{-}difference} - 365 \cdot \mathit{diff}) \bmod 18980) \\ \hfill \textbf{if } (\mathit{diff} \bmod 5) = 0 \\ \textbf{bogus} \hfill \textbf{otherwise} \end{cases}$$

where

$$\begin{aligned} \mathit{haab\text{-}difference} &= \textbf{mayan-haab-difference} \\ &\quad \left(\textbf{mayan-haab-from-fixed} \right. \\ &\quad\quad \left. (0), \mathit{haab} \right) \\ \mathit{tzolkin\text{-}difference} &= \textbf{mayan-tzolkin-difference} \\ &\quad \left(\textbf{mayan-tzolkin-from-fixed}\ (0), \right. \\ &\quad \left. \mathit{tzolkin} \right) \\ \mathit{diff} &= \mathit{tzolkin\text{-}difference} - \mathit{haab\text{-}difference} \end{aligned}$$

For impossible combinations the constant **bogus** is returned.

This function can be used to compute the number of days between a pair of dates on the calendar round or to write a function **mayan-haab-tzolkin-on-or-after**; we leave these to the reader.

References

[1] C. P. Bowditch, *The Numeration, Calendar Systems and Astronomical Knowledge of the Mayas*, Cambridge University Press, Cambridge, 1910.

[2] J. T. Goodman, *The Archaic Maya Inscriptions*, Appendix to volume VIII of *Biologia Centrali-Americanna*, ed. by F. D. Godman and O. Salvin, R. H. Porter and Dulau & Co., London, 1897.

[3] J. S. Justeson, "Ancient Mayan Ethnography: An Overview of Hieroglyphic Sources," chapter 8 in *World Archeo-Astronomy*, A. Aveni, ed., 1989.

[4] F. G. Lounsbury, "Maya Numeration, Computation, and Calendrical Astronomy," *Dictionary of Scientific Bibliography*, volume 15, Supplement 1, pp. 759–818, Charles Scribner's Sons, New York, 1978.

[5] S. G. Morley, *The Ancient Maya*, revised by G. W. Brainerd, Stanford University Press, Stanford, CA, 1963.

[6] O. Ore, *Number Theory and Its History*, McGraw-Hill Book Co., Inc., New York, 1948. Reprinted by Dover Publications, Inc., Mineola, NY, 1987.

[7] L. Satterwaite, "Concepts and Structures of Maya Calendrical Arithmetics," Ph.D. Thesis, University of Pennsylvania, Philadelphia, 1947.

[8] H. J. Spinden, "Central American Calendars and the Gregorian Day," *Proceedings of the National Academy of Sciences* (*USA*), volume 6, pp. 56–59 (1920).

[9] H. J. Spinden, "The Reduction of Maya Dates," *Peabody Museum Papers*, volume VI, no. 4, 1924.

[10] H. J. Spinden, "Maya Dates and What They Reveal," *Science Bulletin* (The Museum of the Brooklyn Institute of Arts and Sciences), volume IV, no. 1, 1930.

[11] J. E. S. Thompson, *Maya Hieroglyphic Writing*, 3rd ed., University of Oklahoma Press, Norman, OK, 1971.

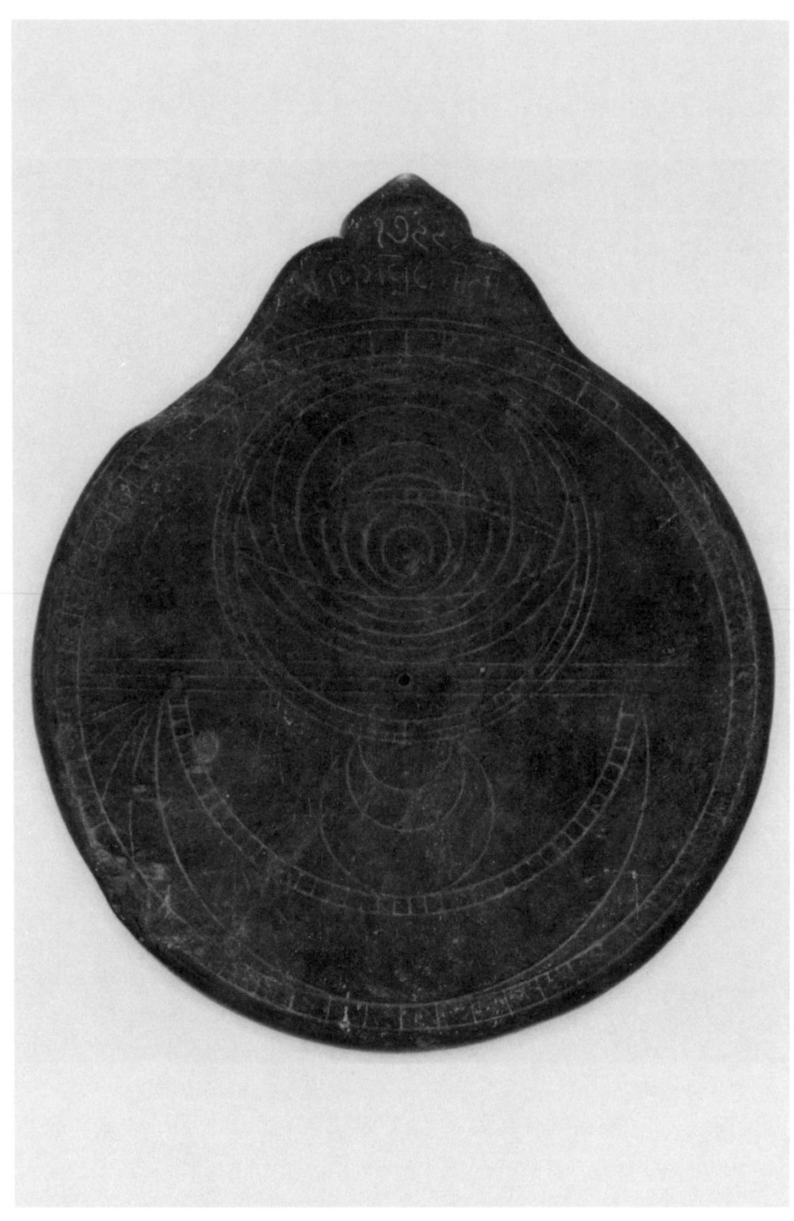

Stone astrolabe from India. (Courtesy of Adler Planetarium & Astronomy Museum, Chicago, IL.)

11

The Old Hindu Calendars

> I sincerely hope that leading Indian pañcāṅg-makers, astronomers and mathematicians will keep their Siddhāntic reckoning as pure as possible and not use the old works for purposes they can never be able to serve, mindful of the sage word: no man putteth a piece of undressed cloth upon an old garment; for that which should fill it up taketh from the garment, and a worse rent is made.
>
> —Walther E. van Wijk: "On Hindu Chronology IV," *Acta Orientalia*, volume IV, p. 72 (1926)

11.1 Structure and History

The Hindus have both solar and lunisolar calendars. In the Hindu lunisolar system, as in other lunisolar calendars, months follow the lunar cycle and are synchronized with the solar year by introducing occasional leap months. However unlike those of other lunisolar calendars such as the Hebrew calendar (described in Chapter 9), Hindu intercalated months do not follow a simple fixed pattern. Moreover, unlike other calendars, a day can be *omitted* any time in a lunar month.

Modern Hindu calendars are based on close approximations to the *true* times of the sun's entrance into the signs of the zodiac and of lunar conjunctions (new moons). Before about 1100 C.E., however, Hindu calendars used *mean* times. Though the basic structure of the calendar is similar for both systems, the mean (*madhyama*) and true (*spaṣṭa*) calendars can differ by a few days or can be shifted by a month. In this chapter we implement the mean system, as described in [4, pp. 360–446], which is arithmetical in character; Chapter 15 is devoted to the more modern astronomical version. For an ancient description of

Hindu astronomy, calendars, and holidays, see the book on India by al-Bīrūnī [1];[1] a more modern reference is [3].

There are various epochs that are, or have been, used as starting points for the enumeration of years in India. For a list of eras, see [5, pp. 39–47, civ–cvi]. In this chapter, we use the expired *Kali Yuga* ("Iron Age") epoch. The *expired* year number is the number of years that have *elapsed* since the onset of the Kali Yuga.[2] As van Wijk [6] explains:

> We count the years of human life in expired years. A child of seven years has already lived more than seven years; but on the famous *18 Brumaire de l'An VIII de la République Française une et indivisible* only 7 years and 47 days of the French Era had elapsed.

The first day of year 0 K.Y.[3] was Friday, January 23, −3101 (Gregorian), or February 18, 3102 B.C.E. (Julian), that is, day R.D. −1,132,959:

$$\textbf{hindu-epoch} \stackrel{\text{def}}{=} \textbf{fixed-from-julian}\left(\boxed{\textbf{february} \mid 18 \mid 3102\ \text{B.C.E.}}\right) \qquad (11.1)$$

Time is measured in days and fractions since this epoch.

The Kali Yuga epoch marks—in Hindu chronology—the onset of the fourth and final stage (lasting 432,000 years) of the 4,320,000-year era beginning with the last recreation of the world. Civil days begin at mean sunrise, reckoned as one quarter of a day past midnight; that is, at 6:00 a.m. The midnight just prior to day 1 of the Hindu calendar is considered to have been the start of a new lunar month; indeed, it was the time of the most recent *mean* conjunction of all the visible planets (the sun, moon, Mercury, Venus, Mars, Jupiter, and Saturn).

The Hindus also have a day count beginning with the first day of the Kali Yuga. To compute it we simply add the R.D. date to the number of days from the onset of the Kali Yuga until R.D. 0; that is,

$$\textbf{hindu-day-count}\ (\textit{date}) \stackrel{\text{def}}{=} \textit{date} - \textbf{hindu-epoch} \qquad (11.2)$$

The day number is called its *ahargaṇa* ("heap of days") and is traditionally used to determine the day of the week by casting off sevens, just as we have done with our R.D. numbering.

[1] There is some confusion of dates in the note (on page 358) by R. Schram to volume II, page 2 of Sachau's translation of this book, where the following equivalences are given: Thursday, February 25, 1031 C.E. (Julian) = 1 Caitra 953 Śaka Era = 28 Ṣafar 422 A.H. = 19 Ispandârmadh-Mâh 399 Anno Persarum, and New Year 400 Anno Persarum = March 9, 1031 C.E. (Julian) = J.D. 2,097,686. In fact, February 25, 1031 C.E. (Julian) = 29 Ṣafar 422 A.H. = J.D. 2,097,686.

[2] For each epoch, there is also a *current* year number, beginning with year 1.

[3] *Kali Yuga* (Iron Age).

The names of the days of the week (dated to the third or fourth century C.E.) are

Sunday	Ravivāra or Ādityavāra
Monday	Chandravāra or Somavāra
Tuesday	Maṅgalavāra or Bhaumavāra
Wednesday	Buddhavāra or Saumyavāra
Thursday	Bṛihaspatvāra or Guruvāra
Friday	Śukravāra
Saturday	Śanivāra

The Hindu value for the (sidereal) year (the mean number of days it takes for the sun to return to the same point vis-à-vis the celestial globe—see Section 12.5) is

$$\textbf{arya-sidereal-year} \stackrel{\text{def}}{=} \frac{1577917500}{4320000} \tag{11.3}$$

or 365.258680555 · · · (civil) days.

A Jovian cycle is also employed. It takes Jupiter about twelve years to circle the sun; the Hindu value is

$$\textbf{arya-jovian-period} \stackrel{\text{def}}{=} \frac{1577917500}{364224} \tag{11.4}$$

days. The Jovian period is divided into twelve equal periods of time, one for each sign of the zodiac. Five revolutions of Jupiter suggest a 60-year cycle of year names, called *samvatsaras*:

(1) Vijaya	(16) Kīlaka	(31) Rudhirodgārin
(2) Jaya	(17) Saumya	(32) Raktāksha
(3) Manmatha	(18) Sādhāraṇa	(33) Krodhana
(4) Durmukha	(19) Virodhakṛit	(34) Kshaya
(5) Hemalamba	(20) Paridhāvin	(35) Prabhava
(6) Vilamba	(21) Pramādin	(36) Vibhava
(7) Vikārin	(22) Ānanda	(37) Śukla
(8) Śarvari	(23) Rākshasa	(38) Pramoda
(9) Plava	(24) Anala	(39) Prajāpati
(10) Śubhakṛit	(25) Piṅgala	(40) Aṅgiras
(11) Śobhana	(26) Kālayukta	(41) Śrīmukha
(12) Krodhin	(27) Siddhārthin	(42) Bhāva
(13) Viśvāvasu	(28) Rāudra	(43) Yuvan
(14) Parābhava	(29) Durmati	(44) Dhātṛi
(15) Plavaṅga	(30) Dundubhi	(45) Īśvara

(46) Bahudhānya	(51) Subhānu	(56) Sarvadhārin
(47) Pramāthin	(52) Tāraṇa	(57) Virodhin
(48) Vikrama	(53) Pārthiva	(58) Vikṛita
(49) Vṛisha	(54) Vyaya	(59) Khara
(50) Chitrabhānu	(55) Sarvajit	(60) Nandana

The Jovian year number corresponding to the start of a solar year is computed from a fixed date as follows:

$$\textbf{jovian-year}\,(\textit{date}) \stackrel{\text{def}}{=} \left(\left\lfloor \frac{\textbf{hindu-day-count}\,(\textit{date})}{\frac{\textbf{arya-jovian-period}}{12}} \right\rfloor \bmod 60 \right) + 1 \tag{11.5}$$

Since a Jovian "year" is somewhat shorter than a solar year, consecutive solar years do not necessarily carry consecutive Jovian names. In that case, every eighty-six years or so the saṃvatsara is said to be "expunged."

The Jovian cycle and all other figures are given in traditional Hindu astronomy as rational numbers. Accordingly, we use rational arithmetic in our calendar functions, as well as in the Lisp code given in Appendix B. The numerators and denominators of the rational numbers obtained during the intermediate calculations exceed 32 binary digits but remain below 2^{63}; thus, they can be reformulated as integer calculations on modern machines.

Different Indian astronomical treatises give slightly varying astronomical constants; in this chapter we follow the (First) Arya Siddhānta of Āryabhaṭa (499 C.E.). There are also many variations in details of the calendars; we describe only one version.

11.2 The Solar Calendar

A solar month is one twelfth of a year:

$$\textbf{arya-solar-month} \stackrel{\text{def}}{=} \frac{\textbf{arya-sidereal-year}}{12} \tag{11.6}$$

The solar (*saura*) months are named after the signs of the zodiac (but differ from region to region), since the mean sun traverses one sign per month:

(1) Mesha	(Aries)	(7) Tulā	(Libra)
(2) Vṛishabha	(Taurus)	(8) Vṛiśchika	(Scorpio)
(3) Mithuna	(Gemini)	(9) Dhanu	(Sagittarius)
(4) Karka	(Cancer)	(10) Makara	(Capricorn)
(5) Siṁha	(Leo)	(11) Kumbha	(Aquarius)
(6) Kanyā	(Virgo)	(12) Mīna	(Pisces)

The solar new year is called *Mesha saṃkrānti*. Each solar month begins on the day of the first sunrise after the calculated time of the new month. If that calculated time is before (or at) sunrise, then it is the first day of the new month; otherwise, it is the last day of the previous month. Hence, even though the (mean) month is a constant, months vary in length. Our R.D. 0 is Makara 19, 3101 K.Y. on the mean solar calendar.

Converting a solar date according to this old Hindu calendar into an R.D. date is straightforward:

$$\textbf{fixed-from-old-hindu-solar}\left(\boxed{\begin{array}{c|c|c} month & day & year \end{array}}\right) \stackrel{\text{def}}{=} \tag{11.7}$$

$$\left\lfloor \textbf{hindu-epoch} + year \cdot \textbf{arya-sidereal-year} + (month - 1) \cdot \textbf{arya-solar-month} + day - \frac{1}{4} \right\rfloor$$

Since *year* is the number of years that have *elapsed* since the epoch, we multiply it by the average length of a year, which is a fraction, and add the number of days (and fractions of a day) in the elapsed months of the current year. That gives the time at which the current month began, to which is added the fixed date of the epoch and the number of days up to and including the given *day*. If the resultant moment is after mean sunrise (6 a.m.), then we have the right fixed date; if it is before sunrise, we need to subtract 1. Subtracting 1/4 of a day from the resultant moment and taking the floor has this effect.

Inverting the process is not much harder:

$$\textbf{old-hindu-solar-from-fixed}\,(date) \stackrel{\text{def}}{=} \tag{11.8}$$

$$\boxed{\begin{array}{c|c|c} month & day & year \end{array}}$$

where

$$rise = \textbf{hindu-day-count}\,(date) + \frac{1}{4}$$

$$year = \left\lfloor \frac{rise}{\textbf{arya-sidereal-year}} \right\rfloor$$

$$month = \left(\left\lfloor \frac{rise}{\textbf{arya-solar-month}} \right\rfloor \bmod 12\right) + 1$$

$$day = \lfloor rise \bmod \textbf{arya-solar-month} \rfloor + 1$$

Here, *rise* is the number of days and the fraction (1/4) of days that have elapsed since the Hindu epoch at mean sunrise—the decisive moment—on fixed date *date*; *year* is the number of mean years that have elapsed at that moment; *month* is the current solar month, counting mean months from the beginning of that solar year; and *day* is the number of the civil day, counting from the beginning of the solar month.

11.3 The Lunisolar Calendar

> Sometimes I cannot help regretting that only so very few readers can rejoice with me in the simplicity of the method and the exactness of its results.
> —*Walther E. van Wijk*: "On Hindu Chronology III," *Acta Orientalia*, volume II, p. 238 (1924)

We follow the south-India method, in which months begin and end at new moons (the *amânta* scheme); in the north, months go from full moon to full moon (the *pûrṇimânta* scheme). The name of a lunar month depends on the solar month that begins during that lunar month. A month is leap, and takes the following month's name, when no solar month begins within it. See Figure 11.1.

The names themselves are based on the longitudinal position of the moon at midmonth:

(1) Chaitra	(7) Āśvina
(2) Vaiśākha	(8) Kārttika
(3) Jyaishṭha	(9) Mārgaśīra
(4) Āshāḍha	(10) Pausha
(5) Śrāvaṇa	(11) Māgha
(6) Bhādrapada	(12) Phālguna

Some regions of India begin the year with Kārttika and use different or shifted month names.

Since a solar month (see Section 12.7) is longer than a lunar month, a lunar month is intercalated whenever the latter is wholly contained within the former. That lunar month and the following take the same name, except that the first is leap, called *adhika* ("added," or *prathama*, first), and the second is *nija* ("regular," or *dvitīya*, second).[4] In the rare event (at the onset of K.Y. 0, and every 360,000 years later) that both the lunar and solar month end at the

[4] In the northern, full-moon scheme, the intercalated month is inserted between the two halves of the ordinary month [2, p. 405].

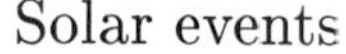

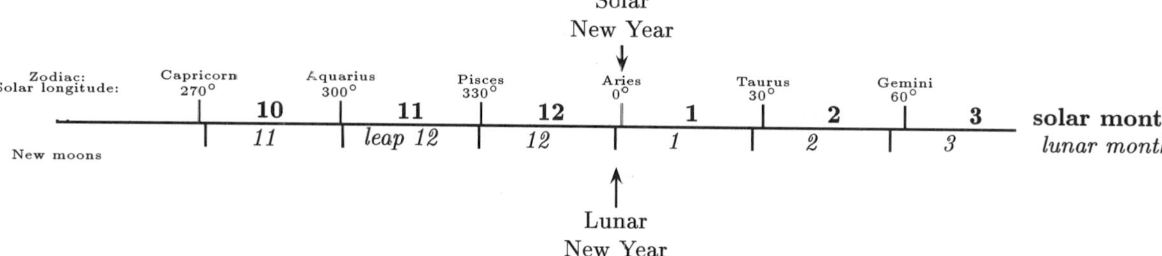

Figure 11.1 The old Hindu lunisolar calendar. Solar events (entries into zodiac constellations) are shown above the time line; lunar events (lunar conjunctions) are shown below. The solar months are shown in boldface numbers; the lunar months, in italic numbers.

same moment and, hence, that the following lunar and solar months both begin at the same moment, we follow the explicit statement of al-Bīrūnī [1, vol. 2, pp. 20–21] that the former lunar month is the intercalated one.

Two constants play a major rôle in lunar computations: the length of a solar month (page 122) and that of the lunar month:

$$\textbf{arya-lunar-month} \stackrel{\text{def}}{=} \frac{1577917500}{53433336} \tag{11.9}$$

that is, $29.53058181\cdots$ days. The lunar cycle is divided into thirty "lunar days,"[5] called *tithis*:

$$\textbf{arya-lunar-day} \stackrel{\text{def}}{=} \frac{\textbf{arya-lunar-month}}{30} \tag{11.10}$$

Because a mean lunar month is less than thirty (civil) days long, a lunar day is somewhat shorter than a day (0.98435 day).

Days within a lunar month are numbered by the lunar day current at sunrise, usually referred to by ordinal number within one fortnight or the other; we use ordinal numbers from 1 to 30. The first fifteen lunar days belong to the *suddha* ("bright," waxing; also *śukla*) fortnight and the second fifteen, to the *bahula* ("dark," waning; also *kṛishna*) fortnight. Just as there are leap months, there are also "lost" days whenever a lunar day begins and ends between one sunrise and the next. R.D. 0 is Pausha 19 (that is, dark 4), 3101 K.Y. on the lunisolar calendar.

To determine the number of the month, we look at the next occurrence of a new moon—the second, if it is a leap month; see where the sun is at that moment; and then give the lunar month the number of that solar month. For the lunar year number, we use the solar year of that solar month. The previous mean new moon is found using formula (1.23); the next new moon is one month later.

We can apply our leap year formulas (1.44) and (1.47) to the calculation of the old Hindu calendar, subject to a few complications:

1. The K.Y. year count begins at 0, not 1.
2. The first lunar year began one month before the onset of the Kali Yuga.
3. The determining time is mean sunrise, not midnight.
4. The relevant solar event—the start of solar month Mīna—occurs in the last month of a lunisolar year, rather than in the first.

[5] This should not be confused with what astronomers call a "lunar day."

Accordingly, we need to adjust the year numbers by 1, the month enumeration by 1, and the day count by 1/4. The first month of a lunar year is that in which the moment "Mīna plus one (lunar) month" occurs. That moment in year 0 was

$$\delta = 2 - \frac{\textbf{arya-solar-month}}{\textbf{arya-lunar-month}} \text{ months}$$

into the first month, because the first lunar year began exactly one month before the solar new year. The average year length is

$$\bar{L} = \frac{\textbf{arya-sidereal-year}}{\textbf{arya-lunar-month}} \text{ months.}$$

By inequality (1.45), Hindu year y is leap if

$$\left(2 - \frac{\textbf{arya-solar-month}}{\textbf{arya-lunar-month}} + y\frac{\textbf{arya-sidereal-year}}{\textbf{arya-lunar-month}}\right) \bmod 1$$
$$\geq 1 - \frac{\textbf{arya-sidereal-year}}{\textbf{arya-lunar-month}} \bmod 1.$$

Multiplying through by **arya-lunar-month** and simplifying we get the following test:

$$\textbf{old-hindu-lunar-leap-year?}\ (\textit{l-year}) \stackrel{\text{def}}{=} \tag{11.11}$$

$$\begin{aligned}&(\,(\,\textit{l-year} \cdot \textbf{arya-sidereal-year} - \\ &\quad \textbf{arya-solar-month}\,)\\ &\bmod \textbf{arya-lunar-month}\,)\\ &\geq \textbf{arya-lunar-month} - \\ &(\textbf{arya-sidereal-year} \bmod \textbf{arya-lunar-month})\end{aligned}$$

We do not, however, require this test for the conversion functions that follow.

Let $\textit{rise} = n + 1/4$ be the moment of sunrise on day n since the onset of the Kali Yuga. The number of months m that have elapsed since the first lunar year is $\lfloor \textit{rise}/\textbf{arya-lunar-month} \rfloor + 1$, which amounts to

$$\textit{rise} - (\textit{rise} \bmod \textbf{arya-lunar-month}) + \textbf{arya-lunar-month}$$

days. By (1.47), the year number (starting from 0) is

$$\left\lceil \frac{m + 1 - \delta}{\bar{L}} \right\rceil - 1.$$

Using the above values for m, δ, and $\bar{L}$ yields

$$y = \left\lceil \frac{m + 1 - \left(2 - \frac{\textbf{arya-solar-month}}{\textbf{arya-lunar-month}}\right)}{\frac{\textbf{arya-sidereal-year}}{\textbf{arya-lunar-month}}} \right\rceil - 1$$

$$= \left\lceil \frac{(m-1) \times \textbf{arya-lunar-month} + \textbf{arya-solar-month}}{\textbf{arya-sidereal-year}} \right\rceil - 1$$

$$= \left\lceil \frac{\textit{new-moon} + \textbf{arya-solar-month}}{\textbf{arya-sidereal-year}} \right\rceil - 1,$$

where *new-moon* is

$$(m-1) \times \textbf{arya-lunar-month}$$

$$= \left\lfloor \frac{\textit{rise}}{\textbf{arya-lunar-month}} \right\rfloor \times \textbf{arya-lunar-month}.$$

Intuitively, the lunisolar year number y is the solar year number in effect at the end of the current month.

The same leap year formula can be used to determine the lunar month name. For this purpose, however, we consider "years" to be a period of either one- or two-month duration: one for ordinary months and two when the month name is shared by a leap month. The average length, A, in lunar months, of such periods is **arya-solar-month/arya-lunar-month**. Formula (1.47) tells us that after m lunar months the number of elapsed periods is

$$z = \left\lceil \frac{m + 1 - \delta}{A} \right\rceil - 1$$

$$= \left\lceil \frac{\textit{new-moon} + \textbf{arya-solar-month}}{\textbf{arya-solar-month}} \right\rceil - 1$$

$$= \left\lceil \frac{\textit{new-moon}}{\textbf{arya-solar-month}} \right\rceil .$$

The inverse, deriving the fixed date from the Hindu lunar date, is a bit more complicated. By equation (1.44), there are $\lfloor 12yA + \delta \rfloor$ months from the beginning of year 0 until the end of elapsed year $y - 1$. Accordingly, the number of months since the Kali Yuga (which began one month after lunar year 0), is

$$\lfloor 12yA + \delta \rfloor - 1 = \left\lfloor 12y \frac{\textbf{arya-solar-month}}{\textbf{arya-lunar-month}} + \left(2 - \frac{\textbf{arya-solar-month}}{\textbf{arya-lunar-month}}\right) \right\rfloor - 1$$

$$= \left\lfloor \frac{(12y - 1) \times \textbf{arya-solar-month}}{\textbf{arya-lunar-month}} \right\rfloor + 1$$

$$= \left\lfloor \frac{\textit{mina}}{\textbf{arya-lunar-month}} \right\rfloor + 1$$

where

$$\begin{aligned} mina &= (12y - 1) \times \textbf{arya-solar-month} \\ &= y \times \textbf{arya-sidereal-year} - \textbf{arya-sidereal-month}. \end{aligned}$$

We use a boolean (true/false) value to indicate whether a month is leap. A date is represented as

month	*leapmonth*	*day*	*year*

where *month* is an integer in the range 1 through 12, *day* is an integer in the range 1 through 30, *year* is an integer, and *leapmonth* is either true or false.

$$\textbf{old-hindu-lunar-from-fixed}\,(date) \stackrel{\text{def}}{=} \tag{11.12}$$

month	*leap*	*day*	*year*

where

$$\begin{aligned} rise &= \textbf{hindu-day-count}\,(date) + \frac{1}{4} \\ new\text{-}moon &= rise - (rise \bmod \textbf{arya-lunar-month}) \\ leap &= \textbf{arya-solar-month} - \textbf{arya-lunar-month} \geq \\ &\quad (new\text{-}moon \bmod \textbf{arya-solar-month}) > 0 \\ month &= \left(\left\lceil \frac{new\text{-}moon}{\textbf{arya-solar-month}} \right\rceil \bmod 12 \right) + 1 \\ day &= \left(\left\lfloor \frac{rise}{\textbf{arya-lunar-day}} \right\rfloor \bmod 30 \right) + 1 \\ year &= \left\lceil \frac{new\text{-}moon + \textbf{arya-solar-month}}{\textbf{arya-sidereal-year}} \right\rceil - 1 \end{aligned}$$

To determine the lunar month, we take z, as derived above, and cast off twelves. A month is leap when it begins closer to the solar month's beginning than the excess of a solar month over a lunar month.

The lunar new year is the first lunar month to begin in the last solar month (*Mīna*) of the prior solar year. To compute the R.D. date from an old Hindu lunar date, we count elapsed lunar months and elapsed lunar days, taking care to check if there was a leap month in the interim. This value is added to the moment of the new year, as determined above:

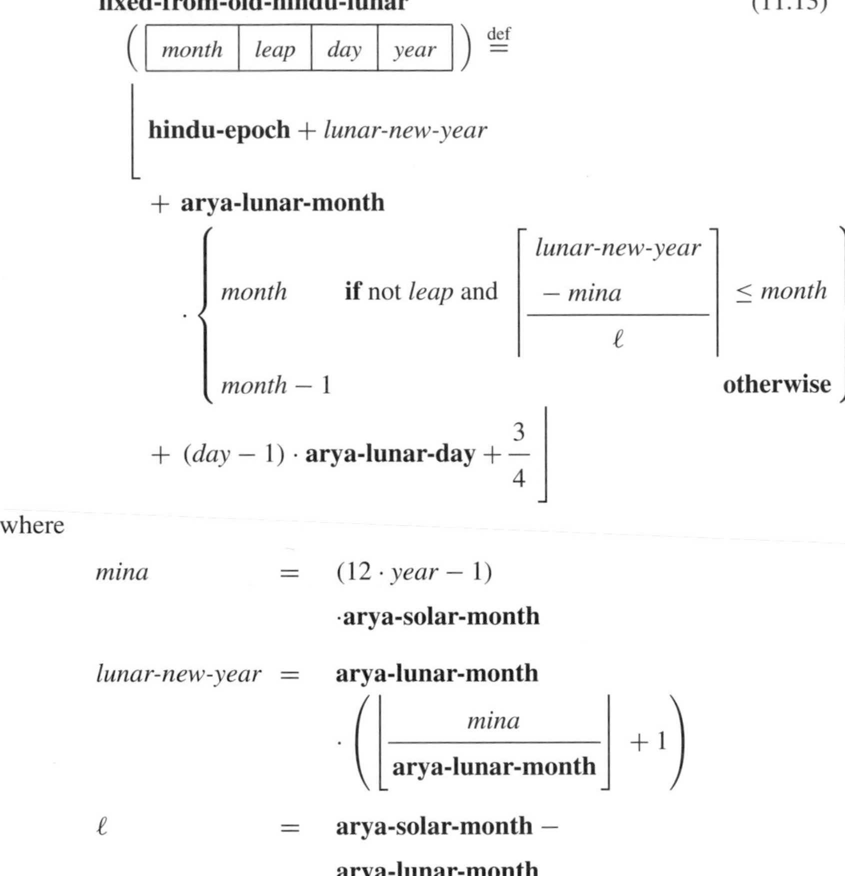

$$\textbf{fixed-from-old-hindu-lunar}\left(\boxed{\textit{month} \mid \textit{leap} \mid \textit{day} \mid \textit{year}}\right) \stackrel{\text{def}}{=} \tag{11.13}$$

$$\Bigl\lfloor \textbf{hindu-epoch} + \textit{lunar-new-year} + \textbf{arya-lunar-month} \cdot \begin{cases} \textit{month} & \textbf{if } \text{not } \textit{leap} \text{ and } \left\lceil \dfrac{\textit{lunar-new-year} - \textit{mina}}{\ell} \right\rceil \leq \textit{month} \\ \textit{month} - 1 & \textbf{otherwise} \end{cases} + (\textit{day} - 1) \cdot \textbf{arya-lunar-day} + \frac{3}{4} \Bigr\rfloor$$

where

$$\textit{mina} = (12 \cdot \textit{year} - 1) \cdot \textbf{arya-solar-month}$$

$$\textit{lunar-new-year} = \textbf{arya-lunar-month} \cdot \left(\left\lfloor \frac{\textit{mina}}{\textbf{arya-lunar-month}} \right\rfloor + 1 \right)$$

$$\ell = \textbf{arya-solar-month} - \textbf{arya-lunar-month}$$

We add 3/4 before taking the floor because the date at midnight is determined by the lunar day that was current at the prior sunrise.

References

[1] al-Bīrūnī (= Abū-Raiḥān Muḥammad ibn ’Aḥmad al-Bīrūnī), *India: An Accurate Description of all Categories of Hindu Thought, as Well those Which are Admissible as those Which Must be Rejected*, circa 1030. Translated and annotated by C. E. Sachau, *Albêrûnî’s India: An Account of the Religion, Philosophy, Literature, Geography, Chronology, Astronomy, Customs, Laws and Astrology of India*, William H. Allen and Co., London, 1910; reprinted under the Authority of the Government of West Pakistan, Lahore, 1962 and by S. Chand & Co., New Delhi, 1964.

[2] H. G. Jacobi, "The Computation of Hindu Dates in Inscriptions, &c.," *Epigraphia Indica: A Collection of Inscriptions Supplementary to the Corpus Inscriptionum Indicarum of the Archæological Survey of India*, J. Burgess, ed., Calcutta, pp. 403–460, p. 481, 1892.

[3] D. Pingree, "History of Mathematical Astronomy in India," *Dictionary of Scientific Biography*, C. C. Gillispie, ed., volume XV, supplement I, pp. 533–633, 1978.

[4] R. Sewell, *The Siddhantas and the Indian Calendar, Being a Continuation of the Author's "Indian Chronography," With an Article by the Late Dr. J. F. Fleet on the Mean Place of the Planet Saturn*, Government of India Central Publication Branch, Calcutta, 1924. This is a reprint of a series of articles in *Epigraphica Indica.*

[5] R. Sewell and S. B. Dîkshit, *The Indian Calendar, with Tables for the Conversion of Hindu and Muhammadan into* A.D. *Dates, and Vice Versa, With Tables of Eclipses Visible in India by R. Schram*, Motilal Banarsidass Publishers, Delhi, 1995. Originally published in 1896.

[6] W. E. van Wijk, *Decimal Tables for the Reduction of Hindu Dates from the Data of the Sūrya-Siddhānta*, Martinus Nijhoff, The Hague, 1938.

Part II

Astronomical Calendars

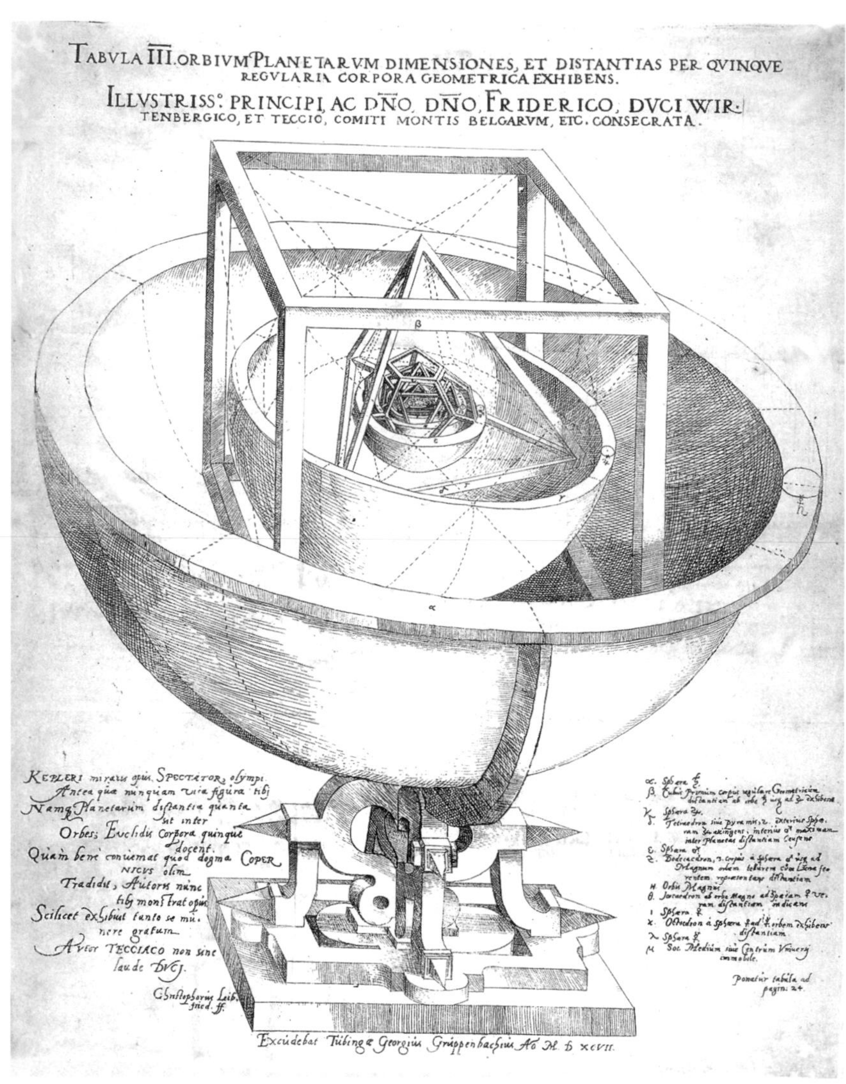

Geometrical explanation of the planetary distances—the mystical harmony of the spheres. From Johannes Kepler's *Prodromus Dissertationum Cosmographicarum Continens Mysterium Cosmographicum* (1596). (Courtesy of the University of Illinois, Urbana, IL.)

12

Time and Astronomy

> Brown's tables fill 650 quarto pages, and even with the tables a man working full time could extract the data just fast enough to keep up with the moon. The advent of the electronic calculator made feasible the direct evaluation of the formulas and. . . improved accuracy.
>
> —Wallace J. Eckert: *Encyclopædia Brittanica*, volume 15, p. 779 (1964)

The calendars in the second part of this book are based on accurate astronomical calculations. This chapter serves to define the necessary astronomical terms and to describe the astronomical functions.

We begin with an explanation of how positions of locations on Earth and of heavenly bodies are specified, and we continue with a discussion of the twenty-four hour day, followed by an examination of the notion of time itself. Then we summarize the different types of weeks, months, and years used by various calendars, along with algorithms that closely approximate the times of astronomical events—notably equinoxes, solstices, and new moons. These astronomical functions are adapted from those in [2] and [3] and require double-precision (64-bit) arithmetic. Most of the algorithms are centered around the present date, for which they are accurate to within about two minutes. Their accuracy decreases for the far distant past or future. More accurate algorithms exist [1], but are extremely complex and not needed for our purposes.

12.1 Position

We specify a location on Earth by giving its latitude and longitude. The *terrestrial latitude* of a geographic location is the angular distance on the earth, measured in degrees from the equator, along the meridian of the location. Similarly, the *terrestrial longitude* of a geographic location is the angular distance on the earth, measured in degrees from the Greenwich meridian (which is taken as 0°). Thus, for example, the location of Jerusalem is described as being 31.8° north, 35.2° east. In the algorithms, we take north as positive latitude and south as negative. For longitudes, we take east from Greenwich as positive and west as negative,[1] so that positive longitude means a time later than Greenwich and a negative longitude means a time earlier than in Greenwich.

The position of heavenly bodies can be measured in a manner corresponding to terrestrial longitude and latitude by projecting meridians on the celestial sphere. *Right ascension* corresponds to longitude, and *declination* to latitude. For marking the position of the sun and moon, however, astronomers use an alternative coordinate system in which (*celestial*) *longitude* is measured along the ecliptic (the sun's apparent path among the stars) and (*celestial*) *latitude* is measured from the ecliptic. Zero longitude is at a position called the *First Point of Aries* (see page 139).

12.2 The Day

> Some, like the Chaldees and the ancient Jews, define such a day as the time between two sunrises; others, like the Athenians, as that between two sunsets; or, like the Romans, from midnight to midnight; or like the Egyptians, from noon to noon. . . . It was necessary. . . to choose some mean and equal day, by which it would be possible to measure regularity of movement without trouble.
>
> —Nicolaus Copernicus: *De revolutionibus orbium coelestium* (III, 26) (1543)

The Earth revolves around its axis, causing the sun, moon, and stars to move across the sky from east to west in the course of a day. Thus, the simplest way of measuring days is from sunrise to sunrise or from sunset to sunset, because sunrise and sunset are unmistakable. The Islamic, Hebrew, and Bahá'í calendars begin their days at sunset, whereas the Hindu day starts and ends with sunrise. The disadvantage of these methods of reckoning days is the wide variation in the beginning/ending times. For example, in London, sunrise occurs anywhere from 3:42 a.m. to 8:06 a.m., and sunset varies from 3:51 p.m. to 8:21 p.m. By contrast, noon (the middle point of the day) and midnight (the middle point of the night) vary only by about half an hour in London. So in many parts of the world, sunset or sunrise definitions of the day have been superseded by a midnight-to-midnight day. For instance, the Chinese in the twelfth century

[1] This is at variance with the standard of the International Astronomical Union, but consistent with common sense and a century of common practice. See [3, p. 89].

B.C.E. began their day with the crowing of the rooster at 2 a.m., but more recently they have been using midnight. A noon-to-noon day is also plausible and indeed is used in the julian day system described in Section 1.4, but it has the disadvantage that the date changes in the middle of the working day.

Even with days measured from midnight to midnight there are seasonal variations. With the advent of mechanical clocks, introduced in the 1600s, the use of *mean* solar time (measured by the average rotation of the Earth, in which a day is 24 hours[2]) was preferred over the *apparent* time as measured by a sundial (during the daytime, at least). The elliptical orbit of the Earth and the inclination of the Earth's axis of rotation with respect to its orbit cause a difference between the time the sun crosses the (upper) meridian (the north-south line, through the zenith, overhead in the sky) and twelve noon on a clock—the difference can be more than 16 minutes. This discrepancy is called the *equation of time*, where the term *equation* has its medieval meaning of "corrective factor."

The equation of time gives the difference between apparent midnight (when the sun crosses the lower meridian that passes through the nadir; this is virtually the same as the midpoint between sunset and sunrise) and mean midnight (0 hours on the 24-hour clock). Similarly, at other times of day the equation of time gives the difference between mean solar time and apparent solar time. In the past, when apparent time was the more readily available, the equation of time conventionally had the opposite sign.

The periodic pattern of the equation of time, shown in Figure 12.1, is sometimes inscribed as part of the analemma on sundials (usually in mirror image). During the twentieth century, the equation of time has zeroes around April 15, June 14, September 1, and December 25; it is at its maximum at the beginning of November and at its minimum in mid-February. The equation of time is needed for the French Revolutionary calendar, and a rough approximation is used in the Hindu calendars. We use the following function for the equation of time:

$$\textbf{equation-of-time}\,(jd) \stackrel{\text{def}}{=} \tag{12.1}$$

$$\frac{\begin{array}{l} y \cdot \sin\left(2 \cdot longitude\right) - 2 \cdot eccentricity \cdot \sin anomaly\, + \\ 4 \cdot eccentricity \cdot y \cdot \sin anomaly \cdot \cos\left(2 \cdot longitude\right) - \\ 0.5 \cdot y^2 \cdot \sin\left(4 \cdot longitude\right) - \\ 1.25 \cdot eccentricity^2 \cdot \sin\left(2 \cdot anomaly\right) \end{array}}{2 \cdot \pi}$$

[2] The twenty-four hour day is sometimes called a *nychthemeron* to distinguish it from the shorter period of daylight.

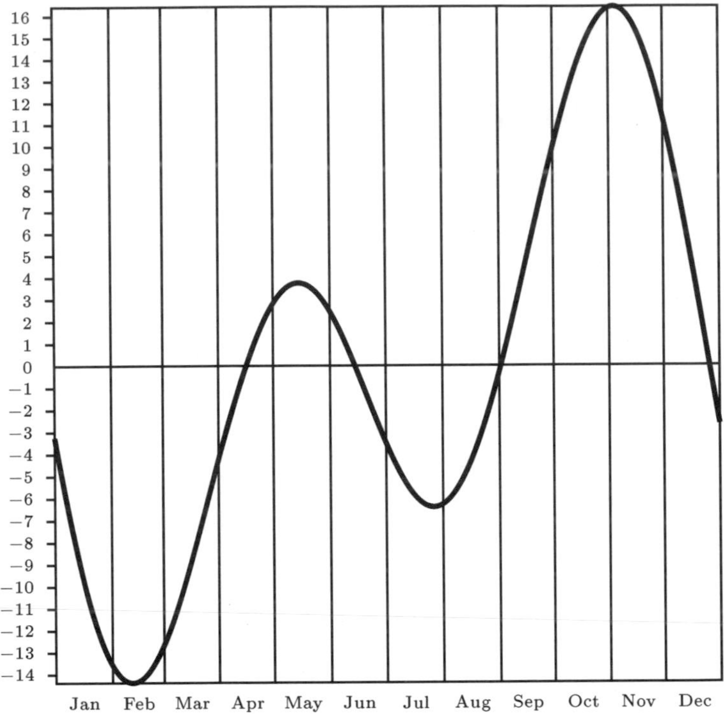

Figure 12.1 The equation of time. The vertical axis is in minutes.

where

$$c = \frac{jd - \mathbf{j2000}}{36525}$$

$$\mathit{longitude} = 280.46645 + 36000.76983 \cdot c + 0.0003032 \cdot c^2$$

$$\mathit{anomaly} = 357.52910 + 35999.05030 \cdot c - 0.0001559 \cdot c^2 - 0.00000048 \cdot c^3$$

$$\mathit{inclination} = 23.43929111 - 0.013004167 \cdot c - 0.00000016389 \cdot c^2 + 0.0000005036 \cdot c^3$$

$$\mathit{eccentricity} = 0.016708617 - 0.000042037 \cdot c - 0.0000001236 \cdot c^2$$

$$y = \tan^2\left(\frac{\mathit{inclination}}{2}\right)$$

The parameter *jd* is a time (day and fraction) given as a julian day number.

The equation of time permits us to convert easily to and from apparent time:

$$\textbf{apparent-from-local}\ (\mathit{moment}) \stackrel{\text{def}}{=} \tag{12.2}$$

$$\mathit{moment} + \textbf{equation-of-time}\ (\mathit{moment})$$

$$\textbf{local-from-apparent}\ (\mathit{moment}) \stackrel{\text{def}}{=} \tag{12.3}$$

$$\mathit{moment} - \textbf{equation-of-time}\ (\mathit{moment})$$

The latter function is slightly inaccurate, because the function **equation-of-time** takes local mean time, not apparent time, as its argument; the difference in the value of the equation of time in those few minutes is negligible, however.

A *sidereal day* is the time it takes for the Earth to rotate once around its axis, namely 23 hours, 56 minutes, and 4.09054 seconds. In the course of one rotation on its axis, the Earth has also revolved somewhat in its orbit around the sun, so the sun is not quite in the same position as it was one rotation prior. This accounts for the difference of almost four minutes with respect to the solar day. The sidereal day is employed in the Hindu calendar, which is based on calculations in terms of *sidereal* longitude, which remains fixed against the backdrop of the stars.

The axis of rotation of the Earth is inclined approximately 23.441884° with respect to the plane of revolution of the Earth around the sun. As a result, the sun, in the course of a year, traces a path through the stars that varies in distance from the celestial north pole (which is near the star Polaris). The ecliptic (the sun's apparent path through the constellations of the zodiac) is inclined the same 23.441884° degrees to the celestial equator (the plane passing through the center of the Earth, perpendicular to the axis of Earth's rotation).

The *vernal equinox* is the moment when the sun crosses the celestial equator from south to north, on approximately March 21 each year. At that time the day and night are 12 hours each all over the world, and the plane containing the Earth's axis and perpendicular to the line connecting the centers of the Earth and sun is tangent to the Earth's orbit around the sun. The point of crossing, from which celestial longitude is measured, is called the *true vernal equinox* or the "First Point of Aries," but it is currently in the constellation Pisces, not Aries, on account of a phenomenon called *precession of the equinoxes*. In its gyroscopic motion, the Earth's rotational axis rotates in a slow circle with period about 25,800 years, mainly as a consequence of the moon's pull. This nearly uniform motion causes the position of the equinoxes to move backwards along the ecliptic. Over the centuries, precession caused the vernal equinox to cease to coincide with the day when the sun enters Aries, as it did some 2300 years ago. Thus, the longitudes of the stars are constantly changing (in addition to the measurable motions of many of the "fixed" stars). Precession also causes the celestial pole to rotate slowly in a circular pattern. This is why the "pole star" has changed over the course of history; in 13,000 B.C.E., Vega was near the pole.

In practice, *sidereal time* is measured by the *hour angle* between the meridian (directly overhead) and the position of the First Point of Aries, the point of intersection of the ecliptic, inclined from south to north, and the *true celestial equator* (the line in the sky above the Earth's equator). This definition of sidereal time is affected by precession of the equinoxes.

In addition to precession, the pole of rotation of the Earth wobbles like a top in an 18.6-year period about its mean position. This effect is called *nutation* and is caused by the gravitational pull of the moon and sun on the unevenly shaped Earth. Nutation causes slight changes in the celestial latitudes and longitudes of stars. The effect (in radians) of nutation on longitude is approximately

$$\textbf{nutation}\,(c) \stackrel{\text{def}}{=} -.0000834 \cdot \sin a - .0000064 \cdot \sin b \tag{12.4}$$

where

$$\begin{aligned} a &= 124.90 - 1934.134 \cdot c + 0.002063 \cdot c^2 \\ b &= 201.11 + 72001.5377 \cdot c + 0.00057 \cdot c^2 \end{aligned}$$

Time, c, is measured in "Julian centuries," which is the number of centuries and fraction thereof before or after noon, January 1, 2000 (Gregorian):

$$\textbf{j2000} \stackrel{\text{def}}{=} \tag{12.5}$$

$$\textbf{jd-from-moment}\left(0.5 + \textbf{fixed-from-gregorian}\left(\boxed{\textbf{january} \mid 1 \mid 2000}\right)\right)$$

The conversion functions **jd-from-moment** and **fixed-from-gregorian** were defined on pages 13 and 36, respectively.

The sidereal day is not constant, mainly because of the retarding effects of tides and the atmosphere, which cause a relatively steady lengthening of the day and contributing what is called a "secular" (that is, steadily changing) term to the length of the day. Nutation causes a periodic variation in the lengths of the sidereal (and solar) day of up to about 0.01 seconds. *Mean sidereal time* smooths out (subtracts) nutation, which can accumulate to a difference of about one second from actual sidereal time as measured by the hour angle.

The moon also causes small oscillations in the length of the day with periods ranging from 12 hours to one (sidereal) month, but these can safely be ignored.

12.3 Subdivisions of the Day

Our civil day is divided into 24 hours, each hour is divided into 60 minutes, and each minute is divided into 60 seconds. Accordingly, we represent the time of day as a triple

$$hour : minute : second$$

where *hour* is an integer in the range 0 to 23, *minute* is an integer in the range 0 to 59, and *second* is a nonnegative real number less than 60. The following function converts the fractional part of a date-time R.D. number *moment* into hours, minutes, and seconds on a 24-hour clock (as used in most parts of the world), taking midnight as 0:00:00 hours:

$$\textbf{time-from-moment}\ (moment) \stackrel{\text{def}}{=} \tag{12.6}$$

$$hour : minute : second$$

where

$$\begin{aligned} hour &= \lfloor moment \cdot 24 \mod 24 \rfloor \\ minute &= \lfloor moment \cdot 24 \cdot 60 \mod 60 \rfloor \\ second &= moment \cdot 24 \cdot 60^2 \mod 60 \end{aligned}$$

Every now and then a *leap second* is added to the year to account for the (only partially predictable) vagaries in the length of an astronomical day, thereby keeping our clocks in tune with the gradually slowing rotation of Earth.

Other cultures subdivided the day differently. For instance, the ancient Egyptians—as well as the Greeks and Romans in classical times—divided the day and night *separately* into twelve equal "hours" each. Since, except at the equator, the length of daylight and nighttime vary with the seasons, the length of such daytime and nighttime hours also vary with the season. These seasonally varying *temporal* (or *seasonal*) hours (*horæ temporales*) are still used for ritual purposes among Moslems and Jews. In London, for example, the length of such an hour varies from about 39 minutes in December to 83 minutes in June. The Hebrew calendar divides the temporal hours into 1080 *ḥalaqim* (parts) of $3\frac{1}{3}$ seconds each; each part is divided into 76 *regaim* (moments).

From the first century B.C.E. until 1670, Chinese astronomers divided the day, which began at midnight, into 12 *shih* and also into 100 *ko*.

The Hindus divide the civil day into 60 *ghaṭikás* of 24 minute duration, each of which is divided into 60 *palas*, each of which is 24 seconds. They also divide the sidereal day into 60 *nádís*, each *nádí* into 60 *vinadis*, and each of the latter into 6 *asus*.

The French Revolutionary calendar divided each day into ten "hours," each "hour" into one hundred "minutes," and each "minute" into one hundred "seconds."

12.4 Time

> What, then, is time? I know well enough what it is, provided that nobody asks me; but if I am asked what it is and try to explain, I am baffled.
> —Saint Augustine: *Confessions* (XI, xiv) (circa 400)

There are four distinct methods of measuring time in use today:

- *Solar time* is based on the solar day, which measures the time between successive transits of the sun across the meridian. We have already seen that this period varies because of the complex motion of the Earth.
- *Sidereal time* is based on the sidereal day and varies less than solar time. It is measured as the right ascension of a point crossing the meridian at any given moment. Thus, *local* sidereal time depends on terrestrial longitude and differs from observatory to observatory.
- *Ephemeris time* takes the motion of the Earth around the sun (or the orbital motions of the moon and planets) as the basic building block. Other forms of *dynamical time* use different frames of reference, which makes a difference in a universe governed by relativity.
- *Atomic time*, a recent time-keeping method, takes the frequency of oscillation of certain atoms as the basic building block. We have no need to consider this most accurate measure of time in this book.

The ordinary method of measuring time is called *universal time*, abbreviated U.T. It is local mean solar time, reckoned from midnight, at the observatory in Greenwich, England, the 0° meridian.[3] The equivalent designation "Greenwich Mean Time," abbreviated G.M.T., has fallen into disfavor with astronomers because of confusion as to whether days begin at midnight or noon.

We use universal time for our time-keeping purposes, expressed as a fraction of a solar day. Converting between universal and local mean time is easy:

$$\textbf{universal-from-local}\,(\textit{l-time}, \textit{zone}) \stackrel{\text{def}}{=} \textit{l-time} - \frac{\textit{zone}}{24 \cdot 60} \tag{12.7}$$

[3] The formal recognition of Greenwich as the "prime meridian" dates from the International Meridian Conference of 1884, but it had been informal practice from 1767. The French, however, continued to treat Paris as the prime meridian until 1911, when they switched to Greenwich, referring to it as "Paris Mean Time, retarded by nine minutes twenty-one seconds" [9, pp. 166–168].

$$\textbf{local-from-universal}\ (\textit{u-time}, \textit{zone}) \stackrel{\text{def}}{=} \qquad (12.8)$$

$$\textit{u-time} + \frac{\textit{zone}}{24 \cdot 60}$$

where time differences or zones are expressed in minutes (of time) after Greenwich. Each longitudinal degree of separation gives rise to a four-minute difference in local time. For example, since the meridian of Paris is $2°20'15''$ east, its local time is 9 minutes, 21 seconds after U.T. As another example, Beijing is $116°25'$ east; the time difference from U.T. is 7:45:40 hours, or 465 minutes, 40 seconds.

From the spread of clocks and pocket watches in Europe until the advent of the railroad, each locale would set its clocks to local mean time. Time zones were first adopted by North American railway companies in the late 1800s, and this is called *standard time* or *zone time*. Most of Western Europe (excluding Great Britain and Finland) is today in one zone; the continental United States (excluding Alaska and Hawaii) is divided into four zones. An incredible list of locations and the times they use today and used historically appears in [7] (for outside the United States) and [6] (for the United States). We ignore the issue of daylight-saving (summer) time, because it is irrelevant to the calendars we discuss.

To determine the difference between local mean time and standard zone time, we can use

$$\textbf{local-from-standard}\ (\textit{s-time}, \textit{offset}) \stackrel{\text{def}}{=} \qquad (12.9)$$

$$\textit{s-time} + \frac{\textit{offset}}{24 \cdot 60}$$

$$\textbf{standard-from-local}\ (\textit{l-time}, \textit{offset}) \stackrel{\text{def}}{=} \qquad (12.10)$$

$$\textit{l-time} - \frac{\textit{offset}}{24 \cdot 60}$$

where *offset* is the difference in minutes between the two times, which in turn depends on the longitude of the location and the difference (in minutes) between U.T. and standard time at that location:

$$\textbf{location-offset}\ (\textit{longitude}, \textit{zone}) \stackrel{\text{def}}{=} 4 \cdot \textit{longitude} - \textit{zone} \qquad (12.11)$$

For example, Jerusalem is $35.2°$ east of Greenwich and it is zone U.T.+120. So to obtain standard time in Jerusalem from local mean time, we add an offset of 20 minutes, 48 seconds.

Sidereal time is usually expressed as an hour angle. Converting between solar and mean sidereal time amounts to evaluating a polynomial:

$$\textbf{sidereal-from-jd}\,(jd) \stackrel{\text{def}}{=} \frac{\sum_i \left(\textit{sidereal-coeff}_{[i]} \cdot c^i\right)}{360} \tag{12.12}$$

where

$$c = \frac{jd - \mathbf{j2000}}{36525}$$

$$\textit{sidereal-coeff} = \left\langle 280.46061837, 36525 \cdot 360.98564736629, 0.000387933, \frac{1}{38710000} \right\rangle$$

The Hindu calendar uses an approximation to this conversion.

Astronomical calculation are typically done using Ephemeris time, on which nutation and *aberration*—the effect of the sun's moving about 20.47 seconds of arc during the eight minutes its light is en route to Earth—have no impact. We therefore need the following functions:

$$\textbf{ephemeris-correction}\,(\textit{moment}) \stackrel{\text{def}}{=} \tag{12.13}$$

$$\begin{cases} \dfrac{\textit{year} - 1933}{24 \cdot 60 \cdot 60} & \textbf{if } 1988 \le \textit{year} \le 2019 \\ \sum_i \left(\textit{coeff-19th}_{[i]} \cdot \theta^i\right) & \textbf{if } 1900 \le \textit{year} \le 1987 \\ \sum_j \left(\textit{coeff-18th}_{[j]} \cdot \theta^j\right) & \textbf{if } 1800 \le \textit{year} \le 1899 \\ \dfrac{196.58333 - 4.0675 \cdot (\textit{year} - 1600) + 0.0219167 \cdot (\textit{year} - 1600)^2}{24 \cdot 60 \cdot 60} & \textbf{if } 1620 \le \textit{year} \le 1799 \\ \dfrac{\dfrac{x^2}{41048480} - 15}{24 \cdot 60 \cdot 60} & \textbf{otherwise} \end{cases}$$

where

$$\textit{year} = \textbf{gregorian-year-from-fixed}\,(\textit{moment})$$

$$\theta = \frac{\textbf{gregorian-date-difference}\left(\boxed{\textbf{january} \mid 1 \mid 1900}, \boxed{\textbf{july} \mid 1 \mid \textit{year}}\right)}{36525}$$

$$\textit{coeff-19th} = \langle -0.00002, 0.000297, 0.025184, -0.181133, 0.553040, -0.861938, 0.677066, -0.212591 \rangle$$

$$\textit{coeff-18th} = \langle -0.000009, 0.003844, 0.083563, 0.865736, 4.867575, 15.845535, 31.332267, 38.291999, 28.316289, 11.636204, 2.043794 \rangle$$

$$x = 0.5 + \textbf{gregorian-date-difference}\left(\boxed{\textbf{january} \mid 1 \mid 1810}, \boxed{\textbf{january} \mid 1 \mid \textit{year}}\right)$$

and

$$\textbf{ephemeris-from-universal}\ (\textit{jd}) \stackrel{\text{def}}{=} \qquad (12.14)$$

$$\textit{jd} + \textbf{ephemeris-correction}\ (\textbf{moment-from-jd}\ (\textit{jd}))$$

where *moment* is a fixed date-time; *jd* is a julian day number in U.T. We approximate the inverse of the previous function by

$$\textbf{universal-from-ephemeris}\ (\textit{jd}) \stackrel{\text{def}}{=} \qquad (12.15)$$

$$\textit{jd} - \textbf{ephemeris-correction}\ (\textbf{moment-from-jd}\ (\textit{jd}))$$

This is inexact, because the correction should take universal time, not Ephemeris time, as the independent variable; the error is quite small, however.

To keep the numbers within reasonable bounds, the astronomical algorithms usually convert dates and times into "Julian centuries," that is, into the number of centuries and fraction thereof before or after noon on January 1, 2000, Ephemeris time:

$$\textbf{julian-centuries}\ (\textit{moment}) \stackrel{\text{def}}{=} \qquad (12.16)$$

$$\frac{\textbf{ephemeris-from-universal}\ (\textit{moment}) - \textbf{j2000}}{36525}$$

12.5 The Year

While the earth remaineth, seedtime and harvest, and cold and heat,
and summer and winter, and day and night shall not cease.
—Genesis 8:22

A *tropical year* is the time it takes for the sun to return to the same position in its apparent path, specifically the First Point of Aries, including the effect of precession. The seasons are governed by the tropical year. The current mean length of a tropical year is 365.242189 days; it is decreasing by about 1.3×10^{-5} days per century. We use

$$\textbf{mean-tropical-year} \stackrel{\text{def}}{=} 365.242199 \tag{12.17}$$

in the French Revolutionary calendar code (Chapter 13), which was its value in about 1900. A *sidereal year* is the time it takes for the Earth to revolve once around the sun, or for the (mean) sun to return to the same position relative to the background of the fixed stars. The sidereal year is 365.25636 days, or about twenty minutes more than the tropical. The modern Hindu calendar (Chapter 15) uses approximations of both the sidereal and tropical year.

To determine the time of equinoxes or solstices, as required for the French Revolutionary (Chapter 13), Chinese (Chapter 14), and proposed Bahá'í (see Chapter 8) calendars, we need to be able to calculate the longitude of the sun at any given time. The following function takes an astronomical time, given as a julian day number *jd*; converts it to Julian centuries; sums a long sequence of periodic terms; adds terms to compensate for aberration (the effect of the sun's motion while its light is traveling towards Earth—see page 147) and nutation (caused by the wobble of the Earth—see page 140); and then converts to degrees:

$$\textbf{solar-longitude}\,(jd) \stackrel{\text{def}}{=} \tag{12.18}$$

$$\textbf{degrees}\left(\left(\,longitude + \textbf{aberration}\,(c) + \textbf{nutation}\,(c)\,\right) \cdot \frac{180}{\pi}\right)$$

where

$$\begin{aligned}
c &= \textbf{julian-centuries}\,(jd) \\
longitude &= 4.9353929 + 628.33196168 \cdot c + \\
&\quad\; 0.0000001 \cdot \sum \left(\tilde{x} \cdot \sin\left((\tilde{y} + \tilde{z} \cdot c) \cdot \frac{180}{\pi}\right)\right) \\
\tilde{x} &= (\textit{see}\text{ Table 12.1}) \\
\tilde{y} &= (\textit{see}\text{ Table 12.1}) \\
\tilde{z} &= (\textit{see}\text{ Table 12.1})
\end{aligned}$$

Table 12.1 *Arguments for* **solar-longitude (page 146)**

$\tilde{x}$	$\tilde{y}$	$\tilde{z}$	$\tilde{x}$	$\tilde{y}$	$\tilde{z}$
403406	4.721964	0.01621043	195207	5.937458	628.30348067
119433	1.115589	628.30821524	112392	5.781616	628.29634302
3891	5.5474	1256.605691	2819	1.512	1256.60984
1721	4.1897	628.324766	0	1.163	0.00813
660	5.415	1256.5931	350	4.315	575.3385
334	4.553	−0.33931	314	5.198	7771.37715
268	5.989	786.04191	242	2.911	0.05412
234	1.423	393.02098	158	0.061	−0.34861
132	2.317	1150.67698	129	3.193	157.74337
114	2.828	52.9667	99	0.52	588.4927
93	4.65	52.9611	86	4.35	−39.807
78	2.75	522.3769	72	4.5	550.7647
68	3.23	2.6108	64	1.22	157.7385
46	0.14	1884.9103	38	3.44	−77.5655
37	4.37	2.6489	32	1.14	1179.0627
29	2.84	550.7575	28	5.96	−79.6139
27	5.09	1884.8981	27	1.72	21.3219
25	2.56	1097.7103	24	1.92	548.6856
21	0.09	254.4393	21	5.98	−557.3143
20	4.03	606.9774	18	4.47	21.3279
17	0.79	1097.7163	14	4.24	−77.5282
13	2.01	1884.9191	13	2.65	2.0781
13	4.98	294.2463	12	0.93	−0.0799
10	2.21	469.4114	10	3.59	−0.6829
10	1.5	214.6325	10	2.55	1572.084

and

$$\textbf{degrees}\,(\theta) \stackrel{\text{def}}{=} \theta \mod 360 \tag{12.19}$$

is used to normalize the sun's longitude to the range 0° to 360°.

To avoid cluttering the page with subscripts, we use vector notation, with the intention that the operations within the sum are performed on like-indexed elements of $\tilde{x}$, $\tilde{y}$, and $\tilde{z}$ displayed in Table 12.1. This function is accurate to within ten minutes of arc for current times.

Aberration is calculated as follows:

$$\textbf{aberration}\,(c) \stackrel{\text{def}}{=} \tag{12.20}$$

$$0.0000017 \cdot \cos(177.63 + 35999.01848 \cdot c) - 0.0000973$$

where c is the time in Julian centuries and the result is in radians.

To determine the time of an equinox or solstice, we need a special operator to express a bisection search [8, section 3.2]. We define

$$y \approx \underset{\xi \in [\mu : \nu]}{\overset{\phi(l,u)}{\textbf{MIN}}} \{\psi(\xi)\} \quad \text{means that} \quad \begin{array}{c} \mu \leq l < y < u \leq \nu, \\ \phi(l,u), \neg\psi(l), \text{ and } \psi(u) \end{array} \tag{12.21}$$

That is, we search for a y satisfying the definiens under the assumption that the region $[\mu : \nu]$ can be split into two intervals $[\mu : x)$ and $[x : \nu]$, such that ψ is false throughout the former and true in the latter. Then y must be close enough to x so that it lies in an interval $(l : u)$, sandwiching x, small enough to satisfy the test $\phi(l, u)$. We implement the definition using a straightforward bisection search of the interval $[\mu : \nu]$:

$$\textbf{MIN}\,(\mu, \nu, \phi, \psi) \stackrel{\text{def}}{=} \tag{12.22}$$

$$\begin{cases} x & \textbf{if } \phi\,(\mu, \nu) \\ \textbf{MIN}\,(\mu, x, \phi, \psi) & \\ \qquad \textbf{if} \text{ not } \phi\,(\mu, \nu) \text{ and } \psi\,(x) & \\ \textbf{MIN}\,(x, \nu, \phi, \psi) & \textbf{otherwise} \end{cases}$$

where

$$x = \frac{\nu + \mu}{2}$$

If ψ is true of the midpoint x, then we "go left" and let the new upper bound ν be x. On the other hand, if ψ is false, we "go right" and let the new lower bound μ be x. This process continues until the interval $[\mu : \nu]$ is small enough that ϕ is true, at which point the midpoint is returned. At each stage of the search, $\psi(\mu)$ is false and $\psi(\nu)$ is true.

Using the **MIN** operator we can determine the time of an equinox or solstice by devising a generic function that takes a date *jd* (in J.D. and U.T.) and number of degrees l and searches for the moment when next the longitude of the sun is a multiple of l degrees; l must be a proper divisor of 360°. The search is bisection within an interval beginning with time *jd* and ending long enough past *jd* to insure that the sun passes through exactly one multiple of l. The process terminates when the time is ascertained within one hundred-thousandth of a day (about 0.9 seconds):

$$\textbf{date-next-solar-longitude}\,(jd, l) \stackrel{\text{def}}{=} \tag{12.23}$$

$$\underset{x \in [jd\,:\,up]}{\overset{p\,(start,\,end)}{\textbf{MIN}}} \left\{ \begin{array}{ll} l \geq \textbf{solar-longitude}\,(x) & \textbf{if } next = 0 \\ \textbf{solar-longitude}\,(x) \geq next & \textbf{otherwise} \end{array} \right\}$$

Table 12.2 *The solar longitudes and approximate dates of equinoxes and solstices*

Name	Solar Longitude	Approximate Date
Vernal (spring) equinox	0°	March 21
Summer solstice	90°	June 21
Autumnal (fall) equinox	180°	September 23
Winter solstice	270°	December 22

where

$$\begin{aligned} next &= \mathbf{degrees}\left(l \cdot \left\lceil \frac{\mathbf{solar\text{-}longitude}\,(jd)}{l} \right\rceil\right) \\ p\,(start, end) &= 0.00001 \geq end - start \\ up &= jd + \frac{l}{360} \cdot 400 \end{aligned}$$

The only complication is handling the discontinuity from 360° to 0°.

The equinoxes and solstices occur when the sun's longitude is a multiple of 90°. Specifically, Table 12.2 gives the names, solar longitudes, and approximate Gregorian dates.

To use **date-next-solar-longitude** to determine, say, the R.D. date of the winter solstice for 1996 in Urbana, Illinois (which is U.T.−360 minutes), we write

$$\mathbf{urbana\text{-}winter}\,(g\text{-}year) \stackrel{\text{def}}{=} \tag{12.24}$$

$$\mathbf{moment\text{-}from\text{-}jd}\left(\mathbf{apparent\text{-}from\text{-}local}\left(\mathbf{local\text{-}from\text{-}universal}\left(\mathbf{date\text{-}next\text{-}solar\text{-}longitude}\left(\mathbf{universal\text{-}from\text{-}local}\left(\mathbf{jd\text{-}from\text{-}moment}\left(\mathbf{fixed\text{-}from\text{-}gregorian}\left(\boxed{\mathbf{december} \mid 15 \mid g\text{-}year}\right)\right), -360\right), 90\right), -360\right)\right)\right)$$

For 1996 this gives us the answer R.D. 729014.3385970318, which is 8:07:35 a.m. local mean time on December 21, 1996 (Gregorian), within a minute of the exact time.

12.6 Sunrise and Sunset

We occasionally need the approximate time of sunrise. We write a general function to calculate the local mean time of sunrise/sunset at *latitude*, *longitude* (in non-polar regions) for fixed *date*:

$$\textbf{solar-moment}\,(\mathit{date}, \mathit{latitude}, \mathit{longitude}, \mathit{rise\text{-}or\text{-}set}) \stackrel{\text{def}}{=} \tag{12.25}$$

$$\left(\frac{\mathit{local} + \mathit{right\text{-}ascension}}{360} - 0.27592 - 0.00273792 \cdot \mathit{approx}\right) \bmod 1$$

where

$$\begin{aligned}
\mathit{approx} &= \textbf{day-number}\,(\textbf{gregorian-from-fixed}\,(\mathit{date})) + 0.5 + \\
&\quad \mathit{rise\text{-}or\text{-}set} + \frac{\mathit{longitude}}{-360} \\
\mathit{anomaly} &= 0.9856 \cdot \mathit{approx} - 3.289 \\
\mathit{sun} &= \textbf{degrees} \\
&\quad (\mathit{anomaly} + 1.916 \cdot \sin \mathit{anomaly} + 282.634 \\
&\qquad + 0.020 \cdot \sin(2 \cdot \mathit{anomaly})) \\
\mathit{right\text{-}ascension} &= \textbf{arctan}\left(\cos 23.441884 \cdot \tan \mathit{sun}, \left\lfloor \frac{\mathit{sun}}{90} \right\rfloor + 1\right) \\
\mathit{declination} &= \arcsin(\sin 23.441884 \cdot \sin \mathit{sun}) \\
\mathit{local} &= \operatorname{signum}(\mathit{rise\text{-}or\text{-}set}) \cdot \arccos\left(\frac{r}{\cos \mathit{declination} \cdot \cos \mathit{latitude}}\right) \\
r &= \cos 90.833333 - \sin \mathit{declination} \cdot \sin \mathit{latitude}
\end{aligned}$$

This uses

$$\textbf{arctan}\,(x, \mathit{quad}) \stackrel{\text{def}}{=} \tag{12.26}$$

$$\begin{cases} \mathit{deg} & \textbf{if } \mathit{quad} = 1 \text{ or } \mathit{quad} = 4 \\ \mathit{deg} + 180 & \textbf{otherwise} \end{cases}$$

where

$$\mathit{deg} = \arctan x$$

to find the arc tangent of x appropriate for the quadrant *quad* in which the sun is located.

The function **solar-moment** gives the local mean time of sunrise when *rise-or-set* is -0.25 and sunset when it is 0.25. Hence we can write

$$\textbf{sunrise}\,(\textit{date}, \textit{latitude}, \textit{longitude}) \stackrel{\text{def}}{=} \textbf{solar-moment}\,(\textit{date}, \textit{latitude}, \textit{longitude}, -0.25) \tag{12.27}$$

and, although we have no need of it, we approximate the local mean time of sunset with

$$\textbf{sunset}\,(\textit{date}, \textit{latitude}, \textit{longitude}) \stackrel{\text{def}}{=} \textbf{solar-moment}\,(\textit{date}, \textit{latitude}, \textit{longitude}, 0.25) \tag{12.28}$$

To convert these local times to standard time we would use **standard-from-local** (page 143). For example, to calculate the local standard time of sunset in Urbana, Illinois (latitude 40.1° north, longitude 88.2° west, 360 minutes before U.T.), we could write

$$\textbf{urbana-sunset}\,(\textit{g-date}) \stackrel{\text{def}}{=} \textbf{time-from-moment}\left(\textbf{standard-from-local}\,(\textbf{sunset}\,(d, \textit{latitude}, \textit{longitude}), \textit{offset})\right) \tag{12.29}$$

where

$$\begin{aligned} d &= \textbf{fixed-from-gregorian}\,(\textit{g-date}) \\ \textit{longitude} &= -88.2 \\ \textit{latitude} &= 40.1 \\ \textit{ut-diff} &= -360 \\ \textit{offset} &= \textbf{location-offset}\,(\textit{longitude}, \textit{ut-diff}) \end{aligned}$$

12.7 The Month

> You have already seen... how much computation is involved, how many additions and subtractions are still necessary, despite our having exerted ourselves greatly to invent approximations that do not require complicated calculations. For the path of the moon is convoluted. Hence wise men have said: the sun knows its way, the moon does not....
>
> —Moses Maimonides: *Mishneh Torah, Book of Seasons*, 17:23 (1178)

The *new moon* is defined as the time when the sun and moon have the same longitude; it is not necessarily the time of their closest encounter, as viewed from Earth, because the orbits of the Earth and moon are not coplanar. The time from new moon (*conjunction* of sun and moon) to new moon (a *lunation*) is called the *synodic month*. Its value today ranges from approximately 29.27 to 29.84 days [4], with a mean currently of 29.530589 (mean) days:

$$\textbf{mean-synodic-month} \stackrel{\text{def}}{=} 29.530588853 \tag{12.30}$$

The mean and true times of the new moon can differ by up to about fourteen hours.

The synodic month is not constant, but is decreasing in mean length by about 3.5×10^{-7} days per century. Approximations of this value are used in all the lunar and lunisolar calendars, except the Chinese, which uses precise values in its calculations. The net effect of the decreases in synodic month and tropical year is to increase the number of months from its current value of about 12.3682670 per year, by 0.3×10^{-6} months per century.

The *sidereal month* is the time it takes the moon to make one revolution around the Earth. Its mean value is 27.32166 days. In the interim, the Earth has moved in its orbit around the sun, so the difference in longitude between the sun and moon has increased, which is why the synodic month is longer. The mean values of these types of month should satisfy the equation

$$\frac{1}{\text{sidereal month}} - \frac{1}{\text{synodic month}} = \frac{1}{\text{sidereal year}}.$$

The *anomalistic month* is the time between consecutive perigees (points at which the moon is closest to Earth). The anomalistic month averages 27.55455 days. Approximations to these values are used in calculating the position of the moon for the modern Hindu lunisolar calendar.

We also use a notion of a *solar month*, the time for the sun's position in the sky to traverse one sign of the zodiac (30° of longitude). Its mean value is one-twelfth of a solar year. Solar months play an important rôle in the Chinese calendar (which uses tropical longitude) and the Hindu calendar (which uses sidereal longitude).

The time of new moon can be determined directly using sums of periodic terms. We use the function

$$\textbf{new-moon-at-or-after}\ (jd) \stackrel{\text{def}}{=} \tag{12.31}$$

$$\textbf{new-moon-time}\ (approx + error)$$

where

$$
\begin{aligned}
date &= \textbf{gregorian-from-fixed}\ (\lfloor \textbf{moment-from-jd}\ (jd) \rfloor) \\
approx &= \lfloor y \cdot 12.3685 \rfloor - 1
\end{aligned}
$$

$$\begin{aligned}
\mathit{error} &= \sum_{k \geq \mathit{approx}}^{p(k)} 1 \\
p(k) &= \textbf{new-moon-time}(k) < \mathit{jd} \\
y &= \mathit{date}_{\textbf{year}} + \frac{\textbf{day-number}(\mathit{date})}{365.25} - 2000
\end{aligned}$$

which, in turn, uses

$$\textbf{new-moon-time}(k) \stackrel{\text{def}}{=} \tag{12.32}$$

$$\textbf{universal-from-ephemeris}(\mathit{jde} + \mathit{correction} + \mathit{additional})$$

where

$$\begin{aligned}
c &= \frac{k}{1236.85} \\
\mathit{jde} &= 2451550.09765 + \\
&\quad \textbf{mean-synodic-month} \cdot 1236.85 \cdot c + 0.0001337 \cdot c^2 \\
&\quad - 0.000000150 \cdot c^3 + 0.00000000073 \cdot c^4 \\
e &= 1 - 0.002516 \cdot c - 0.0000074 \cdot c^2 \\
\mathit{solar\text{-}anomaly} &= 2.5534 + 29.10535669 \cdot 1236.85 \cdot c - \\
&\quad 0.0000218 \cdot c^2 - 0.00000011 \cdot c^3 \\
\mathit{lunar\text{-}anomaly} &= 201.5643 + 385.81693528 \cdot 1236.85 \cdot c + \\
&\quad 0.0107438 \cdot c^2 + 0.00001239 \cdot c^3 - 0.000000058 \cdot c^4 \\
\mathit{moon\text{-}argument} &= 160.7108 + 390.67050274 \cdot 1236.85 \cdot c - \\
&\quad 0.0016341 \cdot c^2 - 0.00000227 \cdot c^3 + 0.000000011 \cdot c^4 \\
\omega &= 124.7746 + (-1.56375580) \cdot 1236.85 \cdot c + \\
&\quad 0.0020691 \cdot c^2 + 0.00000215 \cdot c^3 \\
\mathit{correction} &= -.00017 \cdot \sin\omega + \\
&\quad \sum \left(\tilde{v} \cdot e^{\tilde{w}} \cdot \sin \left(\tilde{x} \cdot \mathit{solar\text{-}anomaly} + \tilde{y} \cdot \mathit{lunar\text{-}anomaly} + \right.\right. \\
&\qquad \left.\left. \tilde{z} \cdot \mathit{moon\text{-}argument} \right) \right) \\
\mathit{additional} &= \sum \left(\tilde{l} \cdot \sin\left(\tilde{i} + \tilde{j} \cdot k + \tilde{n} \cdot c^2 \right) \right) \\
\tilde{v} &= (\textit{see}\ \text{Table 12.3})
\end{aligned}$$

Table 12.3 *Arguments for* **new-moon-time** *(pages 153–154)*

$\tilde{v}$	$\tilde{w}$	$\tilde{x}$	$\tilde{y}$	$\tilde{z}$	$\tilde{v}$	$\tilde{w}$	$\tilde{x}$	$\tilde{y}$	$\tilde{z}$
−0.40720	0	0	1	0	0.17241	1	1	0	0
0.01608	0	0	2	0	0.01039	0	0	0	2
0.00739	1	−1	1	0	−0.00514	1	1	1	0
0.00208	2	2	0	0	−0.00111	0	0	1	−2
−0.00057	0	0	1	2	0.00056	1	1	2	0
−0.00042	0	0	3	0	0.00042	1	1	0	2
0.00038	1	1	0	−2	−0.00024	1	−1	2	0
−0.00007	0	2	1	0	0.00004	0	0	2	−2
0.00004	0	3	0	0	0.00003	0	1	1	−2
0.00003	0	0	2	2	−0.00003	0	1	1	2
0.00003	0	−1	1	2	−0.00002	0	−1	1	−2
−0.00002	0	1	3	0	0.00002	0	0	4	0

Table 12.4 *Arguments for* **new-moon-time** *(pages 153–154)*

$\tilde{i}$	$\tilde{j}$	$\tilde{n}$	$\tilde{l}$	$\tilde{i}$	$\tilde{j}$	$\tilde{n}$	$\tilde{l}$
299.77	0.107408	−0.009173	0.000325	251.88	0.016321	0	0.000165
251.83	26.641886	0	0.000164	349.42	36.412478	0	0.000126
84.66	18.206239	0	0.000110	141.74	53.303771	0	0.000062
207.14	2.453732	0	0.000060	154.84	7.306860	0	0.000056
34.52	27.261239	0	0.000047	207.19	0.121824	0	0.000042
291.34	1.844379	0	0.000040	161.72	24.198154	0	0.000037
239.56	25.513099	0	0.000035	331.55	3.592518	0	0.000023

$\tilde{w}$ = (*see* Table 12.3)

$\tilde{x}$ = (*see* Table 12.3)

$\tilde{y}$ = (*see* Table 12.3)

$\tilde{z}$ = (*see* Table 12.3)

$\tilde{i}$ = (*see* Table 12.4)

$\tilde{j}$ = (*see* Table 12.4)

$\tilde{n}$ = (*see* Table 12.4)

$\tilde{l}$ = (*see* Table 12.4)

which gives the J.D. (in U.T.) of the kth new moon after (before if k is negative) the new moon of January 6, 2000 (Gregorian). To find a new moon preceding a given date, we can use

new-moon-before $(jd) \stackrel{\text{def}}{=}$ (12.33)

$$\textbf{new-moon-at-or-after}\\ (\textbf{new-moon-at-or-after}\ (jd)\ -45)$$

Alternatively, one can determine the time of new moon indirectly from the longitude of the moon. The moon's longitude is significantly more difficult to compute than that of the sun, because it is nonnegligibly affected by the pull of the sun, Venus, and Jupiter. The function for longitude of the moon is given by

$$\textbf{lunar-longitude}\ (u\textit{-time}) \stackrel{\text{def}}{=} \tag{12.34}$$

$$\textbf{degrees}\left(\textit{mean-moon} + \textit{longitude} + \textit{venus} + \textit{jupiter} + \textit{flat-earth} + \textbf{nutation}\ (c) \cdot \frac{180}{\pi}\right)$$

where

$$c = \textbf{julian-centuries}\ (u\textit{-time})$$

$$\textit{mean-moon} = \textbf{degrees}\left(218.3164591 + 481267.88134236 \cdot c - .0013268 \cdot c^2 + \frac{c^3}{538841} - \frac{c^4}{65194000}\right)$$

$$\textit{elongation} = \textbf{degrees}\left(297.8502042 + 445267.1115168 \cdot c - .00163 \cdot c^2 + \frac{c^3}{545868} - \frac{c^4}{113065000}\right)$$

$$\textit{solar-anomaly} = \textbf{degrees}\left(357.5291092 + 35999.0502909 \cdot c - .0001536 \cdot c^2 + \frac{c^3}{24490000}\right)$$

$$\textit{lunar-anomaly} = \textbf{degrees}\left(134.9634114 + 477198.8676313 \cdot c + 0.008997 \cdot c^2 + \frac{c^3}{69699} - \frac{c^4}{14712000}\right)$$

$$
\begin{aligned}
\textit{moon-from-node} &= \mathbf{degrees}\left(93.2720993 + 483202.0175273 \cdot c - .0034029 \cdot c^2 - \frac{c^3}{3526000} + \frac{c^4}{863310000}\right)\\
e &= 1 - 0.002516 \cdot c - 0.0000074 \cdot c^2\\
\textit{longitude} &= \frac{1}{1000000} \cdot \sum \left(\tilde{v} \cdot e^{|\tilde{x}|} \cdot \sin\left(\tilde{w} \cdot \textit{elongation} + \tilde{x} \cdot \textit{solar-anomaly} + \tilde{y} \cdot \textit{lunar-anomaly} + \tilde{z} \cdot \textit{moon-from-node} \right)\right)\\
\textit{venus} &= \frac{3958}{1000000} \cdot \sin(119.75 + c \cdot 131.849)\\
\textit{jupiter} &= \frac{318}{1000000} \cdot \sin(53.09 + c \cdot 479264.29)\\
\textit{flat-earth} &= \frac{1962}{1000000} \cdot \sin(\textit{mean-moon} - \textit{moon-from-node})\\
\tilde{v} &= (\textit{see } \text{Table 12.5})\\
\tilde{w} &= (\textit{see } \text{Table 12.5})\\
\tilde{x} &= (\textit{see } \text{Table 12.5})\\
\tilde{y} &= (\textit{see } \text{Table 12.5})\\
\tilde{z} &= (\textit{see } \text{Table 12.5})
\end{aligned}
$$

(The normalizing function **degrees** is used to bring the arguments to trigonometric functions into their typically most accurate range.)

Using **lunar-longitude**, one can determine the time of the new moon, or other phases of the moon, by searching for a time prior to *jd* when the solar and lunar longitudes differ by the desired amount, *phase*:

$$
\mathbf{lunar\text{-}phase\text{-}at\text{-}or\text{-}before}\,(\textit{phase}, \textit{jd}) \stackrel{\text{def}}{=} \tag{12.35}
$$

$$
\underset{x \in [\textit{low} : \textit{up}]}{\overset{p(l,u)}{\mathbf{MIN}}} \left\{ \textit{phase} \le \mathbf{lunar\text{-}solar\text{-}angle}\,(x) \le \textit{phase} + 90 \right\}
$$

Table 12.5 *Arguments for* **lunar-longitude** *(pages 155–156)*

$\tilde{v}$	$\tilde{w}$	$\tilde{x}$	$\tilde{y}$	$\tilde{z}$	$\tilde{v}$	$\tilde{w}$	$\tilde{x}$	$\tilde{y}$	$\tilde{z}$
6288774	0	0	1	0	1274027	2	0	−1	0
658314	2	0	0	0	213618	0	0	2	0
−185116	0	1	0	0	−114332	0	0	0	2
58793	2	0	−2	0	57066	2	−1	−1	0
53322	2	0	1	0	45758	2	−1	0	0
−40923	0	1	−1	0	−34720	1	0	0	0
−30383	0	1	1	0	15327	2	0	0	−2
−12528	0	0	1	2	10980	0	0	1	−2
10675	4	0	−1	0	10034	0	0	3	0
8548	4	0	−2	0	−7888	2	1	−1	0
−6766	2	1	0	0	−5163	1	0	−1	0
4987	1	1	0	0	4036	2	−1	1	0
3994	2	0	2	0	3861	4	0	0	0
3665	2	0	−3	0	−2689	0	1	−2	0
−2602	2	0	−1	2	2390	2	−1	−2	0
−2348	1	0	1	0	2236	2	−2	0	0
−2120	0	1	2	0	−2069	0	2	0	0
2048	2	−2	−1	0	−1773	2	0	1	−2
−1595	2	0	0	2	1215	4	−1	−1	0
−1110	0	0	2	2	−892	3	0	−1	0
−810	2	1	1	0	759	4	−1	−2	0
−713	0	2	−1	0	−700	2	2	−1	0
691	2	1	−2	0	596	2	−1	0	−2
549	4	0	1	0	537	0	0	4	0
520	4	−1	0	0	−487	1	0	−2	0
−399	2	1	0	−2	−381	0	0	2	−2
351	1	1	1	0	−340	3	0	−2	0
330	4	0	−3	0	327	2	−1	2	0
−323	0	2	1	0	299	1	1	−1	0
294	2	0	3	0	0	2	0	−1	−2

where

$$close = \textbf{degrees}\,(\textbf{lunar-solar-angle}\,(jd) - phase) < 40$$

$$yesterday = jd - 1$$

$$orig = 2451550.26 + \textbf{mean-synodic-month} \cdot \frac{phase}{360}$$

$$\epsilon = 0.000001$$

$$\tau = yesterday - ((yesterday - orig) \bmod \textbf{mean-synodic-month})$$

$$p(l, u) = u - l < \epsilon$$

$$low = \begin{cases} jd - 4 & \textbf{if } close \\ \tau - 2 & \textbf{otherwise} \end{cases}$$

$$up = \begin{cases} jd & \textbf{if } close \\ \tau + 2 & \textbf{otherwise} \end{cases}$$

and

$$\textbf{lunar-solar-angle}\,(jd) \stackrel{\text{def}}{=} \textbf{degrees}\left(\textbf{lunar-longitude}\,(jd) - \textbf{solar-longitude}\,(jd)\right) \tag{12.36}$$

The search normally begins around the last time the *mean* moon had that phase before the first new moon of the twenty-first century, which is January 6th, just after 6 p.m. That moment τ is calculated using equation (1.23). However, if the true phase in question occurs just before or after the given date, this calculation may give a time that is off by a month (whenever the mean phase is on the other side of *jd*). To avoid this problem, we check whether the phase at time *jd* is just past *phase*, in which case we search the period immediately preceding *jd*, rather than around τ.

For the computation of specific phases of the moon, new moon, first quarter, full moon, and last quarter, we can use **lunar-phase-at-or-before**, along with the following set of constants:

$$\textbf{new} \stackrel{\text{def}}{=} 0 \tag{12.37}$$

$$\textbf{full} \stackrel{\text{def}}{=} 180 \tag{12.38}$$

$$\textbf{first-quarter} \stackrel{\text{def}}{=} 90 \tag{12.39}$$

$$\textbf{last-quarter} \stackrel{\text{def}}{=} 270 \tag{12.40}$$

all expressed in degrees. We define

$$\textbf{new-moon-at-or-before}\,(jd) \stackrel{\text{def}}{=} \textbf{lunar-phase-at-or-before}\,(\textbf{new}, jd) \tag{12.41}$$

$$\textbf{full-moon-at-or-before}\,(jd) \stackrel{\text{def}}{=} \tag{12.42}$$

$$\textbf{lunar-phase-at-or-before}\ (\textbf{full}, jd)$$

$$\textbf{first-quarter-moon-at-or-before}\ (jd) \stackrel{\text{def}}{=} \textbf{lunar-phase-at-or-before}\ (\textbf{first-quarter}, jd) \tag{12.43}$$

$$\textbf{last-quarter-moon-at-or-before}\ (jd) \stackrel{\text{def}}{=} \textbf{lunar-phase-at-or-before}\ (\textbf{last-quarter}, jd) \tag{12.44}$$

For obscure reasons, when two full moons occur within one Gregorian calendar month, every 2–3 years, the second is termed a *blue moon*. This event is analogous to the conditions for a leap month on the Chinese calendar and Hindu lunisolar calendars, which mandate a leap month whenever two new moons occur within the same solar month.

References

[1] P. Bretagnon and G. Francou, "Planetary Theories in Rectangular and Spherical Coordinates—VSOP87 Solutions," *Astronomy and Astrophysics*, volume 202, pp. 309–315, 1988.

[2] P. Bretagnon and J.-L. Simon, *Planetary Programs and Tables from −4000 to +2800*, Willmann-Bell, Inc., Richmond, VA, 1986.

[3] J. Meeus, *Astronomical Algorithms*, Willmann-Bell, Inc., Richmond, VA, 1991.

[4] J. Meeus, "Les durées extrêmes de la lunaison," *L'Astronomie* (Société Astronomique de France), volume 102, pp. 288–289, July–August, 1988.

[5] P. K. Seidelmann, B. Guinot, and L. E. Doggett, "Time," Chapter 2 in *Explanatory Supplement to the Astronomical Almanac*, P. K. Seidelmann, ed., U.S. Naval Observatory, University Science Books, Mill Valley, CA, 1992.

[6] T. G. Shanks, *The American Atlas*, 5th ed., ACS Publications, San Diego, CA, 1995.

[7] T. G. Shanks, *The International Atlas*, ACS Publications, San Diego, CA, 1985.

[8] R. D. Skeel and J. B. Keiper, *Elementary Numerical Computing with Mathematica*, McGraw-Hill, New York, 1993.

[9] D. Sobel, *Longitude*, Walker, New York, 1995.

Print of the French Revolutionary calendar month of Vendémiaire by Laurent Guyot, after Jean-Jacques Lagrenée, the younger, Paris. (Courtesy of Bibliothèque Nationale de France, Paris.)

13

The French Revolutionary Calendar

Of the Republican calendar, the late John Quincy Adams said: "This system has passed away and is forgotten. This incongruous composition of profound learning and superficial frivolity, of irreligion and morality, of delicate imagination and coarse vulgarity, is dissolved." Unfortunately the effects of this calendar, though it was used for only about twelve years, have not passed away. It has entailed a permanent injury on history and on science.

—Joseph Lovering: *Proceedings of the American Academy of Arts and Sciences,* p. 350 (1872)[1]

The French Revolutionary calendar (*Le Calendrier Républicain*) was instituted by the National Convention of the French Republic in October 1793. Its epoch was R.D. 654,415, that is, Saturday, September 22, 1792 (Gregorian), the day of the autumnal equinox of that year, and also the first day following the establishment of the Republic. The calendar went into effect on Sunday, November 24, 1793 (Gregorian) and was used by the French until Tuesday, December 31, 1805 (Gregorian); on Wednesday, January 1, 1806 (Gregorian), the Revolutionary calendar was abandoned by Napoleonic edict and France reverted to the Gregorian calendar, but the Revolutionary calendar was used again during May 6–23, 1871.

Following the example of several ancient calendars, including the Coptic and Ethiopic (see Chapter 5), the French Revolutionary calendar divided the year into 12 months containing exactly 30 days each, followed by a period of five monthless days (six in leap years). The poetic names of the twelve months, coined by Fabre d'Églantine, were taken from the seasons in which

[1] Les auteurs ne souscrivent pas nécessairement aux opinions des auteurs des citations.

they occurred:[2]

(1) Vendémiaire (vintage)	(7) Germinal (seed)
(2) Brumaire (fog)	(8) Floréal (blossom)
(3) Frimaire (sleet)	(9) Prairial (pasture)
(4) Nivôse (snow)	(10) Messidor (harvest)
(5) Pluviôse (rain)	(11) Thermidor (heat)
(6) Ventôse (wind)	(12) Fructidor (fruit)

An English wit who was "disgusted with the 'namby pamby' style of the French calendar" dubbed them Slippy, Drippy, Nippy, Showery, Flowery, Bowery, Hoppy, Croppy, Poppy, Wheezy, Sneezy, Freezy [2, volume I, pp. 38–39].

As usual, we use

month	*day*	*year*

to represent the date, treating the monthless days as a thirteenth month, as in the Mayan haab calendar (Chapter 10).

Although not relevant to our calculations, each month was divided into three *décades* (decades) of ten days each; the tenth day was considered a day of rest. This made the new calendar unpopular, because under the Gregorian calendar the workers had had every seventh day off. The ten days were named by their ordinal position in the decade:

(1) Primidi	(6) Sextidi
(2) Duodi	(7) Septidi
(3) Tridi	(8) Octidi
(4) Quartidi	(9) Nonidi
(5) Quintidi	(10) Decadi

The five or six monthless days that were added at the end of each year were holidays called *sansculottides*, celebrating various attributes of the Revolution:

[2] Native American, old Vedic, and Gezer names of months have similar flavor. Also, in the mid-eighteenth century Linnæus published *The Calendar of Flora* consisting of the twelve months Reviving Winter (December 22–March 19), Thawing (March 19–April 12), Budding (April 12–May 9), Leafing (May 9–May 25), Flowering (May 25–June 20), Fruiting (June 20–July 12), Ripening (July 12–August 4), Reaping (August 4–August 28), Sowing (August 28–September 22), Shedding (September 22–October 28), Freezing (October 28–November 5), and Dead Winter (November 5–December 22). See *Miscellaneous Tracts Relating to Natural History, Husbandry, and Physick to which is added the Calendar of Flora*, by B. Stillingfleet, R. and J. Dodsley, London, 1762. Stillingfleet is today best-remembered as the original "bluestocking"; see the *Oxford English Dictionary*, 2nd ed., Oxford University Press, Oxford, 1989. We are indebted to Evan Melhado for pointing out the Linnæus and Stillingfleet references.

(1) Jour de la Vertu (virtue day)
(2) Jour du Génie (genius day)
(3) Jour du Labour (labor day)
(4) Jour de la Raison (reason day)
(5) Jour de la Récompense (reward day)
{(6) Jour de la Révolution (revolution day)}

The leap year structure is given in curly brackets.

13.1 The Original Form

Originally, the calendar was kept in synchronization with the solar year by setting the first day of Vendémiaire to occur at the autumnal equinox. That is, there was no leap year rule per se; a leap year occurred when successive autumnal equinoxes were 366 days apart, which happens roughly every four years. However, the pattern is not regular, and the precise calculation of the equinox is not easy, so the original rule was changed to the simple Gregorian-like rule that we discuss in the following section. In this section we give the original form of the calendar.

To implement the original form of the calendar we need to determine the moment of the autumnal equinox in Paris. Since the meridian of Paris is $2°20'15''$ east, it is 9 minutes, 21 seconds after U.T., so we define

$$\textbf{french-time-zone} \stackrel{\text{def}}{=} 9 + \frac{21}{60} \tag{13.1}$$

We need the autumnal equinox on or before a given R.D. d. This is a bit intricate, because without computing the equinox we cannot know whether dates near the equinox are just before or just after it. We solve this problem by computing the solar longitude at the end of R.D. d; call this $\theta(d+1)$. If that solar longitude is in the range $150° < \theta(d+1) < 180°$, d is about a year after the desired autumnal equinox, so we use **date-next-solar-longitude** to give us the equinox after $d' = d - 370$. If $\theta(d+1)$ is outside that range, we are less than a year after the desired autumnal equinox, and we can use formula (1.23) to compute a date a few days before the last autumnal equinox (which will occur a few days after 260 days into the solar year). Thus we write

french-autumnal-equinox-on-or-before (13.2)

$(\mathit{date}) \stackrel{\text{def}}{=}$

$$\textbf{fixed-from-jd}\left(\textbf{apparent-from-local}\left(\textbf{local-from-universal}\left(\textbf{date-next-solar-longitude}\left(\textbf{universal-from-local}\left(\textbf{jd-from-moment}\left(d'\right), \textbf{french-time-zone}\right), 90\right), \textbf{french-time-zone}\right)\right)\right)$$

where

$$\theta = \textbf{solar-longitude}\left(\textbf{universal-from-local}\left(\textbf{jd-from-moment}\left(\textit{date}+1\right), \textbf{french-time-zone}\right)\right)$$

$$d' = \begin{cases} \textit{date} - 370 & \textbf{if } 150 < \theta < 180 \\ \textit{date} - ((\textit{date} - 260) \bmod \textbf{mean-tropical-year}) & \textbf{otherwise} \end{cases}$$

We need to convert to apparent time (by adding the equation of time to the time of the equinox) so that the time of the equinox can be compared to clock-time midnight in Paris, because in the eighteenth century the French used *true* (apparent) local midnight (that is, when the sun would be at its nadir) for determining the start of the day (see page 139).

We define

$$\textbf{french-epoch} \stackrel{\text{def}}{=} \qquad (13.3)$$

$$\textbf{fixed-from-gregorian}\left(\boxed{\textbf{september} \mid 22 \mid 1792}\right)$$

Now we can convert from a French Revolutionary date to an R.D. date by

$$\textbf{fixed-from-french}\left(\boxed{\textit{month} \mid \textit{day} \mid \textit{year}}\right) \stackrel{\text{def}}{=} \qquad (13.4)$$

$$\textit{new-year} - 1 + 30 \cdot (\textit{month} - 1) + \textit{day}$$

where

$$\textit{new-year} = \textbf{french-autumnal-equinox-on-or-before}\left(\left\lceil \textbf{french-epoch} + \textbf{mean-tropical-year} \cdot (\textit{year} - 1) \right\rceil\right)$$

and in the other direction by

$$\textbf{french-from-fixed}\ (\textit{date}) \stackrel{\text{def}}{=} \boxed{\textit{month} \mid \textit{day} \mid \textit{year}} \tag{13.5}$$

where

$$\textit{new-year} = \textbf{french-autumnal-equinox-on-or-before}\ (\textit{date})$$

$$\textit{year} = \text{round}\left(\frac{\textit{new-year} - \textbf{french-epoch}}{\textbf{mean-tropical-year}}\right) + 1$$

$$\textit{month} = \left\lfloor \frac{\textit{date} - \textit{new-year}}{30} \right\rfloor + 1$$

$$\textit{day} = ((\textit{date} - \textit{new-year}) \bmod 30) + 1$$

13.2 The Modified Form

A simpler, arithmetical leap year rule for the French Revolutionary calendar was proposed by Gilbert Romme in 1795:

> Every 4th year is a leap year, except
> Every 100th year is not a leap year, except
> Every 400th year is a leap year, except
> Every 4000th year is not a leap year,

giving an average of $1460969/4000 = 365.24225$ days per year, an error of about 1 day in 20,000 years. Although the calendar was abandoned before this rule could be adopted, we show how to implement this strictly arithmetical form of the calendar.

We do not need to use it, but we define

$$\textbf{modified-french-leap-year?}\ (\textit{f-year}) \stackrel{\text{def}}{=} \tag{13.6}$$

$$(\textit{f-year} \bmod 4) = 0$$
$$\text{and } (\textit{f-year} \bmod 400) \notin \{100, 200, 300\}$$
$$\text{and } (\textit{f-year} \bmod 4000) \neq 0$$

Conversion of a French Revolutionary date to an R.D. date is thus done by summing all days before that date, including the number of days before the calendar began, 365 days for each prior year, all prior leap days (using the inclusion/exclusion method described for the Gregorian calendar—see page 36), and the number of prior days in the present year:

$$\textbf{fixed-from-modified-french}\left(\boxed{\textit{month} \mid \textit{day} \mid \textit{year}}\right) \stackrel{\text{def}}{=} \tag{13.7}$$

$$\textbf{french-epoch} - 1 + 365 \cdot (\textit{year} - 1) + \left\lfloor \frac{\textit{year} - 1}{4} \right\rfloor - \left\lfloor \frac{\textit{year} - 1}{100} \right\rfloor + \left\lfloor \frac{\textit{year} - 1}{400} \right\rfloor - \left\lfloor \frac{\textit{year} - 1}{4000} \right\rfloor + 30 \cdot (\textit{month} - 1) + \textit{day}$$

Calculating the French Revolutionary date from the R.D. *date* involves sequentially determining the year, month, and day of the month. The year is first approximated within one of its true value and then found precisely by checking the three possible years. The month is then found exactly by division, and the day of the month is determined by subtraction:

$$\textbf{modified-french-from-fixed}\,(\textit{date}) \stackrel{\text{def}}{=} \boxed{\textit{month} \mid \textit{day} \mid \textit{year}} \tag{13.8}$$

where

$$\textit{approx} = \left\lfloor \frac{\textit{date} - \textbf{french-epoch}}{\frac{1460969}{4000}} \right\rfloor$$

$$\textit{year} = \textit{approx} - 1 + \left(\sum_{y \geq \textit{approx}}^{p(y)} 1 \right)$$

$$\textit{month} = \left\lfloor \frac{\textit{date} - \textbf{fixed-from-modified-french}\left(\boxed{1 \mid 1 \mid \textit{year}}\right)}{30} \right\rfloor + 1$$

$$day = date - \textbf{fixed-from-modified-french}\left(\boxed{month \mid 1 \mid year}\right) + 1$$

$$p(y) = date \geq \textbf{fixed-from-modified-french}\left(\boxed{1 \mid 1 \mid y}\right)$$

References

[1] *Le Calendrier Républicain*, Bureau des Longitudes et Observatoire de Paris, Paris, 1994.

[2] J. Brady, *Clavis Calendaria; or, a Compendious Analysis of the Calendar: Illustrated with Ecclesiastical, Historical, and Classical Anecdotes*, 3rd ed., printed privately for the author, London, 1815.

[3] M. Hamer, "A Calendar for All Seasons," *New Scientist*, volume 124, no. 1696/1697, pp. 9–12, December 23/30, 1989.

Blue and white glazed jar from the reign of K'ang Hsi (1662–1722), showing plum blossoms against a background of melting ice and used to hold a gift of fragrant tea for New Year's Day. (Courtesy of the Victoria & Albert Museum, London.)

14

The Chinese Calendar

> The complexity of calendars is due simply to the incommensurability of the fundamental periods on which they are based.... Calendars based on [the synodic month], depending only on lunations, make the seasons unpredictable, while calendars based on [the tropical year] cannot predict the full moons, the importance of which in ages before the introduction of artificial illuminants was considerable. The whole history of calendar-making, therefore, is that of successive attempts to reconcile the irreconcilable, and the numberless systems of intercalated months, and the like, are thus of minor scientific interest. The treatment here will therefore be deliberately brief.
>
> —Joseph Needham: *Science and Civilisation in China,* volume 3, p. 390 (1959)

14.1 Structure

The Chinese calendar is a lunisolar calendar based on astronomical events, not arithmetical rules. Days begin at civil midnight. Months are lunar, beginning on the day of the new moon and ending on the day before the next new moon. Years contain twelve or thirteen such months, with the number of months determined by the number of new moons between successive winter solstices. The details of the Chinese calendar have varied greatly—there have been more than fifty calendar reforms—since its inception in the fourteenth century B.C.E.;[1] the version we implement here is the latest version,

[1] The three most significant of these reforms were the following: In 104 B.C.E., the rule that the lunar month without a major solar term is intercalary was established, and *mean* values were used for both solar and lunar months, much like the old Hindu calendar described in Chapter 11. In 619 C.E., the use of *true* new moons was introduced. In 1645 C.E., the use of *true* solar months was introduced.

established in 1645 C.E., the second year of the Qing dynasty.[2] We discuss some common misconceptions of the Chinese calendar at the end of this chapter.

Although the Chinese year consists of true lunar months, the arrangement of those months depends on the sun's course through the twelve zodiacal signs. Specifically, the Chinese divide the solar year into 24 solar terms: twelve major solar terms called *zhongqi* and twelve minor solar terms called *jieqi*. These terms correspond to 15° segments of solar longitude, with the major terms starting at $k \times 30°$ of solar longitude and the minor terms starting at $k \times 30° + 15°$ of solar longitude, $0 \leq k < 12$; the names of the twenty-four terms are shown in Table 14.1.

The dates of the terms in Table 14.1 are only approximate; the true motion of the sun varies, and thus to implement the Chinese calendar we need to calculate the precise date of a given solar longitude. We use the solar longitude function (Chapter 12) to determine the index of the last major solar term on or before a given date:

$$\textbf{current-major-solar-term}\ (\textit{date}) \stackrel{\text{def}}{=} \tag{14.1}$$

$$\left(2 + \left\lfloor \frac{s}{30} \right\rfloor\right) \text{ amod } 12$$

where

$$s = \textbf{solar-longitude}\left(\textbf{universal-from-local}\left(\textbf{jd-from-moment}\ (\textit{date}),\ \textbf{chinese-time-zone}\ (\textit{date})\right)\right)$$

[2] Specifically, we follow the principles of Baolin Liu, the former calendrist of the Purple Mountain Observatory, Nanjing, China, as given in [7]; for a summary of this manuscript, see [1]. Our Lisp functions accurately reproduce [6, 3rd printing], of which Liu is the primary author, for 1907 onward; they reproduce Hsu's table [5] for 1907 onward, except for 2033; Hsu used the first printing of [6], which was later corrected (there are two possible leap months, the one beginning on August 25 or the one beginning on December 22; Hsu takes the first of these as a leap month, forcing the solstice into the tenth month, thus violating Liu's basic principle given on page 174).

For years 1645–1906, our Lisp functions very occasionally err because of disagreements by a few minutes in the astronomical calculations (the Chinese used seventeenth-century models of the solar system until 1913, so their calculated times of solar and lunar events were not as accurate as ours); nevertheless, our calculated dates for Chinese New Year agree with Hsu's table for 1644–2050.

Table 14.1 *The solar terms of the Chinese year—major terms (zhongqi) are given in boldface, minor terms (jieqi) are given in lightface. Adapted from [1]*

Index	Chinese name	English name	Solar longitude	Approximate Gregorian date
1.	Lichun	Beginning of Spring	315°	February 4
1.	**Yushui**	**Rain Water**	**330°**	**February 19**
2.	Jingzhe	Waking of Insects	345°	March 6
2.	**Chunfen**	**Spring Equinox**	**0°**	**March 21**
3.	Qingming	Pure Brightness	15°	April 5
3.	**Guyu**	**Grain Rain**	**30°**	**April 30**
4.	Lixia	Beginning of Summer	45°	May 6
4.	**Xiaoman**	**Grain Full**	**60°**	**May 21**
5.	Mangzhong	Grain in Ear	75°	June 6
5.	**Xiazhi**	**Summer Solstice**	**90°**	**June 21**
6.	Xiaoshu	Slight Heat	105°	July 7
6.	**Dashu**	**Great Heat**	**120°**	**July 23**
7.	Liqiu	Beginning of Autumn	135°	August 8
7.	**Chushu**	**Limit of Heat**	**150°**	**August 23**
8.	Bailu	White Dew	165°	September 8
8.	**Qiufen**	**Autumnal Equinox**	**180°**	**September 23**
9.	Hanlu	Cold Dew	195°	October 8
9.	**Shuangjiang**	**Descent of Frost**	**210°**	**October 24**
10.	Lidong	Beginning of Winter	225°	November 8
10.	**Xiaoxue**	**Slight Snow**	**240°**	**November 22**
11.	Daxue	Great Snow	255°	December 7
11.	**Dongzhi**	**Winter Solstice**	**270°**	**December 22**
12.	Xiaohan	Slight Cold	285°	January 6
12.	**Dahan**	**Great Cold**	**300°**	**January 20**

We define

$$\textbf{chinese-time-zone}\,(date) \stackrel{\text{def}}{=} \begin{cases} 465 + \dfrac{40}{60} & \textbf{if } year < 1929 \\ 480 & \textbf{otherwise} \end{cases} \tag{14.2}$$

where

$$year \;=\; \textbf{gregorian-year-from-fixed}\,(date)$$

because before 1929 local mean time of Beijing was used—since Beijing is at longitude 116°25′ east, the time difference from U.T. was 7:45:40 hours $= 465\frac{40}{60}$ minutes. After 1928, however, China adopted the standard time zone, and calendar makers used the 120° meridian, or 8:00:00 hours = 480 minutes after U.T.[3]

Although not needed for date conversion, a printed Chinese calendar usually indicates the major and minor solar terms. The solar longitude functions in Chapter 12 also allow us to calculate the first date on or after a given R.D. date when the solar longitude will be a multiple of l degrees:

$$\textbf{chinese-date-next-solar-longitude}\,(d, l) \stackrel{\text{def}}{=} \tag{14.3}$$

$$\begin{aligned}&\textbf{fixed-from-jd}\\&\quad\big(\textbf{local-from-universal}\\&\qquad\big(\textbf{date-next-solar-longitude}\\&\qquad\quad\big(\textbf{universal-from-local}\\&\qquad\qquad\big(\textbf{jd-from-moment}\,(d),\\&\qquad\qquad\ \ \textbf{chinese-time-zone}\,(d)\big), l\big),\\&\qquad\ \textbf{chinese-time-zone}\,(d)\big)\big)\end{aligned}$$

from which we can determine the date of the major solar term on or after a given date:

$$\textbf{major-solar-term-on-or-after}\,(\mathit{date}) \stackrel{\text{def}}{=} \tag{14.4}$$

$$\textbf{chinese-date-next-solar-longitude}\,(\mathit{date}, 30)$$

We can also compute the index of the last minor solar term prior to a given date:

$$\textbf{current-minor-solar-term}\,(\mathit{date}) \stackrel{\text{def}}{=} \tag{14.5}$$

$$\left(3 + \left\lfloor \frac{s - 15}{30} \right\rfloor\right) \text{ amod } 12$$

where

$$\begin{aligned}s &= \textbf{solar-longitude}\\&\qquad\big(\textbf{universal-from-local}\\&\qquad\quad\big(\textbf{jd-from-moment}\,(\mathit{date}),\\&\qquad\quad\ \ \textbf{chinese-time-zone}\,(\mathit{date})\big)\big)\end{aligned}$$

and the date of the minor solar term on or after a given date:

$$\textbf{minor-solar-term-on-or-after}\,(\mathit{date}) \stackrel{\text{def}}{=} \tag{14.6}$$

[3] Actual practice for the year 1928 is uncertain.

$$\begin{cases} \textbf{chinese-date-next-solar-longitude}\,(d, 15) & \textbf{if } (\text{round}\,(s) \mod 30) = 0 \\ d & \textbf{otherwise} \end{cases}$$

where

$$d = \textbf{chinese-date-next-solar-longitude}\,(\mathit{date}, 15)$$

$$s = \textbf{solar-longitude}\,(\textbf{universal-from-local}\,(\textbf{jd-from-moment}\,(d),\ \textbf{chinese-time-zone}\,(d)))$$

Because Chinese months begin on the day of the new moon in Beijing, we must be able to calculate that, too. We use the functions **new-moon-at-or-after** and **new-moon-before** to tell us the julian day number of the first new moon on or after julian day *jd* in universal time, and the function **universal-from-local** and **local-from-universal** to convert between local and universal time (Chapter 12). With these functions we can write

$$\textbf{chinese-new-moon-on-or-after}\,(\mathit{date}) \stackrel{\text{def}}{=} \tag{14.7}$$

$$\textbf{fixed-from-jd}\,(\textbf{local-from-universal}\,(\textbf{new-moon-at-or-after}\,(\textbf{universal-from-local}\,(\textbf{jd-from-moment}\,(\mathit{date}),\ \textbf{chinese-time-zone}\,(\mathit{date}))),\ \textbf{chinese-time-zone}\,(\mathit{date})))$$

$$\textbf{chinese-new-moon-before}\,(\mathit{date}) \stackrel{\text{def}}{=} \tag{14.8}$$

fixed-from-jd
(**local-from-universal**
(**new-moon-before**
(**universal-from-local**
(**jd-from-moment** (*date*) ,
chinese-time-zone (*date*))) ,
chinese-time-zone (*date*)))

14.2 Numbering the Months

Once we can calculate the solar terms and new moons, we are ready to compute the arrangement of months in a Chinese year. The basic rule that determines the calendar is

The winter solstice (dongzhi) always occurs during the eleventh month of the year.

To enforce this rule for a given Chinese year, we must compute the dates of the winter solstices for the corresponding Gregorian year y and the preceding Gregorian year $y-1$. For example, in 1989 the winter solstice occurred at 9:23 p.m. U.T. on December 21, which is December 22 (R.D. 726,458) in Beijing. The next winter solstice is at 3:08 a.m. U.T. on December 22, 1990 (R.D. 726,823), which is the same date in Beijing. The list of the new moons with R.D. dates d such that $726{,}458 < d \leq 726{,}823$ is

(i)	R.D. 726,464	(December 28, 1989)
(ii)	R.D. 726,494	(January 27, 1990)
(iii)	R.D. 726,523	(February 25, 1990)
(iv)	R.D. 726,553	(March 27, 1990)
(v)	R.D. 726,582	(April 25, 1990)
(vi)	R.D. 726,611	(May 24, 1990)
(vii)	R.D. 726,641	(June 23, 1990)
(viii)	R.D. 726,670	(July 22, 1990)
(ix)	R.D. 726,699	(August 20, 1990)
(x)	R.D. 726,729	(September 19, 1990)
(xi)	R.D. 726,758	(October 18, 1990)
(xii)	R.D. 726,788	(November 17, 1990)
(xiii)	R.D. 726,818	(December 17, 1990)

These thirteen dates are the beginnings of months on the Chinese calendar during December 23, 1989 to December 22, 1990.

The average length of a lunar month is about 29.53 days, varying from approximately 29.27 to 29.84. Because there can be 365 or 366 days between successive solstices, there will be either 12 or 13 new moons: Fewer than twelve new moons is impossible, because the longest period containing at most eleven new moons is just short of twelve lunar months, or at most $12 \times 29.84 < 358$ days; more than thirteen new moons is also impossible, because the shortest period containing at least 14 new moons contains 13 full lunar months, or at least $13 \times 29.27 > 380$ days. The 12 or 13 months thus found form the months following the eleventh month of the preceding Chinese year to the eleventh month of the Chinese year in question.

Months on the Chinese calendar are numbered one to twelve; a leap month duplicates the number of the preceding month. The possible numberings of the twelve or thirteen months from the winter solstice of Gregorian year $y - 1$ to the following winter solstice are thus as shown in Figure 14.1. It is clear from this figure that if there are only twelve new moons, they must be numbered 12, 1, 2, ..., 11; but if there are thirteen new moons, which one is the leap month? The answer follows from the rule:

The leap month of a 13-month Chinese year is the first month that does not contain a major solar term—that is, the first lunar month that is wholly within a solar month.

There *must* be such a lunar month, because the period from one winter solstice to the next contains only twelve major solar terms, yet there are thirteen lunar months. (This is an application of the famous "Dirichlet box principle" or "pigeonhole principle"—see, for example, [8, section 4.8].)

We can test for a leap year by computing its first new moon, computing its last new moon, and rounding $(\textit{last-new-moon} - \textit{first-new-moon})/29.53$ to the nearest integer—if the value obtained is 12, the year is a leap year with thirteen months.

How do we know that month (i) in Figure 14.1 is permitted to be leap month 11? What if a prior month that Chinese year was a leap month? That is impossible, because the two-solar-year period between the winter solstice of Gregorian year $y-2$ and the winter solstice of Gregorian year y can contain either 24 or 25 lunar months; since the period from the winter solstice of Gregorian year $y - 1$ to the winter solstice of Gregorian year y has thirteen months, the period from the winter solstice of Gregorian year $y - 2$ to the winter solstice of Gregorian year $y - 1$ can have only twelve lunar months and hence no leap month. Thus, the first month without a major solar term will be the leap month, regardless of

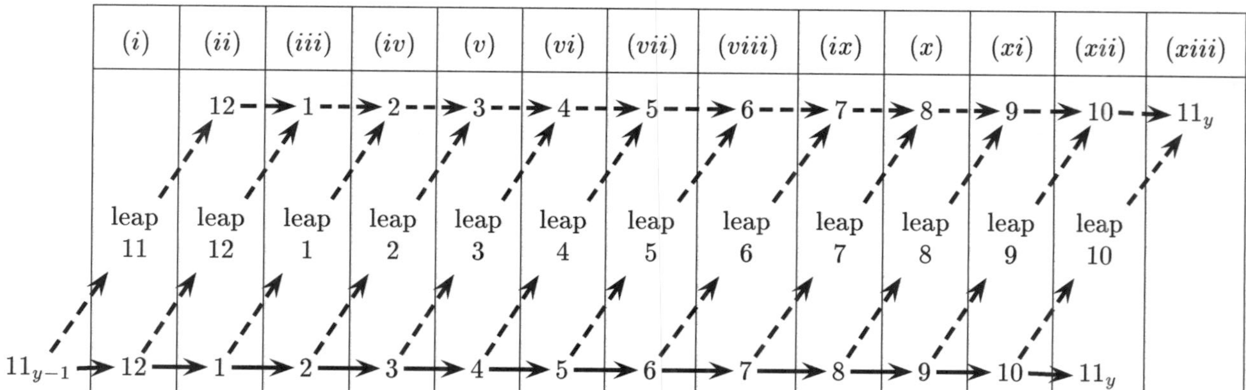

Figure 14.1 The theoretical possible numberings of the lunar months (i)–(xiii) for the Chinese calendar in the Gregorian year y. Each column corresponds to the new moon beginning a lunar month, and each column contains the number of that lunar month. The winter solstice of Gregorian year $y - 1$ occurs in the lunar month numbered 11_{y-1} [that is, in the month before the new moon (i)] and the winter solstice for Gregorian year y occurs in the lunar month numbered 11_y [that is, in the month of the new moon (xii) or (xiii)]. The solid arrows show the only possible numbering when there are twelve new moons between the two solstices. Dashed lines show possible numberings when there are thirteen new moons between two solstices. The relatively swift movement of the sun in the winter means that in current practice, because *true* solar terms are used, there can be no leap months 12 or 1, and leap month 11 is very rare. Before 1645, when *mean* solar terms were used, any month could be followed by a leap month.

the year. To determine whether a given month lacks a major solar term, we use

$$\textbf{no-major-solar-term?}\ (date) \stackrel{\text{def}}{=} \tag{14.9}$$

$$\textbf{current-major-solar-term}\ (date) \\ = \textbf{current-major-solar-term} \\ (\textbf{chinese-new-moon-on-or-after}\ (date + 1))$$

Because we want only the first month missing a major term to be a leap month, we also need

$$\textbf{prior-leap-month?}\ \left(m', m\right) \stackrel{\text{def}}{=} \tag{14.10}$$

$$m \geq m' \\ \text{and} \left\{ \begin{array}{l} \textbf{prior-leap-month?} \\ \quad \left(m', \textbf{chinese-new-moon-before} \right. \\ \qquad \left. (m) \right) \\ \text{or } \textbf{no-major-solar-term?}\ (m) \end{array} \right\}$$

which determines whether there is a Chinese leap month after lunar month m' and at or before lunar month m.

Figure 14.2 shows the structure of the Chinese calendar for 1984–85. Notice that the winter solstice is in the eleventh month (but just barely), as required, and the month following the tenth month is a leap month containing no major solar term.

Continuing our example of 1989–90, we have the following dates for the major solar terms:

12.	Dahan	R.D. 726,487	(January 20, 1990)
1.	Yushui	R.D. 726,517	(February 19, 1990)
2.	Chunfen	R.D. 726,547	(March 21, 1990)
3.	Guyu	R.D. 726,577	(April 20, 1990)
4.	Xiaoman	R.D. 726,608	(May 21, 1990)
5.	Xiazhi	R.D. 726,639	(June 21, 1990)
6.	Dashu	R.D. 726,671	(July 23, 1990)
7.	Chushu	R.D. 726,702	(August 23, 1990)
8.	Qiufen	R.D. 726,733	(September 23, 1990)
9.	Shuangjiang	R.D. 726,764	(October 24, 1990)
10.	Xiaoxue	R.D. 726,793	(November 22, 1990)
11.	Dongzhi	R.D. 726,823	(December 22, 1990)

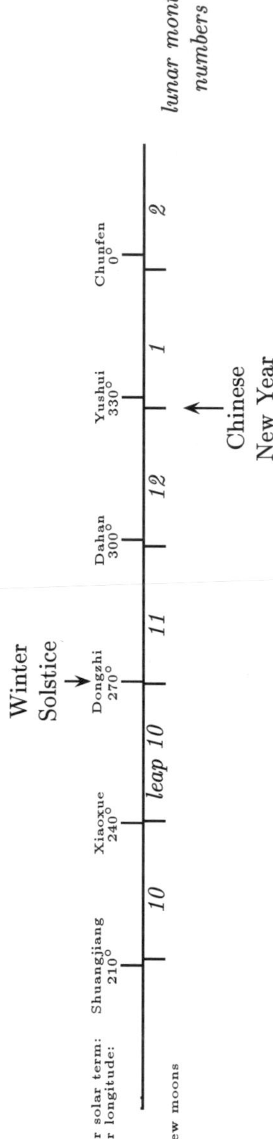

Figure 14.2 The Chinese calendar for 1984–85. Division into major solar terms is shown above the time line; new moons are shown below. Chinese month numbers are in italic.

Collating this list with the list of new moons, we find

	(i)	R.D. 726,464	(December 28, 1989)
12.	Dahan	R.D. 726,487	(January 20, 1990)
	(ii)	R.D. 726,494	(January 27, 1990)
1.	Yushui	R.D. 726,517	(February 19, 1990)
	(iii)	R.D. 726,523	(February 25, 1990)
2.	Chunfen	R.D. 726,547	(March 21, 1990)
	(iv)	R.D. 726,553	(March 27, 1990)
3.	Guyu	R.D. 726,577	(April 20, 1990)
	(v)	R.D. 726,582	(April 25, 1990)
4.	Xiaoman	R.D. 726,608	(May 21, 1990)
	(vi)	R.D. 726,611	(May 24, 1990)
5.	Xiazhi	R.D. 726,639	(June 21, 1990)
	(vii)	R.D. 726,641	(June 23, 1990)
	(viii)	R.D. 726,670	(July 22, 1990)
6.	Dashu	R.D. 726,671	(July 23, 1990)
	(ix)	R.D. 726,699	(August 20, 1990)
7.	Chushu	R.D. 726,702	(August 23, 1990)
	(x)	R.D. 726,729	(September 19, 1990)
8.	Qiufen	R.D. 726,733	(September 23, 1990)
	(xi)	R.D. 726,758	(October 18, 1990)
9.	Shuangjiang	R.D. 726,764	(October 24, 1990)
	(xii)	R.D. 726,788	(November 17, 1990)
10.	Xiaoxue	R.D. 726,793	(November 22, 1990)
	(xiii)	R.D. 726,818	(December 17, 1990)
11.	Dongzhi	R.D. 726,823	(December 22, 1990)

Hence, month (vii) from June 23 to July 21, 1990 is a leap month; that is, the numbering of the thirteen months (i)–(xiii) must be (see Figure 14.1)

Month 12	R.D. 726,464	(December 28, 1989)
Month 1	R.D. 726,494	(January 27, 1990)
Month 2	R.D. 726,523	(February 25, 1990)
Month 3	R.D. 726,553	(March 27, 1990)
Month 4	R.D. 726,582	(April 25, 1990)
Month 5	R.D. 726,611	(May 24, 1990)
Leap month 5	R.D. 726,641	(June 23, 1990)
Month 6	R.D. 726,670	(July 22, 1990)
Month 7	R.D. 726,699	(August 20, 1990)
Month 8	R.D. 726,729	(September 19, 1990)

Month 9	R.D. 726,758	(October 18, 1990)
Month 10	R.D. 726,788	(November 17, 1990)
Month 11	R.D. 726,818	(December 17, 1990)

14.3 Conversions to and from Fixed Dates

Ancient Chinese texts say that "the calendar and the pitch pipes have such a close fit, that you could not slip a hair between them."
—Giorgio de Santillana and Hertha von Dechend: *Hamlet's Mill*, p. 4 (1969)

By tradition, Chinese years go in cycles of sixty, each year having a special sexagenary name (discussed in the next section), with the first year of the first cycle commencing in year −2636 (Gregorian). So we define

$$\textbf{chinese-epoch} \stackrel{\text{def}}{=} \textbf{fixed-from-gregorian}\left(\boxed{\textbf{february} \mid 15 \mid -2636}\right) \tag{14.11}$$

Although it is not traditional to count these cycles, we do so for convenience to identify a year uniquely. The conversion between Chinese dates and R.D. dates can now be done by

$$\textbf{chinese-from-fixed}\,(date) \stackrel{\text{def}}{=} \boxed{cycle \mid year \mid month \mid leap\text{-}month \mid day} \tag{14.12}$$

where

$$g\text{-}year = \textbf{gregorian-year-from-fixed}\,(date)$$

$$s_1 = \textbf{major-solar-term-on-or-after}\left(\textbf{fixed-from-gregorian}\left(\boxed{\textbf{december} \mid 15 \mid g\text{-}year-1}\right)\right)$$

$$s_2 = \textbf{major-solar-term-on-or-after}\left(\textbf{fixed-from-gregorian}\left(\boxed{\textbf{december} \mid 15 \mid g\text{-}year}\right)\right)$$

$$m_1 = \begin{cases} \textbf{chinese-new-moon-on-or-after}\,(s_1 + 1) & \textbf{if } s_1 \le date < s_2 \\ \textbf{chinese-new-moon-on-or-after}\,(s_2 + 1) & \textbf{otherwise} \end{cases}$$

$$m_2 = \begin{cases} \textbf{chinese-new-moon-before}\,(s_2 + 1) & \textbf{if } s_1 \le date < s_2 \\ \textbf{chinese-new-moon-before}\left(\textbf{major-solar-term-on-or-after}\left(\textbf{fixed-from-gregorian}\left(\boxed{\textbf{december} \mid 15 \mid \textit{g-year}+1}\right)\right) + 1\right) & \textbf{otherwise} \end{cases}$$

$$m = \textbf{chinese-new-moon-before}\,(date + 1)$$

$$\textit{leap-year} = \text{round}\left(\frac{m_2 - m_1}{\textbf{mean-synodic-month}}\right) = 12$$

$$\textit{month} = \left(\text{round}\left(\frac{m - m_1}{\textbf{mean-synodic-month}}\right) - \begin{cases} 1 & \textbf{if } \textit{leap-year} \text{ and } \textbf{prior-leap-month?}\,(m_1, m) \\ 0 & \textbf{otherwise} \end{cases}\right) \text{ amod } 12$$

$$
\begin{aligned}
\textit{leap-month} &= \textit{leap-year} \text{ and } \textbf{no-major-solar-term?}\ (m) \\
&\quad \text{and not } \textbf{prior-leap-month?}\ \big(m_1,\ \textbf{chinese-new-moon-before}\ (m)\big) \\
\textit{elapsed-years} &= \textbf{gregorian-year-from-fixed}\ (\textit{date}) \\
&\quad - \textbf{gregorian-year-from-fixed}\ (\textbf{chinese-epoch}) \\
&\quad + \begin{cases} 1 & \textbf{if } \textit{month} < 11 \text{ or } \textit{date} > \textbf{fixed-from-gregorian}\ \left(\boxed{\textbf{july} \mid 1 \mid \textit{g-year}}\right) \\ 0 & \textbf{otherwise} \end{cases} \\
\textit{cycle} &= \left\lfloor \frac{\textit{elapsed-years} - 1}{60} \right\rfloor + 1 \\
\textit{year} &= \textit{elapsed-years} \text{ amod } 60 \\
\textit{day} &= \textit{date} - m + 1
\end{aligned}
$$

A similar, but more specific calculation determines Chinese New Year:

$$
\textbf{chinese-new-year}\ (\textit{g-year}) \stackrel{\text{def}}{=} \tag{14.13}
$$

$$
\begin{cases}
\textbf{chinese-new-moon-on-or-after}\ (m_2 + 1) & \textbf{if } \text{round}\left(\dfrac{m_{11} - m_1}{\textbf{mean-synodic-month}}\right) = 12 \\
& \text{and } \{\textbf{no-major-solar-term?}\ (m_1) \text{ or } \textbf{no-major-solar-term?}\ (m_2)\} \\
m_2 & \textbf{otherwise}
\end{cases}
$$

where

$$
s_1 = \textbf{major-solar-term-on-or-after}\ \left(\textbf{fixed-from-gregorian}\ \left(\boxed{\textbf{december} \mid 15 \mid \textit{g-year}-1}\right)\right)
$$

$$s_2 = \textbf{major-solar-term-on-or-after}\left(\textbf{fixed-from-gregorian}\left(\boxed{\textbf{december} \mid 15 \mid \textit{g-year}}\right)\right)$$

$$m_1 = \textbf{chinese-new-moon-on-or-after}\ (s_1 + 1)$$

$$m_2 = \textbf{chinese-new-moon-on-or-after}\ (m_1 + 1)$$

$$m_{11} = \textbf{chinese-new-moon-before}\ (s_2 + 1)$$

Finally, to convert a Chinese date to an R.D. date,

$$\textbf{fixed-from-chinese}\left(\boxed{\textit{cycle} \mid \textit{year} \mid \textit{month} \mid \textit{leap} \mid \textit{day}}\right) \stackrel{\text{def}}{=} \textit{prior-new-moon} + \textit{day} - 1 \tag{14.14}$$

where

$$\textit{g-year} = (\textit{cycle} - 1) \cdot 60 + \textit{year} - 1 + \textbf{gregorian-year-from-fixed}\ (\textbf{chinese-epoch})$$

$$\textit{new-year} = \textbf{chinese-new-year}\ (\textit{g-year})$$

$$p = \textbf{chinese-new-moon-on-or-after}\ (\textit{new-year} + (\textit{month} - 1) \cdot 29)$$

$$d = \textbf{chinese-from-fixed}\ (p)$$

$$\textit{prior-new-moon} = \begin{cases} p & \textbf{if } \textit{month} = d_{\textbf{month}} \text{ and } \textit{leap} = d_{\textbf{leap}} \\ \textbf{chinese-new-moon-on-or-after}\ (p + 1) & \textbf{otherwise} \end{cases}$$

The use of Gregorian dates and functions in our Chinese calendar functions is merely a computational simplification. We could have eliminated such use to get "pure" Chinese calendar algorithms, but at considerable cost in terms of the clarity of the functions.

14.4 The Sexagesimal Cycle of Names

The Chinese calendar uses a cycle of sixty names for years. The name is formed by combining a *celestial stem* with a *terrestrial branch*. The (untranslatable) celestial stems are

(1) Jia	(6) Ji
(2) Yi	(7) Geng
(3) Bing	(8) Xin
(4) Ding	(9) Ren
(5) Wu	(10) Gui

and the terrestrial branches are

(1) Zi	(Rat)	(7) Wu	(Horse)
(2) Chou	(Ox)	(8) Wei	(Sheep)
(3) Yin	(Tiger)	(9) Shen	(Monkey)
(4) Mao	(Hare)	(10) You	(Fowl)
(5) Chen	(Dragon)	(11) Xu	(Dog)
(6) Si	(Snake)	(12) Hai	(Pig)

Names are assigned sequentially, running through the two lists simultaneously: The first name is Jia-zi, the second is Yi-chou, the third is Bing-yin, and so on. Since the least common multiple of 10 and 12 is 60, the cycle of names repeats after the sixtieth name, Gui-hai. Representing the name as a pair of numbers giving the celestial stem and the terrestrial branch, respectively, and using equation (1.31), we can thus obtain the nth name of the sexagenary cycle of names by the function

$$\textbf{chinese-sexagesimal-name}\,(n) \stackrel{\text{def}}{=} \langle n \ \text{amod} \ 10, n \ \text{amod} \ 12\rangle \tag{14.15}$$

and the name of Chinese year y in any cycle is then

$$\textbf{chinese-name-of-year}\,(y) \stackrel{\text{def}}{=} \textbf{chinese-sexagesimal-name}\,(y) \tag{14.16}$$

This representation can be inverted, to give the year within a cycle corresponding to a given sexagesimal name, as described on page 20.

At one time the Chinese used the same sequence of sixty names to name days and months, as well. For days we have simply

$$\textbf{chinese-name-of-day}\,(\textit{date}) \stackrel{\text{def}}{=} \textbf{chinese-sexagesimal-name}\,(\textbf{fixed-from-chinese}\,(\textit{date}) + 15) \tag{14.17}$$

Leap months were unnamed, so we can write

$$\textbf{chinese-name-of-month}\,(y, m) \stackrel{\text{def}}{=} \textbf{chinese-sexagesimal-name}\,(12 \cdot y + m + 44) \tag{14.18}$$

14.5 Common Misconceptions

> Please note... Islamic and Chinese new year dates are approximate.
>
> —American Express Publishing Company: *1995 Pocket Diary*

Not much has been written in Western languages about the Chinese calendar, but much of what has been written is ill-informed, out of date, or oversimplified. For instance, the nineteen-year Metonic cycle is not used to determine leap years. Since 1645, true, not mean, behavior of the moon and sun is used in calculations, and as a consequence, months twelve and one cannot be followed by a leap month—in particular, Chinese New Year is not always the second new moon after the winter solstice, as is sometimes claimed. The calculations are done for the 120° east meridian (after 1928); calendars for other oriental countries may use other points of reference.

14.6 Holidays

We have already seen how to determine Chinese New Year in the course of our conversions of Chinese dates to R.D. dates. Because the Chinese calendar is consistently aligned with the Gregorian calendar, the determination of holidays is handled, as on the Hebrew calendar, by observing that fixed dates on the Chinese calendar occur in fixed seasons of the year. We observe that

$$\text{Chinese new year occurring in the winter of Gregorian year } y$$
$$= y + 1 - \textbf{gregorian-year-from-fixed}(\textbf{chinese-epoch}).$$

For example, the Chinese year that began in the winter of 1 (Gregorian) was 2637 (cycle 44, year 57). This means that holidays occurring in the spring, summer, and fall of the Gregorian year y occur in the Chinese year $y + 2637$, while holidays in the winter occur in either Chinese year $y + 2637$ or $y + 2636$, depending whether they are before or after January 1; such holidays need to be handled like Islamic holidays (Section 6.2).

Some of the holidays on the Chinese calendar are the Lantern Festival (fifteenth day of first month), the Dragon Festival (fifth day of the fifth month), the Mid-Autumn Festival (fifteenth day of the eighth month), and the Double-Ninth Festival (ninth day of the ninth month). For example, to find the R.D. date of the Dragon Festival in a Gregorian year, we would use

$$\textbf{dragon-festival}\,(g\text{-}year) \stackrel{\text{def}}{=} \tag{14.19}$$

$$\textbf{fixed-from-chinese}\left(\boxed{\,cycle\,}\boxed{\,year\,}\boxed{\,5\,}\boxed{\,\text{false}\,}\boxed{\,5\,}\right)$$

where

$$
\begin{aligned}
\textit{elapsed-years} &= \textit{g-year} - \textbf{gregorian-year-from-fixed}\\
&\qquad\qquad(\textbf{chinese-epoch})\\
&\quad + 1\\
\textit{cycle} &= \left\lfloor \frac{\textit{elapsed-years} - 1}{60} \right\rfloor + 1\\
\textit{year} &= \textit{elapsed-years} \ \text{amod}\ 60
\end{aligned}
$$

References

[1] L. E. Doggett, "Calendars," *Explanatory Supplement to the Astronomical Almanac*, P. K. Seidelmann, ed., University Science Books, Mill Valley, CA, pp. 575–608, 1992.

[2] H. Fritsche, *On Chronology and the Construction of the Calendar with Special Regard to the Chinese Computation of Time Compared with the European*, R. Laverentz, St. Petersburg, 1886.

[3] P. Hoang, *A Notice of the Chinese Calendar and a Concordance with the European Calendar*, 2nd ed., Catholic Mission Press, Shanghai, 1904.

[4] P. Hoang, *Concordance des Chronologies Néoméniques Chinoise et Europèene*, 12th edition, Kuangchi Press, Taiwan, 1968.

[5] H. C. Hsu, *Hsin pien Chung-kuo san chien nien li jih chien so piao (The Newly Compiled Chinese 3000-Year Calendar Indexing Table)*, Jen min chiao yu chu pan she, Hsin hua shu tien tsung tien ko chi fa hsing so fa hsing (People's Education Publication Society), Beijing, 1992.

[6] Purple Mountain Observatory, *Hsin pien wan nien li (The Newly Compiled Perpetual Chinese Calendar) (1840–2050)*, Ko hsuo pu chi chu pan she (Popular Science Press), Beijing, 1984. Third and subsequent printings correct the structure of the year 2033.

[7] B. L. Liu and F. R. Stephenson, "The Chinese Calendar and Its Operational Rules," manuscript, 1990.

[8] C. L. Liu, *Elements of Discrete Mathematics*, 2nd. ed., McGraw-Hill Book Co., Inc., New York, 1985.

[9] J. Needham, *Science and Civilisation in China, Vol. 3: Mathematics and the Sciences of the Heavens and the Earth*, Cambridge University Press, Cambridge, 1959.

[10] F. R. Stephenson and B. L. Liu, "A Brief Contemporary History of the Chinese Calendar," manuscript, 1990.

[11] W. C. Welch, *Chinese-American Calendar for the 102 Chinese Years Commencing January 24, 1849 and Ending February 5, 1951*, U.S. Department of Labor, Bureau of Immigration, United States Government Printing Office, Washington, 1928.

Twelfth-century black stone slab from Andhra Pradesh, India, depicting the twelve signs of the zodiac surrounding a full-blown lotus representing the sun. (Courtesy of the Prince of Wales Museum of Western India, Bombay.)

15

The Modern Hindu Calendars

Adhika months are the cream of the Indian Calendar, while *kshaya* are its *crème de la crème*. Figures of speech apart, it is certainly true that the success or failure of any computer in deducing *adhika* and *kshaya* months is the measure of the success or failure, as a whole, with the Indian Calendar. How far the present method satisfies this ordeal, will be for competent judges to decide.

—Dewan Bahadur L. D. Swamikannu Pillai: *Indian Chronology* (1911)

Today, numerous calendars are used in India for different purposes. The Gregorian calendar is used by the government for civil matters; the Islamic calendar is used by Moslems; the Hindus employ both solar and lunisolar calendars. Indeed, there are over thirty variations of the Hindu calendar in active use. In 1957, an attempt was made to revise the traditional calendar to follow the pattern of the Gregorian leap year structure [1]. The proposed reform has not, however, been accepted.

The best known of several related systems used on the Indian subcontinent is the classical Hindu calendar of the (Present) *Sūrya-Siddhānta* (circa 1000), said to have been revealed to Maya the Assyrian in the year 2,163,102 B.C.E. This work introduced a calendar based on approximations to the true times of astronomical events, rather than the mean values used in the earlier, simpler calendar described in Chapter 11. This calendar is somewhat similar to the Chinese, beginning its months according to the actual time of new moon; however, the Chinese calendar today uses modern astronomical methods to determine these times, whereas the Hindu calendar applies fixed, ancient methods to approximate the true positions of the sun and moon.

In the mean Hindu calendar (Chapter 11), the calculations are simple. The necessary computational mechanisms for the true system are, by contrast, very complex; van Wijk [10, p.13] has compared the old and new Hindu calendar systems in the following words:

> From a chronological point of view the substitution for the mean calendric system of one based on the true movements of the sun and moon, was anything but an improvement, as it destabilized the foundations of the time reckoning. Indeed, the system may have had the charm of adapting daily life as nearly as the astronomical knowledge permitted to the movement of the heavenly bodies, but on the other hand it broke ties with history, as there was no unity of elements or systems. The very complexity of the system is proof of its primitiveness.

For the Hindu calendar, as for other calendars, experts have attempted over the centuries to reduce hand calculations to table lookup and the very simplest arithmetical operations, avoiding nuisances like large numbers or even signed numbers, but requiring logarithms and a multiplicity of tables covering various periods of time. However, shortcuts for humans are unnecessary complications for computers, and we avoid all of them. Unlike table-based methods, the use of rational numbers gives perfect fidelity to the sources. We believe that an algorithmic description is the simplest and most concise way of describing the rules; it has allowed us to condense many pages of words and tables into a few hundred lines of computer code.

The modern Hindu calendar depends on the computed positions of the sun and moon, taking into account that solar and lunar motions vary in speed across the celestial sphere. We refer to these positions as "true," though they are not true in the astronomical sense but rather approximate the irregular motions of the sun and moon. The length of a Hindu solar month varies from 29.318 days to 31.644; that of a Hindu lunar month varies from 29.305 to 29.812 days. The sidereal month is the mean time it takes for the moon to return to the same (longitudinal) point vis-à-vis the stars, and is given as $27.3216692\cdots$ days. The synodic month takes the motion of the sun into account; it is the mean time between new moons (lunar conjunctions) and is taken to be $29.5305836989\cdots$ days. (See Section 12.7.) The mean values for these times are given in the *Sūrya-Siddhānta* as rational numbers:

$$\textbf{hindu-sidereal-year} \stackrel{\text{def}}{=} 365 + \frac{279457}{1080000} \tag{15.1}$$

$$\textbf{hindu-sidereal-month} \stackrel{\text{def}}{=} 27 + \frac{4644439}{14438334} \tag{15.2}$$

$$\textbf{hindu-synodic-month} \stackrel{\text{def}}{=} 29 + \frac{7087771}{13358334} \tag{15.3}$$

The modern and old Hindu solar calendars have the same basic structure. Each solar month begins when the sun enters a new sign of the zodiac. Hindu astronomy uses the sidereal year and measures solar longitude from the constellation Aries, not from the equinoctial point (which is today in Pisces; see Section 12.1). If the sign is entered before sunrise, then the day is day one of a new month; otherwise, it is the last day of the previous month. However, because the solar months vary in length, we cannot know when successive months begin without calculating the position of the sun. The result is that a solar month can have 29, 30, 31, or 32 days. The solar day begins at sunrise. Since it is the zodiacal position of the sun at sunrise that determines the month name, we will have to compute sunrise as well.

As with the old Hindu calendar (Chapter 11), lunar month names are determined by the (first) zodiacal sign entered by the sun during the month. When no sign is entered, the month is considered leap; leap months take the same name as the *following* month. This method of reckoning also leads occasionally to lost months. When, very rarely, a solar month elapses with no new moon, a lunar month is skipped (called *kshaya*). There is a 19- to 141-year gap between occurrences of skipped months; they occur in the winter, near perihelion, when the apparent motion of the sun is fastest. As in the Chinese calendar with its similar leap month scheme (see page 175), a lunisolar year must have either twelve or thirteen months. Thus, a year with a skipped month perforce contains either one leap month (as in 1963[1]) or—extremely rarely—two leap months (as in 4576 K.Y. = 1475–1476 C.E. and in 5083 K.Y. = 1982–1983 C.E.[2]).

The month names (page 124) are derived from asterisms (star groups) along the ecliptic. They are a subset of the original names for the (unequal) division of the ecliptic into twenty-seven or twenty-eight lunar stations "mansions," one for each day of the sidereal month. The lunar month name is that of the asterism in which the full moon occurs. The exact star groups were already uncertain in the time of al-Bīrūnī; one suggestion is given in Table 15.3.

Day numbers are determined by the lunar day, or *tithi*, current at sunrise (see Chapter 11). The varying motion of the moon—a lunar day ranges in length

[1] In 1897, Sewell and Dîkshit [7] wrote: "We are led by these peculiarities to suppose that there will be no suppressed month till at earliest A.D. 1944, and possibly not till A.D. 1963." Pillai's [4] reaction was: "There is no reason why this matter should be treated as one for conjecture, since anybody familiar with the present method can calculate that the next *Kshaya* month will be in A.D. 1963."

[2] From 1300 until 1980, only Kārtikka, Mārgaśīra, and Pausha have been skipped, but according to our calculations Māgha should have been omitted in 5083 K.Y. This is a close call, since the sun entered Māgha on February 13, 1983 at 4:10:18 a.m., and the new moon occurred half an hour later at 4:43:56. The prior new moon was on January 14th at 9:03:53 a.m., which was before the sun entered Makara at 5:26:14 p.m. Āśvina and Phālguna were leap.

Table 15.1 *Suggested correspondence of lunar stations and asterisms*
Boldface indicates stations after which lunar months are named. The Greek letters indicate the relative brightness of the star in its constellation. (Popular names are given in parentheses.) Thus, α Tauri is the brightest star in Taurus, called Aldebaran ("the follower" in Arabic), a red star of first magnitude in the eye of the bull and part of the Hyades. The 28th station, omitted from some lists, is unnumbered.

	Lunar station		Prominent star	Associated deity
1.	**Aśvinī**	α	Arietis (Hamal)	Aśvinau
2.	Bharaṇī	35	Arietis	Yama
3.	**Kṛittikâ**	η	Tauri (Alcyone)	Agni
4.	Rohiṇī	α	Tauri (Aldebaran)	Prajāpati
5.	**Mṛigaśiras**	λ	Orionis (Meissa)	Soma
6.	Ārdrā	α	Orionis (Betelgeuse)	Rudra
7.	Punarvasu	β	Geminorum (Pollux)	Aditi
8.	**Pushya**	δ	Cancri (Asellus Australis)	Bṛhaspati
9.	Āśleshā	α	Cancri (Acubens)	Sarpāḥ
10.	**Maghā**	α	Leonis (Regulus)	Pitaraḥ
11.	Pūrva Phalgunī	δ	Leonis (Zosma)	Aryaman
12.	**Uttara Phalgunī**	β	Leonis (Denebola)	Bhaga
13.	Hasta	γ	Corvi (Gienah)	Savitṛ
14.	**Chitrā**	α	Virginis (Spica)	Indra
15.	Svāti	α	Bootis (Arcturus)	Vāyu
16.	**Viśākhā**	α	Libræ (Zubenelgenubi)	Indrāgni
17.	Anurādhā	δ	Scorpii (Dschubba)	Mitra
18.	**Jyeshṭhā**	α	Scorpii (Antares)	Indra
19.	Mūla	γ	Scorpii	Pitaraḥ
20.	Pūrva Āshāḍhā	δ	Sagittarii (Kaus Media)	Āpaḥ
21.	**Uttara Āshāḍhā**	σ	Sagittarii (Nunki)	Viśve devāḥ
	Abhijit	α	Lyræ (Vega)	Brahmā
22.	**Śravaṇā**	α	Aquilæ (Altair)	Viṣṇu
23.	Dhanishthā	α	Delphini (Sualocin)	Vasavaḥ
24.	Śatatārakā	λ	Aquarii	Indra
25.	Pūrva Bhādrapadā	α	Pegasi (Markab)	Aja Ekapād
26.	**Uttara Bhādrapadā**	α	Andromedæ (Alpheratz)	Ahirbudhnya
27.	Revatī	ζ	Piscium	

from 21.5 to 26.2 hours—can cause two sunrises to fall within one lunar day, or (every two months, or so) for a lunar day to begin and end between one sunrise and the next. This situation leads to a unique aspect of the Hindu scheme: Consecutive days can bear the *same* ordinal number (an "intercalated" day), and any number can be skipped (an "extracalated" day). In the case of days, the second of two days with the same number is considered extra (*adhika*). A day may therefore be named "Second 7 in the dark half of the first Mārgaśīra."

Suppose we can determine the longitudes of the sun and moon, relative to the celestial sphere, at any given time. To determine the Hindu lunar date of any given day, we perform the following sequence of operations:

1. Determine the phase of the moon at sunrise of the given day, by taking the difference of longitudes between the positions of the sun and moon. Dividing the difference in degrees by 12 gives an integer in the range 0 . . . 29, corresponding to (one less than) the ordinal number of the lunar day current at sunrise.
2. Compare the current day number with that of the previous. If they are the same, then it is a leap day (and "*adhika*" is appended to the number).
3. Determine when the last new moon on or before sunrise of the current day occurred.
4. Determine the position of the sun at that new moon. The zodiacal sign in which it occurs establishes the name (that of the next sign) of the current month.
5. Compare the current month name with that of the next new moon. If they are the same, then it is a leap month (and "*adhika*" is appended to the month's name).

In contrast, the calculations of the old (mean) Hindu lunisolar calendar can result in added months and lost days, but not lost months nor added days. Since the mean lunar month is shorter than the mean solar month, there is never a situation on the mean calendar in which an expunged lunar month is called for. Similarly, because a civil day is longer than a thirtieth of a mean synodic month, leap days were never needed.

15.1 Hindu Astronomy

> It seems to [some people] there is nothing against their supposing, for instance, the heavens immobile and the earth as turning on the same axis from west to east very nearly one revolution a day. . . . But it has escaped their notice . . . that in light of what happens to us in the air such a notion would seem altogether absurd.
>
> —Ptolemy: *Almagest* (I, 7)

From the time of Ptolemy's *Almagest* until the Keplerian Revolution, it was well known that the motions of the seven heavenly bodies visible to the naked eye (the sun, the moon, Mercury, Venus, Mars, Jupiter, and Saturn) can best be described by combinations of circular motions, that is, cycles and epicycles. Elliptical motion is indeed exactly characterized by one retrograde epicycle; the distinction between elliptical motion and epicyclical motion is conceptual. The Hindu calendar approximations are based on such epicycles.

To find the true position of the sun and moon we need to adjust its mean longitude by the contribution of the epicycle. The heavenly body is assumed to remain on the *deferent* (the main circle), but to be "pulled" in one direction or the other by "winds" and "cords of air" originating on the epicycle. Assuming the center of the epicycle is at longitude β and the *anomaly* (angle of the heavenly body around the epicycle, measured from the furthest point from Earth along the epicycle) is α, the angular position is approximately

$$\beta + \arcsin(r \sin\alpha),$$

where r is the ratio of radii of epicycle and deferent. Figure 15.1 illustrates this arrangement.

The *Sūrya-Siddhānta* and earlier Hindu astronomical tracts give a table of sines for angles of 0° to 90°, in increments of 225 minutes of arc, and interpolation is used for intermediate values. The sines, shown in Table 15.2, are given as integers in the range 0 ... 3438 (that is, in terms of a radius of 3438 units) and is a close approximation to the true sine.[3] We implement the table by means of the following ad-hoc function:

$$\textbf{hindu-sine-table}\,(\mathit{entry}) \stackrel{\text{def}}{=} \text{round}\,(\mathit{exact} + \mathit{error}) \tag{15.4}$$

where

$$\begin{aligned} \mathit{exact} &= 3438 \cdot \sin\left(\mathit{entry} \cdot \frac{225}{60}\right) \\ \mathit{error} &= 0.215 \cdot \text{signum}\,(\mathit{exact}) \cdot \text{signum}\,(|\mathit{exact}| - 1716) \end{aligned}$$

Linear interpolation is used for in-between values:

$$\textbf{hindu-sine}\,(\theta) \stackrel{\text{def}}{=} \tag{15.5}$$

$$\mathit{fraction} \cdot \textbf{hindu-sine-table}\,(\lceil \mathit{entry} \rceil) + (1 - \mathit{fraction}) \cdot \textbf{hindu-sine-table}\,(\lfloor \mathit{entry} \rfloor)$$

where

$$\begin{aligned} \mathit{entry} &= \frac{\theta}{225} \\ \mathit{fraction} &= \mathit{entry} \bmod 1 \end{aligned}$$

[3] A radius of 3438 and 5600 minutes in a quadrant imply a value of $\frac{5600\times4}{3438\times2} \approx 3.141361$ for π. A recurrence is given in the *Sūrya-Siddhānta* for producing this table of sines, namely

$$\sin(n+1)\alpha = n\alpha - \frac{1}{225}\sum_{i<n}(n-i)\sin(n\alpha)$$

where $\alpha = 225'$. The table given in *Sūrya-Siddhānta*, however, is more accurate than this formula and, as seen in Table 15.2, is correct, except for erratic rounding. The recurrence would be precise with $(225/3438)^2 \approx 1/223.5$ instead of 1/225. See Burgess's comments in [8, p. 335].

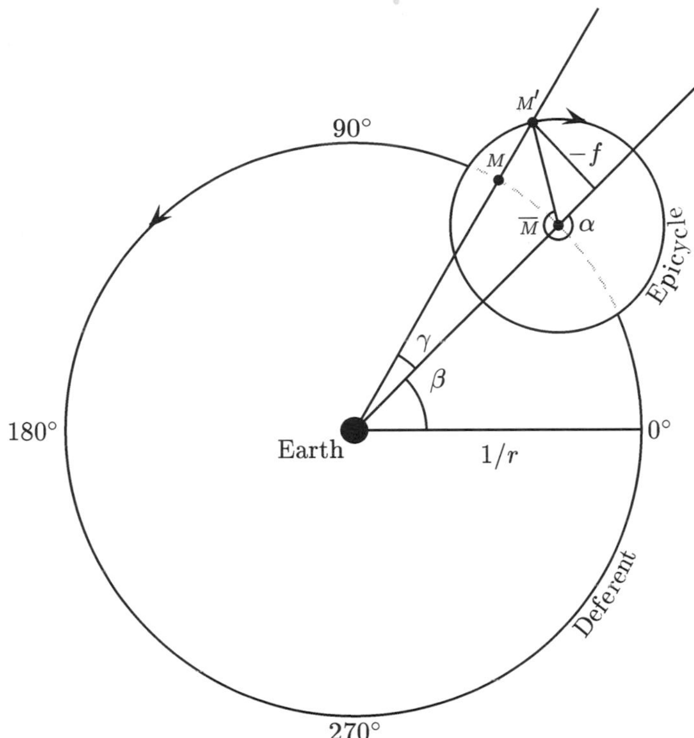

Figure 15.1 The mean position of the moon, $\overline{M}$, revolves in a circle, called the *deferent*, of radius $1/r$ at a steady rate (once every mean sidereal month). At the same time, a "being" M' rotates around a epicycle of unit radius centered at $\overline{M}$, in the opposite direction of the motion of $\overline{M}$, so that it returns to the apogee (the point at which it is farthest from Earth, where the epicycle intersects a line from Earth through $\overline{M}$) in a period called the *anomalistic month*. Let β be the longitude of $\overline{M}$, α be the angle of M' from the apogee, called the *anomaly*, and f be $\sin\alpha$, which we call the *offset*. The true longitude of the moon, M, on the deferent along a radius from Earth to M', is $\beta+\gamma$, where $\sin\gamma \approx -fr = -(\sin\alpha)r$. Thus we have for the *equation of center* $\gamma = 360^\circ - \arcsin(r\sin\alpha) = \arcsin(r\sin\alpha)$. In addition, the ratio r changes as $\overline{M}$ revolves around Earth (see the text). The figure is not drawn to scale.

To invert **hindu-sine** we use,

$$\textbf{hindu-arcsin}\,(\mathit{units}) \stackrel{\text{def}}{=} \tag{15.6}$$

$$\begin{cases} -\,\textbf{hindu-arcsin}\,(-\,\mathit{units}) & \textbf{if } \mathit{units} < 0 \\ 225\cdot\left(\mathit{pos} - 1 + \dfrac{\mathit{units} - \mathit{val}}{\textbf{hindu-sine-table}\,(\mathit{pos}) - \mathit{val}}\right) & \\ & \textbf{otherwise} \end{cases}$$

Table 15.2 *Hindu sine table (with radius 3438)*

Table entry	Angle (minutes)	Hindu sine	Precise value	Table entry	Angle (minutes)	Hindu sine	Precise value
0	0	0	0.00	13	2925	2585	2584.83
1	225	225	224.86	14	3150	2728	2727.55
2	450	449	448.75	15	3375	2859	2858.59
3	675	671	670.72	16	3600	2978	2977.40
4	900	890	889.82	17	3825	3084	3083.45
5	1125	1105	1105.11	18	4050	3177	3176.30
6	1350	1315	1315.67	19	4275	3256	3255.55
7	1575	1520	1520.59	20	4500	3321	3320.85
8	1800	1719	1719.00	21	4725	3372	3371.94
9	2025	1910	1910.05	22	4950	3409	3408.59
10	2250	2093	2092.92	23	5175	3431	3430.64
11	2475	2267	2266.83	24	5400	3438	3438.00
12	2700	2431	2431.03				

where

$$pos = \sum_{k \geq 0}^{p(k)} 1$$

$$val = \textbf{hindu-sine-table}\,(pos - 1)$$

$$p\,(k) = units > \textbf{hindu-sine-table}\,(k)$$

Again, interpolation is used for intermediate values not appearing in the table.

To determine the position of the mean sun or moon, we have the generic function

$$\textbf{mean-position}\,(ky\text{-}time, period) \stackrel{\text{def}}{=} \tag{15.7}$$

$$21600 \cdot \left(\frac{ky\text{-}time}{period} \bmod 1\right)$$

which calculates the longitude in arcminutes (of which there are 21,600 in a circle) at a given moment *ky-time* since the Hindu epoch, when the period of rotation is *period* days. The visible planets were, according to the *Sūrya-Siddhānta*, in true conjunction at the end of creation, 1,955,880,000 years (sidereal, not tropical—the difference is slight; see Section 12.5) prior to the onset of the Kali Yuga:

$$\textbf{hindu-creation} \stackrel{\text{def}}{=} \tag{15.8}$$

$$1955880000 \cdot \textbf{hindu-sidereal-year}$$

Thus, the anomaly is taken to be zero at the end of creation. The size of the sun's epicycle is $\frac{14}{360}$ of its deferent; for the moon the ratio is larger: $\frac{32}{360}$. The period of revolution of the (cords of air around the) epicycles are:

$$\textbf{hindu-anomalistic-year} \stackrel{\text{def}}{=} \frac{1577917828000}{4320000000 - 387} \tag{15.9}$$

$$\textbf{hindu-anomalistic-month} \stackrel{\text{def}}{=} \frac{1577917828}{57753336 - 488199} \tag{15.10}$$

for the sun and moon, respectively. These values are derived from the stated speed of rotation of the apses, $\frac{387}{1000}$ times in 4,320,000 years (= 15,779,178,828 days) for the sun and 488,199 times in the same period for the moon.[4] The anomalistic month is the corrected (*bija*) value introduced in the mid-sixteenth century by Gaṇesa Daivajna and still in use today, not that originally given in the *Sūrya-Siddhānta*.

To complicate matters, in the scheme of *Sūrya-Siddhānta*, the epicycle actually shrinks as it revolves (almost as if there were an epicycle on the epicycle). For both the sun and moon, the change amounts to $\frac{1}{42}$ of the maximum size and reaches its minimum value when entering the even quadrants. Changes in the size of the epicycle are reflected in the following function:

$$\begin{aligned}&\textbf{true-position} \\ &\quad (\textit{ky-time}, \textit{period}, \textit{size}, \textit{anomalistic}, \textit{change}) \stackrel{\text{def}}{=} \\ &\quad (\textit{long} - \textit{equation}) \bmod 21600\end{aligned} \tag{15.11}$$

where

$$\begin{aligned}
\textit{long} &= \textbf{mean-position}\,(\textit{ky-time}, \textit{period}) \\
\textit{days} &= \textit{ky-time} + \textbf{hindu-creation} \\
\textit{offset} &= \textbf{hindu-sine} \\
&\qquad (\textbf{mean-position}\,(\textit{days}, \textit{anomalistic})) \\
\textit{contraction} &= |\textit{offset}| \cdot \textit{change} \cdot \frac{\textit{size}}{3438} \\
\textit{equation} &= \textbf{hindu-arcsin}\,(\textit{offset} \cdot (\textit{size} - \textit{contraction}))
\end{aligned}$$

[4] Whereas we compute the anomaly from creation, traditionally one precomputes the position of perihelion at some base date, and the time between true and mean new year for that base, called *sodhya*, since the solar anomaly changes very slowly. "The difference in the sun's equation of the centre and true longitude, caused by the shift of the apsin, is exceedingly small and may well be ignored" [6, p. 55].

which adjusts the mean longitudinal position (center of the epicycle) by the equation of motion (the longitudinal displacement caused by epicyclic motion), and normalizes the resultant angle θ to the range $0 \leq \theta < 21{,}600$ minutes of arc by using the modulus function. Hindu longitudes are sidereal (relative to the fixed stars, not to the precessing equinoctial point) and have as their origin a point near ζ Piscium (Revatī, the sixth brightest star—actually a binary star—in constellation Pisces, near the ecliptic), but this has no impact on the calculations.

Plugging in the relevant constants, we have

$$\textbf{hindu-solar-longitude}\,(\textit{ky-time}) \stackrel{\text{def}}{=} \tag{15.12}$$
$$\textbf{true-position}\left(\textit{ky-time}, \textbf{hindu-sidereal-year}, \frac{14}{360}, \textbf{hindu-anomalistic-year}, \frac{1}{42}\right)$$

from which the zodiacal position follows:

$$\textbf{hindu-zodiac}\,(\textit{ky-time}) \stackrel{\text{def}}{=} \tag{15.13}$$
$$\left\lfloor \frac{\textbf{hindu-solar-longitude}\,(\textit{ky-time})}{1800} \right\rfloor + 1$$

The position of the moon is calculated in a similar fashion:

$$\textbf{hindu-lunar-longitude}\,(\textit{ky-time}) \stackrel{\text{def}}{=} \tag{15.14}$$
$$\textbf{true-position}\left(\textit{ky-time}, \textbf{hindu-sidereal-month}, \frac{32}{360}, \textbf{hindu-anomalistic-month}, \frac{1}{42}\right)$$

Now we have all the information needed to determine the phase of the moon at any given time. It is simply the difference in longitudes:

$$\textbf{hindu-lunar-phase}\,(\textit{ky-time}) \stackrel{\text{def}}{=} \tag{15.15}$$
$$(\textbf{hindu-lunar-longitude}\,(\textit{ky-time}) - \textbf{hindu-solar-longitude}\,(\textit{ky-time})) \bmod 21600$$

This translates into the number of the lunar day by dividing the difference by one-thirtieth of a full circle (that is, 720 arcminutes):

$$\textbf{lunar-day}\,(\textit{ky-time}) \stackrel{\text{def}}{=} \qquad (15.16)$$

$$\left\lfloor \frac{\textbf{hindu-lunar-phase}\,(\textit{ky-time})}{720} \right\rfloor + 1$$

To find the time of the new moon, we need to search for the time when the difference in longitudes of the sun and moon is nil. The exact time can be found by bisection (see page 148):

$$\textbf{hindu-new-moon}\,(\textit{ky-time}) \stackrel{\text{def}}{=} \qquad (15.17)$$

$$\begin{cases} \textbf{hindu-new-moon}\,(\lfloor \textit{ky-time} \rfloor - 20) & \textbf{if } \textit{try} > \textit{ky-time} \\ \textit{try} & \textbf{otherwise} \end{cases}$$

where

$$\begin{aligned}
\textit{tomorrow} &= \textit{ky-time} + 1 \\
\textit{estimate} &= \textit{tomorrow} - (\textit{tomorrow} \bmod \textbf{hindu-synodic-month}) \\
\textit{try} &= \underset{x \in [\textit{low}:\textit{up}]}{\overset{p(l,u)}{\textbf{MIN}}} \left\{ \textbf{hindu-lunar-phase}\,(x) < 10800 \right\} \\
p\,(l, u) &= \textit{ky-time} < l \\
&\quad \text{or } \{ u \leq \textit{ky-time} \\
&\quad\quad \text{and } \textbf{hindu-zodiac}\,(l) = \textbf{hindu-zodiac}\,(u) \} \\
\textit{low} &= \textit{estimate} - \frac{2}{3} \\
\textit{up} &= \textit{estimate} + \frac{2}{3}
\end{aligned}$$

Since the month's length is variable, we do not know a priori whether the result of the search will be in the past or future. Thus, we may end up looking a second time.

15.2 Calendars

> I dare not hope that I have made myself quite clear, simply because [my explanation] involves too many fractions and details. To tell the truth it took me several days to get familiar with the [calendar] system.... Several of my Brahmin friends themselves were unable to explain the intricacies of the Hindu calendar.... But let me not leave the impression that these attempts on the part of the Brahmins of old to reconcile the seemingly irreconcilable have been futile.... There can be no doubt that, from the point of view of correctness and exactitude, the Hindu calendars are by far the nearest approaches to the actual machinery of astronomical phenomena governing life on our planet. The only fault of the Hindu calendars is that they are unintelligible to the common man.
>
> —Hashim Amir Ali: *Facts and Fancies* (1946)

To determine the Hindu year for a given R.D. date (or time), it is not enough to take the quotient of the number of days elapsed with the mean length of a year. A correction must be applied based on where the sun actually is, vis-à-vis the start of the zodiac, at the time of mean solar New Year:

$$\textbf{hindu-calendar-year}\,(\textit{ky-time}) \stackrel{\text{def}}{=} \tag{15.18}$$

$$\begin{cases} \textit{year} - 1 \ \textbf{if}\ \textit{real} > 20000 > 1000 > \textit{mean} \\ \textit{year} + 1 \ \textbf{if}\ \textit{mean} > 20000 > 1000 > \textit{real} \\ \textit{year} \qquad\qquad \textbf{otherwise} \end{cases}$$

where

$$\begin{aligned} \textit{mean} &= 21600 \cdot \left(\frac{\textit{ky-time}}{\textbf{hindu-sidereal-year}} \bmod 1 \right) \\ \textit{real} &= \textbf{hindu-solar-longitude}\,(\textit{ky-time}) \\ \textit{year} &= \left\lfloor \frac{\textit{ky-time}}{\textbf{hindu-sidereal-year}} \right\rfloor \end{aligned}$$

If the mean solar longitude (computed in arcminutes) at the given time is just past 0°, while the true longitude is almost 360°, then the year number obtained by dividing by the mean year length is too high. Conversely, if the mean longitude is a bit less than 360°, but the true longitude is already past 0°, then we add 1 to the mean year number.

The Kali Yuga era is used today only for calculations. Instead, one commonly used starting point is the Śaka era, in which (elapsed) year 0 began with the vernal equinox of 79 C.E., or 3179 K.Y.:

$$\textbf{hindu-solar-era} \stackrel{\text{def}}{=} 3179 \tag{15.19}$$

$$\textbf{hindu-solar-from-fixed}\,(date) \stackrel{\text{def}}{=} \boxed{month \mid day \mid year} \tag{15.20}$$

where

$$
\begin{aligned}
ky\text{-}time &= \textbf{hindu-day-count}\,(date)\\
rise &= \textbf{hindu-sunrise}\,(ky\text{-}time)\\
month &= \textbf{hindu-zodiac}\,(rise)\\
year &= \textbf{hindu-calendar-year}\,(rise) - \textbf{hindu-solar-era}\\
approx &= ky\text{-}time - 3 - \left\lfloor \frac{\textbf{hindu-solar-longitude}\,(rise) \bmod 1800}{60} \right\rfloor\\
begin &= approx + \left(\sum_{i \geq approx}^{p(i)} 1 \right)\\
day &= ky\text{-}time - begin + 1\\
p\,(i) &= \textbf{hindu-zodiac}\,(\textbf{hindu-sunrise}\,(i)) \neq month
\end{aligned}
$$

For example, R.D. 0 is the 19th day of Makara (the 10th month) of year −78 S.E.,[5] the same month and day as for the mean solar calendar (page 123). The function **hindu-day-count** (page 120) gives the number of days *ky-time* since the start of the Kali Yuga. The calculation of **hindu-sunrise** will be taken up in the next section. To determine the day of the month, we underestimate the day when the sun entered the current zodiacal sign (*approx*) and search forward for the start of the month *begin*.

Unlike the mean calendar, determining the R.D. date now requires search, for which we also need to compare solar dates:

$$\textbf{hindu-solar-precedes?} \tag{15.21}$$
$$\left(\boxed{month_1 \mid day_1 \mid year_1}, \boxed{month_2 \mid day_2 \mid year_2} \right) \stackrel{\text{def}}{=}$$

[5] Śaka (Scythian) era (expired).

$$
\begin{aligned}
& year_1 < year_2 \\
& \quad \text{or } \Big\{ year_1 = year_2 \\
& \qquad\qquad \text{and } \Big\{ month_1 < month_2 \\
& \qquad\qquad\qquad \text{or } \{ month_1 = month_2 \text{ and } day_1 < day_2 \} \Big\} \Big\}
\end{aligned}
$$

$$
\textbf{fixed-from-hindu-solar}\,(s\text{-}date) \stackrel{\text{def}}{=} \tag{15.22}
$$

$$
\begin{cases}
try & \textbf{if hindu-solar-from-fixed} \\
 & \quad (try) = s\text{-}date \\
\textbf{bogus} & \textbf{otherwise}
\end{cases}
$$

where

$$
\begin{aligned}
month &= s\text{-}date_{\textbf{month}} \\
day &= s\text{-}date_{\textbf{day}} \\
year &= s\text{-}date_{\textbf{year}} \\
approx &= \Big\lfloor \left(year + \textbf{hindu-solar-era} + \frac{month - 1}{12} \right) \\
&\qquad \cdot \textbf{hindu-sidereal-year} \\
&\qquad + \textbf{hindu-epoch} + day - 9 \Big\rfloor \\
try &= approx + \left(\sum_{i \geq approx}^{p(i)} 1 \right) \\
p(i) &= \textbf{hindu-solar-precedes?} \\
&\qquad (\textbf{hindu-solar-from-fixed}\,(i)\,,\, s\text{-}date)
\end{aligned}
$$

This function begins its linear search for the fixed date corresponding to the Hindu solar date *s-date* from R.D. date *approx*, obtained by adding the average number of days in the elapsed years and months, plus the elapsed number of days ($day - 1$) in the current month, minus 8 days, mainly to account for shorter than average months. When a given Hindu date does not occur, the constant **bogus** is returned.

As explained earlier, there are both leap months and leap days on the true Hindu lunisolar calendar; hence, we use quintuples

month	*leapmonth*	*day*	*leapday*	*year*

for lunisolar dates. For the lunar year, we use another common era, the Vikrama, which differs from the Kali Yuga by 3044 years:

$$\textbf{hindu-lunar-era} \stackrel{\text{def}}{=} 3044 \tag{15.23}$$

$$\textbf{hindu-lunar-from-fixed}\ (\mathit{date}) \stackrel{\text{def}}{=} \tag{15.24}$$

month	*leapmonth*	*day*	*leapday*	*year*

where

$$\begin{aligned}
\mathit{ky\text{-}time} &= \textbf{hindu-day-count}\ (\mathit{date}) \\
\mathit{rise} &= \textbf{hindu-sunrise}\ (\mathit{ky\text{-}time}) \\
\mathit{day} &= \textbf{lunar-day}\ (\mathit{rise}) \\
\mathit{leapday} &= \mathit{day} = \textbf{lunar-day} \\
&\qquad (\textbf{hindu-sunrise}\ (\mathit{ky\text{-}time} - 1)) \\
\mathit{last\text{-}new\text{-}moon} &= \textbf{hindu-new-moon}\ (\mathit{rise}) \\
\mathit{next\text{-}new\text{-}moon} &= \textbf{hindu-new-moon}\ (\lfloor \mathit{last\text{-}new\text{-}moon} \rfloor + 35) \\
\mathit{solar\text{-}month} &= \textbf{hindu-zodiac}\ (\mathit{last\text{-}new\text{-}moon}) \\
\mathit{leapmonth} &= \mathit{solar\text{-}month} = \textbf{hindu-zodiac}\ (\mathit{next\text{-}new\text{-}moon}) \\
\mathit{month} &= (\mathit{solar\text{-}month} + 1) \ \ \text{amod}\ \ 12 \\
\mathit{year} &= \textbf{hindu-calendar-year}\ (\mathit{next\text{-}new\text{-}moon}) - \\
&\quad \textbf{hindu-lunar-era} - \\
&\quad \left\{ \begin{array}{ll} -1 \ \textbf{if}\ \mathit{leapmonth} \text{ and } \mathit{month} = 1 & \\ 0 & \textbf{otherwise} \end{array} \right\}
\end{aligned}$$

This function uses the Hindu approximations to true times of new moons, true position of the sun at new moon, and true phase of the moon at sunrise (*rise*) to determine the *month* and *day*. The lunisolar month name and year number *year* are those of the solar month and year in effect one solar month after the beginning (*last-new-moon*) of the current lunar month. The function checks whether it is a leap month (*leapmonth*) with the same name as the following month (*next-new-moon*), or a leap day (*leapday*) with the same ordinal number as the previous day. Our fixed date R.D. 0 is the 4th day of the dark half (that is, lunar day 19) of Māgha (the 11th month) in year 57 V.E.;[6] neither the day

[6] Vikrama era (expired).

nor month is leap. This date is one month later than on the mean calendar (see page 126).

To invert the process and derive the R.D. date from a lunar date, we first find a lower bound on the possible R.D. date and then perform a bisection search for the exact correspondence. As Jacobi [2, p. 409] explains: "The problem must be solved indirectly, *i.e.,* we must ascertain approximately the day on which the given *tithi* was likely to end, and then calculate . . . the *tithi* that really ends on that day."

We need to compare the five components of lunar dates lexicographically:

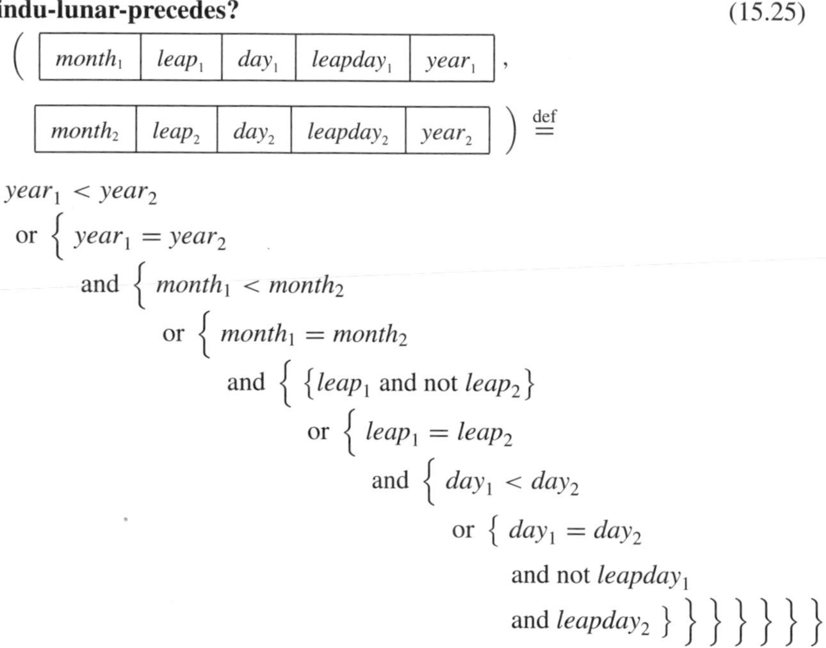

hindu-lunar-precedes? (15.25)

$$\left(\boxed{month_1 \mid leap_1 \mid day_1 \mid leapday_1 \mid year_1},\ \boxed{month_2 \mid leap_2 \mid day_2 \mid leapday_2 \mid year_2}\right) \stackrel{\text{def}}{=}$$

$$year_1 < year_2 \text{ or } \left\{ year_1 = year_2 \text{ and } \left\{ month_1 < month_2 \text{ or } \left\{ month_1 = month_2 \text{ and } \left\{ \{leap_1 \text{ and not } leap_2\} \text{ or } \left\{ leap_1 = leap_2 \text{ and } \left\{ day_1 < day_2 \text{ or } \left\{ day_1 = day_2 \text{ and not } leapday_1 \text{ and } leapday_2 \right\} \right\} \right\} \right\} \right\} \right\} \right\}$$

With this we can convert to a fixed date:

fixed-from-hindu-lunar (*l-date*) $\stackrel{\text{def}}{=}$ (15.26)

$$\begin{cases} try & \textbf{if hindu-lunar-from-fixed} \\ & \quad (try) = l\text{-}date \\ try + 1 & \textbf{if hindu-lunar-from-fixed} \\ & \quad (try + 1) = l\text{-}date \\ try - 1 & \textbf{if hindu-lunar-from-fixed} \\ & \quad (try - 1) = l\text{-}date \\ \textbf{bogus} & \textbf{otherwise} \end{cases}$$

where

$$
\begin{aligned}
\textit{year} &= \textit{l-date}_{\mathbf{year}}\\
\textit{month} &= \textit{l-date}_{\mathbf{month}}\\
\textit{leap} &= \textit{l-date}_{\mathbf{leap\text{-}month}}\\
\textit{leap-day} &= \textit{l-date}_{\mathbf{leap\text{-}day}}\\
\textit{day} &= \textit{l-date}_{\mathbf{day}}\\
\textit{ky year} &= \textit{year} + \mathbf{hindu\text{-}lunar\text{-}era}\\
\textit{mean} &= \mathbf{fixed\text{-}from\text{-}old\text{-}hindu\text{-}lunar}\\
&\qquad \left(\boxed{\textit{month}}\,\boxed{\textit{leap}}\,\boxed{\textit{day}}\,\boxed{\textit{ky-year}}\right)\\
\textit{approx} &= \begin{cases}
\textit{mean} + \mathbf{hindu\text{-}synodic\text{-}month} \\
\qquad \textbf{if hindu-lunar-precedes?} \\
\qquad\quad \left(\mathbf{hindu\text{-}lunar\text{-}from\text{-}fixed}\right. \\
\qquad\qquad \left.(\textit{mean} + 15), \textit{l-date}\right) \\
\textit{mean} - \mathbf{hindu\text{-}synodic\text{-}month} \\
\qquad \textbf{if hindu-lunar-precedes?} \\
\qquad\quad \left(\textit{l-date}, \mathbf{hindu\text{-}lunar\text{-}from\text{-}fixed}\right. \\
\qquad\qquad \left.(\textit{mean} - 15)\right) \\
\textit{mean} & \textbf{otherwise}
\end{cases}\\
\textit{try} &= \underset{d \in [\textit{approx} - 4\,:\,\textit{approx} + 4]}{\overset{p(l,u)}{\mathbf{MIN}}} \left\{ \begin{array}{l}
\text{not } \textbf{hindu-lunar-precedes?} \\
\quad \left(\mathbf{hindu\text{-}lunar\text{-}from\text{-}fixed}\right. \\
\qquad \left.(\lfloor d \rfloor), \textit{l-date}\right)
\end{array} \right\}\\
p(l,u) &= u - l \le 2
\end{aligned}
$$

We use the conversion function of the old Hindu lunisolar calendar to estimate the fixed date. That estimate may be a month off in either direction, because a true new moon might occur before a true solar month begins although the mean new moon occurs after the mean sun enters the next zodiacal constellation, or vice versa. After the correct month is determined, a search is still necessary because of the variability in month length. If the given Hindu date does not occur, the constant **bogus** is returned.

15.3 Sunrise

> It should, however, be remarked that if the interval between true sunrise and the end of a *tithi*, &c. is *very* small ... the case must be regarded as doubtful; though our calculations materially agree with those of the Hindus, still an almanac-maker avails himself of abbreviations which in the end may slightly influence the result.
>
> —Hermann Jacobi: "The Computation of Hindu Dates in Inscriptions, & c.," *Epigraphia Indica*, p. 436 (1892)

It remains to compute the actual time of sunrise for any particular day. We use the standard location, Ujjain, a city holy to the Hindus situated at 23°9′ north, 75°46′6″ east. Other locales employ local variants of the calendar which depend on the zodiacal constellation and lunar phase in effect at true local sunrise. Despite the comment of van Wijk [10, p. 24], "The rules the Sūrya-Siddhānta gives for calculating the time of true sunrise are exceedingly complicated, and inapplicable in practice," the fact that no one seems to bother with all the corrections mandated for the calculation of local sunrise, and the inaccuracy of the methods, we include them here exactly as ordained by the *Sūrya-Siddhānta* (see [12]).

Three corrections to mean sunrise (6 a.m.) are necessary:

1. The latitude of the location affects the time of sunrise by an amount that also depends on the season. This is called the "ascensional difference":

$$\textbf{ascensional-difference}\,(\textit{ky-time}, \textit{latitude}) \stackrel{\text{def}}{=} \qquad (15.27)$$

$$\textbf{hindu-arcsin}\left((-3438)\cdot\frac{\textit{earth-sine}}{\textit{diurnal-radius}}\right)$$

where

$$\textit{sin-decl} = \frac{1397}{3438}\cdot\textbf{hindu-sine}\,(\textbf{tropical-longitude}\,(\textit{ky-time}))$$

$$\textit{diurnal-radius} = \textbf{hindu-sine}\,(5400 - \textbf{hindu-arcsin}\,(\textit{sin-decl}))$$

$$\textit{tan} = \frac{\textbf{hindu-sine}\,(\textit{latitude})}{\textbf{hindu-sine}\,(5400 + \textit{latitude})}$$

$$\textit{earth-sine} = \textit{sin-decl}\cdot\textit{tan}$$

and is given here in arcminutes. This computation requires *tropical longitude*, which is affected by precession of the equinoxes. The value given in the *Sūrya-Siddhānta* for the maximum precession is 27°, and it is said to cycle once every 7200 years:[7]

$$\textbf{tropical-longitude}\,(\textit{ky-time}) \stackrel{\text{def}}{=} \left(\textbf{hindu-solar-longitude}\,(\textit{ky-time}) - \textit{precession}\right) \bmod 21600 \tag{15.28}$$

where

$$\begin{aligned} \textit{midnight} &= \lfloor \textit{ky-time} \rfloor \\ \textit{precession} &= 1620 - \left| 1620 - \left(6480 \cdot \frac{600}{1577917828} \cdot \textit{midnight} \bmod 6480 \right) \right| \end{aligned}$$

2. There is a small difference between the length of the sidereal day (one rotation of the Earth) and the solar day (from midnight to midnight) which amounts to almost a minute in a quarter of a day (see page 139). The function

$$\textbf{solar-sidereal-difference}\,(\textit{ky-time}) \stackrel{\text{def}}{=} \textbf{daily-motion}\,(\textit{ky-time}) \cdot \textbf{rising-sign}\,(\textit{ky-time}) \cdot \frac{1}{1800} \tag{15.29}$$

gives the difference for one day in arcminutes. It comprises a factor for the speed of the sun along the ecliptic:

$$\textbf{daily-motion}\,(\textit{ky-time}) \stackrel{\text{def}}{=} \textit{mean-motion} \cdot (\textit{equation-of-motion-factor} + 1) \tag{15.30}$$

where

$$\begin{aligned} \textit{mean-motion} &= \frac{21600}{\textbf{hindu-sidereal-year}} \\ \textit{anomaly} &= \textbf{mean-position}\left(\textbf{hindu-creation} + \textit{ky-time}, \textbf{hindu-anomalistic-year}\right) \end{aligned}$$

[7] The correct value is about 26,000 years with no maximum; see page 139.

$$\begin{aligned}
\textit{epicycle} &= \frac{14}{360} - \frac{|\textbf{hindu-sine}\,(\textit{anomaly})|}{3713040} \\
\textit{entry} &= \left\lfloor \frac{\textit{anomaly}}{225} \right\rfloor \\
\textit{sine-table-step} &= \textbf{hindu-sine-table}\,(\textit{entry}+1) - \\
&\quad\ \textbf{hindu-sine-table}\,(\textit{entry}) \\
\textit{equation-of-motion-factor} &= \left(-\frac{\textit{epicycle}}{225}\right) \cdot \textit{sine-table-step}
\end{aligned}$$

which depends on the solar anomaly, and a tabulated factor that depends on the distance of the sun from the celestial equator:

$$\textbf{rising-sign}\,(\textit{ky-time}) \stackrel{\text{def}}{=} \qquad (15.31)$$
$$\langle 1670, 1795, 1935, 1935, 1795, 1670\rangle_{[\,i\,]}$$

where

$$i = \left\lfloor \frac{\textbf{tropical-longitude}\,(\textit{ky-time})}{1800} \right\rfloor \bmod 6$$

3. The *equation of time* gives the difference between local and civil midnight caused by the uneven (apparent) motion of the sun through the seasons (see page 139). The *Sūrya-Siddhānta* uses the following very rough approximation:

$$\textbf{hindu-equation-of-time}\,(\textit{ky-time}) \stackrel{\text{def}}{=} \qquad (15.32)$$
$$\textbf{daily-motion}\,(\textit{ky-time}) \cdot \textit{equation-sun} \cdot \frac{\textbf{hindu-sidereal-year}}{21600} \cdot \frac{1}{21600}$$

where

$$\begin{aligned}
\textit{offset} &= \textbf{hindu-sine} \\
&\quad\ (\,\textbf{mean-position} \\
&\quad\quad (\,\textbf{hindu-creation} + \textit{ky-time}, \\
&\quad\quad\ \ \textbf{hindu-anomalistic-year}\,)\,) \\
\textit{equation-sun} &= \textit{offset} \cdot \left(\frac{|\textit{offset}|}{3713040} - \frac{14}{360}\right)
\end{aligned}$$

Putting the above together, we have

$$\textbf{hindu-sunrise}\ (\textit{ky-time}) \stackrel{\text{def}}{=} \tag{15.33}$$

$$\textit{ky-time} + \frac{1}{4} + \textbf{hindu-equation-of-time}\ (\textit{ky-time}) + \frac{1577917828/1582237828}{21600} \cdot \left(\textbf{ascensional-difference}\ (\textit{ky-time}, 1389) + \frac{\textbf{solar-sidereal-difference}\ (\textit{ky-time})}{4} \right)$$

The factor $\frac{1,577,917,828}{1,582,237,828} \approx 0.9972697$ converts a sidereal hour angle to solar time. The argument 1389 to **ascensional-difference** is the latitude of Ujjain in minutes of arc, and must be changed to get the time of sunrise at other latitudes. For locations other than Ujjain, the difference in longitude would also affect the local time of astronomical events by four seconds for every minute of longitude.

15.4 Alternatives

An alternative to the calculations we have presented would be to use the same accurate astronomical functions used for the Chinese calendar. Indeed, some Indian calendar makers have substituted such ephemeris data for the traditional methods, but they are the exception. In this regard, van Wijk wrote [11, p. 72]:

> Every year a great number of pañcāṅgs [almanacs] is still printed all over India, and some are calculated entirely after the prescriptions of the *Sūrya-Siddhānta* (or of another Siddhānta or Karaṇa), and some take their astronomical data from the Greenwich Nautical Almanac. Now there is something in favour of both ways, and one who wishes to know the exact moment of conjunctions, &c., must certainly use the second type. But that which is won on the one side is lost on the other: the Indians are possessors of an old tradition, and they ought to preserve that and glorify it. . . .

Though it is generally agreed that one should follow the rules dictated by the *Sūrya-Siddhānta* for calculating lunar days, for sunrise it seems that most calendars use tabulated times, not the approximate values obtained by following the strictures of the *Sūrya-Siddhānta*, which can be off by more than sixteen minutes. Thus, one would get better agreement with published Hindu calendars by incorporating modern computations of local sunrise, in place of those we gave in the previous section. To use astronomical sunrise at the Hindu "prime meridian," we would need to substitute the following calculation for **hindu-sunrise**:

$$\textbf{sunrise-at-ujjain}\,(\textit{ky-time}) \stackrel{\text{def}}{=} \qquad (15.34)$$

$$\textit{ky-time} + \textbf{sunrise}\,(d, \textit{latitude}, \textit{longitude})$$

where

$$d = \textit{ky-time} + \textbf{hindu-epoch}$$

$$\textit{latitude} = \frac{1389}{60}$$

$$\textit{longitude} = \frac{4546}{60}$$

We should also point out that the "infinite" precision of our algorithms is, from a mathematical point of view, specious, since the "true" motions are only approximations, and the sine table used to calculate the epicyclic adjustments is accurate to only three decimal places. There is therefore nothing gained by our keeping the fractions obtained by interpolation and calculation to greater accuracy than the table lookup methods, other than fidelity to the traditional sources. (Our formulas, as stated, can involve numbers with over 400 digits!) Double-precision arithmetic suffices for all practical purposes.

15.5 Holidays

> In what manner the *Hindus* contrive so far to reconcile the lunar and solar years, as to make them proceed concurrently in their ephemerides, might easily have been shown by exhibiting a version of their *Nadíyu* or *Varánes* almanack; but their modes of intercalation form no part of my present subject, and would injure the simplicity of my work, without throwing any light on the religion of the *Hindus*.
>
> —Sir William Jones: "Asiatick Researches," *Transactions of the Bengal Society*, volume 3, p. 259 (1801)

As with the Hindu calendars, so too with the holidays; there is a plethora of regional holidays and local variants of widespread holidays. The most complete reference in English is [9], but sufficient details to handle exceptional circumstances (leap months, skipped months, leap days, omitted days, and borderline cases) are lacking.

Certain hours, days, and months are more auspicious than others. For example, Wednesday and Saturday are "unlucky" days, as is the dark half of each month. Leap months and civil days containing lost lunar days are considered inauspicious. Astronomical events, such as actual or computed solar and lunar eclipses and planetary conjunctions, are usually auspicious.

The chief solar festivals are solar new year (Sowramana Ugadi) on Mesha 1, the day following the Hindu vernal equinox, and Ayyappa Jyothi Darshanam (Pongal) on Makara 1 and on the preceding day, celebrating the winter solstice. Solar new year in Gregorian year y is always in year $y - 78$ S.E. and the winter solstice of Gregorian year y occurs in year $y - 79$ S.E.; thus, the computation of the corresponding R.D. dates is straightforward.

The precise times of solar and lunar events are usually included in published Indian calendars. The fixed moment of entry of the sun into a Hindu zodiacal sign, called the *saṃkrānti*, can be computed in the following manner:

$$\textbf{samkranti}\,(\textit{g-year}, m) \stackrel{\text{def}}{=} \textit{begin} + \textbf{hindu-epoch} \qquad (15.35)$$

where

$$\begin{aligned}
\textit{diff} &= \textbf{hindu-solar-era} + \\
&\quad \textbf{gregorian-from-fixed}\,(\textbf{hindu-epoch})_{\textbf{year}} \\
\textit{h-year} &= \textit{g-year} - \textit{diff} \\
\textit{ny} &= \textbf{fixed-from-hindu-solar}\left(\boxed{m \mid 1 \mid \textit{h-year}}\right) - \\
&\quad \textbf{hindu-epoch} \\
\textit{begin} &= \underset{x \in \left[\textit{ny} - \frac{7}{8} : \textit{ny} + \frac{3}{8}\right]}{\overset{p\,(\textit{start},\,\textit{end})}{\textbf{MIN}}} \left\{ \begin{array}{ll} \textbf{hindu-solar-longitude}\,(x) < 180^\circ & \textbf{if } m = 1 \\ \textbf{hindu-solar-longitude}\,(x) \geq (m-1) \cdot 180^\circ & \textbf{otherwise} \end{array} \right\} \\
p\,(\textit{start}, \textit{end}) &= \frac{1}{1000000} \geq \textit{end} - \textit{start}
\end{aligned}$$

This is simply a bisection search for the moment before sunrise of the first day (*ny* days since the epoch) of the *m*th solar month of the Hindu solar year beginning in Gregorian year *g-year* when the true (sidereal) solar longitude is $m \times 1800'$. Mesha saṃkrānti, when the longitude of the sun is zero by Hindu reckoning, is, then,

$$\textbf{mesha-samkranti}\,(g\text{-}year) \stackrel{\text{def}}{=} \textbf{samkranti}\,(g\text{-}year, 1) \tag{15.36}$$

This function gives 8:21:10 a.m. on April 14 as the time of Mesha saṃkrānti in 1983.

Most Indian holidays, however, depend on the lunar date. Festivals are usually celebrated on the day a specified lunar day is current at sunrise; other events may depend on the phase of the moon at noon, sunset, or midnight. Some lunar holidays require that the specified lunar day be current at noon, rather than at sunrise. Sometimes, if the lunar day in question begins at least $\frac{1}{15}$ of a day before sunset of one day and ends before sunset of the next, the corresponding holiday is celebrated on the first day [4, section 113]. For example, *Naga Panchamī* (a day of snake worship) is normally celebrated on Śrāvaṇa 5 but is advanced one day if lunar day 5 begins in the first 1.2 temporal hours of day 4 and ends within the first tenth of day 5. Technically, such determinations require computation of the time of sunset in a manner analogous to that of sunrise.

The search for the new moon, listed on page 199, is halted once the position of the moon (and sun) at the time of conjunction has been narrowed down to a particular constellation on the zodiac. When greater accuracy is needed, and for the arbitrary phases needed for holiday calculations, we use the following function—the inverse of equation (15.15)—which gives the moment at which the kth lunar day occurred prior to *ky-time* days since the Hindu epoch:

$$\textbf{lunar-day-start}\,(ky\text{-}time, k, accuracy) \stackrel{\text{def}}{=} \tag{15.37}$$

$$\begin{cases} \textbf{lunar-day-start}\,(ky\text{-}time - 20, k, accuracy) & \\ & \textbf{if } try > ky\text{-}time \\ try & \textbf{otherwise} \end{cases}$$

where

$$\begin{aligned} tomorrow &= ky\text{-}time + 1 \\ part &= \frac{k-1}{30} \cdot \textbf{hindu-synodic-month} \\ estimate &= tomorrow - \\ &\quad ((tomorrow - part) \bmod \textbf{hindu-synodic-month}) \end{aligned}$$

$$
\begin{aligned}
try &= \underset{x \in [low : up]}{\overset{p(l,u)}{\mathbf{MIN}}} \left\{ 0 < \textit{diff-x} < 10800 \text{ or } \textit{diff-x} < -10800 \right\} \\
p(l, u) &= \textit{ky-time} < l \text{ or } u - l < \textit{accuracy} \\
\textit{diff-x} &= \textbf{hindu-lunar-phase}\,(x) - (k-1) \cdot 720 \\
low &= \textit{estimate} - \frac{2}{3} \\
up &= \textit{estimate} + \frac{2}{3}
\end{aligned}
$$

The value of *estimate* is yet another instance of equation (1.23), giving the most recent mean moment when $k - 1$ thirtieths of a lunar month had elapsed. For the time of new moon, k should be 1; $k = 16$ for the time of full moon.

The beginning of the lunisolar new year (Chandramana Ugadi), usually Chaitra 1, is the day of the first sunrise after the new moon preceding Mesha saṃkrānti, or the prior new moon in the case when the first month of the lunar year is leap:

$$
\textbf{hindu-lunar-new-year}\,(\textit{g-year}) \stackrel{\text{def}}{=} \tag{15.38}
$$

$$
\textbf{hindu-epoch} + \textit{h-day} + \left\{ \begin{array}{ll} 0 & \textbf{if } \textit{new-moon} < \textit{rise} \\ & \quad \text{or } \textbf{lunar-day} \\ & \qquad (\textbf{hindu-sunrise}\,(\textit{h-day} + 1)) = 2 \\ 1 & \textbf{otherwise} \end{array} \right\}
$$

where

$$
\begin{aligned}
mesha &= \textbf{mesha-samkranti}\,(\textit{g-year}) \\
m_1 &= \textbf{lunar-day-start} \\
& \qquad (\textbf{hindu-day-count}\,(mesha)\,,\,1, \epsilon) \\
m_0 &= \textbf{lunar-day-start}\,(m_1 - 27, 1, \epsilon) \\
\textit{new-moon} &= \left\{ \begin{array}{ll} m_0 \ \textbf{if hindu-zodiac}\,(m_0) = \textbf{hindu-zodiac}\,(m_1) & \\ m_1 & \textbf{otherwise} \end{array} \right. \\
\textit{h-day} &= \lfloor \textit{new-moon} \rfloor
\end{aligned}
$$

$$rise = \textbf{hindu-sunrise}\,(h\text{-}day)$$

$$\epsilon = \frac{1}{100000}$$

If the first lunar day of the new year is wholly contained in the interval between one sunrise and the next, then this function returns the fixed date on which the new moon occurs, which is also the last day of the previous lunisolar year, Phālguna 30.[8]

The major Hindu lunar holidays include: the Birthday of Rāma (Rāma Navami), celebrated on Chaitra 9; Varalakshmi Vratam on the Friday prior to Śrāvaṇa 15; the Birthday of Krishna (Janmashtami) on Śrāvaṇa 23; Ganesh Chaturthi, held on Bhādrapada 4;[9] Durga Ashtami on Āśvina 8; Saraswati Puja on Āśvina 9, when books are worshipped in honor of the goddess of eloquence and arts, Sarasvatī; Dasra on Āśvina 10; Diwali, a major autumn festival celebrated Āśvina 29–Kārttika 1 (Kārttika 1 is the main day of festivity and marks the beginning of the year in some regions); the festival Karthikai Deepam on Kārttika 15; the main festival of the year, Vaikunta Ekadashi on Mārgaśīra 11, honoring Vishnu; Maha Shivaratri, the Great Night of Shiva, celebrated on the day that the 29th lunar day of Mārgaśīra is current at midnight, and preceded by a day of fasting by devotees of Shiva; and the spring festival, Holi, which takes place in the evening of the 15th lunar day of Phālguna.

In general, holidays are not held in leap months. When a month is skipped, its holidays are usually celebrated in the following month. Festivals are generally celebrated on the second of two days with the same lunar day number; if a day is expunged, the festival takes place on the civil day containing that lunar day.

For some holidays, the location of the moon may be more important in some regions than the lunar date. A lunar mansion, called *nakṣatra*, is associated

8 The results obtained with our functions are in complete agreement with Sewell and Dîkshit's tables [7] for added and expunged months from 1500 C.E. to 1900. Furthermore, our functions are in agreement with the calculations in [4, pp. 97–101] for the earlier disputed years considered there. They also agree on the date of the lunisolar new years in the period 1500–1900, except for Spring 1600, when the first new moon of 1657 V.E. occurred on March 5 (Julian) after sunrise, but the second lunar day began at 6:07 a.m. on March 6. Reckoning with mean sunrise, as in [7, p. lxxxii], March 6 is the first day of the new year, since at 6 a.m. that day the new moon was still in its first tithi. However, at the true time of sunrise, 6:14 according to the *Sūrya-Siddhānta*, or 6:08 using our astronomical code, lunar day 1 had already ended and, therefore, the new year is considered to start on the previous day.

9 According to [3], the precise rule is that Ganesh Chaturthi is celebrated on the day in which lunar day 4 is current in whole or in part during the midday period that extends from 1.2 temporal hours before noon until 1.2 temporal hours after noon. If, however, that lunar day is current during midday on two consecutive days, or if it extends from after midday on one day until before midday of the next, then it is celebrated on the former day.

with each civil day and is determined by the (sidereal) longitude of the moon at sunrise:

$$\textbf{lunar-mansion}\ (date) \stackrel{\text{def}}{=} \left\lfloor \frac{\textbf{hindu-lunar-longitude}\ (rise)}{800} \right\rfloor + 1 \quad (15.39)$$

where

$$rise = \textbf{hindu-sunrise}\ (\textbf{hindu-day-count}\ (date))$$

Their names were given in Table 15.3.

The function **lunar-day-start** can also be used to determine the time of onset of *karanas*, which are each half of a lunar day in duration, by using fractions for k. The most recent occurrence of the nth karana ($1 \le n \le 60$), prior to day d, begins within ϵ of **lunar-day-start**$(d,\ (n+1)/2,\ \epsilon)$. The names of the karanas follow the repeating pattern shown in Table 15.3. The following function gives the column number of the nth karana:

$$\textbf{karana}\ (n) \stackrel{\text{def}}{=} \begin{cases} 0 & \textbf{if } n = 1 \\ n - 50 & \textbf{if } n > 57 \\ (n-1) \text{ amod } 7 & \textbf{otherwise} \end{cases} \quad (15.40)$$

A *yoga* is the varying period of time during which the solar and lunar longitudes increase a *total* of 800 arcminutes (13°20′).[10] A full circle contains twenty-seven segments of 800 minutes, corresponding to the 27 yogas:

(1) Viṣkamba	(10) Gaṇḍa	(19) Parigha
(2) Prīti	(11) Vṛddhi	(20) Śiva
(3) Ayuṣmān	(12) Dhruva	(21) Siddha
(4) Saubhāgya	(13) Vyāghāta	(22) Sādhya
(5) Śobhana	(14) Harṣaṇa	(23) Śubha
(6) Atigaṇḍa	(15) Vajra	(24) Śukla
(7) Sukarmān	(16) Siddhi	(25) Brahman
(8) Dhṛti	(17) Vyatipāta	(26) Indra
(9) Śūla	(18) Varīyas	(27) Vaidhṛti

Since a full revolution of the sun or moon has no net effect on the yoga, we need only consider their longitudes, counted in increments of 800′,

[10] Certain conjunctions of calendrical and astronomical events are also termed "yogas."

Table 15.3 *The repeating pattern of names of karanas (half-days)*

Karanas	0	1	2	3	4	5	6	7	8	9	10
1–8	Kiṃstughna	Bava	Vālava	Kaulava	Taitila	Gara	Vaṇija	Viṣṭi			
9–15		Bava	Vālava	Kaulava	Taitila	Gara	Vaṇija	Viṣṭi			
16–22		Bava	Vālava	Kaulava	Taitila	Gara	Vaṇija	Viṣṭi			
23–29		Bava	Vālava	Kaulava	Taitila	Gara	Vaṇija	Viṣṭi			
30–36		Bava	Vālava	Kaulava	Taitila	Gara	Vaṇija	Viṣṭi			
37–43		Bava	Vālava	Kaulava	Taitila	Gara	Vaṇija	Viṣṭi			
44–50		Bava	Vālava	Kaulava	Taitila	Gara	Vaṇija	Viṣṭi			
51–60		Bava	Vālava	Kaulava	Taitila	Gara	Vaṇija	Viṣṭi	Śakuni	Nāga	Catuṣpada

modulo 27:

$$\textbf{yoga}\ (\textit{ky-time}) \stackrel{\text{def}}{=} \tag{15.41}$$

$$\left\lfloor \frac{\textbf{hindu-solar-longitude}\ (\textit{ky-time}) + \textbf{hindu-lunar-longitude}\ (\textit{ky-time})}{800} \bmod 27 \right\rfloor + 1$$

Inverting this function to determine the time of the last occurrence of a given yoga is similar to **lunar-day-start**.

There are also numerous days of lesser importance that depend on the lunisolar calendar. Certain combinations of events are also significant. For example, whenever lunar day 8 falls on Wednesday, the day is sacred:

$$\textbf{sacred-wednesdays-in-gregorian}\ (\textit{g-year}) \stackrel{\text{def}}{=} \tag{15.42}$$

$$\textbf{sacred-wednesdays}\left(\textbf{fixed-from-gregorian}\left(\boxed{\textbf{january} \mid 1 \mid \textit{g-year}}\right), \textbf{fixed-from-gregorian}\left(\boxed{\textbf{december} \mid 31 \mid \textit{g-year}}\right)\right)$$

This uses the following function to collect all such Wednesdays between fixed dates *start* and *end*:

$$\textbf{sacred-wednesdays}\ (\textit{start}, \textit{end}) \stackrel{\text{def}}{=} \tag{15.43}$$

$$\begin{cases} \langle\,\rangle & \textbf{if } \textit{start} > \textit{end} \\ \begin{Bmatrix} \langle \textit{wed} \rangle \ \textbf{if } \textit{h-date}_{\textbf{day}} = 8 \\ \langle\,\rangle \quad \textbf{otherwise} \end{Bmatrix} \ \| \ \textbf{sacred-wednesdays}\ (\textit{wed}+1, \textit{end}) & \textbf{otherwise} \end{cases}$$

where

$$\textit{wed} = \textbf{kday-on-or-after}\ (\textit{start}, \textbf{wednesday})$$

$$\textit{h-date} = \textbf{hindu-lunar-from-fixed}\ (\textit{wed})$$

There are also auspicious and inauspicious days that depend on the position of the planets. These can be calculated in much the same way as that of the moon, but with an additional epicyclic motion to contend with (see [5]).

The *panchang* is the traditional five-part Hindu calendar, comprising for each civil day: its lunar day (*tithi*), day of the week, *nakṣatra* (stellar position of the moon), *yoga*, and *karana* (based on the lunar phase). We have provided functions for each component.

References

[1] Calendar Reform Committee, *Report of the Calendar Reform Committee*, New Delhi, 1955.

[2] H. G. Jacobi, "The Computation of Hindu Dates in Inscriptions, & c.," J. Burgess, ed., *Epigraphia Indica: A Collection of Inscriptions Supplementary to the Corpus Inscriptionum Indicarum of the Archæological Survey of India*, Calcutta, pp. 403–460, p. 481, 1892.

[3] F. Kielhorn, "Festal Days of the Hindu Lunar Calendar," *The Indian Antiquary*, volume XXVI, pp. 177–187, 1897.

[4] D. B. L. D. S. Pillai, *Indian Chronology, Solar, Lunar, and Planetary. A Practical Guide*, Madras, 1911.

[5] D. Pingree, "History of Mathematical Astronomy in India," C. C. Gillispie, ed., *Dictionary of Scientific Biography*, volume XV, supplement I, 1978, pp. 533–633.

[6] R. Sewell, *The Siddhantas and the Indian Calendar*, Government of India Central Publication Branch, Calcutta, 1924.

[7] R. Sewell and S. B. Dîkshit, *The Indian Calendar, With Tables for the Conversion of Hindu and Muhammadan into* A.D. *Dates, and Vice Versa, with Tables of Eclipses Visible in India by R. Schram*, Motilal Banarsidass Publishers, Delhi, 1995. Originally published in 1896.

[8] *Sūrya-Siddhānta*, circa 1000. Translated by E. Burgess with notes by W. D. Whitney, *Journal of the American Oriental Society*, volume 6, 1860. A new edition, edited by P. Gangooly with an introduction by P. Sengupta, was published by Calcutta University, 1935. Reprinted by Indological Book House, Varanasi, India, 1977; also reprinted by Wizards Book Shelf, Minneapolis, 1978.

[9] M. M. Underhill, *The Hindu Religious Year*, Association Press, Calcutta and Oxford University Press, London, 1921.

[10] W. E. van Wijk, *Decimal Tables for the Reduction of Hindu Dates from the Data of the Sūrya-Siddhānta*, Martinus Nijhoff, The Hague, 1938.

[11] W. E. van Wijk, "On Hindu Chronology IV: Decimal Tables for Calculating the Exact Moments of Beginning of Mean and True Tithis, Karaṇas, Nakṣatras and Yogas, According to the Sūrya-Siddhānta; Together With Some Miscellaneous Notes on the Subject of Hindu Chronology," *Acta Orientalia*, volume IV, pp. 55–80, 1926.

[12] W. E. van Wijk, "On Hindu Chronology V: Decimal Tables for Calculating True Local Time, According to the Sūrya-Siddhānta," *Acta Orientalia*, volume V, pp. 1–27, 1927.

Coda

The following description of the presentation of the annual calendar in China is taken from Peter (Pierre) Hoang (*A Notice of the Chinese Calendar and a Concordance with the European Calendar*, 2nd ed., Catholic Mission Press, Shanghai, 1904):

Every year, on the 1st of the 2nd month, the Board of Mathematics presents to the Emperor three copies of the *Annual Calendar* for the following year, namely in Chinese, in Manchou and in Mongolian. Approbation being given, it is engraved and printed. Then on the 1st of the 4th month, two printed copies in Chinese are sent to the *Fan-t'ai* (Treasurer) of each province, that of Chih li excepted; one of which, stamped with the seal of the Board of Mathematics, is to be preserved in the archives of the Treasury, while the other is used for engraving and printing for public use in the province.

On the 1st day of the 10th month, early in the morning, the Board of Mathematics goes to offer Calendars to the Imperial court. The copies destined to the Emperor and Empresses are borne upon a sedan-like stand painted with figures of dragons (*Lung t'ing*), those for the Princes, the Ministers and officers of the court being carried on eight similar stands decorated with silk ornaments (*Ts'ai-t'ing*). They are accompanied by the officers of the Board with numerous attendants and the Imperial band of music. On arriving at the first entrance of the palace, the Calendars for the Emperor are placed upon an ornamented stand, those for other persons being put upon two other stands on each side. The copies for the Emperor and his family are not stamped with the seal of the Board of Mathematics, while the others are. The middle stand is taken into the palace, where the officers of the Board make three genuflections, each followed by three prostrations, after which the Calendars are handed to the eunuchs who present them to the Emperor, the Empress-mother, the Empress and other persons of the seraglio, two copies being given to each, viz. one in Chinese and one in Manchou. The master of ceremonies then proceeds to the entrance of the palace where the two other stands were left, and where the Princes, the Ministers with the civil and military mandarins, both Manchous and Mongols all in robes of state are in attendance. The master of ceremonies reads the Imperial decree of publication of the Calendars, namely: "The Emperor presents you all with the Annual Calendar of the year, and promulgates it throughout the Empire," which proclamation is heard kneeling. Then follow three genuflections and nine prostrations, after which all receive the Calendar on their knees, the Princes two copies, one in Chinese and one in Manchou, the ministers and other officers only one, each in his own language. Lastly the Corean envoy, who must attend every year on that day, is presented kneeling with one hundred Chinese copies, to take home with him.

In the provinces, the *Fan-t'ai* (Treasurer), after getting some printed copies of the Calendar stamped with a special seal, also on the 1st of the 10th month, sends them on a sedan-like stand to the Viceroy or Governor, accompanied by the mandarin called *Li-wen-t'ing*, who is instructed with the printing of the Calendar. The Viceroy or Governor receives them to the sound of music and of three cannon shots. The Calendars being set upon a stand between two tapers in the tribunal, the Viceroy or Governor, in robes of state, approaches the stand, and turning towards that quarter where Peking is situated, makes three genuflections and nine prostrations, after which ceremony he reverently receives the Calendars. The Treasurer sends the Calendar to all the civil and military Mandarins, all of whom, except those of inferior degree, receive it with the same forms. Any copies left are sold to the people. The reprinting of the Calendar is forbidden under a penalty (except in *Fu-chien* and *Kuang-tong* where it is tolerated). If therefore any copy is found without seal or with a false one, its author is sought after and punished. Falsification of the Calendar is punished with death; whoever reprints the *Annual Calendar* is liable to 100 blows and two months cangue.

Now that's a society that takes calendars (and copyrights) seriously!

Appendix A

Function, Parameter, and Constant Types

In this appendix we list all of the types of objects used in our calendar functions. After giving a list of the types themselves, we list, for each function, the types of its parameters and of its result. Then, we give a similar list for all constants.

A.1 Types

Name	Type or range	Supertype
amplitude	$[-1:1]$	*real*
angle	$[0:360)$	*real*
arcminute	$[0:21600)$	*rational*
bahai-cycle	$1\ldots19$	*positive-integer*
bahai-date	⟨*bahai-major*, *bahai-cycle*, *bahai-year*, *bahai-month*, *bahai-day*⟩	*list-of-integers*
bahai-day	$1\ldots19$	*positive-integer*
bahai-major	*integer*	
bahai-month	$1\ldots20$	*positive-integer*
bahai-year	$1\ldots19$	*positive-integer*
boolean	*true*, *false*	
chinese-cycle	*integer*	
chinese-date	⟨*chinese-cycle*, *chinese-year*, *chinese-month*, *chinese-leap-month*, *chinese-day*⟩	*list*
chinese-day	$1\ldots31$	*positive-integer*
chinese-leap	*boolean*	
chinese-month	$1\ldots12$	*positive-integer*
chinese-year	$1\ldots60$	*positive-integer*
coptic-date	⟨*coptic-month*, *coptic-day*, *coptic-year*⟩	*standard-date*
coptic-day	$1\ldots31$	*positive-integer*
coptic-month	$1\ldots13$	*positive-integer*
coptic-year	*integer*	
day-of-week	$0\ldots6$	*non-negative-integer*
ethiopic-date	⟨*ethiopic-month*, *ethiopic-day*, *ethiopic-year*⟩	*standard-date*
ethiopic-day	$1\ldots31$	*positive-integer*
ethiopic-month	$1\ldots13$	*positive-integer*
ethiopic-year	*integer*	
fixed-date	*integer*	
fraction-of-day	$[0,1)$	*real*
french-date	⟨*french-month*, *french-day*, *french-year*⟩	*standard-date*
french-day	$1\ldots30$	*positive-integer*
french-month	$1\ldots13$	*positive-integer*
french-year	*integer*	

Name	Type or range	Supertype
gregorian-date	⟨*gregorian-month, gregorian-day, gregorian-year*⟩	*standard-date*
gregorian-day	1 . . . 31	*positive-integer*
gregorian-month	1 . . . 12	*positive-integer*
gregorian-year	*integer*	
hebrew-date	⟨*hebrew-month, hebrew-day, hebrew-year*⟩	*standard-date*
hebrew-day	1 . . . 30	*positive-integer*
hebrew-month	1 . . . 13	*positive-integer*
hebrew-year	*integer*	
hindu-lunar-date	⟨*hindu-lunar-month, hindu-lunar-leap-month, hindu-lunar-day, hindu-lunar-leap-day, hindu-lunar-year*⟩	*list*
hindu-lunar-day	1 . . . 30	*positive-integer*
hindu-lunar-leap-day	*boolean*	
hindu-lunar-leap-month	*boolean*	
hindu-lunar-month	1 . . . 12	*positive-integer*
hindu-lunar-year	*integer*	
hindu-moment	*rational*	*moment*
hindu-solar-date	⟨*hindu-solar-month, hindu-solar-day, hindu-solar-year*⟩	*standard-date*
hindu-solar-day	1 . . . 31	*positive-integer*
hindu-solar-month	1 . . . 12	*positive-integer*
hindu-solar-year	*integer*	
hindu-year	*integer*	
hour	0 . . . 23	*non-negative-integer*
integer		*rational*
islamic-date	⟨*islamic-month, islamic-day, islamic-year*⟩	*standard-date*
islamic-day	1 . . . 30	*positive-integer*
islamic-month	1 . . . 12	*positive-integer*
islamic-year	*integer*	
iso-date	⟨*iso-week, iso-day, iso-year*⟩	*list-of-integers*
iso-day	1 . . . 7	*positive-integer*
iso-week	1 . . . 53	*positive-integer*
iso-year	*integer*	
julian-centuries	*real*	
julian-date	⟨*julian-month, julian-day, julian-year*⟩	*standard-date*
julian-day	1 . . . 31	*positive-integer*
julian-day-number	*real*	
julian-month	1 . . . 12	*positive-integer*
julian-year	*non-zero-integer*	
list-of-fixed-dates	*list-of-integers*	
list-of-integers		*list*
list-of-non-negative-integers		*list-of-integers*
list-of-pairs		*list*
list-of-reals		*list*
mayan-baktun	*integer*	
mayan-haab-date	⟨*mayan-haab-day, mayan-haab-month*⟩	*list-of-non-negative-integers*
mayan-haab-day	0 . . . 19	*non-negative-integer*
mayan-haab-month	1 . . . 19	*positive-integer*
mayan-katun	0 . . . 19	*non-negative-integer*
mayan-kin	0 . . . 19	*non-negative-integer*
mayan-long-count-date	⟨*mayan-baktun, mayan-katun, mayan-tun, mayan-uinal, mayan-kin*⟩	*list-of-integers*
mayan-tun	0 . . . 17	*non-negative-integer*
mayan-tzolkin-date	⟨*mayan-tzolkin-number, mayan-tzolkin-name*⟩	*list-of-non-negative-integers*
mayan-tzolkin-name	1 . . . 20	*non-negative-integer*
mayan-tzolkin-number	1 . . . 13	*non-negative-integer*
mayan-uinal	0 . . . 19	*non-negative-integer*
minute	0 . . . 59	*non-negative-integer*
moment	*real*	
non-negative-integer	0, 1, . . .	*integer*

Name	Type or range	Supertype
non-zero-integer	$\ldots, -2, -1, 1, 2, \ldots$	*integer*
non-zero-real	$(-\infty : 0) \cup (0 : \infty)$	*real*
old-hindu-date	⟨*old-hindu-month*, *old-hindu-leap*, *old-hindu-day*, *old-hindu-year*⟩	*list*
old-hindu-day	$1 \ldots 31$	*positive-integer*
old-hindu-leap	*boolean*	
old-hindu-lunar-date	⟨*old-hindu-lunar-month*, *old-hindu-lunar-leap*, *old-hindu-lunar-day*, *old-hindu-lunar-year*⟩	*list*
old-hindu-lunar-day	$1 \ldots 30$	*positive-integer*
old-hindu-lunar-leap	*boolean*	
old-hindu-lunar-month	$1 \ldots 12$	*positive-integer*
old-hindu-lunar-year	*integer*	
old-hindu-month	$1 \ldots 12$	*positive-integer*
old-hindu-year	*integer*	
omer-count	$\langle 0 \ldots 7, 0 \ldots 6 \rangle$	*list-of-non-negative-integers*
persian-date	⟨*persian-month*, *persian-day*, *persian-year*⟩	*standard-date*
persian-day	$1 \ldots 31$	*positive-integer*
persian-month	$1 \ldots 12$	*positive-integer*
persian-year	*non-zero-integer*	
phase	$[0 : 360)$	*angle*
positive-integer	$1, 2, \ldots$	*integer*
quadrant	$1 \ldots 4$	*positive-integer*
radian	$[0 : 2\pi)$	*real*
rational		*real*
real	$(-\infty : \infty)$	
second	$[0 : 60)$	*real*
standard-date	⟨*standard-month*, *standard-day*, *standard-year*⟩	*list-of-integers*
standard-day	$1 \ldots 31$	*positive-integer*
standard-month	$1 \ldots 12$	*positive-integer*
standard-year	*integer*	
string		
weekday	$0 \ldots 6$	*non-negative-integer*

A.2 Function Types

Function	Parameter type(s)	Result type
aberration	*julian-centuries*	*radian*
adjusted-mod	⟨*integer*, *positive-integer*⟩	*positive-integer*
advent	*gregorian-year*	*fixed-date*
apparent-from-local	*moment*	*moment*
arccos-degrees	*amplitude*	*angle*
arcsin-degrees	*amplitude*	*angle*
arctan-degrees	⟨*real*, *quadrant*⟩	*angle*
ascensional-difference	⟨*hindu-moment*, *arcminute*⟩	*arcminute*
bahai-cycle	*bahai-date*	*bahai-cycle*
bahai-date	⟨*bahai-major*, *bahai-cycle*, *bahai-year*, *bahai-month*, *bahai-day*⟩	*bahai-date*
bahai-day	*bahai-date*	*bahai-day*
bahai-from-fixed	*fixed-date*	*bahai-date*
bahai-major	*bahai-date*	*bahai-major*
bahai-month	*bahai-date*	*bahai-month*
bahai-new-year	*gregorian-year*	*fixed-date*
bahai-year	*bahai-date*	*bahai-year*
bce	*standard-year*	*julian-year*
binary-search	⟨—, *real*, —, *real*, —, *real*→*boolean*, ⟨*real*, *real*⟩→*boolean*⟩	*real*
birkath-ha-hama	*gregorian-year*	*list-of-fixed-dates*
ce	*standard-year*	*julian-year*
chinese-cycle	*chinese-date*	*chinese-cycle*

Function	Parameter type(s)	Result type
chinese-date	⟨*chinese-cycle, chinese-year, chinese-month, chinese-leap, chinese-day*⟩	*chinese-date*
chinese-date-next-solar-longitude	⟨*fixed-date angle*⟩	*fixed-date*
chinese-day	*chinese-date*	*chinese-day*
chinese-from-fixed	*fixed-date*	*chinese-date*
chinese-leap	*chinese-date*	*chinese-leap*
chinese-month	*chinese-date*	*chinese-month*
chinese-name-of-day	*chinese-date*	⟨1 . . . 10, 1 . . . 12⟩
chinese-name-of-month	*chinese-month*	⟨1 . . . 10, 1 . . . 12⟩
chinese-name-of-year	*chinese-year*	⟨1 . . . 10, 1 . . . 12⟩
chinese-new-moon-before	*fixed-date*	*fixed-date*
chinese-new-moon-on-or-after	*fixed-date*	*fixed-date*
chinese-new-year	*gregorian-year*	*fixed-date*
chinese-sexagesimal-name	*integer*	⟨1 . . . 10, 1 . . . 12⟩
chinese-time-zone	*fixed-date*	*real*
chinese-year	*chinese-date*	*chinese-year*
christmas	*gregorian-year*	*fixed-date*
coptic-christmas	*gregorian-year*	*list-of-fixed-dates*
coptic-date	⟨*coptic-month, coptic-day, coptic-year*⟩	*coptic-date*
coptic-from-fixed	*fixed-date*	*coptic-date*
coptic-in-gregorian	⟨*coptic-month, coptic-day, gregorian-year*⟩	*list-of-fixed-dates*
coptic-leap-year?	*coptic-year*	*boolean*
cosine-degrees	*angle*	*amplitude*
current-major-solar-term	*fixed-date*	*integer*
current-minor-solar-term	*fixed-date*	*integer*
daily-motion	*hindu-moment*	*arcminute*
date-next-solar-longitude	⟨*julian-day-number, angle*⟩	*julian-day-number*
day-number	*gregorian-date*	*non-negative-integer*
day-of-week-from-fixed	*fixed-date*	*day-of-week*
daylight-savings-end	*gregorian-year*	*fixed-date*
daylight-savings-start	*gregorian-year*	*fixed-date*
days-in-hebrew-year	*hebrew-year*	353,354,355,383, 384,385
days-remaining	*gregorian-date*	*non-negative-integer*
degrees	*real*	*angle*
degrees-to-radians	*real*	*radian*
dragon-festival	*gregorian-year*	*fixed-date*
easter	*gregorian-year*	*fixed-date*
eastern-orthodox-christmas	*gregorian-year*	*list-of-fixed-dates*
election-day	*gregorian-year*	*fixed-date*
ephemeris-correction	*moment*	*fraction-of-day*
ephemeris-from-universal	*julian-day-number*	*julian-day-number*
epiphany	*gregorian-year*	*fixed-date*
equation-of-time	*moment*	*fraction-of-day*
ethiopic-date	⟨*ethiopic-month, ethiopic-day, ethiopic-year*⟩	*ethiopic-date*
ethiopic-from-fixed	*fixed-date*	*ethiopic-date*
feast-of-ridvan	*gregorian-year*	*fixed-date*
first-quarter-moon-at-or-before	*julian-day-number*	*julian-day-number*
fixed-from-bahai	*bahai-date*	*fixed-date*
fixed-from-chinese	*chinese-date*	*fixed-date*
fixed-from-coptic	*coptic-date*	*fixed-date*
fixed-from-ethiopic	*ethiopic-date*	*fixed-date*
fixed-from-french	*french-date*	*fixed-date*
fixed-from-gregorian	*gregorian-date*	*fixed-date*
fixed-from-hebrew	*hebrew-date*	*fixed-date*
fixed-from-hindu-lunar	*old-hindu-lunar-date*	*fixed-date* (or **bogus**)
fixed-from-hindu-solar	*hindu-solar-date*	*fixed-date* (or **bogus**)
fixed-from-islamic	*islamic-date*	*fixed-date*
fixed-from-iso	*iso-date*	*fixed-date*
fixed-from-jd	*julian-day-number*	*fixed-date*
fixed-from-julian	*julian-date*	*fixed-date*
fixed-from-mayan-long-count	*mayan-long-count-date*	*fixed-date*
fixed-from-modified-french	*french-date*	*fixed-date*

Function	Parameter type(s)	Result type
fixed-from-old-hindu-lunar	*hindu-lunar-date*	*fixed-date*
fixed-from-old-hindu-solar	*hindu-solar-date*	*fixed-date*
fixed-from-persian	*persian-date*	*fixed-date*
french-autumnal-equinox-on-or-before	*fixed-date*	*fixed-date*
french-date	⟨*french-month*, *french-day*, *french-year*⟩	*french-date*
french-from-fixed	*fixed-date*	*french-date*
full-moon-at-or-before	*julian-day-number*	*julian-day-number*
gregorian-date	⟨*gregorian-month*, *gregorian-day*, *gregorian-year*⟩	*gregorian-date*
gregorian-date-difference	⟨*gregorian-date*, *gregorian-date*⟩	*integer*
gregorian-from-fixed	*fixed-date*	*gregorian-date*
gregorian-leap-year?	*gregorian-year*	*boolean*
gregorian-year-from-fixed	*fixed-date*	*gregorian-year*
hebrew-birthday	⟨*hebrew-date*, *hebrew-year*⟩	*fixed-date*
hebrew-calendar-elapsed-days	*hebrew-year*	*integer*
hebrew-date	⟨*hebrew-month*, *hebrew-day*, *hebrew-year*⟩	*hebrew-date*
hebrew-from-fixed	*fixed-date*	*hebrew-date*
hebrew-leap-year?	*hebrew-year*	*boolean*
hebrew-new-year-delay	*hebrew-year*	0,1,2
hindu-arcsin	−3438 ... 3438	*arcminute*
hindu-calendar-year	*hindu-moment*	*hindu-solar-year*
hindu-day-count	*fixed-date*	*integer*
hindu-equation-of-time	*hindu-moment*	*hindu-moment*
hindu-lunar-date	⟨*hindu-lunar-month*, *hindu-lunar-leap-month*, *hindu-lunar-day*, *hindu-lunar-leap-day*, *hindu-lunar-year*⟩	*hindu-lunar-date*
hindu-lunar-day	*hindu-lunar-date*	*hindu-lunar-day*
hindu-lunar-from-fixed	*fixed-date*	*hindu-lunar date*
hindu-lunar-leap-day	*hindu-lunar-date*	*hindu-lunar-leap-day*
hindu-lunar-leap-month	*hindu-lunar-date*	*hindu-lunar-leap-month*
hindu-lunar-longitude	*hindu-moment*	*arcminute*
hindu-lunar-month	*hindu-lunar-date*	*hindu-lunar-month*
hindu-lunar-new-year	*gregorian-year*	*fixed-date*
hindu-lunar-phase	*hindu-moment*	*arcminute*
hindu-lunar-precedes?	⟨*hindu-lunar-date*, *hindu-lunar-date*⟩	*boolean*
hindu-lunar-year	*hindu-lunar-date*	*hindu-lunar-year*
hindu-new-moon	*hindu-moment*	*hindu-moment*
hindu-sine	*arcminute*	−3438 ... 3438
hindu-sine-table	*integer*	*arcminute*
hindu-solar-date	⟨*hindu-solar-month*, *hindu-solar-day*, *hindu solar-year*⟩	*hindu-solar-date*
hindu-solar-from-fixed	*fixed-date*	*hindu-solar-date*
hindu-solar-longitude	*hindu-moment*	*arcminute*
hindu-solar-precedes?	⟨*hindu-solar-date*, *hindu-solar-date*⟩	*boolean*
hindu-sunrise	*hindu-moment*	*hindu-moment*
hindu-zodiac	*hindu-moment*	*hindu-solar-month*
independence-day	*gregorian-year*	*fixed-date*
islamic-date	⟨*islamic-month*, *islamic-day*, *islamic-year*⟩	*islamic-date*
islamic-from-fixed	*fixed-date*	*islamic-date*
islamic-in-gregorian	⟨*islamic-month*, *islamic-day*, *gregorian-year*⟩	*list-of-fixed-dates*
islamic-leap-year?	*islamic-year*	*boolean*
iso-date	⟨*iso-week*, *iso-day*, *iso-year*⟩	*iso-date*
iso-day	*iso-date*	*day-of-week*
iso-from-fixed	*fixed-date*	*iso-date*

Function	Parameter type(s)	Result type
iso-week	*iso-date*	*iso-week*
iso-year	*iso-date*	*iso-year*
jd-from-moment	*moment*	*julian-day-number*
jovian-year	*fixed-date*	1...60
julian-centuries	*moment*	*moment*
julian-date	⟨*julian-month, julian-day, julian-year*⟩	*julian-date*
julian-from-fixed	*fixed-date*	*julian-date*
julian-in-gregorian	⟨*julian-month, julian-day, gregorian-year*⟩	*list-of-fixed-dates*
julian-leap-year?	*julian-year*	*boolean*
karana	1...60	0...10
kday-after	⟨*fixed-date, weekday*⟩	*fixed-date*
kday-before	⟨*fixed-date, weekday*⟩	*fixed-date*
kday-nearest	⟨*fixed-date, weekday*⟩	*fixed-date*
kday-on-or-after	⟨*fixed-date, weekday*⟩	*fixed-date*
kday-on-or-before	⟨*fixed-date, weekday*⟩	*fixed-date*
labor-day	*gregorian-year*	*fixed-date*
last-day-of-hebrew-month	⟨*hebrew-month, hebrew-year*⟩	*hebrew-day*
last-month-of-hebrew-year	*hebrew-year*	*hebrew-month*
last-quarter-moon-at-or-before	*julian-day-number*	*julian-day-number*
local-from-apparent	*moment*	*moment*
local-from-standard	⟨*moment, minute*⟩	*moment*
local-from-universal	⟨*moment, minute*⟩	*moment*
location-offset	⟨*angle, minute*⟩	*minute*
long-heshvan?	*hebrew-year*	*boolean*
lunar-day	*hindu-moment*	*hindu-lunar-day*
lunar-day-start	⟨*hindu-moment, rational, real*⟩	*hindu-moment*
lunar-longitude	*moment*	*angle*
lunar-mansion	*fixed-date*	*positive-integer*
lunar-phase-at-or-before	⟨*phase, julian-day-number*⟩	*julian-day-number*
lunar-solar-angle	*julian-day-number*	*phase*
major-solar-term-on-or-after	*fixed-date*	*fixed-date*
mawlid-an-nabi	*gregorian-year*	*list-of-fixed-dates*
mayan-baktun	*mayan-long-count-date*	*mayan-baktun*
mayan-haab-date	⟨*mayan-haab-day, mayan-haab-month*⟩	*mayan-haab-date*
mayan-haab-day	*mayan-haab-date*	*mayan-haab-day*
mayan-haab-difference	⟨*mayan-haab-date, mayan-haab-date*⟩	*integer*
mayan-haab-from-fixed	*fixed-date*	*mayan-haab-date*
mayan-haab-month	*mayan-haab-date*	*mayan-haab-month*
mayan-haab-on-or-before	⟨*mayan-haab-date, fixed-date*⟩	*fixed-date*
mayan-haab-tzolkin-on-or-before	⟨*mayan-haab-date, mayan-tzolkin-date, fixed-date*⟩	*fixed-date* (or **bogus**)
mayan-katun	*mayan-long-count-date*	*mayan-katun*
mayan-kin	*mayan-long-count-date*	*mayan-kin*
mayan-long-count-date	⟨*mayan-baktun, mayan-katun, mayan-tun, mayan-uinal, mayan-kin*⟩	*mayan-long-count-date*
mayan-long-count-from-fixed	*fixed-date*	*mayan-long-count-date*
mayan-tun	*mayan-long-count-date*	*mayan-tun*
mayan-tzolkin-date	⟨*mayan-tzolkin-number, mayan-tzolkin-name*⟩	*mayan-tzolkin-date*
mayan-tzolkin-difference	⟨*mayan-tzolkin-date, mayan-tzolkin-date*⟩	*integer*
mayan-tzolkin-from-fixed	*fixed-date*	*mayan-tzolkin-date*
mayan-tzolkin-name	*mayan-tzolkin-date*	*mayan-tzolkin-name*
mayan-tzolkin-number	*mayan-tzolkin-date*	*mayan-tzolkin-number*
mayan-tzolkin-on-or-before	⟨*mayan-tzolkin-date, fixed-date*⟩	*fixed-date*
mayan-uinal	*mayan-long-count-date*	*mayan-uinal*
mean-position	⟨*hindu-moment, rational*⟩	*arcminute*
memorial-day	*gregorian-year*	*fixed-date*
mesha-samkranti	*gregorian-year*	*moment*
minor-solar-term-on-or-after	*fixed-date*	*fixed-date*
modified-french-from-fixed	*fixed-date*	*french-year*
modified-french-leap-year?	*french-year*	*boolean*
moment-from-jd	*julian-day-number*	*moment*
naw-ruz	*gregorian-year*	*fixed-date*

Function	Parameter type(s)	Result type
new-moon-before	*julian-day-number*	*julian-day-number*
new-moon-at-or-after	*julian-day-number*	*julian-day-number*
new-moon-at-or-before	*julian-day-number*	*julian-day-number*
new-moon-time	*integer*	*julian-day-number*
nicaean-rule-easter	*julian-year*	*fixed-date*
no-major-solar-term?	*fixed-date*	*boolean*
nth-kday	⟨*integer, weekday, fixed-date*⟩	*fixed-date*
nutation	*julian-centuries*	*radian*
old-hindu-lunar-date	⟨*old-hindu-lunar-month, old-hindu-lunar-leap, old-hindu-lunar-day, old-hindu-lunar-year*⟩	*old-hindu-lunar-date*
old-hindu-lunar-day	*old-hindu-lunar-date*	*old-hindu-lunar-day*
old-hindu-lunar-from-fixed	*fixed-date*	*old-hindu-lunar-date*
old-hindu-lunar-leap	*old-hindu-lunar-date*	*old-hindu-lunar-leap*
old-hindu-lunar-leap-year?	*old-hindu-lunar-year*	*boolean*
old-hindu-lunar-month	*old-hindu-lunar-date*	*old-hindu-lunar-month*
old-hindu-lunar-year	*old-hindu-lunar-date*	*old-hindu-lunar-year*
old-hindu-solar-from-fixed	*fixed-date*	*hindu-solar-date*
omer	*fixed-date*	*omer-count* (or **bogus**)
passover	*gregorian-year*	*fixed-date*
pentecost	*gregorian-year*	*fixed-date*
persian-date	⟨*persian-month, persian-day, persian-year*⟩	*persian-date*
persian-from-fixed	*fixed-date*	*persian-date*
persian-leap-year?	*persian-year*	*boolean*
persian-year-from-fixed	*fixed-date*	*persian-year*
poly	⟨*real, list-of-reals*⟩	*real*
prior-leap-month?	⟨*fixed-date, fixed-date*⟩	*boolean*
purim	*gregorian-year*	*fixed-date*
quotient	⟨*real, non-zero-real*⟩	*integer*
radians-to-degrees	*radian*	*angle*
rising-sign	*hindu-moment*	*integer*
sacred-wednesdays	*gregorian-year*	*list-of-fixed-dates*
sacred-wednesdays-in-gregorian	*gregorian-year*	*list-of-fixed-dates*
samkranti	⟨*gregorian-year, hindu-solar-month*⟩	*moment*
yom-ha-zikaron	*gregorian-year*	*fixed-date*
sh-ela	*gregorian-year*	*fixed-date*
short-kislev?	*hebrew-year*	*boolean*
sidereal-from-jd	*julian-day-number*	*julian-day-number*
sigma	⟨*list-of-pairs, list-of-reals→real*⟩	*real*
sin-degrees	*angle*	*amplitude*
solar-longitude	*julian-day-number*	*angle*
solar-moment	⟨*fixed-date, angle, angle, real*⟩	*moment*
solar-sidereal-difference	*hindu-moment*	*arcminute*
standard-day	*standard-date*	*standard-day*
standard-from-local	⟨*moment, minute*⟩	*moment*
standard-month	*standard-date*	*standard-month*
standard-year	*standard-date*	*standard-year*
sum	⟨*integer→real*, —, *integer, integer→boolean*⟩	*real*
sunrise	⟨*fixed-date, angle, angle*⟩	*moment*
sunrise-at-ujjain	*hindu-moment*	*hindu-moment*
sunset	⟨*fixed-date, angle, angle*⟩	*moment*
ta-anith-esther	*gregorian-year*	*fixed-date*
tangent-degrees	*angle*	*real*
time-from-moment	*moment*	⟨*hour, minute, second*⟩
time-of-day	⟨*hour, minute, second*⟩	*moment*
tisha-b-av	*gregorian-year*	*fixed-date*
tropical-longitude	*hindu-moment*	*arcminute*
true-position	⟨*hindu-moment, rational, positive-integer, rational, non-negative-integer*⟩	*arcminute*
universal-from-ephemeris	*julian-day-number*	*julian-day-number*

Function	Parameter type(s)	Result type
universal-from-local	⟨*moment*, *minute*⟩	*moment*
yahrzeit	⟨*hebrew-date*, *hebrew-year*⟩	*fixed-date*
yoga	*hindu-moment*	1 . . . 27
yom-kippur	*gregorian-year*	*fixed-date*

A.3 Constant Types and Values

Constant	Type	Value
april	*standard-month*	4
arya-jovian-period	*rational*	131493125/30352
arya-lunar-day	*rational*	26298625/26716668
arya-lunar-month	*rational*	131493125/4452778
arya-sidereal-year	*rational*	210389/576
arya-solar-month	*rational*	210389/6912
august	*standard-month*	8
bahai-epoch	*fixed-date*	673222
bogus	*string*	"bogus"
chinese-epoch	*fixed-date*	−963099
coptic-epoch	*fixed-date*	103605
december	*standard-month*	12
ethiopic-epoch	*fixed-date*	2430
false	*boolean*	false
february	*standard-month*	2
first	*integer*	1
first-quarter	*phase*	90
french-epoch	*fixed-date*	654415
french-time-zone	*rational*	187/20
friday	*weekday*	5
full	*phase*	180
gregorian-epoch	*fixed-date*	1
hebrew-epoch	*fixed-date*	−1373427
hindu-anomalistic-month	*rational*	1577917828/57265137
hindu-anomalistic-year	*rational*	1577917828000/4319999613
hindu-creation	*integer*	714402296627
hindu-epoch	*fixed-date*	−1132959
hindu-lunar-era	*standard-year*	3044
hindu-sidereal-month	*rational*	394479457/14438334
hindu-sidereal-year	*rational*	394479457/1080000
hindu-solar-era	*standard-year*	3179
hindu-synodic-month	*rational*	394479457/13358334
islamic-epoch	*fixed-date*	227015
j2000	*julian-day-number*	2451545.0
january	*standard-month*	1
jd-start	*moment*	−1721424.5
julian-epoch	*fixed-date*	−1
july	*standard-month*	7
june	*standard-month*	6
last	*integer*	−1
last-quarter	*phase*	270
march	*standard-month*	3
may	*standard-month*	5
mayan-epoch	*fixed-date*	−1137142
mayan-haab-at-epoch	*mayan-haab-date*	⟨8, 18⟩
mayan-tzolkin-at-epoch	*mayan-tzolkin-date*	⟨4, 20⟩
mean-synodic-month	*real*	29.530588853
mean-tropical-year	*real*	365.242199
monday	*weekday*	1

Constant	Type	Value
new	*phase*	0
november	*standard-month*	11
october	*standard-month*	10
persian-epoch	*fixed-date*	226896
pi	*real*	3.141592653589793
saturday	*weekday*	6
september	*standard-month*	9
sunday	*weekday*	0
thursday	*weekday*	4
tuesday	*weekday*	2
wednesday	*weekday*	3

Astronomical clock, designed and made in Norway by Rasmus Sornes between 1958 and 1964. It computes sidereal time, apparent solar time, mean solar time, Gregorian date (taking the leap rule fully into account), solar and lunar eclipses, precession, and the positions of all planets. (Courtesy of The Time Museum, Rockford, IL.)

Appendix B

Lisp Implementation

> It has been often said that a person does not really understand something until he teaches it to someone else. Actually a person does not *really* understand something until he can teach it to a *computer*, i.e., express it as an algorithm.
>
> —Donald E. Knuth: "Computer Science and its Relation to Mathematics," *American Mathematical Monthly*, volume 81, p. 327 (1974)

This appendix contains the complete Common Lisp implementation of the calendar functions described in the text. The functions in the text were automatically typeset from the definitions in this appendix. We will gladly provide these Lisp functions in electronic form to those who agree to the terms of the License Agreements and Limited Warranty on page xxi of this book and accompanying the electronic version of the code. Send an empty electronic mail message to `reingold@cs.uiuc.edu` with the subject line containing precisely the phrase `send-cal`; your message will be answered automatically. The code (and errata for this book) are also available over the World Wide Web at

`http://emr.cs.uiuc.edu/home/reingold/calendar-book/index.html`

Please bear in mind the limits of the License, that the copyright on this book includes the code, and that a patent is pending on certain related program elements and their output. *Also please keep in mind that if the result of any calculation is critical, it should be verified by independent means.*

For licensing information about nonpersonal and other uses, contact the authors at the electronic mail address above. The code is distributed in the hope that it may be useful, but without any warranty as to the accuracy of its output and with liability limited to return of the price of this book, which restrictions are set forth on page xxi.

B.1 Lisp Preliminaries

For readers unfamiliar with Lisp, this section provides the bare necessities. A complete description can be found in [1].

All functions in Lisp are written in prefix notation. If `f` is a defined function, then

```
(f e0 e1 e2 ... en)
```

applies `f` to the $n+1$ arguments `e0`, `e1`, `e2`, ..., `en`. Thus, for example, + adds a list of numbers:

```
(+ 1 -2 3)
```

adds the three numbers and returns the value 2. The Lisp functions `-`, `*`, and `/` work similarly, to subtract, multiply, and divide, respectively, a list of numbers. In a similar fashion, <= ($\leq$) checks that the three numbers are in nondecreasing order and yields true (`t` in Lisp) if the relations hold. For instance,

```
(<= 1 2 3)
```

evaluates to `t`. The Lisp functions =, /= ($\neq$), <, >, and >= ($\geq$) are similar.

Lists are Lisp's main data structure. To construct a list `(e0 e1 e2 ... en)` the expression

```
(list e0 e1 e2 ... en)
```

is used. The function `nth`, used as `(nth i l)`, extracts the ith element of the list `l`, indexing from zero; the predicate `member`, used as `(member x l)`, tests if `x` is an element of `l`. To get the first (indexed zero), second, third, fourth, or fifth elements of a list, we use the functions `first`, `second`, `third`, `fourth`, and `fifth`, respectively. The empty list is represented by `nil`.

Constants are defined with the `defconstant` command, which has the syntax

```
(defconstant constant-name
   expression)
```

For example,

```
(defconstant sunday
  ;; TYPE day-of-week
  ;; Residue class for Sunday.
  0)
```

```
(defconstant monday
  ;; TYPE day-of-week
  ;; Residue class for Monday.
  (1+ sunday))
```

```
(defconstant tuesday
  ;; TYPE day-of-week
  ;; Residue class for Tuesday.
  (+ sunday 2))
```

```
(defconstant wednesday
  ;; TYPE day-of-week
  ;; Residue class for Wednesday.
  (+ sunday 3))
```

```
(defconstant thursday
  ;; TYPE day-of-week
  ;; Residue class for Thursday.
  (+ sunday 4))
```

```
(defconstant friday
  ;; TYPE day-of-week
  ;; Residue class for Friday.
  (+ sunday 5))
```

```
(defconstant saturday
  ;; TYPE day-of-week
  ;; Residue class for Saturday.
  (+ sunday 6))
```

The function `1+` increments a number by one (the similar function `1-` decrements by one).

Notice that semicolons mark the start of comments. "Type" information is given in comments for each of these functions. Although Common Lisp has its own system of type declarations, we prefer the simpler, untyped Lisp but annotate each function and constant to aid the reader in translating our code into a typed language. The base types are defined in Table A.1 beginning on page 221.

To distinguish in the code between empty lists (`nil`) and the truth value "false," we define

```
(defconstant false
  ;; TYPE boolean
  ;; Constant representing false.
  nil)
```

We also use a constant to signify an error value:

```
(defconstant bogus
  ;; TYPE string
  ;; Used to denote nonexistent dates.
  "bogus")
```

Functions are defined using the `defun` command, which has the following syntax:

```
(defun function-name (param1 ... paramn)
   expression)
```

For example, we compute the day of the week of an R.D. date (page 17) with

```
(defun day-of-week-from-fixed (date)
  ;; TYPE fixed-date -> day-of-week
  ;; The residue class of the day of the week of date.
  (mod date 7))
```

and we implement julian day calculations (equations 1.2–1.5) by writing

```
(defconstant jd-start
  ;; TYPE moment
  ;; Fixed time of start of the julian day number.
  -1721424.5)
```

```
(defun moment-from-jd (jd)
  ;; TYPE julian-day-number -> moment
  ;; Fixed time of astronomical (julian) day number jd.
  (+ jd jd-start))
```

```
(defun jd-from-moment (moment)
  ;; TYPE moment -> julian-day-number
  ;; Astronomical (julian) day number of fixed moment moment.
  (- moment jd-start))
```

```
(defun fixed-from-jd (jd)
  ;; TYPE julian-day-number -> fixed-date
  ;; Fixed date of astronomical (julian) day number jd.
  (floor (moment-from-jd jd)))
```

As another example of a function definition, we can define a function (inconveniently named in Common Lisp) to return the (truncated) integer quotient of two integers, $\lfloor m/n \rfloor$:

```
(defun quotient (m n)
  ;; TYPE (real non-zero-real) -> integer
  ;; Whole part of m/n.
  (floor m n))
```

The `floor` function can also be called with one argument:

```
(floor x)
```

is $\lfloor x \rfloor$, the greatest integer less than or equal to x.

As a final example of a function definition, note that the Common Lisp function `mod` *always returns a nonnegative value for a positive divisor*; we use this property occasionally, but we also need a function like `mod`, with its values adjusted so that the modulus of a multiple of the divisor is the divisor itself rather than 0. To define this function, denoted "amod" in the text, we write

```
(defun adjusted-mod (m n)
  ;; TYPE (integer positive-integer) -> positive-integer
  ;; Positive remainder of m/n with n instead of 0.
  (1+ (mod (1- m) n)))
```

For convenience in expressing our calendar functions in Lisp, we introduce a macro to compute sums (the few instances in which we use macros and not functions avoid the issue of passing functions to functions). The expression

```
(sum f i k p)
```

computes

$$\sum_{i \geq k,\, p(i)} f(i);$$

that is, the expression $f(i)$ is summed for all $i = k, k+1, \ldots$, continuing only as long as the condition $p(i)$ holds. The sum is 0 if $p(k)$ is false. The (mysterious-looking) Common Lisp definition of `sum` is as follows:

```
(defmacro sum (expression index initial condition)
  ;; TYPE ((integer->real) * integer (integer->boolean))
  ;; TYPE -> real
  ;; Sum expression for index = initial and successive
  ;; integers, as long as condition holds.
  (let* ((temp (gensym)))
    '(do ((,temp 0 (+ ,temp ,expression))
          (,index ,initial (1+ ,index)))
         ((not ,condition) ,temp))))
```

The Common Lisp construct `let*` defines a sequence of constants (possibly in terms of previously defined constants) and ends with an expression whose value is returned by the construct.

A summation macro `sigma` and a summation function **poly** for polynomials are used in the astronomical code:

```
(defmacro sigma (list body)
  ;; TYPE (list-of-pairs (list-of-reals->real))
  ;; TYPE -> real
  ;; list is of the form ((i1 l1)..(in ln)).
  ;; Sum of body for indices i1..in
  ;; running simultaneously thru lists l1..ln.
  '(apply '+ (mapcar (function (lambda
                                   ,(mapcar 'car list)
                                   ,body))
                     ,@(mapcar 'cadr list))))
```

```
(defun poly (x a)
  ;; TYPE (real list-of-reals) -> real
  ;; Sum powers of x with coefficients (from order 0 up)
  ;; in list a.
  (if (equal a nil)
      0
    (+ (first a) (* x (poly x (cdr a))))))
```

The function `if` has three arguments: a Boolean condition, a then-expression, and an else-expression. The `cond` statement lists a sequence of tests and values, like a generalized case statement.

We use binary search—see equation (12.21)—expressed as the macro **binary-search**:

```
(defmacro binary-search (l lo h hi x test end)
  ;; TYPE (* real * real * (real->boolean)
  ;; TYPE  ((real real)->boolean)) -> real
  ;; Bisection search for x in lo..hi such that end holds.
  ;; test determines when to go left.
  (let* ((left (gensym)))
    '(do* ((,x false (/ (+ ,h ,l) 2))
           (,left false ,test)
           (,l ,lo (if ,left ,l ,x))
           (,h ,hi (if ,left ,x ,h)))
          (,end (/ (+ ,h ,l) 2)))))
```

B.2 Basic Code

To extract a particular component from a date, we use, when necessary, the functions **standard-month**, **standard-day**, and **standard-year**. For example:

```
(defun standard-month (date)
  ;; TYPE standard-date -> standard-month
  ;; Month field of date = (month day year).
  (first date))
```

```
(defun standard-day (date)
  ;; TYPE standard-date -> standard-day
  ;; Day field of date = (month day year).
  (second date))
```

```
(defun standard-year (date)
  ;; TYPE standard-date -> standard-year
  ;; Year field of date = (month day year).
  (third date))
```

Such constructors and selectors could be more efficiently defined as macros.

We also have

```
(defun time-of-day (hour minute second)
  ;; TYPE (hour minute second) -> moment
  (list hour minute second))
```

B.3 Cycles of Days

```
(defun kday-on-or-before (date k)
  ;; TYPE (fixed-date weekday) -> fixed-date
  ;; Fixed date of the k-day on or before fixed date.
  ;; k=0 means Sunday, k=1 means Monday, and so on.
  (- date (day-of-week-from-fixed (- date k))))
```

```
(defun kday-on-or-after (date k)
  ;; TYPE (fixed-date weekday) -> fixed-date
  ;; Fixed date of the k-day on or after fixed date.
  ;; k=0 means Sunday, k=1 means Monday, and so on.
  (kday-on-or-before (+ date 6) k))
```

```
(defun kday-nearest (date k)
  ;; TYPE (fixed-date weekday) -> fixed-date
  ;; Fixed date of the k-day nearest fixed date.  k=0
  ;; means Sunday, k=1 means Monday, and so on.
  (kday-on-or-before (+ date 3) k))
```

```
(defun kday-after (date k)
  ;; TYPE (fixed-date weekday) -> fixed-date
  ;; Fixed date of the k-day after fixed date.  k=0
  ;; means Sunday, k=1 means Monday, and so on.
  (kday-on-or-before (+ date 7) k))
```

```
(defun kday-before (date k)
  ;; TYPE (fixed-date weekday) -> fixed-date
  ;; Fixed date of the k-day before fixed date.  k=0
  ;; means Sunday, k=1 means Monday, and so on.
  (kday-on-or-before (1- date) k))
```

B.4 The Gregorian Calendar

```
(defun gregorian-date (month day year)
  ;; TYPE (gregorian-month gregorian-day gregorian-year)
  ;; TYPE -> gregorian-date
  (list month day year))
```

```
(defconstant gregorian-epoch
  ;; TYPE fixed-date
  ;; Fixed date of start of the (proleptic) Gregorian
  ;; calendar.
  1)
```

```
(defconstant january
  ;; TYPE standard-month
  ;; January on Julian/Gregorian calendar.
  1)
```

```
(defconstant february
  ;; TYPE standard-month
  ;; February on Julian/Gregorian calendar.
  (1+ january))
```

```
(defconstant march
  ;; TYPE standard-month
  ;; March on Julian/Gregorian calendar.
  (+ january 2))
```

```
(defconstant april
  ;; TYPE standard-month
  ;; April on Julian/Gregorian calendar.
  (+ january 3))
```

```
(defconstant may
  ;; TYPE standard-month
  ;; May on Julian/Gregorian calendar.
  (+ january 4))
```

```
(defconstant june
  ;; TYPE standard-month
  ;; June on Julian/Gregorian calendar.
  (+ january 5))
```

```
(defconstant july
  ;; TYPE standard-month
  ;; July on Julian/Gregorian calendar.
  (+ january 6))
```

```
(defconstant august
  ;; TYPE standard-month
  ;; August on Julian/Gregorian calendar.
  (+ january 7))
```

```
(defconstant september
  ;; TYPE standard-month
  ;; September on Julian/Gregorian calendar.
  (+ january 8))
```

```
(defconstant october
  ;; TYPE standard-month
  ;; October on Julian/Gregorian calendar.
  (+ january 9))
```

```
(defconstant november
  ;; TYPE standard-month
  ;; November on Julian/Gregorian calendar.
  (+ january 10))
```

```
(defconstant december
  ;; TYPE standard-month
  ;; December on Julian/Gregorian calendar.
  (+ january 11))
```

```
(defun gregorian-leap-year? (g-year)
  ;; TYPE gregorian-year -> boolean
  ;; True if year is a leap year on the Gregorian calendar.
  (and (= (mod g-year 4) 0)
       (not (member (mod g-year 400)
                    (list 100 200 300)))))
```

```
(defun fixed-from-gregorian (g-date)
  ;; TYPE gregorian-date -> fixed-date
  ;; Fixed date equivalent to the Gregorian date.
  (let* ((month (standard-month g-date))
         (day (standard-day g-date))
         (year (standard-year g-date)))
      (+ (1- gregorian-epoch); Days before start of calendar
         (* 365 (1- year)); Ordinary days since epoch
         (quotient (1- year)
                   4); Julian leap days since epoch...
         (-          ; ...minus century years since epoch...
          (quotient (1- year) 100))
         (quotient   ; ...plus years since epoch divisible...
          (1- year) 400)  ; ...by 400.
         (quotient        ; Days in prior months this year...
          (- (* 367 month) 362); ...assuming 30-day Feb
          12)
         (if (<= month 2) ; Correct for 28- or 29-day Feb
             0
           (if (gregorian-leap-year? year)
               -1
             -2))
         day)))          ; Days so far this month.
```

```
(defun gregorian-year-from-fixed (date)
  ;; TYPE fixed-date -> gregorian-year
  ;; Gregorian year corresponding to the fixed date.
  (let* ((d0        ; Prior days.
          (- date gregorian-epoch))
         (n400      ; Completed 400-year cycles.
          (quotient d0 146097))
         (d1        ; Prior days not in n400.
          (mod d0 146097))
         (n100      ; 100-year cycles not in n400.
          (quotient d1 36524))
         (d2        ; Prior days not in n400 or n100.
          (mod d1 36524))
         (n4        ; 4-year cycles not in n400 or n100.
          (quotient d2 1461))
         (d3        ; Prior days not in n400, n100, or n4.
          (mod d2 1461))
         (n1        ; Years not in n400, n100, or n4.
          (quotient d3 365))
         (d4        ; Prior days not in n400, n100, n4, or n1.
          (1+ (mod d3 365)))
         (year (+ (* 400 n400)
```

```
                 (* 100 n100)
                 (* 4 n4)
                 n1)))
    (if (or (= n100 4) (= n1 4))
        year      ; Date is December 31 in year.
      (1+ year)))); Date is ordinal day (1+ d4) in (1+ year).
```

```
(defun gregorian-from-fixed (date)
  ;; TYPE fixed-date -> gregorian-date
  ;; Gregorian (month day year) corresponding to fixed date.
  (let* ((year (gregorian-year-from-fixed date))
         (prior-days; This year
          (- date (fixed-from-gregorian
                   (gregorian-date january 1 year))))
         (correction; To simulate a 30-day Feb
          (if (< date (fixed-from-gregorian
                       (gregorian-date march 1 year)))
              0
            (if (gregorian-leap-year? year)
                1
              2)))
         (month     ; Assuming a 30-day Feb
          (quotient
           (+ (* 12 (+ prior-days correction)) 373)
           367))
         (day       ; Calculate the day by subtraction.
          (1+ (- date
                 (fixed-from-gregorian
                  (gregorian-date month 1 year))))))
    (gregorian-date month day year)))
```

```
(defun gregorian-date-difference (g-date1 g-date2)
  ;; TYPE (gregorian-date gregorian-date) -> integer
  ;; Number of days from Gregorian date g-date1 until g-date2.
  (- (fixed-from-gregorian g-date2)
     (fixed-from-gregorian g-date1)))
```

```
(defun day-number (g-date)
  ;; TYPE gregorian-date -> non-negative-integer
  ;; Day number in year of Gregorian date g-date.
  (gregorian-date-difference
   (gregorian-date december 31 (1- (standard-year g-date)))
   g-date))
```

```
(defun days-remaining (g-date)
  ;; TYPE gregorian-date -> non-negative-integer
  ;; Days remaining in year after Gregorian date g-date.
  (gregorian-date-difference
   g-date
   (gregorian-date december 31 (standard-year g-date))))
```

```
(defun independence-day (year)
  ;; TYPE gregorian-year -> fixed-date
  ;; Fixed date of American Independence Day in
  ;; Gregorian year.
  (fixed-from-gregorian (gregorian-date july 4 year)))
```

```
(defun nth-kday (n k date)
  ;; TYPE (integer weekday fixed-date) -> fixed-date
  ;; Fixed date of n-th k-day after Gregorian date.  If
  ;; n>0, return the n-th k-day on or after date.
  ;; If n<0, return the n-th k-day on or before date.
```

```
  ;; A k-day of 0 means Sunday, 1 means Monday, and so on.
  (if (> n 0)
      (+ (* 7 n)
         (kday-before (fixed-from-gregorian date) k))
    (+ (* 7 n)
       (kday-after (fixed-from-gregorian date) k))))
```

```
(defconstant first
  ;; TYPE integer
  ;; Index for selecting a k-day.
  1)
```

```
(defconstant last
  ;; TYPE integer
  ;; Index for selecting a k-day.
  -1)
```

```
(defun labor-day (g-year)
  ;; TYPE gregorian-year -> fixed-date
  ;; Fixed date of American Labor Day in Gregorian
  ;; year--the first Monday in September.
  (nth-kday first monday (gregorian-date september 1 g-year)))
```

```
(defun memorial-day (g-year)
  ;; TYPE gregorian-year -> fixed-date
  ;; Fixed date of American Memorial Day in Gregorian
  ;; year--the last Monday in May.
  (nth-kday last monday (gregorian-date may 31 g-year)))
```

```
(defun election-day (g-year)
  ;; TYPE gregorian-year -> fixed-date
  ;; Fixed date of American Election Day in Gregorian
  ;; year--the Tuesday after the first Monday in November.
  (nth-kday first tuesday (gregorian-date november 2 g-year)))
```

```
(defun daylight-savings-start (g-year)
  ;; TYPE gregorian-year -> fixed-date
  ;; Fixed date of the start of American daylight savings
  ;; time in Gregorian year--the first Sunday in April.
  (nth-kday first sunday (gregorian-date april 1 g-year)))
```

```
(defun daylight-savings-end (g-year)
  ;; TYPE gregorian-year -> fixed-date
  ;; Fixed date of the end of American daylight savings time
  ;; in Gregorian year--the last Sunday in October.
  (nth-kday last sunday (gregorian-date october 31 g-year)))
```

```
(defun christmas (g-year)
  ;; TYPE gregorian-year -> fixed-date
  ;; Fixed date of Christmas in Gregorian year.
  (fixed-from-gregorian (gregorian-date december 25 g-year)))
```

```
(defun advent (g-year)
  ;; TYPE gregorian-year -> fixed-date
  ;; Fixed date of Advent in Gregorian year.
  (kday-nearest (fixed-from-gregorian
                 (gregorian-date november 30 g-year))
                sunday))
```

```
(defun epiphany (g-year)
  ;; TYPE gregorian-year -> fixed-date
  ;; Fixed date of Epiphany in Gregorian year.
  (+ 12 (christmas (1- g-year))))
```

B.5 The ISO Calendar

```
(defun iso-date (week day year)
  ;; TYPE (iso-week iso-day iso-year) -> iso-date
  (list week day year))
```

```
(defun iso-week (date)
  ;; TYPE iso-date -> iso-week
  (first date))
```

```
(defun iso-day (date)
  ;; TYPE iso-date -> day-of-week
  (second date))
```

```
(defun iso-year (date)
  ;; TYPE iso-date -> iso-year
  (third date))
```

```
(defun fixed-from-iso (i-date)
  ;; TYPE iso-date -> fixed-date
  ;; Fixed date equivalent to ISO (week day year).
  (let* ((week (iso-week i-date))
         (day (iso-day i-date))
         (year (iso-year i-date)))
    ;; Add fixed date of Sunday preceding date plus day
    ;; in week.
    (+ (nth-kday
        week sunday
        (gregorian-date december 28 (1- year))) day)))
```

```
(defun iso-from-fixed (date)
  ;; TYPE fixed-date -> iso-date
  ;; ISO (week day year) corresponding to the fixed date.
  (let* ((approx ; Year may be one too small.
          (gregorian-year-from-fixed (- date 3)))
         (year (if (>= date
                       (fixed-from-iso
                        (iso-date 1 1 (1+ approx))))
                   (1+ approx)
                 approx))
         (week (1+ (quotient
                    (- date
                       (fixed-from-iso (iso-date 1 1 year)))
                    7)))
         (day (adjusted-mod date 7)))
    (iso-date week day year)))
```

B.6 The Julian Calendar

In the Lisp code we use $-n$ for year n B.C.E. (Julian):

```
(defun bce (n)
  ;; TYPE standard-year -> julian-year
  ;; Negative value to indicate a BCE Julian year.
  (- n))
```

and positive numbers for C.E. (Julian) years:

```
(defun ce (n)
  ;; TYPE standard-year -> julian-year
  ;; Positive value to indicate a CE Julian year.
  n)
```

```
(defun julian-date (month day year)
  ;; TYPE (julian-month julian-day julian-year)
  ;; TYPE -> julian-date
  (list month day year))
```

```
(defun julian-leap-year? (j-year)
  ;; TYPE julian-year -> boolean
  ;; True if year is a leap year on the Julian calendar.
  (= (mod j-year 4) (if (> j-year 0) 0 3)))
```

```
(defconstant julian-epoch
  ;; TYPE fixed-date
  ;; Fixed date of start of the Julian calendar.
  (fixed-from-gregorian (gregorian-date december 30 0)))
```

```
(defun fixed-from-julian (j-date)
  ;; TYPE julian-date -> fixed-date
  ;; Fixed date equivalent to the Julian date.
  (let* ((month (standard-month j-date))
         (day (standard-day j-date))
         (year (standard-year j-date))
         (y (if (< year 0)
                (1+ year) ; No year zero
              year)))
    (+ (1- julian-epoch)    ; Days before start of calendar
       (* 365 (1- y))      ; Ordinary days since epoch.
       (quotient (1- y) 4); Leap days since epoch...
       (quotient           ; Days in prior months this year...
        (- (* 367 month) 362); ...assuming 30-day Feb
        12)
       (if (<= month 2)    ; Correct for 28- or 29-day Feb
           0
         (if (julian-leap-year? year)
             -1
           -2))
       day)))              ; Days so far this month.
```

```
(defun julian-from-fixed (date)
  ;; TYPE fixed-date -> julian-date
  ;; Julian (month day year) corresponding to fixed date.
  (let* ((approx     ; Nominal year.
          (quotient (+ (* 4 (- date julian-epoch)) 1464)
                    1461))
         (year (if (<= approx 0)
                   (1- approx) ; No year 0.
                 approx))
         (prior-days; This year
          (- date (fixed-from-julian
                   (julian-date january 1 year))))
         (correction; To simulate a 30-day Feb
          (if (< date (fixed-from-julian
                       (julian-date march 1 year)))
              0
            (if (julian-leap-year? year)
                1
              2)))
         (month     ; Assuming a 30-day Feb
          (quotient
           (+ (* 12 (+ prior-days correction)) 373)
           367))
         (day       ; Calculate the day by subtraction.
          (1+ (- date
                 (fixed-from-julian
                  (julian-date month 1 year))))))
    (julian-date month day year)))
```

```
(defun julian-in-gregorian (j-month j-day g-year)
  ;; TYPE (julian-month julian-day gregorian-year)
  ;; TYPE -> list-of-fixed-dates
  ;; List of the fixed dates of Julian month, day
  ;; that occur in Gregorian year.
  (let* ((jan1 (fixed-from-gregorian
                 (gregorian-date january 1 g-year)))
         (dec31 (fixed-from-gregorian
                  (gregorian-date december 31 g-year)))
         (y (standard-year (julian-from-fixed jan1)))
         ;; The possible occurrences in one year are
         (date1 (fixed-from-julian
                  (julian-date j-month j-day y)))
         (date2 (fixed-from-julian
                  (julian-date j-month j-day (1+ y)))))
    (append
     (if ; date1 occurs in current year
         (<= jan1 date1 dec31)
         ;; Then that date; otherwise, none
         (list date1) nil)
     (if ; date2 occurs in current year
         (<= jan1 date2 dec31)
         ;; Then that date; otherwise, none
         (list date2) nil))))
```

In languages like Lisp that allow functions as parameters, one could write a generic version of this function to collect holidays of any given calendar and pass `fixed-from-julian` to it as an additional parameter. We have deliberately avoided this and similar advanced language features, in the interests of portability.

```
(defun eastern-orthodox-christmas (g-year)
  ;; TYPE gregorian-year -> list-of-fixed-dates
  ;; List of zero or one fixed dates of Eastern Orthodox
  ;; Christmas in Gregorian year.
  (julian-in-gregorian december 25 g-year))
```

```
(defun nicaean-rule-easter (j-year)
  ;; TYPE julian-year -> fixed-date
  ;; Fixed date of Easter in positive Julian year, according
  ;; to the rule of the Council of Nicaea.
  (let* ((shifted-epact ; Age of moon for April 5.
          (mod (+ 14 (* 11 (mod j year 19)))
               30))
         (paschal-moon  ; Day after full moon on
                        ; or after March 21.
          (- (fixed-from-julian (julian-date april 19 j-year))
             shifted-epact)))
    ;; Return the Sunday following the Paschal moon
    (kday-after paschal-moon sunday)))
```

```
(defun easter (g-year)
  ;; TYPE gregorian-year -> fixed-date
  ;; Fixed date of Easter in Gregorian year.
  (let* ((century (1+ (quotient g-year 100)))
         (shifted-epact        ; Age of moon for April 5...
          (mod
           (+ 14 (* 11 (mod g-year 19));   ...by Nicaean rule
              (- ;...corrected for the Gregorian century rule
               (quotient (* 3 century) 4))
              (quotient; ...corrected for Metonic
                       ; cycle inaccuracy.
               (+ 5 (* 8 century)) 25))
```

```
           30))
         (adjusted-epact       ;  Adjust for 29.5 day month.
          (if (or (= shifted-epact 0)
                  (and (= shifted-epact 1)
                       (< 10 (mod g-year 19))))
              (1+ shifted-epact)
            shifted-epact))
         (paschal-moon; Day after full moon on
                      ; or after March 21.
          (- (fixed-from-gregorian
              (gregorian-date april 19 g-year))
             adjusted-epact)))
    ;; Return the Sunday following the Paschal moon.
    (kday-after paschal-moon sunday)))
```

```
(defun pentecost (g-year)
  ;; TYPE gregorian-year -> fixed-date
  ;; Fixed date of Pentecost in Gregorian year.
  (+ (easter g-year) 49))
```

B.7 The Coptic and Ethiopic Calendars

```
(defun coptic-date (month day year)
  ;; TYPE (coptic-month coptic-day coptic-year) -> coptic-date
  (list month day year))
```

```
(defconstant coptic-epoch
  ;; TYPE fixed-date
  ;; Fixed date of start of the Coptic calendar.
  (fixed-from-julian (julian-date august 29 (ce 284))))
```

```
(defun coptic-leap-year? (c-year)
  ;; TYPE coptic-year -> boolean
  ;; True if year is a leap year on the Coptic calendar.
  (= (mod c-year 4) 3))
```

```
(defun fixed-from-coptic (c-date)
  ;; TYPE coptic-date -> fixed-date
  ;; Fixed date of Coptic date.
  (let* ((month (standard-month c-date))
         (day (standard-day c-date))
         (year (standard-year c-date)))
    (+ coptic-epoch -1  ; Days before start of calendar
       (* 365 (1- year)); Ordinary days in prior years
       (quotient year 4); Leap days in prior years
       (* 30 (1- month)); Days in prior months this year
       day)))           ; Days so far this month
```

```
(defun coptic-from-fixed (date)
  ;; TYPE fixed-date -> coptic-date
  ;; Coptic equivalent of fixed date.
  (let* ((year ; Calculate the year by cycle-of-years formula
          (quotient (+ (* 4 (- date coptic-epoch)) 1463)
                    1461))
         (month; Calculate the month by division.
          (1+ (quotient
               (- date (fixed-from-coptic
                        (coptic-date 1 1 year)))
               30)))
         (day  ; Calculate the day by subtraction.
          (- date -1
             (fixed-from-coptic
              (coptic-date month 1 year)))))
    (coptic-date month day year)))
```

```
(defun ethiopic-date (month day year)
  ;; TYPE (ethiopic-month ethiopic-day ethiopic-year)
  ;; TYPE -> ethiopic-date
  (list month day year))
```

```
(defconstant ethiopic-epoch
  ;; TYPE fixed-date
  ;; Fixed date of start of the Ethiopic calendar.
  (fixed-from-julian (julian-date august 29 (ce 7))))
```

```
(defun fixed-from-ethiopic (e-date)
  ;; TYPE ethiopic-date -> fixed-date
  ;; Fixed date of Ethiopic date.
  (let* ((month (standard-month e-date))
         (day (standard-day e-date))
         (year (standard-year e-date)))
    (+ ethiopic-epoch
       (- (fixed-from-coptic
           (coptic-date month day year)) coptic-epoch))))
```

```
(defun ethiopic-from-fixed (date)
  ;; TYPE fixed-date -> ethiopic-date
  ;; Ethiopic equivalent of fixed date.
  (coptic-from-fixed
   (+ date (- coptic-epoch ethiopic-epoch))))
```

```
(defun coptic-in-gregorian (c-month c-day g-year)
  ;; TYPE (coptic-month coptic-day gregorian-year)
  ;; TYPE -> list-of-fixed-dates
  ;; List of the fixed dates of Coptic month, day
  ;; that occur in Gregorian year.
  (let* ((jan1 (fixed-from-gregorian
                (gregorian-date january 1 g-year)))
         (dec31 (fixed-from-gregorian
                 (gregorian-date december 31 g-year)))
         (y (standard-year (coptic-from-fixed jan1)))
         ;; The possible occurrences in one year are
         (date1 (fixed-from-coptic
                 (coptic-date c-month c-day y)))
         (date2 (fixed-from-coptic
                 (coptic-date c-month c-day (1+ y)))))
    (append
     (if ; date1 occurs in current year
         (<= jan1 date1 dec31)
         ;; Then that date; otherwise, none
         (list date1) nil)
     (if ; date2 occurs in current year
         (<= jan1 date2 dec31)
         ;; Then that date; otherwise, none
         (list date2) nil))))
```

```
(defun coptic-christmas (g-year)
  ;; TYPE gregorian-year -> list-of-fixed-dates
  ;; List of zero or one fixed dates of Coptic Christmas
  ;; in Gregorian year.
  (coptic-in-gregorian 4 29 g-year))
```

B.8 The Islamic Calendar

```
(defun islamic-date (month day year)
  ;; TYPE (islamic-month islamic-day islamic-year)
  ;; TYPE -> islamic-date
  (list month day year))
```

```
(defconstant islamic-epoch
  ;; TYPE fixed-date
  ;; Fixed date of start of the Islamic calendar.
  (fixed-from-julian (julian-date july 16 (ce 622))))
```

```
(defun islamic-leap-year? (i-year)
  ;; TYPE islamic-year -> boolean
  ;; True if year is an Islamic leap year.
  (< (mod (+ 14 (* 11 i-year)) 30) 11))
```

```
(defun fixed-from-islamic (i-date)
  ;; TYPE islamic-date -> fixed-date
  ;; Fixed date equivalent to Islamic date.
  (let* ((month (standard-month i-date))
         (day (standard-day i-date))
         (year (standard-year i-date)))
    (+ day                        ; Days so far this month.
       (ceiling                   ; Days in prior months.
        (* 29.5 (1- month)))
       (* (1- year) 354)          ; Nonleap days in prior years.
       (quotient                  ; Leap days in prior years.
        (+ 3 (* 11 year)) 30)
       islamic-epoch -1)))  ; Days before start of calendar.
```

```
(defun islamic-from-fixed (date)
  ;; TYPE fixed-date -> islamic-date
  ;; Islamic date (month day year) corresponding to fixed
  ;; date.
  (let* ((year  ; Divide elapsed days by average year length.
          (quotient (+ (* 30 (- date islamic-epoch)) 10646)
                    10631))
         (month ; Months alternate between 29 and 30 days
          (min 12 ; Last month can be longer
               (1+ (ceiling
                    (/ (- date 29
                          (fixed-from-islamic
                           (islamic-date 1 1 year)))
                       29.5)))))
         (day            ; Calculate the day by subtraction.
          (1+ (- date (fixed-from-islamic
                       (islamic-date month 1 year))))))
      (islamic-date month day year)))
```

```
(defun islamic-in-gregorian (i-month i-day g-year)
  ;; TYPE (islamic-month islamic-day gregorian-year)
  ;; TYPE -> list-of-fixed-dates
  ;; List of the fixed dates of Islamic month, day
  ;; that occur in Gregorian year.
  (let* ((jan1 (fixed-from-gregorian
                (gregorian-date january 1 g-year)))
         (dec31 (fixed-from-gregorian
                 (gregorian-date december 31 g-year)))
         (y (standard-year (islamic-from-fixed jan1)))
         ;; The possible occurrences in one year are
         (date1 (fixed-from-islamic
                 (islamic-date i-month i-day y)))
         (date2 (fixed-from-islamic
                 (islamic-date i-month i-day (1+ y))))
         (date3 (fixed-from-islamic
                 (islamic-date i-month i-day (+ 2 y)))))
    ;; Combine in one list those that occur in current year
    (append
     (if (<= jan1 date1 dec31)
         (list date1) nil)
     (if (<= jan1 date2 dec31)
```

```
            (list date2) nil)
        (if (<= jan1 date3 dec31)
            (list date3) nil))))
```

```
(defun mawlid-an-nabi (g-year)
  ;; TYPE gregorian-year -> list-of-fixed-dates
  ;; List of fixed dates of Mawlid-an-Nabi occurring in
  ;; Gregorian year.
  (islamic-in-gregorian 3 12 g-year))
```

B.9 The Persian Calendar

```
(defun persian-date (month day year)
  ;; TYPE (persian-month persian-day persian-year)
  ;; TYPE -> persian-date
  (list month day year))
```

```
(defconstant persian-epoch
  ;; TYPE fixed-date
  ;; Fixed date of start of the Persian calendar.
  (fixed-from-julian (julian-date march 19 (ce 622))))
```

```
(defun persian-leap-year? (p-year)
  ;; TYPE persian-year -> boolean
  ;; True if year is a leap year on the Persian calendar.
  (let* ((y ; Years since start of 2820-year cycles
          (if (< 0 p-year)
              (- p-year 474)
            (- p-year 473))); No year zero
         (year ; Equivalent year in the range 474...3263
          (+ (mod y 2820) 474)))
    (< (mod (* (+ year 38)
               682)
            2816)
       682)))
```

```
(defun fixed-from-persian (p-date)
  ;; TYPE persian-date -> fixed-date
  ;; Fixed date equivalent to Persian date.
  (let* ((day (standard-day p-date))
         (month (standard-month p-date))
         (p-year (standard-year p-date))
         (y ; Years since start of 2820-year cycle
          (if (< 0 p-year)
              (- p-year 474)
            (- p-year 473))); No year zero
         (year ; Equivalent year in the range 474...3263
          (+ (mod y 2820) 474)))
    (+ (1- persian-epoch); Days before epoch
       (* 1029983          ; Days in 2820-year cycles
                           ; before Persian year 474
          (quotient y 2820))
       (* 365 (1- year)) ; Nonleap days in prior years this
                           ; 2820-year cycle
       (quotient           ; Leap days in prior years this
                           ; 2820-year cycle
        (- (* 682 year) 110) 2816)
       (if (<= month 7)   ; Days in prior months this year
           (* 31 (1- month))
         (+ (* 30 (1- month)) 6))
       day)))              ; Days so far this month
```

```
(defun persian-year-from-fixed (date)
  ;; TYPE fixed-date -> persian-year
  ;; Persian year corresponding to the fixed date.
  (let* ((d0       ; Prior days since start of 2820-year cycle
                   ; beginning in Persian year 474
          (- date (fixed-from-persian
                   (persian-date 1 1 475))))
         (n2820   ; Completed prior 2820-year cycles
          (quotient d0 1029983))
         (d1       ; Prior days not in n2820--that is, days
                   ; since start of last 2820-year cycle
          (mod d0 1029983))
         (y2820 ; Years since start of last 2820-year cycle
          (if (= d1 1029982)
              ;; Last day of 2820-year cycle
              2820
            ;; Otherwise use cycle of years formula
            (quotient (+ (* 2816 d1) 1031337)
                      1028522)
            ;; If (* 2816 d1) causes integers that are
             ;; too-large, use instead:
            ;; (let ((a (floor d1 366))
            ;;       (b (mod d1 366)))
            ;;  (+ 1 a (quotient
            ;;          (+ (* 2134 a) (* 2816 b) 2815)
            ;;          1028522
            ))
         (year    ; Years since Persian epoch
          (+ 474     ; Years before start of 2820-year cycles
             (* 2820 n2820) ; Years in prior 2820-year cycles
             y2820))); Years since start of last 2820-year
                     ; cycle
    (if (< 0 year)
        year
      (1- year)))); No year zero
```

```
(defun persian-from-fixed (date)
  ;; TYPE fixed-date -> persian-date
  ;; Persian (month day year) corresponding to fixed date.
  (let* ((year (persian-year-from-fixed date))
         (day-of-year (1+ (- date
                             (fixed-from-persian
                              (persian-date 1 1 year)))))
         (month (if (<= day-of-year 186)
                    (ceiling (/ day-of-year 31))
                  (ceiling (/ (- day-of-year 6) 30))))
         (day            ; Calculate the day by subtraction
          (- date (1- (fixed-from-persian
                       (persian-date month 1 year))))))
    (persian-date month day year)))
```

```
(defun naw-ruz (g-year)
  ;; TYPE gregorian-year -> fixed-date
  ;; Fixed date of Persian New Year (Naw-Ruz) in Gregorian
  ;; year.
  (let* ((persian-year
          (1+ (- g-year
                 (gregorian-year-from-fixed
                  persian-epoch)))))
    (fixed-from-persian
     (persian-date 1 1 (if (<= persian-year 0)
                           ;; No Persian year 0
                           (1- persian-year)
                         persian-year)))))
```

B.10 The Bahá'í Calendar

```
(defun bahai-date (major cycle year month day)
  ;; TYPE (bahai-major bahai-cycle bahai-year
  ;; TYPE  bahai-month bahai-day) -> bahai-date
  (list major cycle year month day))
```

```
(defun bahai-major (date)
  ;; TYPE bahai-date -> bahai-major
  (first date))
```

```
(defun bahai-cycle (date)
  ;; TYPE bahai-date -> bahai-cycle
  (second date))
```

```
(defun bahai-year (date)
  ;; TYPE bahai-date -> bahai-year
  (third date))
```

```
(defun bahai-month (date)
  ;; TYPE bahai-date -> bahai-month
  (fourth date))
```

```
(defun bahai-day (date)
  ;; TYPE bahai-date -> bahai-day
  (fifth date))
```

```
(defconstant bahai-epoch
  ;; TYPE fixed-date
  ;; Fixed date of start of Bahai calendar.
  (fixed-from-gregorian (gregorian-date march 21 1844)))
```

```
(defun fixed-from-bahai (b-date)
  ;; TYPE bahai-date -> fixed-date
  ;; Fixed date equivalent to the Bahai date b-date.
  (let* ((major (bahai-major b-date))
         (cycle (bahai-cycle b-date))
         (year (bahai-year b-date))
         (month (bahai-month b-date))
         (day (bahai-day b-date))
         (g-year; Corresponding Gregorian year.
          (+ (* 361 (1- major))
             (* 19 (1- cycle)) year -1
             (gregorian-year-from-fixed bahai-epoch))))
    (+ (fixed-from-gregorian ; Prior years.
        (gregorian-date march 20 g-year))
       (* 19 (1- month))        ; Elapsed months.
       ;; Subtract 14 or 15 if counted ayyam-i-ha.
       (if (/= month 20)
           0
         (if (gregorian-leap-year? (1+ g-year))
             -14
           -15))
       day)))                   ; Days in current month.
```

```
(defun bahai-from-fixed (date)
  ;; TYPE fixed-date -> bahai-date
  ;; Bahai (month day cycle year) corresponding to fixed
  ;; date.
  (let* ((g-year (gregorian-year-from-fixed date))
         (start   ; 1844
          (gregorian-year-from-fixed bahai-epoch))
         (years ; Since start of Bahai calendar.
```

```
              (- g-year start
                 (if (<= (fixed-from-gregorian
                          (gregorian-date january 1 g-year))
                         date
                         (fixed-from-gregorian
                          (gregorian-date march 20 g-year)))
                     1 0)))
             (major (1+ (quotient years 361)))
             (cycle (1+ (quotient (mod years 361) 19)))
             (year (1+ (mod years 19)))
             (days; Since start of year
              (- date (fixed-from-bahai
                       (bahai-date major cycle year 1 1))))
             (month (if (>= date
                            (fixed-from-bahai
                             (bahai-date major cycle year 20 1)))
                        20
                      (1+ (quotient days 19))))
             (day (- date -1
                     (fixed-from-bahai
                      (bahai-date major cycle year month 1)))))
        (bahai-date major cycle year month day)))
```

```
(defun bahai-new-year (g-year)
  ;; TYPE gregorian-year -> fixed-date
  ;; Fixed date of Bahai New Year in Gregorian year.
  (fixed-from-gregorian
   (gregorian-date march 21 g-year)))
```

```
(defun feast-of-ridvan (g-year)
  ;; TYPE gregorian-year -> fixed-date
  ;; Fixed date of Bahai New Year in Gregorian year.
  (let* ((years (- g-year
                   (gregorian-year-from-fixed
                    bahai-epoch)))
         (major (1+ (quotient years 361)))
         (cycle (1+ (quotient (mod years 361) 19)))
         (year (1+ (mod years 19))))
    (fixed-from-bahai
     (bahai-date major cycle year 2 13))))
```

B.11 The Hebrew Calendar

```
(defun hebrew-date (month day year)
  ;; TYPE (hebrew-month hebrew-day hebrew-year) -> hebrew-date
  (list month day year))
```

```
(defun hebrew-leap-year? (h-year)
  ;; TYPE hebrew-year -> boolean
  ;; True if year is a leap year on Hebrew calendar.
  (< (mod (1+ (* 7 h-year)) 19) 7))
```

```
(defun last-month-of-hebrew-year (h-year)
  ;; TYPE hebrew-year -> hebrew-month
  ;; Last month of Hebrew year.
  (if (hebrew-leap-year? h-year)
      13
    12))
```

```
(defconstant hebrew-epoch
  ;; TYPE fixed-date
  ;; Fixed date of start of the Hebrew calendar, that is,
```

```
  ;; Tishri 1, 1 AM.
  (fixed-from-julian (julian-date october 7 (bce 3761))))
```

```
(defun hebrew-calendar-elapsed-days (h-year)
  ;; TYPE hebrew-year -> integer
  ;; Number of days elapsed from the (Sunday) noon prior
  ;; to the epoch of the Hebrew calendar to the mean
  ;; conjunction (molad) of Tishri of Hebrew year h-year,
  ;; or one day later.
  (let* ((months-elapsed  ; Since start of Hebrew calendar.
          (quotient (- (* 235 h-year) 234) 19))
         (parts-elapsed; Fractions of days since prior noon.
          (+ 12084 (* 13753 months-elapsed)))
         (day  ; Whole days since prior noon.
          (+ (* 29 months-elapsed)
             (quotient parts-elapsed 25920)))
        ;; If (* 13753 months-elapsed) causes integers that
        ;; are to large, use instead:
        ;; (parts-elapsed
        ;;  (+ 204 (* 793 (mod months-elapsed 1080))))
        ;; (hours-elapsed
        ;;  (+ 11 (* 12 months-elapsed)
        ;;     (* 793 (quotient months-elapsed 1080))
        ;;     (quotient parts-elapsed 1080)))
        ;; (day
        ;;  (+ (* 29 months-elapsed)
        ;;     (quotient hours-elapsed 24)))
         )
    (if (< (mod (* 3 (1+ day)) 7) 3); Sun, Wed, or Fri
        (1+ day) ; Delay one day.
      day)))
```

```
(defun hebrew-new-year-delay (h-year)
  ;; TYPE hebrew-year -> {0,1,2}
  ;; Delays to start of Hebrew year to keep ordinary year in
  ;; range 353-356 and leap year in range 383-386.
  (let* ((ny0 (hebrew-calendar-elapsed-days (1- h-year)))
         (ny1 (hebrew-calendar-elapsed-days h-year))
         (ny2 (hebrew-calendar-elapsed-days (1+ h-year))))
    (cond
     ((= (- ny2 ny1) 356) 2); Next year would be too long.
     ((= (- ny1 ny0) 382) 1); Previous year too short.
     (t 0))))
```

```
(defun long-heshvan? (h-year)
  ;; TYPE hebrew-year -> boolean
  ;; True if Heshvan is long in Hebrew year.
  (= (mod (days-in-hebrew-year h-year) 10) 5))
```

```
(defun short-kislev? (h-year)
  ;; TYPE hebrew-year -> boolean
  ;; True if Kislev is short in Hebrew year.
  (= (mod (days-in-hebrew-year h-year) 10) 3))
```

```
(defun last-day-of-hebrew-month (h-month h-year)
  ;; TYPE (hebrew-month hebrew-year) -> hebrew-day
  ;; Last day of month in Hebrew year.
  (if (or (member h-month (list 2 4 6 10 13))
          (and (= h-month 12)
               (not (hebrew-leap-year? h-year)))
          (and (= h-month 8) (not (long-heshvan? h-year)))
          (and (= h-month 9) (short-kislev? h-year)))
      29
    30))
```

```
(defun days-in-hebrew-year (h-year)
  ;; TYPE hebrew-year -> {353,354,355,383,384,385}
  ;; Number of days in Hebrew year.  Calls fixed-from-hebrew
  ;; for value that does not in turn require
  ;; days-in-hebrew-year.
  (- (fixed-from-hebrew (hebrew-date 7 1 (1+ h-year)))
     (fixed-from-hebrew (hebrew-date 7 1 h-year))))
```

```
(defun fixed-from-hebrew (h-date)
  ;; TYPE hebrew-date -> fixed-date
  ;; Fixed date of Hebrew date.  This function is designed
  ;; so that it works for Hebrew dates month, day, year even
  ;; if the month has fewer than day days--in that case the
  ;; function returns the (day-1)st day after month 1, year.
  ;; This property is required by the functions
  ;; hebrew-birthday and yahrzeit.
  (let* ((month (standard-month h-date))
         (day (standard-day h-date))
         (year (standard-year h-date)))
    (+ hebrew-epoch            ; Days before fixed date 1.
       (hebrew-calendar-elapsed-days; Days in prior years.
        year)
       (hebrew-new-year-delay year)
       day -1                  ; Days so far this month.
       (if ;; before Tishri
           (< month 7)
           ;; Then add days in prior months this year before
           ;; and after Nisan.
           (+ (sum (last-day-of-hebrew-month m year)
                   m 7 (<= m (last-month-of-hebrew-year year)))
              (sum (last-day-of-hebrew-month m year)
                   m 1 (< m month)))
         ;; Else add days in prior months this year
         (sum (last-day-of-hebrew-month m year)
              m 7 (< m month))))))
```

```
(defun hebrew-from-fixed (date)
  ;; TYPE fixed-date -> hebrew-date
  ;; Hebrew (month day year) corresponding to fixed date.
  ;; The fraction can be approximated by 365.25.
  (let* ((approx    ; Approximate year (may be off by 1)
          (quotient (- date hebrew-epoch) 35975351/98496))
         ;; The value 35975351/98496, the average length of
         ;; a Hebrew year, can be approximated by 365.25
         (year      ; Search forward.
          (+ approx -1 ; Lower bound.
             (sum 1 y approx
                  (>= date
                      (fixed-from-hebrew
                       (hebrew-date 7 1 y))))))
         (start     ; Starting month for search for month.
          (if (< date (fixed-from-hebrew
                       (hebrew-date 1 1 year)))
              7 ; Tishri
            1)) ; Nisan
         (month ; Search forward from either Tishri or Nisan.
          (+ start
             (sum 1 m start
                  (> date
                     (fixed-from-hebrew
                      (hebrew-date m
                             (last-day-of-hebrew-month m year)
                             year))))))
         (day   ; Calculate the day by subtraction.
          (1+ (- date (fixed-from-hebrew
                       (hebrew-date month 1 year))))))
    (hebrew-date month day year)))
```

We are using Common Lisp exact arithmetic for rationals here (and elsewhere). Without that facility, one must rephrase all quotient operations to work with integers only.

The function hebrew-calendar-elapsed-days is called repeatedly during the calculations, often several times for the same year. A more efficient algorithm could avoid such repetition.

```
(defun yom-kippur (g-year)
  ;; TYPE gregorian-year -> fixed-date
  ;; Fixed date of Yom Kippur occurring in Gregorian year.
  (let* ((hebrew-year
          (1+ (- g-year
                 (gregorian-year-from-fixed
                  hebrew-epoch)))))
    (fixed-from-hebrew (hebrew-date 7 10 hebrew-year))))
```

```
(defun passover (g-year)
  ;; TYPE gregorian-year -> fixed-date
  ;; Fixed date of Passover occurring in Gregorian year.
  (let* ((hebrew-year
          (- g-year
             (gregorian-year-from-fixed hebrew-epoch))))
    (fixed-from-hebrew (hebrew-date 1 15 hebrew-year))))
```

```
(defun omer (date)
  ;; TYPE fixed-date -> omer-count
  ;; Number of elapsed weeks and days in the omer at date.
  ;; Returns bogus if that date does not fall during the
  ;; omer.
  (let* ((c (- date
               (fixed-from-hebrew
                (hebrew-date
                 1 15 (standard-year
                       (hebrew-from-fixed date)))))))
    (if (<= 1 c 49)
        (list (quotient c 7) (mod c 7))
      bogus)))
```

```
(defun purim (g-year)
  ;; TYPE gregorian-year -> fixed-date
  ;; Fixed date of Purim occurring in Gregorian year.
  (let* ((hebrew-year
          (- g-year
             (gregorian-year-from-fixed hebrew-epoch)))
         (last-month  ; Adar or Adar II
          (last-month-of-hebrew-year hebrew-year)))
    (fixed-from-hebrew
     (hebrew-date last-month 14 hebrew-year))))
```

```
(defun ta-anith-esther (g-year)
  ;; TYPE gregorian-year -> fixed-date
  ;; Fixed date of Ta'anith Esther occurring in
  ;; Gregorian year.
  (let* ((purim-date (purim g-year)))
    (if ; Purim is on Sunday
        (= (day-of-week-from-fixed purim-date) sunday)
        ;; Then prior Thursday
        (- purim-date 3)
      ;; Else previous day
      (1- purim-date))))
```

```
(defun tisha-b-av (g-year)
  ;; TYPE gregorian-year -> fixed-date
  ;; Fixed date of Tisha B'Av occurring in Gregorian year.
  (let* ((hebrew-year
          (- g-year
             (gregorian-year-from-fixed hebrew-epoch)))
         (ninth-of-av
          (fixed-from-hebrew
           (hebrew-date 5 9 hebrew-year))))
    (if ; Ninth of Av is Saturday
        (= (day-of-week-from-fixed ninth-of-av) saturday)
        ;; Then the next day
        (1+ ninth-of-av)
      ninth-of-av)))
```

```
(defun birkath-ha-hama (g-year)
  ;; TYPE gregorian-year -> list-of-fixed-dates
  ;; List of fixed date of Birkath HaHama occurring in
  ;; Gregorian year, if it occurs.
  (let* ((mar26 (julian-in-gregorian
                 march 26 g-year)))
    (if (and (not (equal mar26 nil))
             (= (mod (standard-year
                      (julian-from-fixed (first mar26)))
                     28)
                21))
        mar26
      nil)))
```

```
(defun yom-ha-zikaron (g-year)
  ;; TYPE gregorian-year -> fixed-date
  ;; Fixed date of Yom HaZikaron occurring in Gregorian year.
  (let* ((hebrew-year
          (- g-year
             (gregorian-year-from-fixed hebrew-epoch)))
         (h; Ordinarily Iyar 4
          (fixed-from-hebrew
           (hebrew-date 2 4 hebrew-year))))
    (if (< wednesday (day-of-week-from-fixed h))
        ;; But prior Wednesday if Iyar 5 is Friday or
        ;; Saturday
        (kday-before h wednesday)
      h)))
```

```
(defun sh-ela (g-year)
  ;; TYPE gregorian-year -> fixed-date
  ;; Fixed date of Sh'ela occurring in Gregorian year.
  (- (first (julian-in-gregorian march 26 (1+ g-year)))
     124))
```

```
(defun hebrew-birthday (birthdate h-year)
  ;; TYPE (hebrew-date hebrew-year) -> fixed-date
  ;; Fixed date of the anniversary of Hebrew birthdate
  ;; occurring in Hebrew year.  This function assumes
  ;; that the function fixed-from-hebrew works for Hebrew
  ;; dates month, day, year even if the month has fewer than
  ;; day days--in that case the function returns the
  ;; (day-1)st day after month 1, year.
  (let* ((birth-day (standard-day birthdate))
         (birth-month (standard-month birthdate))
         (birth-year (standard-year birthdate)))
    (if ; It's Adar in a normal Hebrew year or Adar II
        ; in a Hebrew leap year,
        (= birth-month (last-month-of-hebrew-year birth-year))
        ;; Then use the same day in last month of Hebrew year.
```

```
          (fixed-from-hebrew
           (hebrew-date (last-month-of-hebrew-year h-year)
                        birth-day
                        h-year))
        ;; Else use the normal anniversary of the birth date,
        ;; or the corresponding day in years without that date
        (fixed-from-hebrew
         (hebrew-date birth-month birth-day h-year)))))
```

```
(defun yahrzeit (death-date h-year)
  ;; TYPE (hebrew-date hebrew-year) -> fixed-date
  ;; Fixed date of the anniversary of Hebrew death-date
  ;; occurring in Hebrew year.  This function assumes
  ;; that the function fixed-from-hebrew works for Hebrew
  ;; dates month, day, year even if the month has fewer than
  ;; day days--in that case the function returns the
  ;; (day-1)st day after month 1, year.
  (let* ((death-day (standard-day death-date))
         (death-month (standard-month death-date))
         (death-year (standard-year death-date)))
    (cond
     ;; If it's Heshvan 30 it depends on the first
     ;; anniversary; if that was not Heshvan 30, use
     ;; the day before Kislev 1.
     ((and (= death-month 8)
           (= death-day 30)
           (not (long-heshvan? (1+ death-year))))
      (1- (fixed-from-hebrew
           (hebrew-date 9 1 h-year))))
     ;; If it's Kislev 30 it depends on the first
     ;; anniversary; if that was not Kislev 30, use
     ;; the day before Teveth 1.
     ((and (= death-month 9)
           (= death-day 30)
           (short-kislev? (1+ death-year)))
      (1- (fixed-from-hebrew
           (hebrew-date 10 1 h-year))))
     ;; If it's Adar II, use the same day in last
     ;; month of Hebrew year (Adar or Adar II).
     ((= death-month 13)
      (fixed-from-hebrew
       (hebrew-date (last-month-of-hebrew-year h-year)
                    death-day
                    h-year)))
     ;; If it's the 30th in Adar I and Hebrew year is not a
     ;; Hebrew leap year (so Adar has only 29 days), use the
     ;; last day in Shevat.
     ((and (= death-day 30)
           (= death-month 12)
           (not (hebrew-leap-year? h-year)))
      (fixed-from-hebrew (hebrew-date 11 30 h-year)))
     ;; In all other cases, use the normal anniversary of
     ;; the date of death.
     (t (fixed-from-hebrew
         (hebrew-date death-month death-day h-year))))))
```

B.12 The Mayan Calendars

```
(defun mayan-long-count-date (baktun katun tun uinal kin)
  ;; TYPE (mayan-baktun mayan-katun mayan-tun mayan-uinal
  ;; TYPE  mayan-kin) -> mayan-long-count-date
  (list baktun katun tun uinal kin))
```

```
(defun mayan-baktun (date)
  ;; TYPE mayan-long-count-date -> mayan-baktun
  (first date))
```

```
(defun mayan-katun (date)
  ;; TYPE mayan-long-count-date -> mayan-katun
  (second date))
```

```
(defun mayan-tun (date)
  ;; TYPE mayan-long-count-date -> mayan-tun
  (third date))
```

```
(defun mayan-uinal (date)
  ;; TYPE mayan-long-count-date -> mayan-uinal
  (fourth date))
```

```
(defun mayan-kin (date)
  ;; TYPE mayan-long-count-date -> mayan-kin
  (fifth date))
```

```
(defconstant mayan-epoch
  ;; TYPE fixed-date
  ;; Fixed date of start of the Mayan calendar, according
  ;; to the Goodman-Martinez-Thompson correlation.
  ;; That is, August 11, -3113.
  (fixed-from-jd 584282.5))
```

```
(defun fixed-from-mayan-long-count (count)
  ;; TYPE mayan-long-count-date -> fixed-date
  ;; Fixed date corresponding to the Mayan long count
  ;; count, which is a list (baktun katun tun uinal kin).
  (let* ((baktun (mayan-baktun count))
         (katun (mayan-katun count))
         (tun (mayan-tun count))
         (uinal (mayan-uinal count))
         (kin (mayan-kin count)))
    (+ mayan-epoch      ; Fixed date at Mayan 0.0.0.0.0
       (* baktun 144000); Baktun.
       (* katun 7200)   ; Katun.
       (* tun 360)      ; Tun.
       (* uinal 20)     ; Uinal.
       kin)))           ; Kin (days).
```

```
(defun mayan-long-count-from-fixed (date)
  ;; TYPE fixed-date -> mayan-long-count-date
  ;; Mayan long count date of fixed date.
  (let* ((long-count (- date mayan-epoch))
         (baktun (quotient long-count 144000))
         (day-of-baktun (mod long-count 144000))
         (katun (quotient day-of-baktun 7200))
         (day-of-katun (mod day-of-baktun 7200))
         (tun (quotient day-of-katun 360))
         (day-of-tun (mod day-of-katun 360))
         (uinal (quotient day-of-tun 20))
         (kin (mod day-of-tun 20)))
    (mayan-long-count-date baktun katun tun uinal kin)))
```

```
(defun mayan-haab-date (day month)
  ;; TYPE (mayan-haab-day mayan-haab-month) -> mayan-haab-date
  (list day month))
```

```
(defun mayan-haab-day (date)
  ;; TYPE mayan-haab-date -> mayan-haab-day
  (first date))
```

```
(defun mayan-haab-month (date)
  ;; TYPE mayan-haab-date -> mayan-haab-month
  (second date))
```

```
(defconstant mayan-haab-at-epoch
  ;; TYPE mayan-haab-date
  ;; Haab date at long count 0.0.0.0.0.
  (mayan-haab-date 8 18))
```

```
(defun mayan-haab-from-fixed (date)
  ;; TYPE fixed-date -> mayan-haab-date
  ;; Mayan haab date of fixed date.
  (let* ((long-count (- date mayan-epoch))
         (day-of-haab
          (mod (+ long-count
                  (mayan-haab-day mayan-haab-at-epoch)
                  (* 20 (1- (mayan-haab-month
                             mayan-haab-at-epoch))))
               365))
         (day (mod day-of-haab 20))
         (month (1+ (quotient day-of-haab 20))))
    (mayan-haab-date day month)))
```

```
(defun mayan-haab-difference (h-date1 h-date2)
  ;; TYPE (mayan-haab-date mayan-haab-date) -> integer
  ;; Number of days from Mayan haab date h-date1 to the next
  ;; occurrence of Mayan haab date h-date2.
  (let* ((day1 (mayan-haab-day h-date1))
         (day2 (mayan-haab-day h-date2))
         (month1 (mayan-haab-month h-date1))
         (month2 (mayan-haab-month h-date2)))
    (mod (+ (* 20 (- month2 month1))
            (- day2 day1))
         365)))
```

```
(defun mayan-haab-on-or-before (haab date)
  ;; TYPE (mayan-haab-date fixed-date) -> fixed-date
  ;; Fixed date of latest date on or before fixed date
  ;; that is Mayan haab date haab.
  (- date
     (mod (- date
             (mayan-haab-difference
              (mayan-haab-from-fixed 0) haab))
          365)))
```

```
(defun mayan-tzolkin-date (number name)
  ;; TYPE (mayan-tzolkin-number mayan-tzolkin-name)
  ;; TYPE -> mayan-tzolkin-date
  (list number name))
```

```
(defun mayan-tzolkin-number (date)
  ;; TYPE mayan-tzolkin-date -> mayan-tzolkin-number
  (first date))
```

```
(defun mayan-tzolkin-name (date)
  ;; TYPE mayan-tzolkin-date -> mayan-tzolkin-name
  (second date))
```

```
(defconstant mayan-tzolkin-at-epoch
  ;; TYPE mayan-tzolkin-date
  ;; Tzolkin date at long count 0.0.0.0.0.
  (mayan-tzolkin-date 4 20))
```

```
(defun mayan-tzolkin-from-fixed (date)
  ;; TYPE fixed-date -> mayan-tzolkin-date
  ;; Mayan tzolkin date of fixed date.
  (let* ((long-count (- date mayan-epoch))
         (number
          (adjusted-mod (+ long-count
                           (mayan-tzolkin-number
                            mayan-tzolkin-at-epoch))
                        13))
         (name
          (adjusted-mod (+ long-count
                           (mayan-tzolkin-name
                            mayan-tzolkin-at-epoch))
                        20)))
    (mayan-tzolkin-date number name)))
```

```
(defun mayan-tzolkin-difference (t-date1 t-date2)
  ;; TYPE (mayan-tzolkin-date mayan-tzolkin-date) -> integer
  ;; Number of days from Mayan tzolkin date t-date1 to the
  ;; next occurrence of Mayan tzolkin date t-date2.
  ;; occurrence of Mayan haab date t-date2.
  (let* ((number1 (mayan-tzolkin-number t-date1))
         (number2 (mayan-tzolkin-number t-date2))
         (name1 (mayan-tzolkin-name t-date1))
         (name2 (mayan-tzolkin-name t-date2))
         (number-difference (- number2 number1))
         (name-difference (- name2 name1)))
    (mod (+ number-difference
            (* 13 (mod (* 3 (- number-difference
                               name-difference))
                       20)))
         260)))
```

```
(defun mayan-tzolkin-on-or-before (tzolkin date)
  ;; TYPE (mayan-tzolkin-date fixed-date) -> fixed-date
  ;; Fixed date of latest date on or before fixed date
  ;; that is Mayan tzolkin date tzolkin.
  (- date
     (mod (- date (mayan-tzolkin-difference
                   (mayan-tzolkin-from-fixed 0)
                   tzolkin))
          260)))
```

```
(defun mayan-haab-tzolkin-on-or-before (haab tzolkin date)
  ;; TYPE (mayan-haab-date mayan-tzolkin-date fixed-date)
  ;; TYPE -> fixed-date
  ;; Fixed date of latest date on or before date
  ;; that is Mayan haab date haab and tzolkin date tzolkin;
  ;; returns bogus if such a haab-tzolkin combination is
  ;; impossible.
  (let* ((haab-difference
          (mayan-haab-difference (mayan-haab-from-fixed 0)
                                 haab))
         (tzolkin-difference
          (mayan-tzolkin-difference
           (mayan-tzolkin-from-fixed 0)
           tzolkin))
         (diff (- tzolkin-difference haab-difference)))
    (if (= (mod diff 5) 0)
        (- date
           (mod (- date (+ haab-difference
                           (* 365 diff)))
                18980))
      bogus))); haab-tzolkin combination is impossible.
```

B.13 The Old Hindu Calendars

```
(defconstant hindu-epoch
  ;; TYPE fixed-date
  ;; Fixed date of start of the Hindu calendar (Kali Yuga).
  (fixed-from-julian (julian-date february 18 (bce 3102))))
```

```
(defun hindu-day-count (date)
  ;; TYPE fixed-date -> integer
  ;; Elapsed days (Ahargana) to date since Hindu epoch (K.Y.).
  (- date hindu-epoch))
```

```
(defconstant arya-jovian-period
  ;; TYPE rational
  ;; Number of days in one revolution of Jupiter around the
  ;; Sun.
  1577917500/364224)
```

```
(defun jovian-year (date)
  ;; TYPE fixed-date -> {1-60}
  ;; Year of Jupiter cycle at fixed date.
  (1+ (mod (quotient (hindu-day-count date)
                     (/ arya-jovian-period 12))
           60)))
```

```
(defconstant arya-sidereal-year
  ;; TYPE rational
  ;; Length of Old Hindu solar year.
  1577917500/4320000)
```

```
(defun old-hindu-solar-from-fixed (date)
  ;; TYPE fixed-date -> hindu-solar-date
  ;; Old Hindu solar date equivalent to fixed date.
  (let* ((rise ; Sunrise on Hindu date.
          (+ (hindu-day-count date) 1/4))
         (year    ; Elapsed years.
          (quotient rise arya-sidereal-year))
         (month (1+ (mod (quotient rise arya-solar-month)
                         12)))
         (day (1+ (floor (mod rise arya-solar-month)))))
    (hindu-solar-date month day year)))
```

```
(defun fixed-from-old-hindu-solar (s-date)
  ;; TYPE hindu-solar-date -> fixed-date
  ;; Fixed date corresponding to Old Hindu solar date.
  (let* ((month (standard-month s-date))
         (day (standard-day s-date))
         (year (standard-year s-date)))
    (floor
     (+ hindu-epoch ; Since start of era.
        (* year arya-sidereal-year) ; Days in elapsed years
        (* (1- month) arya-solar-month) ; ...in months.
        day -1/4)))) ; Midnight of day.
```

```
(defun old-hindu-lunar-date (month leap day year)
  ;; TYPE (old-hindu-lunar-month old-hindu-lunar-leap
  ;; TYPE  old-hindu-lunar-day old-hindu-lunar-year)
  ;; TYPE -> old-hindu-lunar-date
  (list month leap day year))
```

```
(defun old-hindu-lunar-month (date)
  ;; TYPE old-hindu-lunar-date -> old-hindu-lunar-month
  (first date))
```

```
(defun old-hindu-lunar-leap (date)
  ;; TYPE old-hindu-lunar-date -> old-hindu-lunar-leap
  (second date))
```

```
(defun old-hindu-lunar-day (date)
  ;; TYPE old-hindu-lunar-date -> old-hindu-lunar-day
  (third date))
```

```
(defun old-hindu-lunar-year (date)
  ;; TYPE old-hindu-lunar-date -> old-hindu-lunar-year
  (fourth date))
```

```
(defconstant arya-solar-month
  ;; TYPE rational
  ;; Length of Old Hindu solar month.
  (/ arya-sidereal-year 12))
```

```
(defconstant arya-lunar-month
  ;; TYPE rational
  ;; Length of Old Hindu lunar month.
  1577917500/53433336)
```

```
(defconstant arya-lunar-day
  ;; TYPE rational
  ;; Length of Old Hindu lunar day.
  (/ arya-lunar-month 30))
```

```
(defun old-hindu-lunar-leap-year? (l-year)
  ;; TYPE old-hindu-lunar-year -> boolean
  ;; True if year is a leap year on the
  ;; old Hindu calendar.
  (>= (mod (- (* l-year arya-sidereal-year)
              arya-solar-month)
           arya-lunar-month)
      (- arya-lunar-month
         (mod arya-sidereal-year arya-lunar-month))))
```

```
(defun old-hindu-lunar-from-fixed (date)
  ;; TYPE fixed-date -> old-hindu-lunar-date
  ;; Old Hindu lunar date equivalent to fixed date.
  (let* ((rise ; Sunrise on Hindu date.
          (+ (hindu-day-count date) 1/4))
         (new-moon ; Beginning of lunar month.
          (- rise (mod rise arya-lunar-month)))
         (leap ; If lunar contained in solar.
          (and (>= (- arya-solar-month arya-lunar-month)
                   (mod new-moon arya-solar-month))
               (> (mod new-moon arya-solar-month) 0)))
         (month ; Next solar month's name.
          (1+ (mod (ceiling (/ new-moon
                               arya-solar-month))
                   12)))
         (day ; Lunar days since beginning of lunar month
          (1+ (mod (quotient rise arya-lunar-day) 30)))
         (year ; Solar year at end of lunar month(s).
          (1- (ceiling (/ (+ new-moon arya-solar-month)
                          arya-sidereal-year)))))
    (old-hindu-lunar-date month leap day year)))
```

```
(defun fixed-from-old-hindu-lunar (l-date)
  ;; TYPE old-hindu-lunar-date -> fixed-date
  ;; Fixed date corresponding to Old Hindu lunar date.
  (let* ((year (old-hindu-lunar-year l-date))
```

```
         (month (old-hindu-lunar-month l-date))
         (leap (old-hindu-lunar-leap l-date))
         (day (old-hindu-lunar-day l-date))
         (mina ; One solar month before solar new year.
          (* (1- (* 12 year)) arya-solar-month))
         (lunar-new-year ; New moon after mina.
          (* arya-lunar-month
             (1+ (quotient mina arya-lunar-month)))))
    (floor
     (+ hindu-epoch
        lunar-new-year
        (* arya-lunar-month
           (if ; If there was a leap month this year.
               (and (not leap)
                    (<= (ceiling (/ (- lunar-new-year mina)
                                    (- arya-solar-month
                                       arya-lunar-month)))
                        month))
               month
             (1- month)))
        (* (1- day) arya-lunar-day) ; Lunar days.
        3/4)))) ; Add one if lunar day begins after sunrise.
```

B.14 Time and Astronomy

```
(defun degrees (theta)
  ;; TYPE real -> angle
  ;; Normalize angle theta to range 0-360 degrees.
  (mod theta 360))
```

```
(defun radians-to-degrees (theta)
  ;; TYPE radian -> angle
  ;; Convert angle theta from radians to degrees.
  (degrees (/ theta pi 1/180)))
```

```
(defun degrees-to-radians (theta)
  ;; TYPE real -> radian
  ;; Convert angle theta from degrees to radians.
  (* (degrees theta) pi 1/180))
```

```
(defun sin-degrees (theta)
  ;; TYPE angle -> amplitude
  ;; Sine of theta (given in degrees).
  (sin (degrees-to-radians theta)))
```

```
(defun cosine-degrees (theta)
  ;; TYPE angle -> amplitude
  ;; Cosine of theta (given in degrees).
  (cos (degrees-to-radians theta)))
```

```
(defun tangent-degrees (theta)
  ;; TYPE angle -> real
  ;; Tangent of theta (given in degrees).
  (tan (degrees-to-radians theta)))
```

```
(defun arctan-degrees (x quad)
  ;; TYPE (real quadrant) -> angle
  ;; Arctangent of x in degrees in quadrant quad.
  (let* ((deg (radians-to-degrees (atan x))))
    (if (or (= quad 1) (= quad 4))
        deg
      (+ deg 180))))
```

```
(defun arcsin-degrees (x)
  ;; TYPE amplitude -> angle
  ;; Arcsine of x in degrees.
  (radians-to-degrees (asin x)))
```

```
(defun arccos-degrees (x)
  ;; TYPE amplitude -> angle
  ;; Arccosine of x in degrees.
  (radians-to-degrees (acos x)))
```

```
(defun time-from-moment (moment)
  ;; TYPE moment -> (hour minute second)
  ;; Time of day (hour minute second) from moment moment.
  (let* ((hour (floor (mod (* moment 24) 24)))
         (minute (floor (mod (* moment 24 60) 60)))
         (second (double-float (mod (* moment 24 60 60) 60))))
    (time-of-day hour minute second)))
```

Common Lisp uses d0 to specify unscaled double-precision constants.

```
(defun equation-of-time (jd)
  ;; TYPE moment -> fraction-of-day
  ;; Equation of time (in days) for julian day number jd.
  ;; Adapted from "Astronomical Algorithms" by Jean Meeus,
  ;; Willmann-Bell, Inc., 1991.
  (let* ((c (/ (- jd j2000) 36525d0))
         (longitude
          (poly c
                (list 280.46645d0 36000.76983d0 0.0003032d0)))
         (anomaly
          (poly c
                (list 357.52910d0 35999.05030d0
                      -0.0001559d0 -0.00000048d0)))
         (inclination
          (poly c
                (list 23.43929111d0 -0.013004167d0
                      -0.00000016389d0 0.0000005036d0)))
         (eccentricity
          (poly c
                (list 0.016708617d0 -0.000042037d0
                      -0.0000001236d0)))
         (y (expt (tangent-degrees (/ inclination 2)) 2)))
    (/ (+ (* y (sin-degrees (* 2 longitude)))
          (* -2 eccentricity (sin-degrees anomaly))
          (* 4 eccentricity y (sin-degrees anomaly)
             (cosine-degrees (* 2 longitude)))
          (* -0.5 y y (sin-degrees (* 4 longitude)))
          (* -1.25 eccentricity eccentricity
             (sin-degrees (* 2 anomaly))))
       2 pi)))
```

```
(defun apparent-from-local (moment)
  ;; TYPE moment -> moment
  ;; Sundial time at local time.
  (+ moment (equation-of-time moment)))
```

```
(defun local-from-apparent (moment)
  ;; TYPE moment -> moment
  ;; Local time from sundial time.
  (- moment (equation-of-time moment)))
```

```
(defun universal-from-local (l-time zone)
  ;; TYPE (moment minute) -> moment
  ;; Universal time from l-time in local time at time-zone
  ;; zone.
  (- l-time (/ zone 24d0 60d0)))
```

```
(defun local-from-universal (u-time zone)
  ;; TYPE (moment minute) -> moment
  ;; Local time from u-time in universal time at time-zone
  ;; zone.
  (+ u-time (/ zone 24d0 60d0)))
```

```
(defun local-from-standard (s-time offset)
  ;; TYPE (moment minute) -> moment
  ;; Local time from standard s-time at distance
  ;; offset (in minutes) from time zone.
  (+ s-time (/ offset 24d0 60d0)))
```

```
(defun standard-from-local (l-time offset)
  ;; TYPE (moment minute) -> moment
  ;; Standard time from local l-time at distance
  ;; offset (in minutes) from time zone.
  (- l-time (/ offset 24d0 60d0)))
```

```
(defun location-offset (longitude zone)
  ;; TYPE (angle minute) -> minute
  ;; Offset of location at longitude
  ;; from standard time at zone.
  (- (* 4 longitude) zone))
```

```
(defun sidereal-from-jd (jd)
  ;; TYPE julian-day-number -> julian-day-number
  ;; Sidereal Time from julian-day-number.
  ;; Adapted from "Astronomical Algorithms"
  ;; by Jean Meeus, Willmann-Bell, Inc., 1991.
  (let* ((c (/ (- jd j2000) 36525))
         (sidereal-coeff
          (list 280.46061837d0 (* 36525 360.98564736629d0)
                0.000387933d0 1/38710000)))
    (/ (poly c sidereal-coeff) 360)))
```

```
(defun ephemeris-correction (moment)
  ;; TYPE moment -> fraction-of-day
  ;; Ephemeris Time minus Universal Time (in days) for
  ;; fixed time.  Adapted from "Astronomical Algorithms"
  ;; by Jean Meeus, Willmann-Bell, Inc., 1991.
  (let* ((year (gregorian-year-from-fixed moment))
         (theta (/ (gregorian-date-difference
                    (gregorian-date january 1 1900)
                    (gregorian-date july 1 year))
                   36525d0))
         (coeff-19th
          (list -0.00002d0 0.000297d0 0.025184d0
                -0.181133d0 0.553040d0 -0.861938d0
                0.677066d0 -0.212591d0))
         (coeff-18th
          (list -0.000009d0 0.003844d0 0.083563d0
                0.865736d0 4.867575d0 15.845535d0
                31.332267d0 38.291999d0 28.316289d0
                11.636204d0 2.043794d0)))
    (cond ((<= 1988 year 2019)
           (/ (- year 1933) 24d0 60d0 60d0))
          ((<= 1900 year 1987)
           (poly theta coeff-19th))
          ((<= 1800 year 1899)
           (poly theta coeff-18th))
          ((<= 1620 year 1799)
           (/ (poly (- year 1600)
                    (list 196.58333d0 -4.0675d0 0.0219167d0))
              24d0 60d0 60d0))
          (t (let* ((x (+ 0.5d0
```

```
                              (gregorian-date-difference
                               (gregorian-date january 1 1810)
                               (gregorian-date january 1 year)))))
                    (/ (- (/ (* x x) 41048480d0) 15)
                       24d0 60d0 60d0))))))
```

```
(defun ephemeris-from-universal (jd)
  ;; TYPE julian-day-number -> julian-day-number
  ;; Ephemeris time at Universal time.
  (+ jd (ephemeris-correction (moment-from-jd jd))))
```

```
(defun universal-from-ephemeris (jd)
  ;; TYPE julian-day-number -> julian-day-number
  ;; Universal time from Ephemeris time.
  (- jd (ephemeris-correction (moment-from-jd jd))))
```

```
(defun julian-centuries (moment)
  ;; TYPE moment -> moment
  ;; Julian centuries since j2000 at Universal time.
  (/ (- (ephemeris-from-universal moment) j2000)
     36525d0))
```

```
(defconstant j2000
  ;; TYPE julian-day-number
  ;; Julian day number (2451545) of Gregorian year 2000.
  (jd-from-moment
   (+ 0.5d0 (fixed-from-gregorian
             (gregorian-date january 1 2000)))))
```

```
(defun nutation (c)
  ;; TYPE julian-centuries -> radian
  ;; Longitudinal nutation in radians at c Julian centuries.
  (let* ((A (poly c (list 124.90d0 -1934.134d0 0.002063d0)))
         (B (poly c (list 201.11d0 72001.5377d0 0.00057d0))))
    (+ (* -.0000834d0 (sin-degrees A))
       (* -.0000064d0 (sin-degrees B)))))
```

```
(defun aberration (c)
  ;; TYPE julian-centuries -> radian
  ;; Aberration in radians at c Julian centuries.
  (- (* 0.0000017d0 (cosine-degrees
                     (+ 177.63d0 (* 35999.01848d0 c))))
     0.0000973d0))
```

```
(defconstant mean-tropical-year
  ;; TYPE real
  365.242199d0)
```

```
(defun solar-longitude (jd)
  ;; TYPE julian-day-number -> angle
  ;; Longitude of sun on astronomical (julian) day number jd.
  ;; Adapted from "Planetary Programs and Tables from -4000
  ;; to +2800" by Pierre Bretagnon and Jean-Louis Simon,
  ;; Willmann-Bell, Inc., 1986.
  (let* ((c       ; Ephemeris time in Julian centuries
          (julian-centuries jd))
         (coefficients
          (list 403406 195207 119433 112392 3891 2819 1721 0
                660 350 334 314 268 242 234 158 132 129 114
                99 93 86 78 72 68 64 46 38 37 32 29 28 27 27
                25 24 21 21 20 18 17 14 13 13 13 12 10 10 10
                10))
         (multipliers
```

```
           (list 0.01621043d0 628.30348067d0 628.30821524d0
                 628.29634302d0 1256.605691d0 1256.60984d0
                 628.324766d0 0.00813d0 1256.5931d0
                 575.3385d0 -0.33931d0 7771.37715d0
                 786.04191d0 0.05412d0 393.02098d0 -0.34861d0
                 1150.67698d0 157.74337d0 52.9667d0
                 588.4927d0 52.9611d0 -39.807d0 522.3769d0
                 550.7647d0 2.6108d0 157.7385d0 1884.9103d0
                 -77.5655d0 2.6489d0 1179.0627d0 550.7575d0
                 -79.6139d0 1884.8981d0 21.3219d0 1097.7103d0
                 548.6856d0 254.4393d0 -557.3143d0 606.9774d0
                 21.3279d0 1097.7163d0 -77.5282d0 1884.9191d0
                 2.0781d0 294.2463d0 -0.0799d0 469.4114d0
                 -0.6829d0 214.6325d0 1572.084d0))
          (addends
           (list 4.721964d0 5.937458d0 1.115589d0 5.781616d0
                 5.5474d0 1.512d0 4.1897d0 1.163d0 5.415d0
                 4.315d0 4.553d0 5.198d0 5.989d0 2.911d0
                 1.423d0 0.061d0 2.317d0 3.193d0 2.828d0
                 0.52d0 4.65d0 4.35d0 2.75d0 4.5d0 3.23d0
                 1.22d0 0.14d0 3.44d0 4.37d0 1.14d0 2.84d0
                 5.96d0 5.09d0 1.72d0 2.56d0 1.92d0 0.09d0
                 5.98d0 4.03d0 4.47d0 0.79d0 4.24d0 2.01d0
                 2.65d0 4.98d0 0.93d0 2.21d0 3.59d0 1.5d0
                 2.55d0))
          (longitude
           (+ 4.9353929d0
              (* 628.33196168d0 c)
              (* 0.0000001d0
                 (sigma ((x coefficients)
                         (y addends)
                         (z multipliers))
                        (* x (sin (+ y (* z c))))))))
     (radians-to-degrees
      (+ longitude (aberration c) (nutation c)))))
```

```
(defun date-next-solar-longitude (jd l)
  ;; TYPE (julian-day-number angle) -> julian-day-number
  ;; Julian day number of the first date at or after julian
  ;; day number jd (in Greenwich) when the solar longitude
  ;; will be a multiple of l degrees; l must be a proper
  ;; divisor of 360.
  (let* ((next (double-float
                (degrees
                 (* l (ceiling (/ (solar-longitude jd)
                                  l)))))))
    (binary-search
     start jd
     end   (+ jd (* (/ l 360) 400d0))
     x     (if (= next 0); Discontinuity at next=0
               ;; Then test for drop in longitude
               (>= l (solar-longitude x))
             ;; Else test if we are past the desired
             ;; longitude
             (>= (solar-longitude x) next))
     (>= 0.00001d0 (- end start)))))
```

```
(defun solar-moment (date latitude longitude rise-or-set)
  ;; TYPE (fixed-date angle angle real) -> moment
  ;; Local time (fraction of day) of sunrise/sunset at
  ;; latitude, longitude (in nonpolar regions) for fixed
  ;; date.  rise-or-set is -0.25 for sunrise and +0.25 for
  ;; sunset.
  (let* ((approx  ; Approximate time of event.
          (+ (day-number (gregorian-from-fixed date))
             0.5 rise-or-set (/ longitude -360.0d0)))
```

```lisp
         (anomaly ; Anomaly of sun.
          (- (* 0.9856d0 approx) 3.289d0))
         (sun     ; Longitude of sun.
          (degrees (+ anomaly (* 1.916d0
                                 (sin-degrees anomaly))
                      282.634d0
                      (* 0.020d0
                         (sin-degrees (* 2 anomaly))))))
         (right-ascension ; Right ascension of sun.
          (arctan-degrees
           (* (cosine-degrees 23.441884d0)
              (tangent-degrees sun))
           (1+ (quotient sun 90)))) ; Quadrant.
         (declination ; Declination of sun.
          (arcsin-degrees (* (sin-degrees 23.441884d0)
                             (sin-degrees sun))))
         (local (* (signum rise-or-set)
                   (arccos-degrees
                    (/ (- (cosine-degrees 90.833333d0)
                          (* (sin-degrees declination)
                             (sin-degrees latitude)))
                       (cosine-degrees declination)
                       (cosine-degrees latitude))))))
    (mod (- (/ (+ local right-ascension) 360)
            0.27592d0 (* 0.00273792d0 approx))
         1)))
```

```lisp
(defun sunrise (date latitude longitude)
  ;; TYPE (fixed-date angle angle) -> moment
  ;; Local time (fraction of day) of sunrise at latitude,
  ;; longitude (in nonpolar regions) for fixed date.
  (solar-moment date latitude longitude -0.25d0))
```

```lisp
(defun sunset (date latitude longitude)
  ;; TYPE (fixed-date angle angle) -> moment
  ;; Local time (fraction of day) of sunset at latitude,
  ;; longitude (in nonpolar regions) for fixed date.
  (solar-moment date latitude longitude 0.25d0))
```

```lisp
(defconstant mean-synodic-month
  ;; TYPE real
  29.530588853d0)
```

```lisp
(defun lunar-longitude (u-time)
  ;; TYPE moment -> angle
  ;; Longitude of sun (in degrees) at u-time (Universal time).
  ;; Adapted from "Astronomical Algorithms" by Jean Meeus,
  ;; Willmann-Bell, Inc., 1991.
  (let* ((c (julian-centuries u-time))
         (mean-moon
          (degrees
           (poly c
                 (list 218.3164591d0 481267.88134236d0
                       -.0013268d0 1/538841 -1/65194000))))
         (elongation
          (degrees
           (poly c
                 (list 297.8502042d0 445267.1115168d0
                       -.00163d0 1/545868 -1/113065000))))
         (solar-anomaly
          (degrees
           (poly c
                 (list 357.5291092d0 35999.0502909d0
                       -.0001536d0 1/24490000))))
         (lunar-anomaly
```

```
          (degrees
           (poly c
                 (list 134.9634114d0 477198.8676313d0
                       0.008997d0 1/69699 -1/14712000))))
         (moon-from-node
          (degrees
           (poly c
                 (list 93.2720993d0 483202.0175273d0
                       -.0034029d0 -1/3526000 1/863310000))))
         (e (poly c (list 1 -0.002516d0 -0.0000074d0)))
         (args-lunar-elongation
          (list 0 2 2 0 0 0 2 2 2 2 0 1 0 2 0 0 4 0 4 2 2 1
                1 2 2 4 2 0 2 2 1 2 0 0 2 2 2 4 0 3 2 4 0 2
                2 2 4 0 4 1 2 0 1 3 4 2 0 1 2 2))
         (args-solar-anomaly
          (list 0 0 0 0 1 0 0 -1 0 -1 1 0 1 0 0 0 0 0 0 1 1
                0 1 -1 0 0 0 1 0 -1 0 -2 1 2 -2 0 0 -1 0 0 1
                -1 2 2 1 -1 0 0 -1 0 1 0 1 0 0 -1 2 1 0 0))
         (args-lunar-anomaly
          (list 1 -1 0 2 0 0 -2 -1 1 0 -1 0 1 0 1 1 -1 3 -2
                -1 0 -1 0 1 2 0 -3 -2 -1 -2 1 0 2 0 -1 1 0
                -1 2 -1 1 -2 -1 -1 -2 0 1 4 0 -2 0 2 1 -2 -3
                2 1 -1 3 -1))
         (args-moon-from-node
          (list 0 0 0 0 0 2 0 0 0 0 0 0 0 -2 2 -2 0 0 0 0 0
                0 0 0 0 0 0 0 2 0 0 0 0 0 0 -2 2 0 2 0 0 0 0
                0 0 -2 0 0 0 0 -2 -2 0 0 0 0 0 0 0 -2))
         (sine-coefficients
          (list 6288774 1274027 658314 213618 -185116 -114332
                58793 57066 53322 45758 -40923 -34720 -30383
                15327 -12528 10980 10675 10034 8548 -7888
                -6766 -5163 4987 4036 3994 3861 3665 -2689
                -2602 2390 -2348 2236 -2120 -2069 2048 -1773
                -1595 1215 -1110 -892 -810 759 -713 -700 691
                596 549 537 520 -487 -399 -381 351 -340 330
                327 -323 299 294 0))
         (longitude
          (* 1/1000000
             (sigma ((v sine-coefficients)
                     (w args-lunar-elongation)
                     (x args-solar-anomaly)
                     (y args-lunar-anomaly)
                     (z args-moon-from-node))
                    (* v (expt e (abs x))
                       (sin-degrees
                        (+ (* w elongation)
                           (* x solar-anomaly)
                           (* y lunar-anomaly)
                           (* z moon-from-node)))))))
         (venus (* 3958/1000000
                   (sin-degrees
                    (+ 119.75d0 (* c 131.849d0)))))
         (jupiter (* 318/1000000
                     (sin-degrees
                      (+ 53.09d0 (* c 479264.29d0)))))
         (flat-earth
          (* 1962/1000000
             (sin-degrees (- mean-moon moon-from-node)))))
    (degrees (+ mean-moon longitude venus jupiter flat-earth
                (radians-to-degrees (nutation c))))))
```

```
(defun new-moon-time (k)
  ;; TYPE integer -> julian-day-number
  ;; Astronomical (julian) day number (at Greenwich) of k-th
  ;; new moon after (or before) the new moon of January 6,
  ;; 2000.  Adapted from "Astronomical Algorithms" by Jean
  ;; Meeus, Willmann-Bell, Inc., 1991.
```

```
  (let* ((c (/ k 1236.85d0))
         (JDE (poly c (list 2451550.09765d0
                            (* mean-synodic-month
                               1236.85d0)
                            0.0001337d0
                            -0.000000150d0
                            0.00000000073d0)))
         (e (poly c (list 1 -0.002516d0 -0.0000074d0)))
         (solar-anomaly
          (poly c (list 2.5534d0 (* 29.10535669d0 1236.85d0)
                        -0.0000218d0 -0.00000011d0)))
         (lunar-anomaly
          (poly c (list 201.5643d0 (* 385.81693528d0
                                      1236.85d0)
                        0.0107438d0 0.00001239d0
                        -0.000000058d0)))
         (moon-argument
          (poly c (list 160.7108d0 (* 390.67050274d0
                                      1236.85d0)
                        -0.0016341d0 -0.00000227d0
                        0.000000011d0)))
         (omega
          (poly c (list 124.7746d0 (* -1.56375580d0 1236.85d0)
                        0.0020691d0 0.00000215d0)))
         (e-factor (list 0 1 0 0 1 1 2 0 0 1 0 1 1 1 0 0 0 0
                         0 0 0 0 0 0))
         (solar-coeff (list 0 1 0 0 -1 1 2 0 0 1 0 1 1 -1 2
                            0 3 1 0 1 -1 -1 1 0))
         (lunar-coeff (list 1 0 2 0 1 1 0 1 1 2 3 0 0 2 1 2
                            0 1 2 1 1 1 3 4))
         (moon-coeff (list 0 0 0 2 0 0 0 -2 2 0 0 2 -2 0 0
                           -2 0 -2 2 2 2 -2 0 0))
         (sine-coeff
          (list -0.40720d0 0.17241d0 0.01608d0 0.01039d0
                0.00739d0 -0.00514d0 0.00208d0
                -0.00111d0 -0.00057d0 0.00056d0
                -0.00042d0 0.00042d0 0.00038d0
                -0.00024d0 -0.00007d0 0.00004d0
                0.00004d0 0.00003d0 0.00003d0
                -0.00003d0 0.00003d0 -0.00002d0
                -0.00002d0 0.00002d0))
         (correction
          (+ (* -.00017d0 (sin-degrees omega))
             (sigma ((v sine-coeff)
                     (w e-factor)
                     (x solar-coeff)
                     (y lunar-coeff)
                     (z moon-coeff))
                    (* v (expt e w)
                       (sin-degrees
                        (+ (* x solar-anomaly)
                           (* y lunar-anomaly)
                           (* z moon-argument)))))))
         (add-const
          (list 299.77d0 251.88d0 251.83d0 349.42d0 84.66d0
                141.74d0 207.14d0 154.84d0 34.52d0 207.19d0
                291.34d0 161.72d0 239.56d0 331.55d0))
         (add-coeff
          (list 0.107408d0 0.016321d0 26.641886d0
                36.412478d0 18.206239d0 53.303771d0
                2.453732d0 7.306860d0 27.261239d0 0.121824d0
                1.844379d0 24.198154d0 25.513099d0
                3.592518d0))
         (add-extra
          (list -0.009173d0 0 0 0 0 0 0 0 0 0 0 0 0 0))
         (add-factor
          (list 0.000325d0 0.000165d0 0.000164d0 0.000126d0
```

```
                 0.000110d0 0.000062d0 0.000060d0 0.000056d0
                 0.000047d0 0.000042d0 0.000040d0 0.000037d0
                 0.000035d0 0.000023d0))
          (additional
           (sigma ((i add-const)
                   (j add-coeff)
                   (n add-extra)
                   (l add-factor))
                  (* l (sin-degrees
                        (+ i (* j k) (* n c c)))))))
     (universal-from-ephemeris (+ JDE correction additional))))
```

```
(defun new-moon-at-or-after (jd)
  ;; TYPE julian-day-number -> julian-day-number
  ;; Astronomical (julian) day number of first new moon at
  ;; or after astronomical (julian) day number jd (in
  ;; Greenwich).  The fractional part is the time of day.
  (let* ((date; Gregorian date, Universal Time
          (gregorian-from-fixed
           (floor (moment-from-jd jd))))
         (approx; Approximate number of new moons since
                ; January 6, 2000
          (1- (floor (* (- (+ (standard-year date)
                              (/ (day-number date) 365.25d0))
                           2000.0d0)
                        12.3685d0)))) ; New moons per year.
         (error (sum 1 k approx (< (new-moon-time k) jd))))
    (new-moon-time (+ approx error))))
```

```
(defun new-moon-before (jd)
  ;; TYPE julian-day-number -> julian-day-number
  ;; Astronomical (julian) day number of last new moon
  ;; before astronomical (julian) day number jd (in
  ;; Greenwich).  The fractional part is the time of day.
  (new-moon-at-or-after (- (new-moon-at-or-after jd) 45)))
```

```
(defun lunar-phase-at-or-before (phase jd)
  ;; TYPE (phase julian-day-number) -> julian-day-number
  ;; Astronomical (julian) day number of last time moon was
  ;; in phase phase (in degrees) at or before astronomical
  ;; (julian) day number jd (in Greenwich).  The fractional
  ;; part is the time of day.
  (let* ((close (< (degrees (- (lunar-solar-angle jd)
                               phase))
                   40))
         (yesterday (1- jd))
         (orig (+ 2451550.26d0
                  (* mean-synodic-month (/ phase 360))))
         (epsilon 0.000001d0)
         (tau (- yesterday
                 (mod (- yesterday orig)
                      mean-synodic-month))))
    (binary-search
     l (if close (- jd 4) (- tau 2))
     u (if close jd (+ tau 2))
     x (<= phase (lunar-solar-angle x) (+ phase 90))
     (< (- u l) epsilon))))
```

```
(defun lunar-solar-angle (jd)
  ;; TYPE julian-day-number -> phase
  ;; Lunar phase, as an angle in degrees, at astronomical
  ;; (julian) day number jd.  An angle of 0 means a new
  ;; moon, 90 degrees means the first quarter, 180 means a
  ;; full moon, and 270 degrees means the last quarter.
  (degrees (- (lunar-longitude jd)
              (solar-longitude jd))))
```

```
(defconstant new
  ;; TYPE phase
  ;; Excess of lunar longitude over solar longitude at new
  ;; moon.
  0)
```

```
(defconstant full
  ;; TYPE phase
  ;; Excess of lunar longitude over solar longitude at full
  ;; moon.
  180)
```

```
(defconstant first-quarter
  ;; TYPE phase
  ;; Excess of lunar longitude over solar longitude at first
  ;; quarter moon.
  90)
```

```
(defconstant last-quarter
  ;; TYPE phase
  ;; Excess of lunar longitude over solar longitude at last
  ;; quarter moon.
  270)
```

```
(defun new-moon-at-or-before (jd)
  ;; TYPE julian-day-number -> julian-day-number
  ;; Astronomical (julian) day number of last new moon
  ;; at or before astronomical (julian) day number jd (in
  ;; Greenwich).  The fractional part is the time of day.
  (lunar-phase-at-or-before new jd))
```

```
(defun full-moon-at-or-before (jd)
  ;; TYPE julian-day-number -> julian-day-number
  ;; Astronomical (julian) day number of last full moon
  ;; at or before astronomical (julian) day number jd (in
  ;; Greenwich).  The fractional part is the time of day.
  (lunar-phase-at-or-before full jd))
```

```
(defun first-quarter-moon-at-or-before (jd)
  ;; TYPE julian-day-number -> julian-day-number
  ;; Astronomical (julian) day number of last first-quarter
  ;; moon at or before astronomical (julian) day number jd
  ;; (in Greenwich).  The fractional part is the time of
  ;; day.
  (lunar-phase-at-or-before first-quarter jd))
```

```
(defun last-quarter-moon-at-or-before (jd)
  ;; TYPE julian-day-number -> julian-day-number
  ;; Astronomical (julian) day number of last last-quarter
  ;; moon at or before astronomical (julian) day number jd
  ;; (in Greenwich).  The fractional part is the time of
  ;; day.
  (lunar-phase-at-or-before last-quarter jd))
```

B.15 The French Revolutionary Calendar

```
(defun french-date (month day year)
  ;; TYPE (french-month french-day french-year) -> french-date
  (list month day year))
```

```
(defconstant french-epoch
  ;; TYPE fixed-date
  ;; Fixed date of start of the French Revolutionary
  ;; calendar.
  (fixed-from-gregorian (gregorian-date september 22 1792)))
```

```
(defconstant french-time-zone
  ;; TYPE minute
  ;; The difference (in minutes) of the Paris time zone
  ;; from Universal Time.
  (+ 9 21/60))
```

```
(defun french-autumnal-equinox-on-or-before (date)
  ;; TYPE fixed-date -> fixed-date
  ;; Fixed date, in Paris local time, of autumnal equinox
  ;; on or before fixed date.
  (let* ((theta; solar longitude at end of date in Paris
          (solar-longitude
           (universal-from-local
            (jd-from-moment (1+ date))
            french-time-zone)))
         (d-prime; date shortly before previous autumnal
                 ; equinox
          (if (< 150d0 theta 180d0); if date is in August or
                                   ; in September before the
                                   ; autumnal equinox...
              (- date 370); ...then pick a date before the
                          ; prior autumnal equinox
            ; ...otherwise, if date is beyond the autumnal
            ; equinox, pick a date before the last autumnal
            ; equinox
            (- date (mod (- date 260) mean-tropical-year)))))
    (fixed-from-jd
     (apparent-from-local
      (local-from-universal
       (date-next-solar-longitude
        (universal-from-local
         (jd-from-moment d-prime)
         french-time-zone)
        90)
       french-time-zone)))))
```

```
(defun fixed-from-french (f-date)
  ;; TYPE french-date -> fixed-date
  ;; Fixed date of French Revolutionary date.
  (let* ((month (standard-month f-date))
         (day (standard-day f-date))
         (year (standard-year f-date))
         (new-year
          (french-autumnal-equinox-on-or-before
           (ceiling (+ french-epoch
                       (* mean-tropical-year
                          (1- year)))))))
    (+ (1- new-year)    ;  Days in prior years
       (* 30 (1- month)); Days in prior months
       day)))           ;  Days this month
```

```
(defun french-from-fixed (date)
  ;; TYPE fixed-date -> french-date
  ;; French Revolutionary date of fixed date.
  (let* ((new-year
          (french-autumnal-equinox-on-or-before date))
         (year (1+ (round (/ (- new-year french-epoch)
                             mean-tropical-year))))
         (month (1+ (quotient (- date new-year) 30)))
```

```
           (day (1+ (mod (- date new-year) 30))))
      (french-date month day year)))
```

```
(defun modified-french-leap-year? (f-year)
  ;; TYPE french-year -> boolean
  ;; True if f-year is a leap year on the French Revolutionary
  ;; calendar.
  (and (= (mod f-year 4) 0)
       (not (member (mod f-year 400) (list 100 200 300)))
       (not (= (mod f-year 4000) 0))))
```

```
(defun fixed-from-modified-french (f-date)
  ;; TYPE french-date -> fixed-date
  ;; Fixed date of French Revolutionary date.
  (let* ((month (first f-date))
         (day (second f-date))
         (year (third f-date)))
    (+ french-epoch -1; Days before start of calendar.
       (* 365 (1- year)); Ordinary days in prior years.
       ; Leap days in prior years.
       (quotient (1- year) 4)
       (- (quotient (1- year) 100))
       (quotient (1- year) 400)
       (- (quotient (1- year) 4000))
       (* 30 (1- month)); Days in prior months this year.
       day))); Days this month.
```

```
(defun modified-french-from-fixed (date)
  ;; TYPE fixed-date -> french-year
  ;; French Revolutionary date (month day year) of fixed
  ;; date.
  (let* ((approx   ; Approximate year (may be off by 1).
          (quotient (- date french-epoch) 1460969/4000))
         (year     ; Search forward.
          (+ approx -1 ; Lower bound
             (sum 1 y approx
                  (>= date
                      (fixed-from-modified-french
                       (french-date 1 1 y))))))
         (month    ; Calculate the month by division.
          (1+ (quotient
               (- date (fixed-from-modified-french
                        (french-date 1 1 year)))
               30)))
         (day      ; Calculate the day by subtraction.
          (1+ (- date
                 (fixed-from-modified-french
                  (french-date month 1 year))))))
    (french-date month day year)))
```

B.16 The Chinese Calendar

```
(defun chinese-date (cycle year month leap day)
  ;; TYPE (chinese-cycle chinese-year chinese-month
  ;; TYPE  chinese-leap chinese-day) -> chinese-date
  (list cycle year month leap day))
```

```
(defun chinese-cycle (date)
  ;; TYPE chinese-date -> chinese-cycle
  (first date))
```

```
(defun chinese-year (date)
  ;; TYPE chinese-date -> chinese-year
  (second date))
```

```
(defun chinese-month (date)
  ;; TYPE chinese-date -> chinese-month
  (third date))
```

```
(defun chinese-leap (date)
  ;; TYPE chinese-date -> chinese-leap
  (fourth date))
```

```
(defun chinese-day (date)
  ;; TYPE chinese-date -> chinese-day
  (fifth date))
```

```
(defun current-major-solar-term (date)
  ;; TYPE fixed-date -> integer
  ;; Last Chinese major solar term (zhongqi) before fixed
  ;; date.
  (let ((s (solar-longitude
            (universal-from-local
             (jd-from-moment date)
             (chinese-time-zone date)))))
    (adjusted-mod (+ 2 (quotient s 30)) 12)))
```

```
(defun chinese-time-zone (date)
  ;; TYPE fixed-date -> real
  ;; The difference (in minutes) of the Beijing time zone
  ;; from Universal Time on fixed date.
  (let* ((year (gregorian-year-from-fixed date)))
    (if (< year 1929)
        (+ 465 40/60)
      480)))
```

```
(defun chinese-date-next-solar-longitude (d l)
  ;; (fixed-date angle) -> fixed-date
  ;; Fixed date (Beijing time) of the first date on or
  ;; after fixed date d (Beijing time) when the solar
  ;; longitude will be a multiple of l degrees.
  (fixed-from-jd
   (local-from-universal
    (date-next-solar-longitude
     (universal-from-local (jd-from-moment d)
                           (chinese-time-zone d))
     l)
    (chinese-time-zone d))))
```

```
(defun major-solar-term-on-or-after (date)
  ;; TYPE fixed-date -> fixed-date
  ;; Fixed date (in Beijing) of the first Chinese major
  ;; solar term (zhongqi) on or after fixed date.  The
  ;; major terms begin when the sun's longitude is a
  ;; multiple of 30 degrees.
  (chinese-date-next-solar-longitude date 30))
```

```
(defun current-minor-solar-term (date)
  ;; TYPE fixed-date -> integer
  ;; Last Chinese minor solar term (jieqi) before date.
  (let* ((s (solar-longitude
             (universal-from-local
              (jd-from-moment date)
              (chinese-time-zone date)))))
    (adjusted-mod (+ 3 (quotient (- s 15) 30)) 12)))
```

```
(defun minor-solar-term-on-or-after (date)
  ;; TYPE fixed-date -> fixed-date
  ;; Fixed date (in Beijing) of the first Chinese minor
  ;; solar term (jieqi) on or after fixed date.  The
  ;; minor terms begin when the sun's longitude is a
  ;; multiple of 30 degrees.
  (let* ((d (chinese-date-next-solar-longitude date 15))
         (s (solar-longitude
             (universal-from-local
              (jd-from-moment d)
              (chinese-time-zone d)))))
    (if (= (mod (round s) 30) 0)
        (chinese-date-next-solar-longitude d 15)
      d)))
```

```
(defun chinese-new-moon-on-or-after (date)
  ;; TYPE fixed-date -> fixed-date
  ;; Fixed date (Beijing) of first new moon on or after
  ;; fixed date.
  (fixed-from-jd
   (local-from-universal
    (new-moon-at-or-after
     (universal-from-local
      (jd-from-moment date)
      (chinese-time-zone date)))
    (chinese-time-zone date))))
```

```
(defun chinese-new-moon-before (date)
  ;; TYPE fixed-date -> fixed-date
  ;; Fixed date (Beijing) of first new moon before
  ;; fixed date.
  (fixed-from-jd
   (local-from-universal
    (new-moon-before
     (universal-from-local
      (jd-from-moment date)
      (chinese-time-zone date)))
    (chinese-time-zone date))))
```

```
(defun no-major-solar-term? (date)
  ;; TYPE fixed-date -> boolean
  ;; True if Chinese lunar month starting on date
  ;; has no major solar term.
  (= (current-major-solar-term date)
     (current-major-solar-term
      (chinese-new-moon-on-or-after (1+ date)))))
```

```
(defun prior-leap-month? (m-prime m)
  ;; TYPE (fixed-date fixed-date) -> boolean
  ;; True if there is a Chinese leap month at or after lunar
  ;; month m-prime and at or before lunar month m.
  (and (>= m m-prime)
       (or (prior-leap-month? m-prime
                              (chinese-new-moon-before m))
           (no-major-solar-term? m))))
```

```
(defconstant chinese-epoch
  ;; TYPE fixed-date
  ;; Fixed date of start of the Chinese calendar.
  (fixed-from-gregorian (gregorian-date february 15 -2636)))
```

```
(defun chinese-from-fixed (date)
  ;; TYPE fixed-date -> chinese-date
  ;; Chinese date (cycle year month leap day) of fixed
```

```
  ;; date.
  (let* ((g-year (gregorian-year-from-fixed date))
         (s1; Prior solstice for most dates
          (major-solar-term-on-or-after
           (fixed-from-gregorian
            (gregorian-date december 15 (1- g-year)))))
         (s2; Following solstice for most dates--can be the
            ; prior solstice if the date is at the end of
            ; the Gregorian year, just after the solstice
          (major-solar-term-on-or-after
           (fixed-from-gregorian
            (gregorian-date december 15 g-year))))
         (m1      ; month after last 11th month
          (if (and (<= s1 date) (< date s2))
              (chinese-new-moon-on-or-after (1+ s1))
            ;; Date is at end of the Gregorian year, just
            ;; after the solstice, so we need the solstice
            ;; of that year
            (chinese-new-moon-on-or-after (1+ s2))))
         (m2      ; next 11th month
          (if (and (<= s1 date) (< date s2))
              (chinese-new-moon-before (1+ s2))
            ;; Date is at end of the Gregorian year, just
            ;; after the solstice, so we need the solstice
            ;; of the following year
            (chinese-new-moon-before
             (1+ (major-solar-term-on-or-after
                  (fixed-from-gregorian
                   (gregorian-date
                    december 15 (1+ g-year))))))))
         (m       ; start of month containing date
          (chinese-new-moon-before (1+ date)))
         (leap-year; if there are 13 new moons (12 full
                   ; lunar months)
          (= (round (/ (- m2 m1) mean-synodic-month)) 12))
         (month   ; month number
          (adjusted-mod
           (-
            ;; ordinal position of month in year
            (round (/ (- m m1) mean-synodic-month))
            ;; minus 1 during or after a leap month
            (if (and leap-year (prior-leap-month? m1 m))
                1
              0))
           12))
         (leap-month    ; it's a leap month if...
          (and leap-year; ...there are 13 months
               (no-major-solar-term? m); no major solar term
               (not (prior-leap-month?; and no prior leap month
                     m1 (chinese-new-moon-before m)))))
         (elapsed-years ; since the epoch
          (+ (- (gregorian-year-from-fixed date)
                (gregorian-year-from-fixed chinese-epoch))
            (if (or (< month 11)
                    (> date (fixed-from-gregorian
                             (gregorian-date july 1 g-year))))
                1 0)))
         (cycle (1+ (quotient (1- elapsed-years) 60)))
         (year (adjusted-mod elapsed-years 60))
         (day (1+ (- date m))))
    (chinese-date cycle year month leap-month day)))
```

```
(defun chinese-new-year (g-year)
  ;; TYPE gregorian-year -> fixed-date
  ;; Fixed date of Chinese New Year in Gregorian year.
  (let* ((s1; prior solstice
          (major-solar-term-on-or-after
```

```
          (fixed-from-gregorian
           (gregorian-date
            december 15 (1- g-year)))))
        (s2; following solstice
         (major-solar-term-on-or-after
          (fixed-from-gregorian
           (gregorian-date december 15 g-year))))
        (m1 ; month after last 11th month--either 12 or
            ; leap 11
         (chinese-new-moon-on-or-after (1+ s1)))
        (m2 ; month after m2--either 1 or leap 12
         (chinese-new-moon-on-or-after (1+ m1)))
        (m11 ; next 11th month
         (chinese-new-moon-before (1+ s2))))
  (if ; Either m1 or m2 is a leap month if there are 13
      ; new moons (12 full lunar months) and either m1 or
      ; m2 has no major solar term
      (and (= (round (/ (- m11 m1) mean-synodic-month)) 12)
           (or (no-major-solar-term? m1)
               (no-major-solar-term? m2)))
      (chinese-new-moon-on-or-after (1+ m2))
    m2)))
```

```
(defun fixed-from-chinese (c-date)
  ;; TYPE chinese-date -> fixed-date
  ;; Fixed date of Chinese date (cycle year month leap
  ;; day).
  (let* ((cycle (chinese-cycle c-date))
         (year (chinese-year c-date))
         (month (chinese-month c-date))
         (leap (chinese-leap c-date))
         (day (chinese-day c-date))
         (g-year; Gregorian year at start of Chinese year
          (+ (* (1- cycle) 60); years in prior cycles
             (1- year)        ; prior years this cycle
             ;; Gregorian year at start of calendar
             (gregorian-year-from-fixed chinese-epoch)))
         (new-year (chinese-new-year g-year))
         (p; new moon before date--a month too early if
            ; there was prior leap month that year
          (chinese-new-moon-on-or-after
           (+ new-year (* (1- month) 29))))
         (d (chinese-from-fixed p))
         (prior-new-moon
          (if  ; If the months match...
              (and (= month (chinese-month d))
                   (equal leap (chinese-leap d)))
              p; ...that's the right month
            ;; otherwise, there was a prior leap month that
            ;; year, so we want the next month
            (chinese-new-moon-on-or-after (1+ p)))))
    (+ prior-new-moon day -1)))
```

```
(defun chinese-sexagesimal-name (n)
  ;; TYPE integer -> ({1--10} {1-12})
  ;; The n-th name of the Chinese sexagesimal cycle.
  (list (adjusted-mod n 10)
        (adjusted-mod n 12)))
```

```
(defun chinese-name-of-year (y)
  ;; TYPE chinese-year -> ({1--10} {1-12})
  ;; Sexagesimal name for Chinese year y of any cycle.
  (chinese-sexagesimal-name y))
```

```
(defun chinese-name-of-day (date)
  ;; TYPE chinese-date -> ({1--10} {1-12})
  ;; Sexagesimal name for Chinese date.
  (chinese-sexagesimal-name
   (+ (fixed-from-chinese date) 15)))
```

```
(defun chinese-name-of-month (y m)
  ;; TYPE chinese-month -> ({1--10} {1-12})
  ;; Sexagesimal name for Chinese month m in year y of any
  ;; cycle.
  (chinese-sexagesimal-name (+ (* 12 y) m 44)))
```

```
(defun dragon-festival (g-year)
  ;; TYPE gregorian-year -> fixed-date
  ;; Fixed date of the Dragon Festival occurring in
  ;; Gregorian year.
  (let* ((elapsed-years
          (1+ (- g-year
                 (gregorian-year-from-fixed
                  chinese-epoch))))
         (cycle (1+ (quotient (1- elapsed-years) 60)))
         (year (adjusted-mod elapsed-years 60)))
    (fixed-from-chinese (chinese-date cycle year 5 false 5))))
```

B.17 The Modern Hindu Calendars

Common Lisp supplies arithmetic with arbitrary rational numbers, and we take advantage of it for implementing the Hindu calendars. With other languages, double precision is required for many of the calculations.

```
(defun hindu-sine-table (entry)
  ;; TYPE integer -> arcminute
  ;; This simulates the Hindu sine table.
  ;; entry is an angle given as a multiplier of 225'.
  (let* ((exact (* 3438 (sin-degrees (* entry 225/60))))
         (error (* 0.215 (signum exact)
                   (signum (- (abs exact) 1716)))))
    (round (+ exact error))))
```

```
(defun hindu-sine (theta)
  ;; TYPE arcminute -> [-3438:3438]
  ;; theta is in minutes of arc.
  ;; Linear interpolation in Hindu table is used.
  (let* ((entry (/ theta 225)) ; Interpolate in table.
         (fraction (mod entry 1)))
    (+ (* fraction
          (hindu-sine-table (ceiling entry)))
       (* (- 1 fraction)
          (hindu-sine-table (floor entry))))))
```

```
(defun hindu-arcsin (units)
  ;; TYPE [-3438:3438] -> arcminute
  ;; Inverse of Hindu sine function.
  (if (< units 0) (- (hindu-arcsin (- units)))
    (let* ((pos (sum 1 k 0 (> units (hindu-sine-table k))))
           (val ; Lower value in table.
            (hindu-sine-table (1- pos))))
      (* 225 (+ pos -1  ; Interpolate.
                (/ (- units val)
                   (- (hindu-sine-table pos) val)))))))
```

```
(defconstant hindu-creation
  ;; TYPE integer
  ;; Days from creation to onset of Hindu epoch.
  (* 1955880000 hindu-sidereal-year))
```

```
(defun mean-position (ky-time period)
  ;; TYPE (hindu-moment rational) -> arcminute
  ;; Position in minutes of arc at ky-time
  ;; in uniform circular orbit of period days.
  (* 21600 (mod (/ ky-time period) 1)))
```

```
(defun true-position (ky-time period size anomalistic change)
  ;; TYPE (hindu-moment rational positive-integer rational
  ;; TYPE  non-negative-integer) -> arcminute
  ;; Longitudinal position (in arcminutes) at ky-time since
  ;; Hindu epoch. period is period of mean motion.  size is
  ;; ratio of radii of epicycle and deferent.  anomalistic
  ;; is the period of retrograde revolution about epicycle.
  ;; change is maximum decrease in epicycle size.
  (let* ((long ; Position of epicycle center
          (mean-position ky-time period))
         (days (+ ky-time hindu-creation)) ; since creation
         (offset ; Sine of anomaly
          (hindu-sine (mean-position days anomalistic)))
         (contraction (* (abs offset) change size 1/3438))
         (equation ; Equation of center
          (hindu-arcsin (* offset (- size contraction)))))
    (mod (- long equation) 21600)))
```

```
(defconstant hindu-sidereal-year
  ;; TYPE rational
  ;; Mean length of Hindu sidereal year.
  (+ 365 279457/1080000))
```

```
(defconstant hindu-sidereal-month
  ;; TYPE rational
  ;; Mean length of Hindu sidereal month.
  (+ 27 4644439/14438334))
```

```
(defconstant hindu-synodic-month
  ;; TYPE rational
  ;; Mean time from new moon to new moon.
  (+ 29 7087771/13358334))
```

```
(defconstant hindu-anomalistic-year
  ;; TYPE rational
  ;; Time from aphelion to aphelion.
  (/ 1577917828000 (- 4320000000 387)))
```

```
(defconstant hindu-anomalistic-month
  ;; TYPE rational
  ;; Time from apogee to apogee, with bija correction.
  (/ 1577917828 (- 57753336 488199)))
```

```
(defun hindu-solar-longitude (ky-time)
  ;; TYPE hindu-moment -> arcminute
  ;; Solar longitude in arcminutes at ky-time since epoch.
  (true-position ky-time hindu-sidereal-year
                 14/360 hindu-anomalistic-year 1/42))
```

```
(defun hindu-zodiac (ky-time)
  ;; TYPE hindu-moment -> hindu-solar-month
  ;; Zodiacal sign of the sun, as integer in range 1..12,
  ;; at ky-time.
  (1+ (quotient (hindu-solar-longitude ky-time) 1800)))
```

```
(defun hindu-lunar-longitude (ky-time)
  ;; TYPE hindu-moment -> arcminute
  ;; Lunar longitude in arcminutes at ky-time.
  (true-position ky-time hindu-sidereal-month
                 32/360 hindu-anomalistic-month 1/42))
```

```
(defun hindu-lunar-phase (ky-time)
  ;; TYPE hindu-moment -> arcminute
  ;; Longitudinal distance between the sun and moon
  ;; in arcminutes at ky-time since Hindu epoch.
  (mod (- (hindu-lunar-longitude ky-time)
          (hindu-solar-longitude ky-time))
       21600))
```

```
(defun lunar-day (ky-time)
  ;; TYPE hindu-moment -> hindu-lunar-day
  ;; Phase of moon (tithi) at ky-time,
  ;; as an integer in the range 1..30.
  (1+ (quotient (hindu-lunar-phase ky-time) 720)))
```

```
(defun hindu-new-moon (ky-time)
  ;; TYPE hindu-moment -> hindu-moment
  ;; Last new moon preceding ky-time since epoch.
  (let* ((tomorrow (1+ ky-time))
         (estimate  ; Can be off by 2/3 day.
          (- tomorrow (mod tomorrow hindu-synodic-month)))
         (try (binary-search ; Search for phase start.
               l (- estimate 2/3)
               u (+ estimate 2/3)
               x (< (hindu-lunar-phase x) 10800)
               (or (< ky-time l) ; Wrong new moon
                   (and (<= u ky-time)
                        (= (hindu-zodiac l)
                           (hindu-zodiac u)))))))
    (if (> try ky-time); Check whether before/after ky-time.
        (hindu-new-moon ; It's previous month.
         (- (floor ky-time) 20))
      try)))
```

```
(defun hindu-solar-date (month day year)
  ;; TYPE (hindu-solar-month hindu-solar-day hindu-solar-year)
  ;; TYPE -> hindu-solar-date
  (list month day year))
```

```
(defconstant hindu-solar-era
  ;; TYPE standard-year
  ;; Years from Kali Yuga until Saka era.
  3179)
```

```
(defun hindu-solar-from-fixed (date)
  ;; TYPE fixed-date -> hindu-solar-date
  ;; Hindu solar date equivalent to fixed date.
  (let* ((ky-time (hindu-day-count date)) ; Hindu date KY.
         (rise    ; Sunrise on Hindu date.
          (hindu-sunrise ky-time))
         (month (hindu-zodiac rise))
         (year (- (hindu-calendar-year rise)
                  hindu-solar-era))
         (approx ; 3 days before start of mean month.
          (- ky-time 3
             (quotient (mod (hindu-solar-longitude rise)
                            1800)
                       60)))
         (begin (+ approx ; Search forward for beginning...
```

```
                    (sum 1 i approx ; ... of month.
                         (/= (hindu-zodiac (hindu-sunrise i))
                             month))))
          (day (- ky-time begin -1)))
     (gregorian-date month day year)))
```

```
(defun hindu-solar-precedes? (s-date1 s-date2)
  ;; TYPE (hindu-solar-date hindu-solar-date) -> boolean
  ;; True if Hindu solar s-date1 precedes s-date2.
  (let* ((month1 (standard-month s-date1))
         (month2 (standard-month s-date2))
         (day1 (standard-day s-date1))
         (day2 (standard-day s-date2))
         (year1 (standard-year s-date1))
         (year2 (standard-year s-date2)))
    (or (< year1 year2)
        (and (= year1 year2)
             (or (< month1 month2)
                 (and (= month1 month2)
                      (< day1 day2)))))))
```

```
(defun hindu-calendar-year (ky-time)
  ;; TYPE hindu-moment -> hindu-solar-year
  ;; Determine solar year at given time ky-time since Hindu
  ;; epoch.
  (let* ((mean; Mean solar longitude (arcminutes) at ky-time.
           (* 21600 (mod (/ ky-time hindu-sidereal-year) 1)))
         (real; True longitude.
          (hindu-solar-longitude ky-time))
         (year; Mean year.
          (quotient ky-time hindu-sidereal-year)))
    (cond ((> real 20000 1000 mean); Really previous year.
           (1- year))
          ((> mean 20000 1000 real); Really next year.
           (1+ year))
          (t year))))
```

```
(defun fixed-from-hindu-solar (s-date)
  ;; TYPE hindu-solar-date -> fixed-date
  ;; Fixed date corresponding to Hindu solar date s-date
  ;; (Saka era).  Returns bogus for nonexistent date.
  (let* ((month (standard-month s-date))
         (day (standard-day s-date))
         (year (standard-year s-date))
         (approx; Approximate date from below
                ; by adding days...
          (floor
           (+ (* (+ year hindu-solar-era ; in months...
                    (/ (1- month) 12))
                 hindu-sidereal-year)    ; ... and years
              hindu-epoch   ; and days before fixed date 0.
              day -9))); Potential discrepancy of mean date.
         (try (+ approx ; Search forward to correct date,
                 (sum 1 i approx; or just past it.
                      (hindu-solar-precedes?
                       (hindu-solar-from-fixed i)
                       s-date)))))
    (if (equal (hindu-solar-from-fixed try) s-date)
        try
      bogus))); Date nonexistent on Hindu solar calendar.
```

```
(defun hindu-lunar-date (month leap-month day leap-day year)
  ;; TYPE (hindu-lunar-month hindu-lunar-leap-month
  ;; TYPE  hindu-lunar-day hindu-lunar-leap-day
  ;; TYPE  hindu-lunar-year) -> hindu-lunar-date
  (list month leap-month day leap-day year))
```

```
(defun hindu-lunar-month (date)
  ;; TYPE hindu-lunar-date -> hindu-lunar-month
  (first date))
```

```
(defun hindu-lunar-leap-month (date)
  ;; TYPE hindu-lunar-date -> hindu-lunar-leap-month
  (second date))
```

```
(defun hindu-lunar-day (date)
  ;; TYPE hindu-lunar-date -> hindu-lunar-day
  (third date))
```

```
(defun hindu-lunar-leap-day (date)
  ;; TYPE hindu-lunar-date -> hindu-lunar-leap-day
  (fourth date))
```

```
(defun hindu-lunar-year (date)
  ;; TYPE hindu-lunar-date -> hindu-lunar-year
  (fifth date))
```

```
(defconstant hindu-lunar-era
  ;; TYPE standard-year
  ;; Years from Kali Yuga until Vikrama era
  3044)
```

```
(defun hindu-lunar-from-fixed (date)
  ;; TYPE fixed-date -> hindu-lunar-date
  ;; Hindu lunar date equivalent to fixed date.
  (let* ((ky-time (hindu-day-count date))   ; Hindu date.
         (rise (hindu-sunrise ky-time)) ; Sunrise that day.
         (day (lunar-day rise)); Day of month.
         (leapday              ; If previous day the same.
          (= day (lunar-day (hindu-sunrise (1- ky-time)))))
         (last-new-moon (hindu-new-moon rise))
         (next-new-moon
          (hindu-new-moon (+ (floor last-new-moon) 35)))
         (solar-month         ; Solar month name.
          (hindu-zodiac last-new-moon))
         (leapmonth       ; If begins and ends in same sign.
          (= solar-month (hindu-zodiac next-new-moon)))
         (month                       ; Month of lunar year.
          (adjusted-mod (1+ solar-month) 12))
         (year ; Solar year at next new moon.
          (- (hindu-calendar-year next-new-moon)
             hindu-lunar-era ; Era
             ;; If month is leap, it belongs to next month's
             ;; year.
             (if (and leapmonth (= month 1)) -1 0))))
    (hindu-lunar-date month leapmonth day leapday year)))
```

```
(defun hindu-lunar-precedes? (l-date1 l-date2)
  ;; TYPE (hindu-lunar-date hindu-lunar-date) -> boolean
  ;; True if Hindu lunar l-date1 precedes l-date2.
  (let* ((month1 (hindu-lunar-month l-date1))
         (month2 (hindu-lunar-month l-date2))
         (leap1 (hindu-lunar-leap-month l-date1))
         (leap2 (hindu-lunar-leap-month l-date2))
         (day1 (hindu-lunar-day l-date1))
         (day2 (hindu-lunar-day l-date2))
         (leapday1 (hindu-lunar-leap-day l-date1))
         (leapday2 (hindu-lunar-leap-day l-date2))
         (year1 (hindu-lunar-year l-date1))
         (year2 (hindu-lunar-year l-date2)))
    (or (< year1 year2)
```

```
        (and (= year1 year2)
             (or (< month1 month2)
                 (and (= month1 month2)
                      (or (and leap1 (not leap2))
                          (and (equal leap1 leap2)
                               (or (< day1 day2)
                                   (and (= day1 day2)
                                        (not leapday1)
                                        leapday2)))))))))
```

```
(defun fixed-from-hindu-lunar (l-date)
  ;; TYPE hindu-lunar-date -> fixed-date
  ;; Fixed date corresponding to Hindu lunar date l-date;
  ;; returns bogus if no such date exists.
  (let* ((year (hindu-lunar-year l-date))
         (month (hindu-lunar-month l-date))
         (leap (hindu-lunar-leap-month l-date))
         (leap-day (hindu-lunar-leap-day l-date))
         (day (hindu-lunar-day l-date))
         (ky-year (+ year hindu-lunar-era))
         (mean; Approximate date.
           (fixed-from-old-hindu-lunar
            (old-hindu-lunar-date month leap day ky-year)))
          (approx; Check if one month off either way.
          (cond ((hindu-lunar-precedes?
                  (hindu-lunar-from-fixed (+ mean 15))
                  l-date)
                 (+ mean hindu-synodic-month))
                ((hindu-lunar-precedes?
                  l-date
                  (hindu-lunar-from-fixed (- mean 15)))
                 (- mean hindu-synodic-month))
                (t mean)))
          (try ; Search for correct date
              ;  or just before or after it.
          (floor (binary-search
                  l (- approx 4)
                  u (+ approx 4)
                  d (not (hindu-lunar-precedes?
                          (hindu-lunar-from-fixed (floor d))
                          l-date))
                  (<= (- u l) 2)))))
    (cond ((equal (hindu-lunar-from-fixed try) l-date)
           try)
          ((equal (hindu-lunar-from-fixed (1+ try)) l-date)
           (1+ try))
          ((equal (hindu-lunar-from-fixed (1- try)) l-date)
           (1- try))
          (t bogus)))); Nonexistent Hindu lunar calendar date.
```

```
(defun ascensional-difference (ky-time latitude)
  ;; TYPE (hindu-moment arcminute) -> arcminute
  ;; Difference between right and oblique ascension
  ;; of sun (in arcminutes) at ky-time at latitude
  ;; (in arcminutes).
  (let* ((sin-decl
          (* 1397/3438
             (hindu-sine (tropical-longitude ky-time))))
         (diurnal-radius
          (hindu-sine (- 5400 (hindu-arcsin sin-decl))))
         (tan ; Tangent of latitude as rational number.
          (/ (hindu-sine latitude)
             (hindu-sine (+ 5400 latitude))))
         (earth-sine (* sin-decl tan)))
    (hindu-arcsin (* -3438 (/ earth-sine diurnal-radius)))))
```

```
(defun solar-sidereal-difference (ky-time)
  ;; TYPE hindu-moment -> arcminute
  ;; Difference between solar and sidereal day at ky-time.
  (* (daily-motion ky-time) (rising-sign ky-time) 1/1800))
```

```
(defun tropical-longitude (ky-time)
  ;; TYPE hindu-moment -> arcminute
  ;; Hindu tropical longitude at ky-time days since epoch.
  ;; Assumes precession with maximum of 27 degrees (1620
  ;; minutes) and period of 7200 sidereal years (=
  ;; 1577917828/600 days).
  (let* ((midnight (floor ky-time)) ; Whole days.
         (precession
          (- 1620
             (abs (- 1620
                     (mod (* 6480 600/1577917828 midnight)
                          6480))))))
    (mod (- (hindu-solar-longitude ky-time) precession)
         21600)))
```

```
(defun rising-sign (ky-time)
  ;; TYPE hindu-moment -> integer
  ;; Tabulated speed of rising of current zodiacal sign.
  (nth (mod (quotient (tropical-longitude ky-time) 1800) 6)
       (list 1670 1795 1935 1935 1795 1670)))
```

```
(defun daily-motion (ky-time)
  ;; TYPE hindu-moment -> arcminute
  ;; Sidereal daily motion (in arcminutes) of sun at ky-time.
  (let* ((mean-motion ; mean daily motion in arcminutes.
          (/ 21600 hindu-sidereal-year))
         (anomaly (mean-position
                   (+ hindu-creation ky-time)
                   hindu-anomalistic-year))
         (epicycle ; Current size of epicycle
          (- 14/360 (/ (abs (hindu-sine anomaly)) 3713040)))
         (entry (quotient anomaly 225))
         (sine-table-step ; Marginal change in anomaly
          (- (hindu-sine-table (1+ entry))
             (hindu-sine-table entry)))
         (equation-of-motion-factor
          (* sine-table-step -1/225 epicycle)))
    (* mean-motion (1+ equation-of-motion-factor))))
```

```
(defun hindu-equation-of-time (ky-time)
  ;; TYPE hindu-moment -> hindu-moment
  ;; Time from mean to true midnight.
  ;; (This is a gross approximation to the correct value.)
  (let* ((offset (hindu-sine (mean-position
                              (+ hindu-creation ky-time)
                              hindu-anomalistic-year)))
         (equation-sun ; Sun's equation of center
               ; Arcsin is not needed since small
          (* offset (- (/ (abs offset) 3713040) 14/360))))
    (* (daily-motion ky-time) equation-sun
       hindu-sidereal-year 1/21600 1/21600)))
```

```
(defun hindu-sunrise (ky-time)
  ;; TYPE hindu-moment -> hindu-moment
  ;; Sunrise at Ujjain (latitude 1389 minutes)
  ;; ky-time (whole) days since Hindu epoch.
  (+ ky-time 1/4 ; Mean sunrise.
     (hindu-equation-of-time ky-time) ; Apparent midnight.
     (* ; Convert sidereal arcminutes to fraction of civil
        1577917828/1582237828 1/21600 ; ... day.
```

```
      (+ (ascensional-difference ky-time 1389)
         (/ (solar-sidereal-difference ky-time) 4)))))
```

```
(defun sunrise-at-ujjain (ky-time)
  ;; TYPE hindu-moment -> hindu-moment
  ;; Astronomical sunrise at Ujjain (latitude 1389 minutes)
  ;; on ky-time (whole) days since Hindu epoch.
  (let* ((d (+ ky-time hindu-epoch))
         (latitude 1389/60)
         (longitude 4546/60))
    (+ ky-time (sunrise d latitude longitude))))
```

```
(defun lunar-day-start (ky-time k accuracy)
  ;; TYPE (hindu-moment rational real) -> hindu-moment
  ;; Time lunar-day (tithi) number k begins before or at
  ;; ky-time in days since onset of Hindu epoch.  k can be
  ;; fractional (for karanas).  accuracy is in fraction of
  ;; (civil) day.
  (let* ((tomorrow (1+ ky-time))
         (part ; Mean time from start of month.
          (* (1- k) 1/30 hindu-synodic-month))
         (estimate ; Mean occurrence of lunar-day.
          (- tomorrow (mod (- tomorrow part)
                           hindu-synodic-month)))
         (try (binary-search ; Search for phase.
               l (- estimate 2/3)
               u (+ estimate 2/3)
               x (let* ((diff-x (- (hindu-lunar-phase x)
                                   (* (1- k) 720))))
                   (or (< 0 diff-x 10800) ; Past the lunar-day
                       (< diff-x -10800)))  ; Over the edge
               (or (< ky-time l) (< (- u l) accuracy)))))
    (if (> try ky-time) ; Too late.
        (lunar-day-start  ; Previous month.
         (- ky-time 20) k accuracy)
      try)))
```

```
(defun lunar-mansion (date)
  ;; TYPE fixed-date -> positive-integer
  ;; Hindu lunar mansion (nakshatra) at sunrise on fixed date.
  (let* ((rise (hindu-sunrise (hindu-day-count date))))
    (1+ (quotient (hindu-lunar-longitude rise) 800))))
```

```
(defun samkranti (g-year m)
  ;; TYPE (gregorian-year hindu-solar-month) -> moment
  ;; Fixed moment of start of m-th solar month
  ;; of Hindu year beginning in Gregorian g-year.
  (let* ((diff (+ hindu-solar-era
                  (standard-year
                   (gregorian-from-fixed hindu-epoch))))
         (h-year (- g-year diff)) ; Since K.Y.
         (ny (- (fixed-from-hindu-solar ; First of month.
                 (hindu-solar-date m 1 h-year))
                hindu-epoch))
         (begin
          (binary-search ; Search for exact time.
             start (- ny 7/8)
             end   (+ ny 3/8)
             x     (if (= m 1) ; Look for 360-0 break.
                       (< (hindu-solar-longitude x)
                          1800)
                     (>= (hindu-solar-longitude x)
                         (* (1- m) 1800)))
             (>= 1/1000000 (- end start)))))
    (+ begin hindu-epoch)))
```

```
(defun mesha-samkranti (g-year)
  ;; TYPE gregorian-year -> moment
  ;; Fixed moment of Mesha samkranti (Vernal equinox)
  ;; in Gregorian g-year.
  (samkranti g-year 1))
```

```
(defun hindu-lunar-new-year (g-year)
  ;; TYPE gregorian-year -> fixed-date
  ;; Fixed date of Hindu luni-solar new year
  ;; in Gregorian g-year.
  (let* ((mesha ; Fixed date of vernal equinox.
          (mesha-samkranti g-year))
         (m1 ; Prior new moon.
          (lunar-day-start (hindu-day-count mesha)
                           1 1/100000))
         (m0 ; New moon before that.
          (lunar-day-start (- m1 27) 1 1/100000))
         (new-moon ; First new moon of year.
          (if ; leap month...
              (= (hindu-zodiac m0) (hindu-zodiac m1))
              m0 m1))
         (h-day (floor new-moon))
         (rise ; Sunrise that day.
          (hindu-sunrise h-day)))
    (+ hindu-epoch h-day
       ;; Next day if new moon after sunrise,
       ;; unless lunar day ends before next sunrise.
       (if (or (< new-moon rise)
               (= (lunar-day
                   (hindu-sunrise (1+ h-day))) 2))
           0 1))))
```

```
(defun karana (n)
  ;; TYPE {1-60} -> {0-10}
  ;; Number (0-10) of the name of the n-th (1-60) Hindu karana.
  (cond ((= n 1) 0)
        ((> n 57) (- n 50))
        (t (adjusted-mod (1- n) 7))))
```

```
(defun yoga (ky-time)
  ;; TYPE hindu-moment -> {1-27}
  ;; Hindu yoga at ky-time days since Hindu epoch.
  (1+ (floor (mod (/ (+ (hindu-solar-longitude ky-time)
                        (hindu-lunar-longitude ky-time))
                     800)
                  27))))
```

```
(defun sacred-wednesdays-in-gregorian (g-year)
  ;; TYPE gregorian-year -> list-of-fixed-dates
  ;; List of Wednesdays in Gregorian year g-year
  ;; that are day 8 of Hindu lunar months.
  (sacred-wednesdays
   (fixed-from-gregorian ; From beginning of year.
    (gregorian-date january 1 g-year))
   (fixed-from-gregorian ; To end.
    (gregorian-date december 31 g-year))))
```

```
(defun sacred-wednesdays (start end)
  ;; TYPE gregorian-year -> list-of-fixed-dates
  ;; List of Wednesdays between fixed dates start and end
  ;; (inclusive) that are day 8 of Hindu lunar months.
  (if (> start end)
      nil
    (let* ((wed (kday-on-or-after start wednesday))
           (h-date (hindu-lunar-from-fixed wed))
```

```
      (append
       (if (= (hindu-lunar-day h-date) 8)
           (list wed)
         nil)
       (sacred-wednesdays (1+ wed) end)))))
```

Reference

[1] G. L. Steele, Jr., *Common LISP: The Language*, 2nd ed. Digital Press, Bedford, MA, 1990.

Appendix C

Some Sample Data

המבין יבין

—Abraham ben David of Posquieres: *Strictures to Maimonides' Mishneh Torah*, Gifts to the Poor 5:11

To aid the reader interested in translating our functions into other programming languages, we give a table of 33 dates from years −1000 to 2100 with their equivalents on all the calendars discussed in the book. For each date we also give the solar longitude at 12:00:00 U.T., the J.D. of the next solstice/equinox (U.T.), the lunar longitude at 00:00:00 U.T., the J.D. of the next new moon (U.T.), and the local (not standard) times of sunrise and sunset for Jerusalem (31.8° north, 35.2° east). All dates and values given are as computed by our functions, and hence may not represent historical reality; furthermore, some of these dates are not meaningful for all calendars.

But go thou thy way till the end be; and thou shalt rest, and shalt stand up to thy lot, at the end of the days.

—Daniel 12:13

R.D.	Weekday	Julian Day	Gregorian	ISO	Julian	Coptic	Ethiopic	Islamic	Persian	Bahá’í	Hebrew
−214193	Sunday	1507231.5	7 24 −586	29 7 −586	7 30 −587	12 6 −870	12 7 −593	12 9 −1245	5 1 −1208	−6 6 3 7 12	5 10 3174
−61387	Wednesday	1660037.5	12 5 −168	49 3 −168	12 8 −169	4 12 −451	4 13 −174	2 23 −813	9 14 −790	−5 9 3 14 13	9 25 3593
25469	Wednesday	1746893.5	9 24 70	39 3 70	9 26 70	1 29 −213	1 29 64	4 1 −568	7 2 −552	−4 2 13 10 17	7 3 3831
49217	Sunday	1770641.5	10 2 135	39 7 135	10 3 135	2 5 −148	2 6 129	4 6 −501	7 9 −487	−4 6 2 11 6	7 9 3896
171307	Wednesday	1892731.5	1 8 470	2 3 470	1 7 470	5 12 186	5 13 463	10 17 −157	10 18 −153	−3 4 13 16 9	10 18 4230
210155	Monday	1931579.5	5 20 576	21 1 576	5 18 576	9 23 292	9 24 569	6 3 −47	2 30 −46	−3 10 6 4 4	3 4 4336
253427	Saturday	1974851.5	11 10 694	45 6 694	11 7 694	3 11 411	3 11 688	7 13 75	8 19 73	−3 16 10 13 7	8 13 4455
369740	Sunday	2091164.5	4 25 1013	16 7 1013	4 19 1013	8 24 729	8 25 1006	10 5 403	2 5 392	−2 14 6 2 17	2 6 4773
400085	Sunday	2121509.5	5 24 1096	21 7 1096	5 18 1096	9 23 812	9 24 1089	5 22 489	3 3 475	−2 18 13 4 8	2 23 4856
434355	Friday	2155779.5	3 23 1190	12 5 1190	3 16 1190	7 20 906	7 21 1183	2 7 586	1 3 569	−1 4 12 1 3	1 7 4950
452605	Saturday	2174029.5	3 10 1240	10 6 1240	3 3 1240	7 7 956	7 8 1233	8 7 637	12 20 618	−1 7 4 20 9	13 8 5000
470160	Friday	2191584.5	4 2 1288	14 5 1288	3 26 1288	7 30 1004	8 1 1281	2 20 687	1 14 667	−1 9 15 1 13	1 21 5048
473837	Sunday	2195261.5	4 27 1298	17 7 1298	4 20 1298	8 25 1014	8 26 1291	7 7 697	2 8 677	−1 10 6 2 19	2 7 5058
507850	Sunday	2229274.5	6 12 1391	23 7 1391	6 4 1391	10 10 1107	10 10 1384	7 1 793	3 22 770	−1 15 4 5 8	4 1 5151
524156	Wednesday	2245580.5	2 3 1436	5 3 1436	1 25 1436	5 29 1152	5 30 1429	7 6 839	11 13 814	−1 17 10 17 16	11 7 5196
544676	Saturday	2266100.5	4 9 1492	14 6 1492	3 31 1492	8 5 1208	8 6 1485	6 1 897	1 21 871	0 1 10 2 1	1 3 5252
567118	Saturday	2288542.5	9 19 1553	38 6 1553	9 9 1553	1 12 1270	1 13 1547	9 30 960	6 28 932	0 4 14 10 12	7 1 5314
569477	Saturday	2290901.5	3 5 1560	9 6 1560	2 24 1560	6 29 1276	6 30 1553	5 27 967	12 14 938	0 5 1 20 4	12 27 5320
601716	Wednesday	2323140.5	6 10 1648	24 3 1648	5 31 1648	10 6 1364	10 7 1641	5 18 1058	3 21 1027	0 9 14 5 6	3 20 5408
613424	Sunday	2334848.5	6 30 1680	26 7 1680	6 20 1680	10 26 1396	10 27 1673	6 2 1091	4 10 1059	0 11 8 6 7	4 3 5440
626596	Friday	2348020.5	7 24 1716	30 5 1716	7 13 1716	11 19 1432	11 20 1709	8 4 1128	5 2 1095	0 13 6 7 12	5 5 5476
645554	Sunday	2366978.5	6 19 1768	24 7 1768	6 8 1768	10 14 1484	10 15 1761	2 3 1182	3 30 1147	0 16 1 5 15	4 4 5528
664224	Monday	2385648.5	8 2 1819	31 1 1819	7 21 1819	11 27 1535	11 27 1812	10 10 1234	5 10 1198	0 18 14 8 2	5 11 5579
671401	Wednesday	2392825.5	3 27 1839	13 3 1839	3 15 1839	7 19 1555	7 19 1832	1 11 1255	1 7 1218	0 19 15 1 7	1 12 5599
694799	Sunday	2416223.5	4 19 1903	16 7 1903	4 6 1903	8 11 1619	8 11 1896	1 21 1321	1 29 1282	1 4 3 2 11	1 22 5663
704424	Sunday	2425848.5	8 25 1929	34 7 1929	8 12 1929	12 19 1645	12 20 1922	3 19 1348	6 3 1308	1 5 10 9 6	5 19 5689
708842	Monday	2430266.5	9 29 1941	40 1 1941	9 16 1941	1 19 1658	1 20 1935	9 8 1360	7 7 1320	1 6 3 11 3	7 8 5702
709409	Monday	2430833.5	4 19 1943	16 1 1943	4 6 1943	8 11 1659	8 11 1936	4 13 1362	1 29 1322	1 6 5 2 11	1 14 5703
709580	Thursday	2431004.5	10 7 1943	40 4 1943	9 24 1943	1 26 1660	1 27 1937	10 7 1362	7 14 1322	1 6 5 11 11	7 8 5704
727274	Tuesday	2448698.5	3 17 1992	12 2 1992	3 4 1992	7 8 1708	7 9 1985	9 13 1412	12 27 1370	1 8 15 20 16	13 12 5752
728714	Sunday	2450138.5	2 25 1996	8 7 1996	2 12 1996	6 17 1712	6 18 1989	10 5 1416	12 6 1374	1 8 19 18 19	12 5 5756
744313	Wednesday	2465737.5	11 10 2038	45 3 2038	10 28 2038	3 1 1755	3 1 2032	10 12 1460	8 19 1417	1 11 5 13 7	8 12 5799
764652	Sunday	2486076.5	7 18 2094	28 7 2094	7 5 2094	11 11 1810	11 12 2087	3 5 1518	4 28 1473	1 14 4 7 6	5 5 5854

R.D.	Mayan Long Count	Mayan Haab	Mayan Tzolkin	Old Hindu Solar	Old Hindu Lunisolar	French Revolutionary Original	French Revolutionary Modified	Chinese	Modern Hindu Solar	Modern Hindu Lunisolar
−214193	6 8 3 13 9	12 11	5 9	5 19 2515	6 *f* 11 2515	11 5 −2378	11 4 −2378	35 11 6 *f* 12	5 18 −664	6 *f* 11 *f* −529
−61387	7 9 8 3 15	3 5	9 15	9 26 2933	9 *f* 26 2933	3 14 −1959	3 13 −1959	42 9 10 *f* 27	9 25 −246	9 *f* 27 *f* −111
25469	8 1 9 8 11	9 4	12 11	7 11 3171	8 *f* 3 3171	1 2 −1721	1 2 −1721	46 7 8 *f* 4	7 8 −8	8 *f* 3 *f* 127
49217	8 4 15 7 19	12 5	9 19	7 17 3236	8 *f* 9 3236	1 10 −1656	1 10 −1656	47 12 8 *f* 9	7 15 57	8 *f* 9 *f* 192
171307	9 1 14 10 9	12 14	3 9	10 19 3570	11 *t* 19 3570	4 19 −1322	4 18 −1322	52 46 11 *f* 20	10 20 391	11 *f* 19 *f* 526
210155	9 7 2 8 17	5 4	7 17	2 28 3677	3 *f* 5 3677	9 1 −1216	9 1 −1216	54 33 4 *f* 5	2 30 498	3 *f* 5 *f* 633
253427	9 13 2 12 9	7 14	2 9	8 17 3795	9 *f* 15 3795	2 19 −1097	2 19 −1097	56 31 10 *f* 15	8 15 616	9 *f* 15 *f* 751
369740	10 9 5 14 2	5 8	4 2	1 26 4114	2 *f* 7 4114	8 5 −779	8 4 −779	61 50 3 *f* 7	1 27 935	2 *f* 6 *f* 1070
400085	10 13 10 1 7	15 10	7 7	2 24 4197	2 *f* 24 4197	9 5 −696	9 5 −696	63 13 4 *f* 24	2 25 1018	3 *t* 23 *f* 1153
434355	10 18 5 4 17	15 8	9 17	12 20 4290	1 *f* 9 4291	7 2 −602	7 1 −602	64 47 2 *f* 9	12 22 1111	1 *f* 8 *f* 1247
452605	11 0 15 17 7	15 8	7 7	12 7 4340	12 *f* 9 4340	6 20 −552	6 20 −552	65 37 2 *f* 9	12 9 1161	1 *f* 8 *f* 1297
470160	11 3 4 13 2	10 10	12 2	12 30 4388	1 *f* 23 4389	7 13 −504	7 13 −504	66 25 2 *f* 23	1 1 1210	1 *f* 22 *f* 1345
473837	11 3 14 16 19	17 11	10 19	1 24 4399	2 *f* 8 4399	8 8 −494	8 8 −494	66 35 3 *f* 9	1 26 1220	2 *f* 8 *f* 1355
507850	11 8 9 7 12	5 15	2 12	3 7 4492	4 *f* 2 4492	9 23 −401	9 23 −401	68 8 5 *f* 2	3 7 1313	4 *f* 1 *f* 1448
524156	11 10 14 12 18	6 9	6 18	10 28 4536	11 *f* 7 4536	5 14 −356	5 13 −356	68 53 1 *f* 8	10 29 1357	11 *f* 7 *f* 1492
544676	11 13 11 12 18	6 13	12 18	1 3 4593	1 *f* 3 4593	7 20 −300	7 19 −300	69 49 3 *f* 4	1 4 1414	2 *t* 3 *f* 1549
567118	11 16 14 1 0	18 3	3 20	6 12 4654	7 *f* 2 4654	13 2 −239	13 1 −239	70 50 8 *f* 2	6 9 1475	7 *f* 2 *f* 1610
569477	11 17 0 10 19	7 12	9 19	11 27 4660	11 *f* 29 4660	6 15 −232	6 14 −232	70 57 1 *f* 29	11 28 1481	11 *f* 28 *t* 1616
601716	12 1 10 2 18	6 18	8 18	3 1 4749	3 *f* 20 4749	9 22 −144	9 22 −144	72 25 4 *t* 20	3 2 1570	3 *f* 20 *f* 1705
613424	12 3 2 12 6	9 1	3 6	3 21 4781	4 *f* 4 4781	10 12 −112	10 12 −112	72 57 6 *f* 5	3 21 1602	4 *f* 4 *f* 1737
626596	12 4 19 4 18	1 3	6 18	4 13 4817	5 *f* 6 4817	11 6 −76	11 6 −76	73 33 6 *f* 6	4 12 1638	5 *f* 6 *f* 1773
645554	12 7 11 16 16	19 1	10 16	3 8 4869	4 *f* 5 4869	10 1 −24	10 1 −24	74 25 5 *f* 5	3 9 1690	4 *f* 5 *f* 1825
664224	12 10 3 14 6	14 4	12 6	4 20 4920	5 *f* 12 4920	11 14 27	11 14 27	75 16 6 *f* 12	4 19 1741	5 *f* 11 *f* 1876
671401	12 11 3 13 3	16 16	13 3	12 13 4939	1 *t* 13 4940	7 6 47	7 6 47	75 36 2 *f* 13	12 15 1760	1 *f* 13 *f* 1896
694799	12 14 8 13 1	14 18	1 1	1 4 5004	1 *f* 23 5004	7 28 111	7 29 111	76 40 3 *f* 22	1 6 1825	1 *f* 22 *f* 1960
704424	12 15 15 8 6	4 7	3 6	5 11 5030	5 *f* 21 5030	12 7 137	12 7 137	77 6 7 *f* 21	5 9 1851	5 *f* 20 *f* 1986
708842	12 16 7 13 4	2 9	1 4	6 15 5042	7 *f* 9 5042	1 7 150	1 7 150	77 18 8 *f* 9	6 13 1863	7 *f* 9 *f* 1998
709409	12 16 9 5 11	4 19	9 11	1 4 5044	1 *f* 15 5044	7 29 151	7 29 151	77 20 3 *f* 15	1 6 1865	1 *f* 14 *f* 2000
709580	12 16 9 14 2	10 9	11 2	6 23 5044	7 *f* 9 5044	1 15 152	1 15 152	77 20 9 *f* 9	6 20 1865	7 *f* 8 *f* 2000
727274	12 18 18 16 16	4 18	12 16	12 2 5092	12 *f* 14 5092	6 27 200	6 27 200	78 9 2 *f* 14	12 3 1913	12 *f* 14 *f* 2048
728714	12 19 2 16 16	4 17	9 16	11 11 5096	12 *f* 7 5096	6 6 204	6 7 204	78 13 1 *f* 7	11 12 1917	12 *f* 7 *f* 2052
744313	13 1 6 4 15	8 12	8 15	7 26 5139	8 *f* 14 5139	2 20 247	2 20 247	78 55 10 *f* 14	7 23 1960	8 *f* 14 *f* 2095
764652	13 4 2 13 14	7 7	2 14	4 2 5195	4 *f* 6 5195	10 30 302	11 1 302	79 51 6 *f* 7	4 1 2016	4 *f* 6 *f* 2151

R.D.	Solar Longitude at 12:00:00 U.T. (degrees)	Next Solstice/Equinox (J.D., U.T.)	Lunar Longitude at 00:00:00 U.T. (degrees)	Next New Moon (J.D., U.T.)	Sunrise in Jerusalem (31.8° N, 35.2° E Local Time)	Sunset in Jerusalem (31.8° N, 35.2° E Local Time)
−214193	84.53777028	1507293.35106933	253.65237163	1507249.87899175	0.21536906 = 05:10:08	0.79339037 = 19:02:29
−61387	220.85420605	1660053.44358385	206.76016760	1660041.49175222	0.28179130 = 06:45:47	0.70544950 = 16:55:51
25469	147.46275212	1746981.28982460	220.88558903	1746920.30266787	0.24240510 = 05:49:04	0.74634083 = 17:54:44
49217	154.79415475	1770722.08639467	287.30894339	1770662.99756638	0.24590144 = 05:54:06	0.73912182 = 17:44:20
171307	254.93761305	1892803.04141963	147.24143065	1892742.93303138	0.29243450 = 07:01:06	0.71698393 = 17:12:27
210155	22.31739308	1931612.40854394	99.62073093	1931605.18791454	0.20816046 = 04:59:45	0.78724026 = 18:53:38
253427	194.52143719	1974892.91108692	41.39250056	1974867.35429782	0.26632230 = 06:23:30	0.71105605 = 17:03:55
369740	357.72014043	2091223.05280459	105.96912584	2091188.23789340	0.22286705 = 05:20:56	0.77472226 = 18:35:36
400085	26.11529660	2121538.11231267	334.11928572	2121516.07027733	0.20679373 = 04:57:47	0.78903246 = 18:56:12
434355	326.33728388	2155870.82314622	98.04134484	2155801.07120215	0.25051906 = 06:00:45	0.75920974 = 18:13:16
452605	314.67491196	2174039.63006866	76.58908373	2174051.68620893	0.26105749 = 06:15:55	0.75343803 = 18:04:57
470160	337.11622593	2191664.51329005	265.77034811	2191592.07345509	0.24078204 = 05:46:44	0.76433481 = 18:20:39
473837	0.52294245	2195316.92862713	128.25956859	2195283.34822989	0.22143083 = 05:18:52	0.77569054 = 18:36:60
507850	43.77130301	2229284.40943015	87.92910153	2229303.16344207	0.20403811 = 04:53:49	0.79564710 = 19:05:44
524156	278.94603527	2245627.12047327	30.92690256	2245603.74432938	0.28638499 = 06:52:24	0.73318076 = 17:35:47
544676	343.38595157	2266173.81749499	48.74090244	2266127.25230070	0.23475474 = 05:38:03	0.76759416 = 18:25:20
567118	140.40943886	2288547.01158583	188.56750234	2288571.01228326	0.24028035 = 05:46:00	0.75091598 = 18:01:19
569477	309.21831286	2290917.17274034	315.96660488	2290903.70252915	0.26528995 = 06:22:01	0.75092375 = 18:01:20
601716	42.57195158	2323151.51873815	312.08365669	2323151.53342300	0.20404552 = 04:53:50	0.79536448 = 19:05:19
613424	61.94890611	2334932.75910771	137.48639909	2334874.26198570	0.20680618 = 04:57:48	0.79831158 = 19:09:34
626596	84.42091655	2348081.47079217	177.48759892	2348044.86952061	0.21580853 = 05:10:46	0.79296897 = 19:01:53
645554	51.09940033	2366980.50059712	136.72150013	2367003.57531350	0.20456163 = 04:54:34	0.79743449 = 19:08:18
664224	92.21106964	2385701.40771425	252.19420187	2385667.38660027	0.21939959 = 05:15:56	0.78902734 = 18:56:12
671401	329.84906937	2392912.66688454	145.05759893	2392843.47043700	0.24696211 = 05:55:38	0.76108161 = 18:15:57
694799	351.41996188	2416288.12830603	290.30601551	2416232.06336741	0.22740816 = 05:27:28	0.77184187 = 18:31:27
704424	115.08198688	2425878.03615487	24.14436512	2425857.99116135	0.22970884 = 05:30:47	0.77298475 = 18:33:06
708842	150.13636923	2430350.73905671	273.76957584	2430288.09697186	0.24457271 = 05:52:11	0.74180613 = 17:48:12
709409	351.71410555	2430897.80003941	191.35860093	2430848.90492601	0.22740816 = 05:27:28	0.77184187 = 18:31:27
709580	157.73162312	2431081.22816813	278.13815111	2431026.58267497	0.24817497 = 05:57:22	0.73473767 = 17:38:01
727274	321.06797077	2448701.86656868	142.34446254	2448715.70938073	0.25495173 = 06:07:08	0.75684059 = 18:09:51
728714	300.62656747	2450162.83533370	43.78789132	2450161.94766557	0.27248681 = 06:32:23	0.74617249 = 17:54:29
744313	193.24413439	2465779.29199040	24.41948060	2465754.07316893	0.26632230 = 06:23:30	0.71105605 = 17:03:55
764652	78.94455226	2486142.96889150	180.48693976	2486100.69129982	0.21280751 = 05:06:27	0.79556694 = 19:05:37

In octo libros De emendatione temporum Index.

A

Oo

First page of the index to Joseph Scaliger's great work on the world's calendars, *De Emendatione Temporum* (1593). (Courtesy of the University of Illinois, Urbana, IL.)

Index

> . . . as two grains of wheat hid in two bushels of chaff: you shall seek all day ere you find them, and when you have them, they are not worth the search.
>
> —William Shakespeare: *Merchant of Venice* (1, i)

Function and constant names are given in **boldface** and page numbers for a function are of four types: The page with the function definition is shown in **boldface**. The page with the type description is shown underlined. The page with the corresponding Lisp code is shown in *italics*. Pages of other occurrences are shown in roman.

Ohe, iam satis est, ohe, libelle,
Iam pervenimus usque ad umbilicos.
Tu procedere adhuc et ire quæris,
Nec summa potes in schida teneri,
Sic tamquam tibi res peracta non sit,
Quae prima quoque pagina peracta est.
Iam lector queriturque deficitque,
Iam librarius hoc et ipse dicit
"Ohe, iam satis est, ohe, libelle."

Martial: *Epigrams*, IV, 89